Europe's Energy Transition

Europe's Energy Transition
Insights for Policy Making

Edited by

Manuel Welsch

Steve Pye

Dogan Keles

Aurélie Faure-Schuyer

Audrey Dobbins

Abhishek Shivakumar

Paul Deane

Mark Howells

ACADEMIC PRESS

An imprint of Elsevier
elsevier.com

Academic Press is an imprint of Elsevier
125 London Wall, London EC2Y 5AS, United Kingdom
525 B Street, Suite 1800, San Diego, CA 92101-4495, United States
50 Hampshire Street, 5th Floor, Cambridge, MA 02139, United States
The Boulevard, Langford Lane, Kidlington, Oxford OX5 1GB, United Kingdom

Notices
Knowledge and best practice in this field are constantly changing. As new research and experience broaden our understanding, changes in research methods, professional practices, or medical treatment may become necessary.

Practitioners and researchers must always rely on their own experience and knowledge in evaluating and using any information, methods, compounds, or experiments described herein. In using such information or methods they should be mindful of their own safety and the safety of others, including parties for whom they have a professional responsibility.

To the fullest extent of the law, neither the Publisher nor the authors, contributors, or editors, assume any liability for any injury and/or damage to persons or property as a matter of products liability, negligence or otherwise, or from any use or operation of any methods, products, instructions, or ideas contained in the material herein.

Library of Congress Cataloging-in-Publication Data
A catalog record for this book is available from the Library of Congress

British Library Cataloguing-in-Publication Data
A catalogue record for this book is available from the British Library

ISBN: 978-0-12-809806-6

For Information on all Academic Press publications
visit our website at https://www.elsevier.com/books-and-journals

Working together
to grow libraries in
developing countries

www.elsevier.com • www.bookaid.org

Publisher: Joe Hayton
Acquisition Editor: Lisa Reading
Editorial Project Manager: Ashlie M. Jackman
Production Project Manager: Anusha Sambamoorthy
Cover Designer: Mark Rogers

Typeset by MPS Limited, Chennai, India

Endorsements

The following endorsements serve to demonstrate the broad audience of this book, both from within and outside of Europe. They cover statements from thought leaders and distinguished energy experts from a diverse range of institutions, including the European Commission, international organizations (IRENA), utilities (Vattenfall), energy agencies (Austrian Energy Agency), independent think tanks (European Policy Center), international energy institutes (JISEA/NREL, IIASA) and universities (Columbia University), as well as scientific journals (Applied Energy).

We would like to thank all of them very much for their interest in reading this book and for finding the time to write the following endorsements.

The energy policy-focused think tank INSIGHT_E is an encounter between two different worlds: policy making, and the research and innovation community. Policy making is often done under pressure from many interest groups and needs to react to events such as geopolitical crises. The world of research on the other hand engages in often timely in-depth studies to provide findings with high levels of certainty. The INSIGHT_E project successfully provided a science–policy interface which brought both worlds closer together, despite the challenges of linking research with policy-making cycles: it required the combination of often fixed deadlines of policy processes with the time needed to produce reasonably reliable results by the researchers.

This book is the final output of this very fruitful encounter. It brings together a selection of the individual assessments done for the European Commission. Further, it complements them with additional research to provide insights into the challenges and opportunities ahead of us on the transition to a low-carbon future.

Dr. Rémy Denos, INSIGHT_E Project Officer at New Energy Technologies Unit, DG Energy, European Commission

The world has embarked on an unprecedented energy transition. Energy efficiency and renewable energy play a key role in this transition and Europe is leading the way. It is an unchartered journey, yet foresight is required as to which path to follow and which framework to put in place to enable such a transition. New technologies, market designs, and business models are needed. This book provides an excellent cutting-edge science-based perspective on various aspects of the energy transition. It helps decision makers to better understand the relation between the physical economy and markets, consumer needs, and technology innovation. Billions are at stake in financial terms, this book is a worthwhile investment to make sure the right decisions are taken.

Dr. Dolf Gielen, Director of the IRENA Innovation and Technology Centre in Bonn International Renewable Energy Agency

A key driving force has gained remarkable momentum in the discussion on energy system transformation: sustainability. The objective to combat climate change is putting environmental considerations higher on the agenda than ever before. In fact, it is already widely believed that integration of sustainability issues will be critical to future commercial success in the energy business. Thus, European utilities are forced to change their business models, factoring in the shift from traditional mostly fossil-based and centralized power generation to a more renewable and increasingly decentralized production landscape. As a result, their traditional long-term investment planning has become even more dependent on regulatory design. More jointed-up thinking between industry and policy makers will be required in order to address current deficiencies originating from the patchwork of energy policies across Europe. Holistic analyses as endeavored by this book are key to establishing the required knowledge amongst stakeholders as common basis to develop the regulatory framework that allows pursuing European sustainability targets in an effective and efficient way.

Dr. Andreas Schuler, Chief Risk Officer, Vice President,
Risk Management, Vattenfall

In times of significant changes in the European energy policy and technology landscape, this book provides a much-needed analysis of the challenges that the European energy system is facing to become more flexible, integrated, affordable, inclusive, and resilient to climate change impacts. The book also addresses potential responses to those challenges, documenting that only with a major transformation in technology, policies, and markets, will the energy system be able to serve well the needs of European citizens and business in the future. It also recognizes that policies in different domains such as renewable energy, energy efficiency, energy markets, and protection of vulnerable consumers have become more and more interlinked and cannot be dealt with in isolation from each other. I recommend reading it.

Dr. Leonardo Barreto, Head of Competence Center "EU and International Projects"
Austrian Energy Agency

The energy system is undergoing a deep, structural, and pervasive transformation, posing a number of challenges to our business models, regulatory frameworks, and behavioral patterns. For Europe, this presents very distinctive challenges, notably due to the EU's unique complexity of multilayer governance. By dissecting the very nature of this double complexity—the energy transition phenomenon and the EU's policy framework—"Europe's Energy Transition: Insights for Policy Making" responded to such a call for a comprehensive approach and provides a precious set of instruments for policy makers, researchers, and analysts at every governance level.

Dr. Fabian Zuleeg, Chief Executive and Chief Economist
European Policy Centre

This book offers a distilled examination of the EU policy landscape and its energy and environmental challenges of the near future. The core of European energy policy on how to achieve an integrated energy market, security of energy supply, and sustainability of the energy sector have been addressed with in-depth and valuable research, in particular, on the issues related to Europe's emission targets, increased impacts of renewable energy on market design and operation, reliability and flexibility of energy systems, and society and consumer demands. The book is a valuable source of comprehensive state-of-the-art and up-to-date major policy-related information with examples on innovation, research, development, and practical applications from the perspective of Europe.

Prof. Jinyue Yan, Editor-in-Chief of Applied Energy
KTH Royal Institute of Technology and Mälardalen University

This book represents a unique, value-added contribution to the ongoing issues related to the transformation of the EU power system. Insights, thoughtful analysis, informed by solid analytics combine to offer decision makers, analysts, academics, and business leaders rich information to chart a pathway forward.

Dr. Doug Arent, Executive Director
Joint Institute for Strategic Energy Analysis (JISEA) at the
National Renewable Energy Laboratory (NREL)

This book provides an important contribution towards European energy policy, regulatory, and investment decision making. Using rigorous analytics to provide practical insights is crucial in such a complex environment.

Dr. Morgan Bazilian, Fellow, Center for Global Energy Policy
Columbia University

While the inevitability of a fundamental energy system transition has been on the radar screen of many energy system analysts, it has yet to become a mainstream policy objective. Several recent international agreements such as the 2030 Agenda for Sustainable Development (with SDG 7 on Affordable and Clean Energy) or the Paris Agreement (with its ambition cycle) on mitigating climate change both concluded in the second half of 2015 and implicitly call for such a deep system transformation. This book explores potential pathways towards meeting long-term sustainable development and climate goals. By doing so, it illuminates the costs and benefits, barriers and attractors of the different options and presents them in a policy-relevant manner.

Dr. Holger Rogner, Associate Editor of Energy Strategy Reviews, Senior Research
Scholar, Transitions To New Technologies
International Institute for Applied Systems Analysis (IIASA)

Contents

SECTION I INTRODUCTION

SECTION II EUROPE'S ENERGY POLICY LANDSCAPE

SECTION VI SOCIETY AND CONSUMER DEMANDS

List of Contributors

Marie-Claire Aoun
Institut Français des Relations Internationales (IFRI), Paris, France

Claude Ayache
InnoEnergy, Brussels, Belgium

Thierry Badouard
Enerdata, Grenoble, France

Claire Baffert
InnoEnergy, Brussels, Belgium

Tomislav Baričević
Energy Institute Hrvoje Požar (EIHP), Zagreb, Croatia

Manuel Baumann
Karlsruhe Institute of Technology (KIT), Karlsruhe, Germany

Robert Bošnjak
Energy Institute Hrvoje Požar (EIHP), Zagreb, Croatia

Jurica Brajković
Energy Institute Hrvoje Požar (EIHP), Zagreb, Croatia

Louise Coffineau
InnoEnergy, Brussels, Belgium

Seán Collins
University College Cork (UCC), Cork, Ireland

Brian Cox
PSI, Villigen, Switzerland

Maïté de Boncourt
Institut Français des Relations Internationales (IFRI), Paris, France

Rocco De Miglio
E4SMA, Turin, Italy

Paul Deane
University College Cork (UCC), Cork, Ireland

Joris Dehler
Karlsruhe Institute of Technology (KIT), Karlsruhe, Germany

Martin Densing
PSI, Villigen, Switzerland

Nathalie Desbrosses
Enerdata, Grenoble, France

Audrey Dobbins
University of Stuttgart, Stuttgart, Germany

Paul Drummond
University College London (UCL), London, United Kingdom

Cherrelle Eid
Institut Français des Relations Internationals (IFRI), Paris, France

Ulrich Fahl
University of Stuttgart, Stuttgart, Germany

Aurélie Faure-Schuyer
Institut Français des Relations Internationales (IFRI), Brussels, Belgium

Wolf Fichtner
Karlsruhe Institute of Technology (KIT), Karlsruhe, Germany

Benjamin Fleischer
University of Stuttgart, Stuttgart, Germany

David Fraboulet
EIT-IE/Commissariat à l'énergie atomique et aux énergies alternatives (CEA), Grenoble, France

Brian Ó. Gallachóir
University College Cork (UCC), Cork, Ireland

James Glynn
University College Cork, Cork, Ireland

Johann Gottschling
University of Stuttgart, Stuttgart, Germany

Rupert Hartel
Karlsruhe Institute of Technology (KIT), Karlsruhe, Germany

Rudolf V. Hemert
Energy Institute Hrvoje Požar (EIHP), Zagreb, Croatia

Mark Howells
KTH Royal Institute of Technology, Stockholm, Sweden

Dražen Jakšić
Energy Institute Hrvoje Požar (EIHP), Zagreb, Croatia

Željko Jurić
Energy Institute Hrvoje Požar (EIHP), Zagreb, Croatia

Ramachandran Kannan
Paul Scherrer Institute, Villigen, Switzerland

Hrvoje Keko
Energy Institute Hrvoje Požar (EIHP), Zagreb, Croatia

Dogan Keles
Karlsruhe Institute of Technology (KIT), Karlsruhe, Germany

Kimon Keramidas
Enerdata, Grenoble, France

Carole Mathieu
Institut Français des Relations Internationales (IFRI), Paris, France

Marko Matosović
Energy Institute Hrvoje Požar (EIHP), Zagreb, Croatia

Christophe McGlade
University College London (UCL), London, United Kingdom

Stanislaw Nagy
AGH University, Kraków, Poland

Bo Normark
InnoEnergy Scandinavia, Stockholm, Sweden

Rajesh Pattupara
Paul Scherrer Institute, Villigen, Switzerland

Damir Pešut
Energy Institute Hrvoje Požar (EIHP), Zagreb, Croatia

Thierry Priem
CEA, Grenoble, France

Steve Pye
University College London (UCL), London, United Kingdom

Lea Renz
Karlsruhe Institute of Technology (KIT), Karlsruhe, Germany

Richard O. Shea
University College Cork (UCC), Cork, Ireland

Abhishek Shivakumar
KTH Royal Institute of Technology, Stockholm, Sweden

Martin Steurer
University of Stuttgart, Stuttgart, Germany

Karmen Stupin
Energy Institute Hrvoje Požar (EIHP), Zagreb, Croatia

Constantinos Taliotis
KTH Royal Institute of Technology, Stockholm, Sweden

Thomas Telsnig
University of Stuttgart, Stuttgart, Germany

Kathrin Volkart
PSI, Villigen, Switzerland

Alfred Voß
University of Stuttgart, Stuttgart, Germany

Manuel Welsch
KTH Royal Institute of Technology, Stockholm, Sweden

Editor Biographies

DR. MANUEL WELSCH

Manuel worked as Deputy Director at the Division of Energy Systems Analysis at KTH Royal Institute of Technology, Stockholm until the end of 2015. There he coordinated the think tank INSIGHT_E, supervised PhD students, and led the development of an EU proposal, securing 4 million EUR. He has published widely including on smart grids, increasing shares of renewable energy and the resource nexus. Further, he was in charge of the development of the energy model OSeMOSYS and significantly improved its functionality, including the modeling of variable generation, storage, and operational reserve requirements.

Prior to KTH, Manuel worked at the Energy and Climate Change Branch of the United Nations Industrial Development Organization (UNIDO), focusing on issues pertaining to UN-Energy. In his preceding jobs, he worked at the Energy Facility of the European Commission, at Bernard Engineers, and at the Uganda Ministry of Water, Lands and Environment. Currently, Manuel is employed as energy planner and economist at the International Atomic Energy Agency (IAEA). There he focuses on strategic environmental assessments and techno-economic and financial energy models to inform decision making.

As lead editor, Manuel was in charge of the overall development process of this book, including the writing of chapters and editing throughout all sections.

STEVE PYE

Steve Pye is a senior researcher at the UCL Energy Institute. His research primarily focuses on how energy systems can transition away from fossil-fuel-based to lower-carbon systems. This includes the economics of such transitions, and the choices for decision makers under uncertainty to enable the large-scale deployment of different technologies that will be needed both now and in the longer term. A further dimension of his research is the assessment of distributional impacts of such transitions, from community impacts due to a changing economy, to higher prices impacting on vulnerable groups, to the challenges for developing countries in moving to sustainable energy systems. Steve has published extensively on the decarbonization of energy systems, both in the academic literature, and in provision of policy reports, primarily for the UK Government. He holds an MSc from Imperial College, and is currently undertaking a PhD at University College Cork.

It is primarily his research on distributional impacts, including the challenge of energy poverty, that Steve has contributed to this book, also writing the conclusions section and reviewing others.

DR. DOGAN KELES

Dr. Dogan Keles graduated as industrial engineer from the Karlsruhe Institute of Technology (KIT) in 2006 and received his doctoral degree at the Economics Department of KIT in 2013 with summa cum laude. During his work at the KIT he analyzed uncertainties in energy markets and developed methods to evaluate energy investments. During his research visit to University of California, Berkeley, he worked on stochastic modeling. Currently, Dogan Keles is head of the research group "energy markets and energy system analysis" at the Institute of Industrial Production (IIP) at the KIT and works on different projects about the design of energy markets, evaluation of energy technologies (under uncertainty), and modeling energy systems. His studies have resulted in different publications in peer-reviewed journals and conference proceedings.

In this book, Dogan acted as the lead editor of the section on the *Impact of Renewable Energies on Market Operation and Design*.

AURÉLIE FAURE-SCHUYER

Aurélie Faure-Schuyer was employed in the investment banks BNP-Paribas, HSBC, and Dexia Asset Management for 15 years. There she worked as a financial analyst covering the energy and commodity sectors (oil companies, oil services, mining companies, electricity, gas and water utilities), and as a sustainable and responsible investment analyst. She graduated from Paris-Dauphine University (Master's Degree in Management), where she studied prices' formation on the crude oil market (master's thesis), before joining the Ecole Nationale Supérieure du Pétrole et des Moteurs (ENSPM), where she studied Energy Economics (1996). Aurélie is a certified financial analyst from the SFAF (Société Française des Analystes Financiers—2000). Recently, she pursued an Executive Master's in Communication and European Politics in IHECS—Brussels. Currently, she focuses on innovation in the business environment of energy companies.

In this book, Aurélie was lead editor of the section on *Europe's Energy Policy Landscape*.

AUDREY DOBBINS

Audrey Dobbins is a research associate at the Institute of Energy Economics and Rational Energy Use (IER), University of Stuttgart in Germany. While in South Africa, she earned a Masters in Energy Studies from the University of Cape Town in 2006. She also worked for an NGO on applied research aiming to improve the energy welfare of residents in informal settlements and to develop and implement Energy and Climate Change Strategies together with cities. Currently, her research focuses on analyzing the significance of energy poverty on the energy system through the application of an energy-economic model. Her research works towards enhancing the energy welfare of vulnerable households and, more broadly, achieving the energy and social objectives of the energy transition in the German context through improved energy planning.

In this book, Audrey was lead editor for the section on *Society and Consumer Demands*.

ABHISHEK SHIVAKUMAR

Abhishek Shivakumar is a researcher at the Division of Energy Systems Analysis at KTH Royal Institute of Technology in Stockholm, Sweden. He also acted as the manager of INSIGHT_E, a think tank informing the European Commission on energy policy. His research covers a wide range of energy issues from valuing the cost of electricity supply interruptions, developing open investment planning toolkits to expand Africa's electricity system, business models to foster Europe's transition to a low-carbon energy system, household DC networks, and indicators to measure the techno-economic potential of demand response. In addition, since 2015 Abhishek has managed the development of OSeMOSYS—an open source energy modeling tool. His work has been used in projects with the European Commission, UNDESA, African Development Bank, and the World Bank. Abhishek holds a dual MS in Energy Technology and Industrial Engineering from KTH (Sweden) and UPC (Spain). Before that, he graduated with a BE in Chemical Engineering from Manipal Institute of Technology in India.

In this book, Abhishek was responsible for the section on *Reliable and Flexible Energy Systems*.

DR. PAUL DEANE

Dr. Paul Deane is a research fellow at University College Cork. His research focuses on European integrated climate and energy policy analysis and low-carbon pathways. He has a PhD degree in the area of energy systems modeling and holds a master's degree in Engineering and Science specializing in wind power meteorology. He has been working and researching in the energy industry for over 12 years. Paul's research aims to understand the transition to low-carbon energy systems from a technical, societal, and economic perspective. He has published in a wide area of disciplines from electricity and gas markets modeling, low-carbon transport, fuel poverty in Europe, and land use. From 2013 he has been a member of the INSIGHT_E group, a European, scientific and multidisciplinary think tank for energy to inform the European Commission and other energy stakeholders. He was a member of Irish government senior officials committee on Climate Change 2015 and currently sits on scientific advisors panel for a number of European energy modeling projects.

In this book, Paul was lead editor for the section on *Energy Supply: A Changing Environment*.

PROF. MARK HOWELLS

Prof. Mark Howells directs the division and holds the chair of Energy Systems Analysis (KTH-dESA) at the Royal Institute of Technology in Sweden, and is an Honorary Affiliate Professor at the University of Technology in Sydney and Editor in Chief of Energy Strategy Reviews. KTH-dESA spearheads the development of some of the world's premier open source energy, resource, and spatial electrification planning tools. Mark has published in Nature Journals; led the European Commission's think tank for Energy; is regularly used by the United Nations as a science-policy expert; and is a key contributor to UNDESA's "Modelling Tools for Sustainable Development Policies." His division contributes to efforts for NASA, IRENA, ABB, the World Bank, and others. Prior to joining KTH-dESA he had an award-winning career with the International Atomic Energy Agency. Mark's graduate and postgraduate studies were undertaken at the University of Cape Town, South Africa. Within that time he was also an international research affiliate at Stanford's Program on Energy and Sustainable Development: spokesperson for the World Energy Council's student program and led RSA's Integrated Energy Planning (IEP) process as well as other national initiatives.

Foreword to this Book

We are living in fast-moving times in the energy sector. The world energy systems are continuously increasing in integration and complexity. Multiple objectives of ensuring energy security, providing affordable energy to all citizens, and spurring competitiveness while mitigating environmental externalities coexist. This is increasingly true also for the European Union. In the IEA World Energy Outlook 2016 central scenario, primary energy demand in the European Union declines by 13% from 2014 to 2040, while electricity increases its share in transport, buildings, and industrial uses. The European Union becomes one of the least carbon-intensive energy economies in the world, driven by decarbonization of the power sector through variable renewables. While traditional energy security concerns, such as natural gas imports, are on the rise, so are concerns on reliability and security of electricity supplies. Integration of variable renewables and coordination of cross-sectoral policies become dominant themes.

In light of this increasing complexity and speed of change, policymakers need more than ever a compass to navigate today's energy sector. Unbiased quantitative and qualitative research is needed to unveil the intricacies of today's energy systems and to provide clear and actionable messages to support policymaking. Of paramount importance is policy-relevant research that takes a whole-system approach, going beyond the traditional sectoral, silos approach.

This book addresses those needs and is based on research that was developed in direct response to the European Commission's requirements. A highly collaborative effort, it covers a range of topics, spanning from the technical performance of energy systems to how to meet societal energy-related demands. The expertise of the authors results in a deep coverage of each topic, while the book's collaborative nature ensures a whole-system approach. As such, it helps fill the gap between high-quality scientific research and policymaking, with essential insights to help moving towards a truly performing energy sector for 21st century Europe.

Laura Cozzi
Co-lead of the World Energy Outlook,
International Energy Agency, Paris

Foreword on INSIGHT_E

An energy think tank informing the European Commission, and the source of research distilled in this book

In the context of a fast-evolving landscape, characterized by geopolitical challenges, the fight against climate change, and globalization processes, energy issues are high on the agenda at all levels—local, national, regional, and of course, global.

The Paris Agreement calls for an urgent response to the observed effect of global warming. The EU was among the first parties to ratify the Paris Agreement, thus enabling its entry into force in November 2016. Energy is at the forefront as this sector represents around two-thirds of greenhouse gas emissions at a global level.

Furthermore, the dependence of the European Union on external supplies exceeds 50% of our overall energy use. Security of supply and prices are therefore intimately linked with our capacity to develop viable and balanced partnerships with our suppliers.

The EU has been and is showing the way in the transition to a secure, sustainable, and competitive energy system. These efforts have been confirmed through measures such as the ambitious Energy and Climate packages for 2020 and 2030, based on scenarios which rely on real figures. The Clean Energy for All Europeans package just adopted on November 30, 2016 completes the set of the Commission's proposals for the energy policy regulatory framework.

Among other goals, the EU wants to increase the share of renewables to 20% by 2020 and to at least 27% by 2030. This change had already started several years ago, the situation is evolving fast with very clear and visible effects in the electricity sector, for example: today, around 30% of EU electricity is from renewables, 11% being from wind and solar. The penetration of renewables contributes to reducing our dependence, our external energy bill, but above all our environmental footprint while creating investments, growth, and local jobs. But this also requires rethinking and redesigning our energy systems from a local to a pan-European one, to make sure that the right signals are provided so that investments take place where and when they are most needed, and so that the energy market is fit to integrate renewable energy, is more flexible, and benefits from better synergies and better efficiencies.

To tackle all these challenges efficiently and correctly, an evidence-based policy is needed, including solid reference scenarios. The INSIGHT_E project has been providing us with a number of ad hoc studies on a number of topics which assist us, aside with other sources, to design our future policies. INSIGHT_E is a very good example on how the research and innovation community can help provide ad hoc and quick studies on topics which policy needs to address urgently.

Dominique Ristori
Director-General for Energy
European Commission, Brussels

Acknowledgments

We are particularly grateful to **Rémy Denos**, INSIGHT_E project officer and primary contact at the European Commission. The INSIGHT_E project and this book have both benefited considerably from Remy's support. Several other policy officers at the Commission significantly enriched our work with their inputs and feedback. In this regard, we especially thank **Jean-Marie Bemtgen**, **Oyvind Vessia**, **Arne Eriksson**, **Eero Ailio**, **Oscar Guinea**, **Javier Castillejos-Alsina** and **Arno Behrens**.

Further, this book greatly benefited from discussions with our Advisory Board, comprised of thought leaders in academia, industry, and research organizations. They are **Ronnie Belmans** (KU Leuven), **Michel Matheu** (EDF), **Dominik Möst** (TU Dresden), **Uwe Remme** (International Energy Agency), and **Ernst Scholtz** (ABB).

The INSIGHT_E project was funded by the European Commission under the Seventh Framework Programme for Research and Technological Development under grant agreement No 612743.

INTRODUCTION

EUROPE'S ENERGY TRANSITION

Manuel Welsch

From a climate policy perspective, 2016 was a historic year. It was the year in which the world's very first comprehensive and legally binding climate deal entered into force, the Paris Agreement. With its ambition to limit global warming to well below 2°C, while pursuing efforts towards 1.5°C, this agreement will directly impact how energy roadmaps and strategies are designed globally. Naturally, in order to deliver on this ambition national pledges on how to achieve this need to match the challenge and, crucially, also have to be implemented. National energy policy making will therefore be assessed in light of these targets, whilst having to demonstrate the feasibility of such a low-carbon future in view of the costs and benefits to society.

The European Union (EU) has an important role in this context. As the third largest emitter of greenhouse gas emissions globally after China and the United States, it has the opportunity to lead by example and be in the driving seat of the global energy transition. While concerted action across all major emitters will be required, a firm signal from Europe to other countries is increasingly important at a time when commitments of other large emitters are uncertain. And the EU remains determined to provide such a signal. Already back in 2011, a roadmap was formulated towards an 80% to 95% reduction of greenhouse gas emissions by 2050. While it may need to be revised in light of the Paris Agreement, it does give a clear strategic direction to where we will be heading, together with the EU's vision to achieve a more secure, affordable, and sustainable Energy Union.

Energy is central to efforts to mitigate climate change, as close to 85% of greenhouse gas emissions in the EU are energy-related. Europe's energy consumption today is largely based on fossil fuels (~70%). A radical energy transformation is thus required by 2050. Currently, the EU consumes 1.2 billion tons of fossil fuels per year (Gtoe). Diverging from commonly applied units but more practical to envision, this equates to 46 train wagons filled with fossil fuels that are being consumed every single minute of the year, day and night[1]. To achieve the transition to a low-carbon energy system, this train would basically have to come to a halt.

While this ultimate goal is well defined, there is no single set of clearly defined actions that need to be implemented to achieve this goal, given the many uncertainties of how our societies and economies will evolve both within Europe and globally. It will therefore be key

---

[1]This corresponds to an endless train constantly supplying the EU at a speed of 49 km/h. The numbers are derived from Eurostat data. Assumptions: 64 tons/85 m^3 VTG Falns waggon for coal as used in Germany; 102 m^3 Greenbrier waggon for oil as used in the United Kingdom; 110 m^3 Greenbrier waggon for gas, assuming all gas was converted to liquefied natural gas (LNG).

Europe's Energy Transition. DOI: http://dx.doi.org/10.1016/B978-0-12-809806-6.00001-8

to diversify efforts and take actions that do not limit the available future low-carbon options, but rather create new choices through support to research, innovation, and development. While the specific choice of actions in the near term will often be a matter of national preference and differ by country, there is a much broader consensus regarding the most promising overarching areas of action, as outlined below.

ELECTRICITY GENERATION

When looking at the three energy-consuming sectors electricity, heating and cooling, and transport, the biggest potential clearly lies in electricity generation. There, almost complete decarbonization is possible, and required. The electricity sector is also the sector where it is most visible that the transition has already gained traction, both within and outside the EU. For example, renewable policies and support schemes in the EU have caused solar photovoltaic (PV) capacity to literally explode from 0 to over 100 GW in the last 15 years, corresponding to around 10% of the total installed capacity. This contributed to the significant reductions of PV system costs, which went down by two-thirds within the period 2008–13 in competitive markets such as Germany and Italy. This trend is expected to continue for some time to come, albeit in a slowed-down fashion: current costs are projected to halve at the latest by 2040. Another example for this transition is the United Kingdom, which was able to reduce the amount of CO_2 emissions per kilowatt hour by around 40% over the last 5 years, largely due to an increasing uptake of renewable energy and reduced coal consumption.

But a successful decarbonization strategy for the power sector will need to rely on a mix of future technologies that has a much wider focus than renewable energy. This requires the consideration of storage technology advancements, the modernization of grids across Europe, and the integration of smarter cities and homes. It will also need to address issues such as the potential role of shale gas, carbon capture and storage (CCS), and also nuclear power for those countries where these are an option. Further, it will need to investigate measures towards a more integrated energy system in general, from supply to consumers, but also across energy forms.

HEATING AND COOLING

Given the significant potential for greenhouse gas emission reductions in electricity generation, it is obvious that other sectors can profit from increasing their use of electricity. Heating and cooling is important in this regard, as half of all fuels consumed in the EU are used to provide heat for buildings and industry. Coupling the electricity and heating and cooling sector is to some extent symbiotic in nature. It not only has the potential to bring down emissions in heating and cooling, but also facilitates the decarbonization of electricity generation. It does so by providing a much needed storage option and source of flexibility to the power sector. Storing heat is orders of magnitude cheaper than storing electricity, and usually the timing of when heating needs to occur is flexible. This allows drawing on and balancing renewable electricity generation in times of oversupply. One way to do so is through heat pumps. The transition to such an increased integration of heat and electricity is probably most visible in Scandinavian countries, where the penetration rate of heat pumps is particularly high. For example, in Sweden with its 4.3 million households, approximately one million heat pumps are installed, mostly in single-family houses. The potential for scaling deployment across Europe is high, both for heating in northern countries as well as for cooling in the south.

In addition to the electrification of heating and cooling, an option to bring down emissions further is through more climate-friendly district heating using locally available carbon-free options, such as solar thermal energy, bioenergy, and waste heat from industrial processes. Adding efficiency measures, such as passive housing standards and refurbishments of old buildings to this mix, emission reductions of around 90% could be achieved in the buildings sector by 2050.

TRANSPORT

Transport is another example where electrification is needed to bring down emissions, as currently 94% of the energy demand in transport is met by oil. It is the source of about a quarter of the EU's greenhouse gas emissions, in addition to being one of the biggest concerns regarding air pollution. In line with the European Commission's Transport White Paper, greenhouse gas emissions will need to reduce by some 60% below 1990 levels by 2050. Electricity can significantly contribute to achieving these emission reductions, and the transition is well on its way and very visible: Tesla has disrupted the scene of conventional market players with its electric, yet luxurious cars, and car-sharing companies around Europe increasingly promote their services by offering electrified cars. Most successful regarding the electrification of transport is the non-EU country Norway, where almost one out of four cars sold in 2015 was electric. By 2025, Norway aims for all new cars to be either electric, hydrogen-powered, or a plug-in hybrid, and Germany is following suit with its goal for all new cars to be emissions free by 2030.

At the level of the EU, electricity is projected to provide some 65% of energy demand in the transport sector by 2050. Emission reductions within the remaining share will need to be tackled in parallel through alternative measures, such as motor efficiency improvements and environmentally sustainable biofuels. This is especially the case for some heavy good transportation and the aviation sector, where electrification is not foreseen as possible.

So while electricity generation will need to be more closely integrated with heating and cooling and transport, another important element of the future European energy system is the closer integration of supply and consumers. Future consumers are envisioned to play a more active part in the transition towards a secure, competitive, and low-carbon energy system, and form a central element of the Energy Union vision. A visible step in this direction is the roll out of smart meters across many households in Europe, and the increasing number of consumers who also generate electricity, e.g., with rooftop PV systems. Further, smart appliances may give consumers control over how flexibly their energy demands are met, for example regarding when to heat their homes. The closer integration of consumers has the potential to be transformative in nature. It can contribute in a novel way to a more balanced utilization of the grid and increased system flexibility, thus facilitating the reliable operation of future power systems with higher shares of variable renewable electricity generation.

While the transition to a low-carbon energy system can already be witnessed now and while the EU continues to be on track to achieve its 2020 energy and climate change goals, this does not mean that we are also well on track towards meeting the targets of the Paris Agreement. Stronger action will be required from 2020 onwards, also to meet the EU greenhouse gas reduction targets for 2030. A further challenge relates to the change in how future energy systems are designed and operated. New market designs and regulatory models are required, e.g., to better integrate consumers and future storage options, and to maintain the secure operation of such a low-carbon energy system. This is crucial, as current markets with their often low and volatile wholesale electricity prices fail to sufficiently incentivize the required infrastructure investments. Furthermore, as consumers participate more actively in markets, their protection will also need to be a priority to avoid misuse of consumer data and to protect those that are vulnerable to energy poverty. Europe's energy transition is thus characterized by many challenges that policy making needs to tackle.

INSIGHTS FOR POLICY MAKING—ABOUT THIS BOOK

Manuel Welsch

As outlined in Chapter 1, Europe's Energy Transition, climate change concerns can be considered as the single largest driver for Europe's envisioned transition to a low-carbon energy system. However, there are also other factors of strategic importance that require consideration, such as ensuring energy security, supply diversification, competitive markets, and affordable access. While European and international energy policy has set clearly defined goals up until 2050, the potential pathways toward achieving these goals are far less clear and depend on many factors, such as geopolitical developments, future resource availabilities, technological progress, demographic changes, behavioral and social trends including public acceptance, and developments in economic sectors other than energy.

Energy policy making therefore has the demanding task of steering this energy transition despite the manifold uncertainties regarding how future circumstances will evolve. An important function is the provision of clarity and direction by establishing clear policy frameworks and market environments that stimulate investments in support of this energy transition. Energy policy making thus needs to anticipate future developments. It needs to reconcile the often competing strategies towards ensuring a reliable and affordable energy system which powers a healthy, competitive, and sustainable economy that meets the needs of society. Informed and up-to-date scientific knowledge can contribute to making this challenging task more achievable.

2.1 IN CLOSE DIALOGUE WITH THE EUROPEAN COMMISSION

In order to provide such scientific knowledge, the European Commission financed the establishment of INSIGHT_E in 2014 as a think tank to provide decision makers with unbiased policy advice and insights on the latest and upcoming energy developments. INSIGHT_E comprises a multidisciplinary team of energy experts from 12 European Institutions and draws on a large network of over 900 stakeholders from 30 countries. The book distills the background research performed by some 50 experts of this think tank and shares the insights gained with a wider audience.

All of INSIGHT_E's research was performed in close dialogue with the European Commission. In the research community, this is a rather unique collaboration. The research is highly topical and responds to the policy needs of the European Commission. At the same time, it is undertaken by independent institutes, ensuring a wholly objective and unbiased perspective. For each topic to be assessed, interinstitutional research teams were set up, combining the expertise of the research institutes involved.

Europe's Energy Transition. DOI: http://dx.doi.org/10.1016/B978-0-12-809806-6.00002-X

Accordingly, this book strives to provide in-depth insights into some of the most pressing elements of the EU policy landscape. It outlines some of the key energy policy challenges the EU faces currently and for many years to come—as opposed to providing an exhaustive introduction to all aspects of energy policy. The close dialogue with the European Commission has ensured that the work done by the think tank and presented in this book directly supported decision-making processes. It has helped the European Commission to take forward their policy program in a range of areas. For example, the work on energy poverty (refer to Section VI) presented new insights that met a critical need by the Commission and resulted in an ongoing debate and engagement of academia with policy makers. This has led to proposed amendments in the "Clean Energy for All Europeans" package from end of 2016 regarding the importance to differentiate between energy poverty and vulnerable customers, stronger protection of household costumers, and measures to actively provide support to those in need. Some of the work presented in this book is also likely to be integrated into upcoming EC Communications.

2.2 AUDIENCE OF THIS BOOK

Stakeholder engagement is a central element of the work within INSIGHT_E. This ensures both the integration of a range of different external viewpoints when performing the analysis, as well as enabling a broad dissemination of findings beyond the European Commission. This book was written in this spirit, and explicitly also targets a nontechnical audience. While technical terms are unavoidable, an effort has been made to introduce new concepts wherever they appear first.

By providing a science–policy interface, this book targets a wide audience interested in gaining strategic insights on how Europe's energy transition may unfold, as also demonstrated by the numerous endorsements in the Preface of this book. This includes:

- Institutions of the European Union and government bodies, such as energy agencies;
- International organizations dealing with energy, such as IRENA, the IEA, or UN organizations;
- Energy industry, such as regulators, transmission system operators, or utilities;
- Research institutes and organizations, such as universities or research centers;
- Civil society, including NGOs and educational institutions.

By analyzing current and future European policy frameworks, insights are presented which are also of interest to a non-European target audience, as some of those challenges assessed will also be relevant to other regions where similar policy instruments are being discussed.

2.3 OUTLINE OF THIS BOOK

This book presents 3 years of research by 12 European research institutions. In the following we provide an overview of how we structured this book.

In Chapter 3, INSIGHT_E—A Think Tank Informing the European Commission, we describe the think tank INSIGHT_E in more detail, including its approach to providing unbiased policy advice, the outputs it delivers, and the institutions it is composed of. The book then presents the current energy landscape in Europe, followed by a set of thematic sections spanning from energy sources to consumption and addressing challenges and policy needs for decision makers. These sections focus on energy supply, renewable market designs, flexible system operation, and society and consumer demands. The book concludes with an outlook on challenges ahead and policy recommendations. The following paragraphs provide more detail on the focus of the subsequent sections of this book.

Section II—Europe's Energy Policy Landscape

This section starts with an introduction to the energy system of the European Union, using energy indicators to assess how the EU's energy system is positioned globally, followed by an overview of European policy developments, including the EU energy policy packages, its vision to achieve an Energy Union, and its energy policy goals to 2030 and 2050. It then continues to assess the level of progress on the main energy policy targets at European and Member State levels and presents the key barriers that need to be overcome to further advance in this regard. Next, the policy instruments and level of progress towards a more competitive internal energy market are described, including the electricity target model, capacity remuneration schemes, and the EU Emissions Trading Scheme. Further, the implications of EU energy policies on energy prices are discussed before presenting the conclusions of this section.

Section III—Energy Supply: A Changing Environment

Global ambitions to limit climate change to a 1.5−2°C increase are difficult to reconcile with the exploitation of indigenous fossil resources. Achieving these ambitions requires large reserves of fossil fuels to remain untouched. In this context, the concept of "carbon budgets" and "unburnable fossil fuels" is introduced in this section. In addition to their economics, the remaining "burnable" fuels are of importance for diversifying the EU's energy supply and ensuring security of supply, as further outlined in this section. In this context, Section III also discusses issues associated with gas imports and related infrastructures, as well as Europe's shale gas potential. An alternative to a diversification of fossil fuel supplies is provided by biofuels, especially in the transport sector—the sector with the largest energy demand in Europe. While surface transport in the EU has benefited from renewable energy policy, biofuels for aviation have not, and are therefore analyzed in more detail in this section. Overall, meeting Europe's emission reduction targets requires a broad mix and range of both technologies and measures, as discussed further in the conclusions of this section.

Section IV—Impact of Renewable Energies on Market Operation and Design

The biggest market impact of ambitions to limit fossil fuel use comes from the increasing shares of renewable energies, which are the focus of this section. While the expansion of renewable energy sources (RES) in the electricity sector has lowered greenhouse gas emissions, it has also caused new challenges. In large electricity markets with high shares of variable RES production, some 100 GWh a year had to be curtailed to avoid damages or outages in the grid infrastructure, as discussed in more detail in this section. Further, the implications of RES on the merit order effect and resulting lower wholesale electricity price levels are investigated. It is further discussed how the merit order effect may increase the missing-money problem for peak load power plants. Energy-only markets may not provide enough incentives to invest in such plants any longer, and new market design options may be required to ensure system reliability. This is analyzed in more detail in a case study on the German electricity market. Finally, this section provides a summary of its main findings, highlighting future research needs.

Section V—Reliable and Flexible Energy Systems

Whatever form an effective market design takes that accommodates larger shares of renewables, it must facilitate a reliable supply of electricity. This requires a power system that is flexible enough to compensate the variability introduced by some renewables. However, increasing shares of variable renewables displace traditional, more flexible supply-side options. This leads to both an increasing need for flexibility and a reducing availability of flexibility within the system. This has created a "flexibility gap," which is addressed in this section. One of the most promising solutions to fill this gap is energy storage, such as pumped hydro power or battery storage. Further, in the medium- to long-term stationary fuel cell and hydrogen (FCH) technologies may emerge as important options. The level of flexibility required is closely linked to the level of reliability demanded by consumers from the power system. However, a clear understanding of the socioeconomic costs of interruptions for consumers across the EU is lacking, as analyzed in this section. Section V then concludes with a summary of the main findings, highlighting future research needs.

Section VI—Society and Consumer Demands

In addition to supply-side measures, a large potential source of system flexibility comes from a more active participation of consumers in the energy transition, as analyzed in this section. Facilitating self-consumption from renewables is an important measure in this regard that may help increase the share of renewable energy. Self-consumption may be facilitated by direct current networks, as they enable a direct integration of the energy produced by households to power their direct current appliances, thus avoiding conversion losses. In addition to electricity consumption, household heat supply offers a significant potential to harness renewable energy, as it makes up the largest share of the energy consumed by the majority of European households. In this context, the potential role of district heating (and cooling) networks is investigated in this section. Further, to ensure an active role for households in the energy transition across all income levels, vulnerable consumers at risk of energy poverty require protection. This section concludes with a summary of the main findings, highlighting the important role for the European Commission to engage consumers in the energy transition.

Section VII—Outlook and Policy Recommendations

A fundamental transformation of Europe's energy system is required in line with global climate deals such as the Paris Agreement and energy strategies of the European Union. To deliver on these ambitions, this transformation must consider a set of challenging issues: effectively decarbonizing the energy system while ensuring the reliability of energy supply, facilitating connected and competitive energy markets, and ensuring consumer protection, particularly for vulnerable groups. This section reflects on these key challenges ahead. It builds on the research and conclusions presented in the preceding sections. It condenses and expands them, and complements them with additional insights gained while delivering INSIGHT_E's analyses for the European Commission. It further suggests future research priorities and contemplates the future role of European energy think tanks such as INSIGHT_E.

INSIGHT_E—A THINK TANK INFORMING THE EUROPEAN COMMISSION

3

Louise Coffineau[1], Manuel Welsch[2], and Claude Ayache[1]

[1]InnoEnergy, Brussels, Belgium [2]KTH Royal Institute of Technology, Stockholm, Sweden

Europe, as other parts of the world, finds itself under pressure to address the major challenges of dependence on energy imports, climate change, increasing strain on energy resources, and the need to ensure access for all consumers to affordable and secure energy. This makes energy policy increasingly complex, as it is influenced by social, economic and environmental factors. While energy policy decisions are fundamentally political decisions, sound, scientific and up-to-date knowledge is critical.

In order to provide such knowledge to decision makers from the European Commission and other energy stakeholders, INSIGHT_E was set up as a scientific and multidisciplinary think tank. It offers unbiased energy policy advice and insights on policy options, including assessments of their potential impact. Moreover, it brings new technology trends to the attention of policy makers, as well as the objectives and activities of important stakeholders that have a key voice in European energy policy making.

The INSIGHT_E consortium is composed of a diverse team of energy experts, comprising major European universities, research institutions, and consultancies as well as a knowledge and innovation community, an independent think tank, and a stakeholder organization, all joining forces in this project. All of them are experienced in delivering high-quality policy advice and have access to a large network of experts, ensuring the representation of the diversity of views that exist within the European energy landscape.

This section first outlines how the need for a think tank like INSIGHT_E emerged. It then highlights its main outputs in Section 3.2, before describing the role of its observatory in more detail in Section 3.3. Following on this, Section 3.4 provides more detail on how it responds to questions posed by the European Commission and introduces the partners that form INSIGHT_E.

3.1 THE NEED FOR MULTIDISCIPLINARY ENERGY POLICY ADVICE

Energy is a complex issue, which affects every part of the society, from the consumer lighting his house and paying his bill to the industrial sector dependent on energy supply. Its multidisciplinarily nature is reflected in EU policy-making processes: the EU's standard decision-making procedure, "co-decision,"[a] affects and is influenced by multilevel and multiregional aspects, as outlined in the following.

---

[a]The "co-decision" procedure is the legislative process requiring that neither the European Parliament nor the Council of the EU may adopt legislation (drafted by the European Commission) without the other's assent.

Europe's Energy Transition. DOI: http://dx.doi.org/10.1016/B978-0-12-809806-6.00003-1

Before the European Commission proposes new policy actions, it assesses the potential economic, social and environmental consequences that they may have through "impact assessments," which analyze the advantages and disadvantages of the possible policy options based on predefined criteria.

Further, many European, national, and local stakeholders take part in the decision-making process. The European Commission consults interested and affected parties such as nongovernmental organizations, local authorities, and representatives of industry and civil society through open consultations. In parallel, the European Commission consults groups of experts in high-level working groups to gather advice on technical issues. These measures are critical to ensuring the efficacy of the future policy decisions, and require significant resources and engagement from the European Commission on these multilevel and multisectoral aspects.

In parallel to EU decision making, the energy landscape itself is adding to this complexity, as it is facing a transition towards a low-carbon energy system. In the overall framework of decarbonizing the energy system, building on the Paris Agreement of the UN Framework Convention on Climate Change, we are witnessing a number of monumental changes: from a deeply centralized energy system towards a more and more fragmented one, giving more space to new actors. Further, the digitalization of our society is giving a new dimension to the energy sector. Soon we will be able to control our energy consumption from our mobile devices and passive consumers are turning into prosumers who both produce as well as consume.

To facilitate new methods of energy production and consumption, the European Commission aims at providing an enabling environment for the market to adopt new technologies, services, and business practices. To do so effectively, the European Commission is reliant on the advice of energy practitioners from a wide range of sectors, who are able to provide answers and insights on some of the most pressing questions concerning Europe's energy transition.

In order to provide such advice, the European Commission called for the creation of a think tank, and the INSIGHT_E's consortium responded to this call. INSIGHT_E was created in 2014 as an independent think tank addressing questions of concern to the European Commission, taking the complexity of the decision-making process and the changing nature of the energy landscape into account.

Knowledge and understanding of the challenges, opportunities, and trends affecting Europe's energy sector is becoming increasingly important and a policy-making prerequisite. To aide in this endeavor, the think tank provides transparent and unbiased research on the topical issues being considered by the European Commission. To ensure the intelligence is comprehensive and holistic, the think tank works with stakeholders from business, academia, trade associations, and NGOs to take into account all the dimensions of the energy system. Inclusion of these sectors in INSIGHT_E's research programs provides the European Commission with broad analyses to inform related policy decisions.

3.2 DELIVERING POLICY ADVICE—THE OUTPUTS OF INSIGHT_E

Today the majority of new energy policies are in support of Europe's energy transition to a decarbonized energy supply. The outputs of INSIGHT-E help to assess this energy transition across all of its dimensions. They include tools and instruments to measure the impact of this transition and to identify its drivers, such as technology innovation, policies and regulations, and market incentives. The resources provided by INSIGHT_E further help to conduct analysis of possible

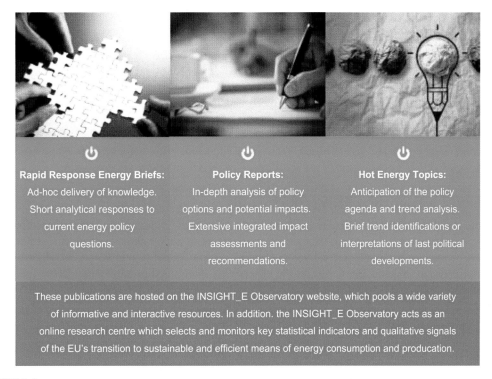

Rapid Response Energy Briefs:
Ad-hoc delivery of knowledge.
Short analytical responses to
current energy policy
questions.

Policy Reports:
In-depth analysis of policy
options and potential impacts.
Extensive integrated impact
assessments and
recommendations.

Hot Energy Topics:
Anticipation of the policy
agenda and trend analysis.
Brief trend identifications or
interpretations of last political
developments.

These publications are hosted on the INSIGHT_E Observatory website, which pools a wide variety of informative and interactive resources. In addition. the INSIGHT_E Observatory acts as an online research centre which selects and monitors key statistical indicators and qualitative signals of the EU's transition to sustainable and efficient means of energy consumption and production.

FIGURE 3.1

The INSIGHT_E outputs.

energy scenarios. One of the main assets of INSIGHT_E is its flexibility, which is represented by its four main types of outputs (see Fig. 3.1).

RAPID RESPONSE ENERGY BRIEFS

Rapid Response Energy Briefs (RREB) are designed to provide answers to the European Commission's most pressing energy queries. INSIGHT_E responds to these queries within 6 weeks to 3 months in the form of a condensed assessment of around 10 pages. For example, these briefs focus on topics such as biofuels for aviation or transport, or the role of shale gas.

HOT ENERGY TOPICS

Hot Energy Topics (HET) are designed to attract the attention of the European Commission on topical or emerging issues that they may not have researched in detail. The consortium usually only works a couple of weeks before publishing a HET, as it has to be up to date and concise, usually at a length of 5−10 pages. As an example, HETs focused on the goals of the UN Climate Change Conference in Paris (COP21) and their implications on the EU's preexisting climate change and clean energy roadmap.

POLICY REPORTS

Policy Reports (PRs) address the European Commission's requests for more in-depth analyses. They allow more time for high-quality research compared to the previous two deliverables. The consortium has 4–6 months to work on a PR after receiving a request from the European Commission. The preparation of a PR usually involves more extensive stakeholder consultations, review, and feedback processes. Its final scope is usually around 60–80 pages. PRs focus on topics such as smart consumers or integrating large shares of renewable energy.

The information provided in all of these three types of publications forms the basis of this book. The content they provide was distilled, rearranged, updated and complemented by new research. All of INSIGHT_E's publications can be accessed on the Observatory.

OBSERVATORY OF THE ENERGY TRANSITION

In order for INSIGHT_E to become a reference in the energy landscape, the Observatory provides access to outputs of the think tank beyond its publications. It combines a set of useful, efficient and responsive tools to give unbiased advice on energy system pathways and scenarios, aligned to the needs of decision makers. The design of the observatory is outlined in more detail in the following.

3.3 THE INSIGHT_E OBSERVATORY OF THE ENERGY TRANSITION

The INSIGHT_E Observatory, available at www.insightenergy.org, was designed as a service provider and knowledge base that is action-oriented, inclusive, and targeted. It serves to internally coordinate the work between partners, while being at the same time a platform for external communication. The Observatory aims to pool expertise, foster debate, and support outreach. Further, it was set up to be complementary to other existing observatories.

ENSURING ITS COMPLEMENTARITY

A review of existing observatories in Europe and beyond reveals that many energy sector organizations engage in activities that fulfill the role of an observatory—i.e., a structure that provides access to energy information and analysis that is either extensive (with regard to the scope, the perspective adopted, or the number of information sources) or intensive in nature (with regard to being accurate and detailed).

Within the considerable number of observatory-like structures that have a European or international scope, some thematic or organizational features emerge. First, there are numerous observatories dedicated specifically to energy markets, focusing on economic perspectives. In this area numerous corporate observatories have flourished in the last decade under the auspices of energy companies or consultancies.

A second topic commonly addressed by observatories is international cooperation in the field of energy, often within regional areas such as the Mediterranean. In this case observatories mostly aim to foster synergies between several countries. However, observatories dedicated to emerging energy technologies are relatively underdeveloped. The French Observatory of Renewable Energies (Observ'ER) has a comparable focus to the INSIGHT_E Observatory, but with a more French than European focus.

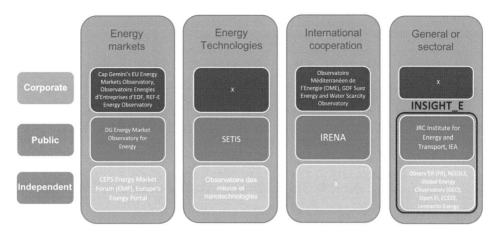

FIGURE 3.2

Overview of institutions and platforms providing observatory functions with an EU dimension.

In general, very few of these observatories, except maybe the ones that are EU-anchored (DG Energy, JRC) or Brussels-based (CEPS EMF), target European policy makers specifically.

The challenge for the Energy Observatory is to avoid duplication, and to make the most of the diversity of the INSIGHT_E consortium in order to provide unique expertise that can't be found in this condensed form anywhere else. Therefore, INSIGHT_E positioned its Observatory as a platform that is institutionally independent in terms of the research provided, yet focused on informing (public) energy policy making in the European Union. It covers all four areas shown in Fig. 3.2, spanning across:

- Energy markets, e.g., when quantifying the merit-order effect in European electricity markets;
- Energy technologies, e.g., when assessing the role of fuel cell and hydrogen technologies and applications;
- International cooperation, e.g., when outlining the energy-related implications of selected Sustainable Development Goals; and
- Sectoral issues of the energy sector, e.g., when investigating the potential role of biofuels for aviation.

All of these and many more topics are covered and freely accessible on the Observatory. It thus is the only independent observatory targeting EU energy policy making with such a broad focus.

OBSERVATORY TOOLS

The INSIGHT_E Observatory's focus is therefore to provide a menu of options to investigate the energy transition. This includes: access to publications, indicators for monitoring the energy transition, webinars, and so-called information corners.

In the following, these instruments and tools of the observatory are described in more detail.

Access to Publications

As outlined previously, INSIGHT_E provides three main types of publications, RREB, HET, and PRs. All of these three outputs are published on the Observatory.

Indicators of the Energy Transition

INSIGHT_E developed indicators to monitor the driving factors of the energy transition of the European Union (Fig. 3.3). This resource is made available as an interactive map on the Observatory which displays key information about each country's energy use.

The indicators help evaluate progress of the energy transition, compare EU countries, and allow identifying of the factors that influence changes in energy consumption and production. In order to deliver consistent outputs, the indicators have been structured around the four cornerstones of the energy transition: environment, economy, society, and security. The interactive resource can be used by the European Commission to inform their decision-making processes and by energy stakeholders to identify trends and patterns in a host of energy-oriented fields.

FIGURE 3.3

Indicators of the energy transition (interactive map) (http://www.insightenergy.org/static_pages/energy_transition_indicators).

By INSIGHT_E, based on Eurostat data.

Webinars

To help expand the outreach of the research by INSIGHT_E, numerous webinars with energy experts and stakeholders are organized to discuss the think tank's outputs. In this context, INSIGHT_E draws on its Energy Policy Advice Network, comprising some 900 + stakeholders from 30 countries. The main objective of the webinars is to inform the participants about the think tank's research and to receive feedback on core research questions. For each webinar, the partners within the INSIGHT_E consortium identify and maps stakeholders which could be interested in participating. Further, all webinars are announced and then published as a video on the Observatory.

Information Corners

To complement the core research outputs of INSIGHT_E, the consortium produces supplementary materials on (1) energy innovation, (2) energy policy, and (3) energy markets, published in "information corners." The energy innovation corner, for example, assesses the technical specificities of particular technologies, their market penetration, and how they can contribute to the energy transition. The policy corner aims to inform EU energy policy making. Lastly, the market corner aims to inform the audience about European and international energy markets.

3.4 BACKGROUND ON INSIGHT_E
INSIGHT_E's MODE OF OPERATION

The design of INSIGHT_E and its mode of operation build on the experiences with a preceding think tank, also financed by the 7th Framework Program of the European Union, called "THINK."[b]

THINK was a 3-year project organized around a Scientific Council of 24 experts covering five energy policy dimensions: Science and Technology, Market and Network Economics, Regulation, Law, and Policy Implementation.

THINK has responded to the European Commission's evolving needs on a half-yearly basis. Each 6 months, the think tank worked on two research projects, with the following processes in place to ensure the high quality of its outputs: an Expert Hearing with an Industrial Council to test the robustness of the work, the Scientific Council with its 24 experts, and a Public Consultation to test the public acceptance of different policy options by involving a broader community. As an output of its work, the consortium has provided clear policy recommendations to the EC through reports covering a broad range of topics.[c]

Building on this successful experience with its high-quality outputs, INSIGHT_E was set up to be more interactive and more responsive by answering quickly and efficiently to questions posed by the European Commission. Adopting this "top-down" approach, the think tank has proven to be a valuable resource to the European Commission, delivering impartial policy advice. It always places high priority on the continuous interactions with the EC as well as with stakeholders of the energy sector. Generating different types of reports, INSIGHT_E satisfies different needs of policy

---

[b]http://www.eui.eu/Projects/THINK/Home.aspx/
[c]http://www.eui.eu/Projects/THINK/Research/Index.aspx

makers ranging from the requirement of in-depth and comprehensive analysis of topics to brief yet informed inputs on specific issues in a timely manner.

To harness external expertise and to share the results of its research with the public, the think tank regularly engages a network of European energy stakeholders in its decision-making processes, research exercises, and outreach activities. From the onset of the project, energy experts from academia, industry, and nongovernmental organizations are helping inform the think tank's program of work and research priorities. Through interviews, questionnaires, meetings, and online webinars, external experts are helping the think tank produce multidisciplinary assessments of technologies and policies that are being considered as part of the energy transition of the European Union.

THE INSIGHT_E CONSORTIUM

The INSIGHT_E consortium has brought together partners with vast expertise in the analysis of and policy advice on the energy system and energy industries, electricity, renewables, oil, coal and gas markets as well as energy efficiency. This in-depth knowledge of the energy sector is complemented by a strong background in economy, trade as well as law and regulatory frameworks.

To be able to ensure this broad level of expertise, the consortium comprises a widely qualified group, composed of a diverse set of bodies:

— Leading European universities;
— Highly experienced European research organizations and consultancies;
— A Knowledge and Innovation Community of the European Institute of Technology;
— A stakeholder organization;
— An independent think tank for research and debate.

The consortium included 12 different partners based in nine different European countries (see Fig. 3.4), as introduced in the following.

KTH Royal Institute of Technology (KTH) is the coordinator of INSIGHT_E. It is responsible for one-third of Sweden's capacity for technical research. Research at KTH is organized in five research platforms encompassing energy, ICT, materials, transport, and life science technology. Within KTH, the Division of Energy Systems Analysis is in charge of INSIGHT_E-related activities. This division combines experience in energy systems analysis and modeling tools such as MESSAGE and LEAP. It further works on the development of the open source energy modeling system OSeMOSYS.

Enerdata is an independent information and consulting firm specialized in the global energy and carbon markets. It has over 25 years of experience in economic issues related to midstream and downstream energy. Enerdata's products cover energy and CO_2 emissions databases, statistics, reports, news, analysis, and forecasts, using globally recognized in-house forecasting models (POLES-Enerdata, MedPro). Within INSIGHT_E, Enerdata takes part in several publications and created the indicators of the Energy Transition, available on the Observatory, in collaboration with EIT InnoEnergy.

The Energy Institute Hrvoje Požar (EIHP) is a nonprofit public institution owned by the Government of Croatia. EIHP provides expert and scientific support to the: strategic development of the energy system and its subsystems; processes of legislative reform and development; advancement of economic relations; and the development of relevant institutions. Within INSIGHT_E, the Institute's main tasks included, inter alia: expert and scientific research in the field of

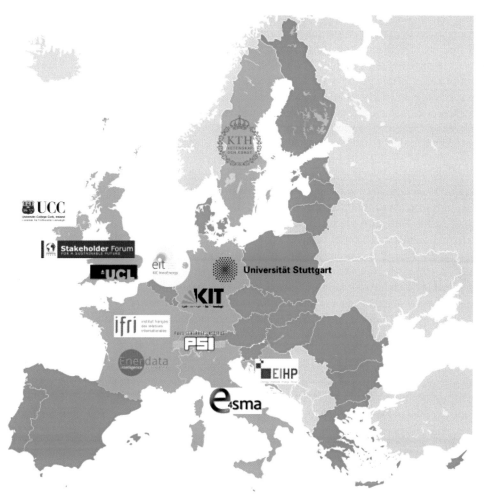

FIGURE 3.4

INSIGHT_E consortium.

energy; management of national energy programs and projects; and communication with experts, scientists, and the general public.

Energy Engineering Economic Environment Systems Modeling and Analysis (E4SMA) provides consulting services in the areas of energy planning, policy, and environment. Its main area of expertise is in supporting the creation of energy, environmental, economic models as a means to represent the complexity of existing energy systems, and to investigate how such systems evolve through scenario-based analysis using simulation or optimization approaches.

EIT InnoEnergy is one of the Knowledge and Innovation Communities (KICs) funded by the European Institute for Innovation and Technology (EIT). EIT InnoEnergy fosters the integration of education, research, and business, strengthening the culture of innovation and entrepreneurship. It is a commercial company with 29 shareholders; all of them key players in the energy sector. EIT InnoEnergy's strategy is to be the leading engine for innovation and entrepreneurship in the field of sustainable energy. Within the INSIGHT_E project, EIT IE is in charge of the Observatory and takes part in different publications.

Institut Français des Relations Internationales (IFRI) is the principal institution for independent research and debate in France that is dedicated to the analysis of international questions and global governance. It is primarily useful for political and economic decision-makers as well as academics, opinion leaders, and civil society representatives. The research that is at the heart of Ifri's activities favors analysis and foresight concerning European and international affairs, and adopts a multidisciplinary approach that takes local, national and global perspectives into consideration.

Karlsruhe Institute of Technology (KIT) bundles the missions of the following two precursory institutions: a university of the state of Baden-Wuerttemberg with teaching and research tasks and a large-scale research institution of the Helmholtz Association conducting program-oriented research on behalf of the Federal Republic of Germany. Within these missions, KIT is operating along the three strategic fields of action of research, teaching, and innovation.

Stakeholder Forum is a nonprofit organization founded in 1987. It is headquartered in London and has an office in New York. Its mission is to enhance open, accountable and participatory decision making at international processes on a diverse range of issues around sustainable development and climate change. Stakeholder Forum works with a diversity of stakeholders globally on: international policy development; stakeholder engagement and consultation; and media and communication. Stakeholder Forum is in charge of dealing with the expert database and organizing webinars within INSIGHT_E.

The Paul Scherrer Institute (PSI) is a multidisciplinary research center for natural sciences and technology and the largest Swiss national research institute. In national and international collaboration with universities, other research institutes, and industry, PSI is active in solid state physics, materials sciences, elementary particle physics, life sciences, nuclear and non-nuclear energy research, and energy-related ecology.

The *Institute of Energy Economics and the Rational Use of Energy (IER)* of the University of Stuttgart contributes to INSIGHT_E with its combination of technical, physical, and human sciences. Today the university is a modern, achievement-orientated institution with a comprehensive range of subjects and a focus on technical and physical disciplines. The university is a much sought-after partner by international and German institutes, state and private funding organizations, and by partners from the economy. Today 4800 employees work in over 150 institutes, 10 faculties, and in its central institutions.

University College Cork (UCC) is a world-class research-led university that plays a key regional and national role in the development of Ireland's knowledge-based economy. UCC's Environmental Research Institute is an interdisciplinary research institute that facilitates and supports environmental, marine, and energy-based research. The current research focus is on building and using energy modeling tools to inform policy decisions.

University College London (UCL) is one of the UK's premier universities and is ranked in the world's top 10, whose staff and former students have included 20 Nobel Prize winners. The UCL Energy Institute is the university's mechanism for bringing together a wide range of perspectives, understandings, and procedures in energy research, transcending the boundaries between academic disciplines. At present, UCL has a research portfolio in energy of more than £10 million.

EUROPE'S ENERGY POLICY LANDSCAPE

INTRODUCTION: EUROPE AS A CONSUMING REGION

4

Aurélie Faure-Schuyer[1], Manuel Welsch[2], and Steve Pye[3]

[1]Institut Français des Relations Internationales (IFRI), Brussels, Belgium [2]KTH Royal Institute of Technology, Stockholm, Sweden [3]University College London (UCL), London, United Kingdom

Across the energy system, a transformation of the global supply—demand dynamic is being observed, especially affecting consumers and producers of fossil fuels such as oil, gas, and coal. This transformation has been visible through a number of crisis, such as the EU 2009 and 2014 gas crises; the 2014 oil price collapse; or the decline in global coal demand in 2015. After a decade of a strong rise in global energy demand, energy markets have been entering a period of lower demand growth. According to BP Statistical Review,[a] global energy demand growth, which grew on average by 2.3% between 2000 and 2014, slowed down to a mere 1.1% in 2015.

In this turbulent environment, the future energy demand in Europe appears to remain relatively constant. Taking into account the limited exploitation of nonconventional energy resources and given the maturity of existing oil- and gas-producing fields, Europe's energy dependency (53% in 2014) is not foreseen to decline in coming years. Given the security concerns combined with the imperative for decarbonization, European countries will remain active in considering new ways of diversifying their conventional energy supplies.

In this changing system, the European Union has formulated a decarbonization agenda to 2050 that shapes the energy policy debate across European countries, which was rapidly taken up in, e.g., Germany and Denmark. The European Union has made strong progress to become one of the leading regions in renewable-based energy. However, many questions remain concerning the structure of the energy mix in this transitional period and on the optimal economic pathway to 2050.

In this context, energy policy strategies also referred to as "energy packages" are explicitly being built over the three dimensions of energy security, affordability, and decarbonization (refer to Section 6.1). The elements of these strategies depend on the specific policy in question (such as energy efficiency, renewables, greenhouse gas emissions, etc.) and what horizon is foreseen (2020, 2030, 2050). During and after the UNFCCC Climate Change Conference in Paris in 2015, Europe's energy and climate policy and diplomacy efforts have been acknowledged on the global scene. However, Europe, together with the rest of the world, will have to remain equally successful in the implementation of the Paris agreement, which will require further internal policy development.

---

[a]BP Energy Outlook, 2016 edition, Outlook to 2035, https://www.bp.com/content/dam/bp/pdf/energy-economics/energy-outlook-2016/bp-energy-outlook-2016.pdf

Europe's Energy Transition. DOI: http://dx.doi.org/10.1016/B978-0-12-809806-6.00004-3

This section presents European energy policy's background, main achievements, and future perspectives. It details to what extent Europe's energy policy is affected by both internal and external dynamics and discusses the historic, legislative, or more structural roots of this policy. It presents the proposal of an Energy Union, aimed at consolidating both, a degree of policy integration within Europe and strategic outward-oriented international policy action. This section further puts Europe's geopolitical role and its internal political dimension in perspective, also considering the infrastructure and systemic transformations required by the energy transition.

Chapter 5, The European Union on the Global Scene—A Snapshot, presents the main statistical energy indicators used in assessing the EU's position on the global scene. Chapter 6, European Energy Policy Objectives, gives an overview of European policy developments. It assesses the level of progress on the main energy policy targets at European and Member State levels. It also presents the key barriers that need to be overcome to further advance the achievement of these targets and discusses the challenges related to the Energy Union. Chapter 7, A Market-Based European Energy Policy, introduces the market policy instruments in place to achieve the targets outlined in Chapter 6, European Energy Policy Objectives. These instruments are grouped under different dimensions of the internal energy market: the electricity target model, and capacity and carbon markets. Chapter 7, A Market-Based European Energy Policy, also discusses the implications of EU energy policies on energy prices, before presenting conclusions in Chapter 8.

THE EUROPEAN UNION ON THE GLOBAL SCENE—A SNAPSHOT

5

Aurélie Faure-Schuyer[1], Manuel Welsch[2], and Steve Pye[3]

[1]Institut Français des Relations Internationales (IFRI), Brussels, Belgium [2]KTH Royal Institute of Technology, Stockholm, Sweden [3]University College London (UCL), London, United Kingdom

On the global energy scene, the European Union (EU) is the fourth largest energy-consuming region after China, the United States, and the rest of Asia (Fig. 5.1). This chapter presents the main developments regarding the EU's energy and electricity supply and its position within international energy markets. It further discusses recent evolutions in consumption and energy dependency. All figures refer to Eurostat office of statistical data (except when credited otherwise).

5.1 PRIMARY ENERGY SOURCES AND INTERACTIONS WITH GLOBAL MARKETS

Over the last decade, the European Union has faced a significant decline in its exploitation of primary energy resources due to the maturity profile of the North Sea oil and gas production (refer to Fig. 5.2). In absolute terms, solid fuels (coking coal and lignite) and crude oil energy production have declined sharply (−25% and −52%, respectively, over the last decade). Overall, the EU-28 primary energy consumption went down by 11% to 1529.6 Mtoe[a] between 2006 and 2015.

The European Union maintains a diversified primary energy consumption structure, relying on imports of fossil energy (crude oil, refined products, natural gas, and hard coal) (refer to Fig. 5.3). Since early 2000, the EU has relied increasingly on hard coal imports and additionally on pipeline natural gas and liquefied natural gas shipments from global gas markets. In total, EU coal imports increased to 205 Mt in 2014,[b] as a result of cheap global coal prices, low carbon prices, and the closure of hard coal mines in Germany.[c] Fossil fuels remain the dominant primary energy mode in the European Union, with a 71% share in 2015 at primary consumption level.

The dominance of fossil fuels in the EU should however not mask the steady growing trend of renewables. Between 1990 and 2013, the proportion of renewables grew from 4.5% in 1990 to

---

[a]Toe: tonnes oil equivalent.
[b]Euracoal Market Report—January 1, 2016; file:///C:/Users/Utilisateur/Downloads/EURACOAL-Market-Report-2016-1%20(1).pdf.
[c]In total all German hard coal mining are scheduled for closure by 2018.

Europe's Energy Transition. DOI: http://dx.doi.org/10.1016/B978-0-12-809806-6.00005-5

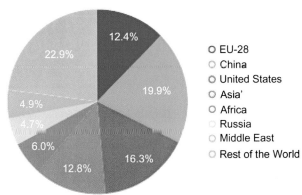

TOTAL 2013: 9173 Mtoe

12.4%

22.9%

19.9%

4.9%

4.7%

6.0%

16.3%

12.8%

O EU-28
O China
O United States
O Asia'
O Africa
○ Russia
○ Middle East
○ Rest of the World

FIGURE 5.1

World energy consumption.

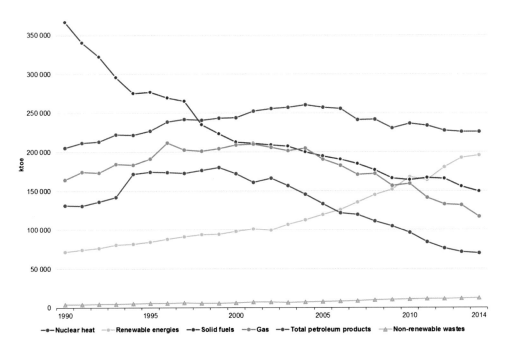

FIGURE 5.2

Gross Inland Energy Consumption in the EU-28.

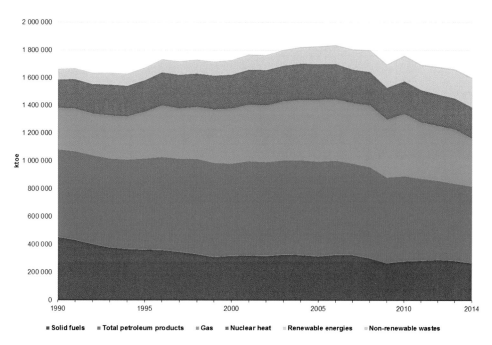

FIGURE 5.3

EU primary energy consumption by fuel.

From Eurostat.

12.6% in 2013, increasing at an average annual rate of 4.5% per year according to the European Environmental Agency.

5.2 ENERGY DEPENDENCY—A KEY CONCERN

As mentioned, the EU is characterized by large imports of oil and petroleum products, gas, and solid fuels. Import dependency measured as the ratio of net imports to gross inland consumption stood at 53% in 2014, increasing from 44% in 1990. As such, it is among the most import-dependent regions of the world (refer to Fig. 5.4) and the single largest importer[d] given its high overall consumption.

On an aggregated level, imports are increasing for all fuels in the European Union, especially gas imports during recent years (Fig. 5.5). However, some stabilization of this overall increase is evident, as the import dependency has been constantly between 52% and 55% since 2005.

---

[d]Energy imports and exports—EU World—Eurostat nrg_100a and International Energy Agency.

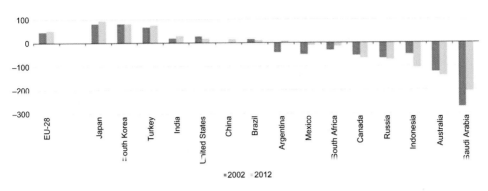

FIGURE 5.4

Energy dependency in different regions of the world.

From Eurostat.

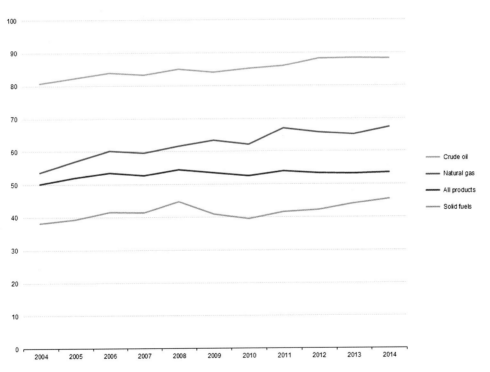

FIGURE 5.5

EU energy dependency by fuel. Domestic production (dark colors) + net imports (light colors).

From Eurostat.

5.3 DIVERSIFIED ELECTRICITY GENERATION COMPARED TO OTHER REGIONS

In the EU's electricity system, fossil fuel-based generation is still the dominant source, generating 40% of the total in 2014. Low-carbon modes of generation are however increasing in importance. Nuclear power accounts for 26% of electricity generation in the EU, with hydro power generation representing 19%, and other renewables accounting for 14%. Nuclear power is present in 14 of the 28 Member States, with especially France and Sweden relying heavily on it. Since Germany's phase out of nuclear power in 2011, newly installed renewables capacities (solar, wind, and biomass) have been acting as compensating factors, while coal-fired power generation has been of continuing importance.

In terms of the installed capacity of renewables, the EU is number two globally behind China. Hydro basins are a strong asset for Europe (in particular in countries such as Norway and in the alpine areas of Austria) in providing large-scale energy storage and balancing variability in demand and renewable generation, especially from wind power. However, the EU's aggregated hydro capacity (136 GW[e]) remains lower than China or Brazil. Overall, installed wind capacity in the EU

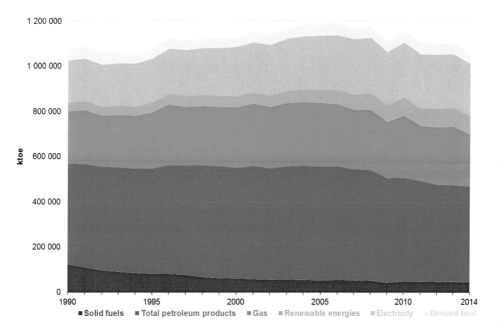

FIGURE 5.6

Trends in EU final energy consumption.

From Eurostat.

[e]Eurelectric—EU-27.

stands at 142 GW and its solar capacity at 40 GW. In several areas, these renewables are continuingly displacing other modes of generation. In particular in Germany, Spain, and Italy, solar-based generation is gaining ground at respectively 6.3%, 4.9%, and 8.7% of the generation mix in 2015. In the same year, wind achieved 22%, 18%, and 5.4% of electricity generation in Germany, Spain, and Italy, respectively. Denmark was the leading country in wind-based electricity generation with 42% of share in the electricity mix.

5.4 FINAL ENERGY CONSUMPTION IN THE EUROPEAN UNION

Gross inland energy consumption stood at 1606 Mtoe in 2014. Since 2005, gross inland consumption has been decoupling from GDP, a trend that accelerated with the 2008−09 financial crisis. Since 2009, energy consumption has been declining, especially in industry and in the residential sector. This is compensated by stable consumption in the transportation sector, which flattened since 2005 as a result of muted GDP growth and efficiency improvements in freight and road transport. The final energy consumption mix by fuel is presented in Fig. 5.6.

While the structure of energy supply differs from one Member State to another, energy consumption trends are less country-specific. In particular, the decoupling of energy consumption from GDP can be considered as a structural driver for the European Union as a whole. It may also be used in founding future scenarios for EU energy policy making.

EUROPEAN ENERGY POLICY OBJECTIVES

Aurélie Faure-Schuyer[1], Manuel Welsch[2], and Steve Pye[3]

[1]*Institut Français des Relations Internationales (IFRI), Brussels, Belgium* [2]*KTH Royal Institute of Technology, Stockholm, Sweden* [3]*University College London (UCL), London, United Kingdom*

European energy policy encompasses a series of policy targets and frameworks that aim at consolidating the European Union's position in the field of clean energy, while ensuring a secure and affordable energy supply, as highlighted in the Lisbon Treaty. This chapter focuses on the way European policy objectives are being translated into a collective action by individual Member States, based on quantified European policy targets.

European energy and climate policy envisages interrelated pillars on renewables penetration, greenhouse gas emissions, and energy efficiency. An introduction to the general framework of European energy policy and reforms is presented in Section 6.1. This provides a background to Section 6.2, which discusses the 2020 energy policy targets and future policy developments towards 2050.

6.1 REFORMING EUROPEAN ENERGY MARKETS AND COORDINATION

THE EU ENERGY PACKAGES

Reforms of the energy markets have occurred through the sequence of three energy legislative developments. These started during the mid-1990s with the First Energy Package in 1996 until the Third (and latest) Energy Package (2020 Climate and Energy Package) of 2009, as illustrated in Fig. 6.1.[a]

The First Directive aimed at introducing competition, with the objective of separating or unbundling former energy monopolies and ensuring the distinction between regulated and nonregulated activities.

The Second Electricity Directive, adopted in June 2003, reinforced procedures whereby energy transmission networks had to be run independently from the production and supply of energy. This was in conformity with the unbundling principle,[b] aimed at limiting risks of systemic conflict of interest deemed inherent in the vertical integration of production, networks, and supply activities.

---

[a]The Climate and Energy package includes the following texts: Regulation (EC) No 443/2009—Reduction of CO_2 Emissions from Light Duty Vehicles/Directive 2009/28/EC—Renewable Energy Sources/Directive 2009/29/EC—Emission Trading Scheme/Directive 2009/30/EC—Fuel Quality Directive/Directive 2009/31/EC—Carbon Capture and Storage/Decision No 406/2009/EC—"effort sharing".

[b]Full ownership, legal, management (or "functional") unbundling.

Europe's Energy Transition. DOI: http://dx.doi.org/10.1016/B978-0-12-809806-6.00006-7

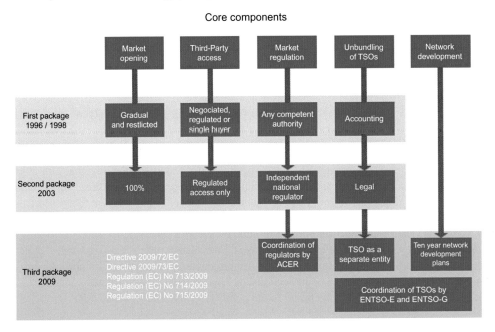

FIGURE 6.1

Development of energy packages.

From European Court of Auditors.

The integration of the electricity and gas markets progressed further with the Third Energy Package,[c] which currently forms the legal basis of the electricity market. It detailed further the role of transmission and distribution system operators, and the separation requirements of generation and supply. European[d] regulation created the Agency for Cooperation of Energy Regulators (ACER), and the European Network of Transmission System Operators (ENTSO),[e] acting together in the creation and adoption of framework guidelines and in the definition of network codes for electricity and gas. ACER issues framework guidelines, while ENTSOe (in electricity) and ENTSOg (in gas) develop network codes based on these guidelines. Network codes become legally binding upon a specific legislative procedure called comitology.[f]

While EU legislation painted a new operating landscape for networks, assets in use today have been inherited from former integrated utility companies. European legislation, however, was not passed without some form of cultural and political resistance to the creation of unbundled operating models, in which networks began their "own lives" within separate entities. Through the new governance role of

[c]Directive 72/2009/EC and Regulation (EC) 714/2009 for electricity.
[d]Regulation (EC) 714/2009 (Article 8).
[e]The ENTSOe covers 41 Transmission System Operators from 34 countries.
[f]A legislative procedure that is reserved for highly technical legislation.

ENTSOe, electricity transmission network operators were able to regain some form of political foothold that they may have lost in the process of unbundling former integrated monopolies.

The promotion of renewables was enhanced with the Renewables Directive of the Third Package, which included a priority dispatch for renewables and the definition of short- to mid-term electricity market models for electricity. This directive was designed with the aim of creating a market-based framework and providing transparent price signals for all technologies including renewables.

This process of reform led to a complete transformation of the energy policy landscape allowing the European Union to advance towards the objective of supplying 20% of the final energy consumption by renewables in 2020. It also led to important transformations at industry sector (utilities) level through the unbundling process, the creation of power electricity exchanges and gas hubs, as well as the phasing out of regulated supply tariffs.

THE ENERGY UNION

In addition to market reforms through the various energy packages, the EU also places a significant emphasis on coordinating and harmonizing its energy transition towards a secure, sustainable, competitive and affordable future energy system. The Energy Union is the most visible outcome of this effort. The Energy Union is a policy initiative that was initially inspired by security of supply concerns in the natural gas market [1]. In 2014−15, it gained a broadened perspective towards the European single energy market and in support of climate policy towards the 2030 and 2050 energy and climate goals. In 2015, it was formally launched as part of the Commission Proposal—COM(2015)80.

The Energy Union comprises five closely related and mutually reinforcing dimensions:

1. Energy security, solidarity, and trust;
2. A fully integrated European energy market;
3. Energy efficiency contributing to moderation of demand;
4. Decarbonizing the economy;
5. Research, innovation, and competitiveness.[g]

Several of these dimensions are investigated later on in this section (e.g., Section 6.2 on renewable energy policy or Section 7.1 on the internal energy market), or are implicitly addressed within other parts of this book (e.g., Section IV on the impact of renewable energies on energy markets).

The Energy Union opens the way for a regionalized approach in the construction of the internal energy market, in particular in areas where cross-border cooperation hinders the completion of the internal energy market. In addition to its internal components, the Energy Union also has a diplomatic dimension with external partners like Russia and the United States as part of its energy security dimension.[h,i]

---

[g]Its innovation policy framework is based on the Integrated Strategic Energy Technology Plan (i.e., the SET Plan).
[h]European Energy Security Strategy (EEES) COM (2014-330).
[i]Security of Supply Package: Revision of Gas Security of Supply Regulation (COM(2016) 52 final)/Communication of an Liquefied Natural Gas Strategy (COM(2016) 49 final)/Heating and Cooling Strategy (COM(2016) 51 final)/Revision of Intergovernmental Agreements (COM(2016) 53 final).

Throughout all of its components, the Energy Union emphasizes that consumers are at its core as active market participants in the energy transition that profit from its benefits and are protected if economically and socially vulnerable.

6.2 ENERGY POLICY GOALS TO 2020 AND 2050

Energy policy legislation is elaborated under the legal provisions of the Lisbon Treaty. This Treaty (entered into force in 2009) recognizes energy as a shared competence between European Union Member States and, therefore, has direct implications on the design and implementation of energy goals. While the European Commission exerts executive power and sets the long-term orientations of energy policies, decisions are implemented under the Council of the European Union's voting procedure involving the European Parliament, as the colegislator. Still, the Lisbon Treaty preserves the sovereignty of Member States over the structure of their energy supply and sources (Art 192).

In this institutional context, the 2020 energy policy targets were formulated to act as incentives for Member States to advance towards their specific national goals for the share of renewables in energy consumption, greenhouse gas emission reductions, and energy efficiency improvements. In addition to national policy ambitions, targets were also formulated outside of National Energy Plans, such as the minimum percentage of interconnection capacities compared to a country's total generation capacity, or efforts to promote carbon capture and storage.

The following subsections outline the 2020 energy policy targets, the level of progress towards achieving these targets, as well as structural barriers to their implementation. Further, the current status of energy policy ambitions for 2030 and 2050 is outlined.

RENEWABLE ENERGY POLICY: SETTING COMMON POLICY CONVERGENCE PATHWAYS TO 2020

The economy-wide European 2020 strategy for growth forms the basis of the energy and climate goals to 2020, which were translated into final legislation in April 2009. The 2020 Climate and Energy Package[j] comprises three main EU targets:

1. 20% share renewables in final energy consumption of which a 10% share of renewables in the transport sector; as part of the Climate and Energy Package, the 2009 Renewable Energy Sources (RES) legislation[k] reinforced the concept of priority dispatch for renewable-based electricity.
2. 20% lower energy consumption, quantified as an EU ceiling measured in terms of primary energy or final energy consumption;
3. 20% reduction in greenhouse gases compared to 1990.

These goals formulated at the level of the European Union (27 countries at that time) were agreed under specific national targets (called National Energy Plans) for each Member State.

---

[j]Directive 2009/31/EC on the geological storage of carbon dioxide; Directive 2009/28/EC on the Effort Sharing Decision in GhG mitigation; Directive 2009/29/EC: Extension of GhG Trading Scheme out to 2013.
[k]Directive (2009/28/CE).

Apart from the energy efficiency objectives, these goals form legally binding regulatory tools out to 2020. The "20−20−20 energy plan" forms a policy framework aiming at catalyzing convergence, while taking into account national specificities.

Under the 2020 legislative process, the degree of convergence still entails some nationally framed approach to policy implementation. For instance, "cooperation mechanisms"[l] that allow Member States to agree on statistical transfers of renewables for complying with target or joint renewable projects have not been used actively.[m] Investment decisions to build up the internal energy market are often considered on a national level through tariff support schemes, rather than through the perspective of a common European market.

LEVEL OF PROGRESS OF THE EUROPEAN UNION TO ACHIEVING THE 2020 TARGETS

According to the European Environmental Agency, the European Union is on track to achieve its 2020 energy and climate policy targets. The progress is detailed below for each of the target:

Greenhouse Gas Emissions: −20% decline compared to 1990

Greenhouse gases were already 19.8% below 1990 levels in 2013, very close to the 20% reduction target set for 2020. According to the European Environmental Agency,[n] the EU may achieve a GHG reduction of 24% below 1990 levels by 2020 with the current measures in place, according to the latest projections from Member States.

Renewable Share: 20% in gross final energy consumption

The 2020 target could be attained if Member States can sustain the speed at which they have been developing RES, so far. However, as we approach 2020, the trajectories for meeting the national targets become steeper, and more costly projects will have to be developed. In the RES-Transport target, the European Union is lagging at an estimated 5.6% in 2014 against a 10% target in 2020, with limited progress in biofuels cars and electric vehicle batteries.

Energy Efficiency: 20% increase compared to 2005, measured in primary and final energy consumption

Since 2005, the EU's primary and final energy consumption have been decreasing at a pace which would be sufficient for the EU to meet its 20% energy efficiency target.

The most important targets indicated in National Energy Plans are those related to the share of renewables and greenhouse gas emissions. This is because energy efficiency targets set out in National Energy Plans constitute nonbinding commitments, despite the fact that Member States are required to report on energy savings.

Overall, there is varying progress at Member States' levels regarding the three 2020 targets. For some Member States like Ireland, Spain, and Portugal, progress has been erratic when measured in terms of renewable capacity growth. Often, this was due to changes in the support tariffs for renewables and related uncertainties for investors. Judging from the latest progress reports, Ireland,

---

[l]European Commission, "Guidance on the use of renewable energy cooperation mechanism," SWD (2013), 440-final.
[m]Cooperation between EU Member States under the RES Directive, Ecofys, November 2014.
[n]European Environment Agency, "Trends and projections in Europe 2015 Tracking progress towards Europe's climate and energy targets," EEA report no 4/2015.

France, the United Kingdom, Luxembourg, the Netherlands, Spain, and Portugal are expected to lag behind their renewable energy targets.

Besides, wider structural barriers still need to be overcome in order to further improve the progress towards achieving the 2020 targets.

CHALLENGES TO THE 2020 POLICY IMPLEMENTATION

Apart from common efforts such as the European Emission Trading Scheme (as discussed in Section 7.4), the 2020 energy policy has been implemented at Member States' level with a certain degree of leeway. To outside observers, the EU renewables policy implementation can therefore resemble a patchwork of administrative rules.

In the various Member States, many different rules still apply regarding land use permission processes, tendering, and grid access responsibility (including priority access or dispatch of RES). This is because areas like renewable support schemes or energy taxation still remain, mostly, a prerogative of Member States.

From a regulatory perspective, some countries have had negative track records in consistently translating energy policy targets into national rules and regulations. For instance, Spain backtracked in July 2013 in changing its feed-in tariffs on wind and solar retroactively,[o] having negative consequences on the investor's sentiment and appreciation of the country's regulatory stability [2]. The "Keep on Track" project underlines that political and economic conditions (regulatory frameworks with regard to the support to renewables) often constitute a strong barrier to a successful policy implementation, equivalent to 38% of all reported barriers in the renewable electricity sector, and above 40% in renewable heating and transport.[p]

In this context, defining economically efficient incentives in order to facilitate the integration of renewables into the grid, the heating or the transport sectors can be considered a complex exercise. One may also ask if the various forms of national policy supports have been carefully evaluated and balanced against their impacts on final customers' bills and consumer affordability.

As an illustration, Germany and Spain have been allocating significant public support to renewables, ultimately largely financed by the final customers. In an analysis of 18 European countries, the Council of European Energy Regulators (CEER) estimated that in 2011 the support for electricity from renewable sources was equivalent to €7/MWh of total final electricity consumption,[q] leading to concerns over the impact of the integration of renewables on final prices (see Section 7.5).

In 2014, the EU antitrust authority (EC Directorate General Competition) released new State Aid Guidelines on Energy and the Environment[r] with important consequences for energy policy. The guidelines aim at moving away from administrative price-setting mechanisms, which can be associated to state aid. They rather encourage new investments in renewables (such as feed-in tariffs) through market-based mechanisms (such as a premium in addition to market prices or auctions). The

---

[o]Royal Decree 413/2014 (RD 413/2014), Order IET/1045/2014.
[p]INSIGHT_E, Hot Energy Topic 10, Analysing RES support mechanisms in the EU post-2020.
[q]http://www.ceer.eu/portal/page/portal/EER_HOME/EER_WORKSHOP/CEER-ERGEG%20EVENTS/CROSS-SECTORAL/EU_SEW_2013/Tab/250613EU%20SEW_CEER_RES.pdf
[r]European Commission (2014/C 200/01).

implementation of these guidelines is currently on-going in the EU Member States. Although the absolute level of remuneration allocated to renewables is likely to be reduced, it is yet unclear if this will lead to acceleration or a slow-down of investments in new renewable power projects.

The success of those options that could be part of the energy transition is closely related to public acceptance. Public opinion regarding renewable energy across Member States varies between regions and can evolve over time. For example, "not in my backyard" (or NIMBY) reactions to wind parks were raised in some regions of the United Kingdom and Denmark. Further, the construction of new high-voltage transmission lines was met with heavy opposition in France and Germany.

As such, many challenges need to be overcome, especially when looking further ahead to increasing levels of ambition for 2030 and 2050.

MOVING TO AN ENERGY AND CLIMATE POLICY FOR 2030

The 2030 EnergyStrategy adopted in 2014 formulates targets for 2030 for: greenhouse gas emission reductions; the share of renewables; and energy efficiency improvements. It was followed by the Clean Energy for All Europeans Package, a legislative proposal from the European Commission, that is underlying three distinct policy targets for 2030:

1. A 40% cut in greenhouse gas emissions (from 1990 levels);
2. At least a 27% share of renewable energy;
3. A binding 30% improvement in energy efficiency compared to 2005.[s]

The 2030 objectives need to maintain a clear pathway towards the objectives agreed by European heads of states for 2050. They will finally be enforced as policy targets in the forthcoming legislative decisions.

2050 ENERGY AND CLIMATE POLICY TARGETS: A CONSENSUS FOR GOING FORWARD?

From a Member State perspective, the cohesion of European energy policy can be seen throughout the agreements of the European Union's Head of States made during European Council meetings. On many occasions (e.g., on March 2007 or June 2010), the European Union, speaking through the voice of the European Council, reiterated its commitment to the decarbonization agenda, which in the early 2000s became one of Europe's most consistent long-term policy goals, together with energy security and affordability.

The European energy and climate policy stated its most ambitious mitigation objective in July 2009, when the leaders of the European Union and the G8 announced an objective to *reduce greenhouse gas emissions by at least 80%* below 1990 levels by 2050. Accordingly, in October 2009 the European Council set the 2050 emissions' abatement objective for the European Union at 80—95% below 1990 levels, the reference year of the Kyoto Protocol.[t]

---

[s]Clean Energy for All Europeans - Com 2016 (860) Final.
[t]Kyoto Protocol of the United Nations Framework Convention on Climate Change: http://unfccc.int/kyoto_protocol/items/2830.php.

Based on these long-term objectives, a number of long-term scenarios have been developed in the Communication from the Commission entitled "Roadmap to 2050."[u] The roadmap to 2050 contemplates a rise in power demand of 40% in the European Union based on 2005, and details the challenges related to the power and energy system transformation.

The roadmap acts as a form of "stakeholder consultation." In reaction to its publication, many reports underlined the degree of uncertainty in calculating investment costs of conventional technologies like nuclear power, or more recent investment areas like offshore wind farms, clean coal, or the roll out of electric vehicles in the transportation sector. The costs of integrating renewables, or—more generally speaking—the costs of the energy transition across the whole energy system have been widely discussed. Further, with the 2050 Roadmap a new debate on the role of flexibility in electricity generation has been opened [3].

This roadmap and long-term decarbonization agenda fulfills different objectives. However, the main one is to instill a sense of internal peer pressure to Europe's policy-making agenda. This fuels the energy and climate debate among Member States, while sending an outward signal in terms of international climate action.

In this context, the EU's decarbonization objective of at least 40% in 2030 compared to 1990 (as included in the nationally determined contributions by the European Union) presented at the Paris Climate Change Conference in December 2015 was set in line with the longer-term objectives of the 2050 Roadmap.

6.3 CONCLUSION: EUROPE IN NEED OF FURTHER REFORM

The European Union and its Member States are on track in achieving their mandated share of renewables in electricity generation by 2020. However, additional efforts will have to be made in the heating/cooling and transportation sectors. While the dynamics introduced by National Energy Plans were largely efficient at national level, both internal regulatory barriers within Member States and a lack of policy coordination at European level can be considered as the strongest determining factors limiting progress towards building a European market for renewables.

In conjunction with difficulties in progressing nationally framed targets, energy markets have become increasingly tough environments with decreasing electricity and low CO_2 prices. While this is partly driven by global market conditions such as decreasing commodity prices, the merit order effect of the increasing penetration of renewables had a significant impact on these developments (see Section IV). This raises new challenges requiring policy adaptations in the form of new energy market designs and models, together with new forms of support schemes for low-carbon technologies.

Chapter 7, A Market-Based European Energy Policy, discusses instruments and market policy adaptations in support of the achievement of the long-term European energy policy targets.

---

[u]European Commission, "Energy roadmap 2050," COM(2011)0885.

REFERENCES

[1] Tusk, D., A united Europe can end Russia's energy stranglehold. Financial Times, April 21, 2014.

[2] Enerdata News, Spain adopts energy reform and removes renewable feed-in tariffs, July 16, 2013.

[3] European Climate Foundation, Roadmap 2050: a practical guide to a prosperous, lowcarbon Europe Volume I: technical and economic assessment, April 2010. <http://www.roadmap2050.eu/attachments/files/Roadmap2050-AllData-MinimalSize.pdf>, slide 68.

A MARKET-BASED EUROPEAN ENERGY POLICY

Aurélie Faure-Schuyer[1], Manuel Welsch[2], and Steve Pye[3]

[1]Institut Français des Relations Internationales (IFRI), Brussels, Belgium [2]KTH Royal Institute of Technology, Stockholm, Sweden [3]University College London (UCL), London, United Kingdom

As mentioned in Chapter 6, European Energy Policy Objectives, the overall objective of European energy policy is to ensure a clean, secure and affordable energy supply. This objective guided the design of the internal market for European energy products and services. The principles of this market were implemented by an EU treaty revision through the single act reform[a] of 1996—consistent with deregulation policies in other infrastructure markets such as telecom and transportation. Its most fundamental goals are to achieve an internal market for energy with a high level of consumer protection, and to facilitate the efficient and secure functioning of this market. In this regards, design principles include ensuring sufficient generation capacity and the development of cross-border infrastructures for energy flows.

European energy policy is founded on a market-based approach, aimed at minimizing regulatory interventions. European market integration and policy harmonization are closely interrelated dynamics requiring efficient coordination between Member States. In 2014, a report from the European Commission[b] highlighted the level of progress regarding the completion of the internal energy market. It underlined the challenges related to infrastructure investment coordination and the implementation of grid code harmonization in the field of electricity.

On many aspects such as regarding prices, and the degree of market opening, varying levels of progresses (or sometimes even lack thereof) were recorded. To European policy makers, the report also pointed out which specific legislative developments will require more attention. Addressing these is especially important with regard to further advancing towards the 2030 and 2050 energy policy framework and the consolidation of the Energy Union (refer to Section 6.1), in particular in relation to the mobilization of investments.

The following subsections will discuss the design principles of the internal energy market (Section 7.1) and the level of progress towards achieving this market (Section 7.2). The chapter then continues by highlighting selected market instruments and developments: the outlook for capacity remuneration schemes in Europe (Section 7.3), the EU Emissions Trading Scheme (Section 7.4) and the implications of EU energy policies on energy prices (Section 7.5).

---

[a]Single Act Reform, 17 February 1996, The Single European Act (SEA) revises the Treaties of Rome in order to add new momentum to European integration and to complete the internal market. It amends the rules governing the operation of the European institutions and expands Community powers, notably in the field of research and development, the environment and common foreign policy.

[b]"Progress towards completing the internal energy market" (COM (2014) 634 final) European Commission.

Europe's Energy Transition. DOI: http://dx.doi.org/10.1016/B978-0-12-809806-6.00007-9

7.1 TOWARDS AN INTERNAL ENERGY MARKET

The European energy policy of moving towards an internal energy market has led to the formulation of the unbundling principle, separating nonregulated from regulated activities. From a market policy perspective, the dynamic that underpins the internal energy market can be defined on three levels that interact with each other:

1. The Internal Energy Market goes along with the definition of a *harmonized market-based framework*, i.e., a set of rules that allow an efficient and transparent functioning of transactions between the main market actors, such as regulators, utilities, suppliers, and consumers.
2. The Internal Energy Market considers *increased trade flows* and equal treatment of these flows across national borders. Market coupling, the merging of balancing zones and interconnections between national markets are fundamental aspects. In May 2014, the Commission proposed to extend its interconnection target from 10% to 15%, measured as the percentage share of gross interconnection capacities compared to the national installed electricity production capacity. (In 2014, the average interconnection level stood at about 8%.)
3. Internal Market and European Union *competition rules* include *the monitoring of wholesale and retail markets* through indicators that allow tracking of the evolution of national markets. These indicators are related to the degree of market opening, the rates of consumers switching suppliers, market concentration (or lack of a dominant position), or the phase out of regulated prices. This pillar has been consolidated by the European State Aid Guidelines in the field of energy and environment [1], which contain criteria for public aid for energy and environment projects outside of the nuclear power sector.

In this context, the *Electricity Target Model* (see also Box 7.1), resulting from the Third Energy Package, envisages the coupling of national markets into a single pan-European market whereby electricity and gas are traded based on their marginal costs. This is also called the energy only market in the case of electricity. The target model aims at facilitating price convergence within the EU and should assure the optimal use of cross-border transmission. The target model for electricity and gas covers a range of underlying market definitions, such as types of products traded, procurement of services, definitions of pricing zones, etc.

This pan-European energy market applies to a region that goes beyond the Union of 28 Member States. It is to be applied in the Members States of the European Economic Area,[c] an area

---

BOX 7.1 THE EU ELECTRICITY TARGET MODEL

The EU Target Model is based on two broad principles [2]:

1. Energy only markets, preferably organized on a zonal basis, where generators' revenues depend on the cost for each marginal unit of energy supplied.
2. Market coupling, linking zonal day-ahead spot markets into a virtual market, allowing congestion constraints limit further trade (using flow-based transmission allocation, based on optimization models).

---

[c]Iceland, Lichtenstein, Norway.

additionally covering Lichtenstein, Iceland, and Norway. This area accounted for 25% of EU energy production in 2013. The internal market is also to be extended to the Energy Community,[d] an international organization that includes transition countries like the Ukraine. The internal energy market therefore has a political dimension in many aspects: it is bringing a cohesive force to a wider group that includes countries that are also important energy partners and contributors to Europe's energy import security. To this extent, there are many uncertainties surrounding the United Kingdom's vote in 2016 to exit from the European Union.

7.2 LEVEL OF PROGRESS IN MARKET INTEGRATION

In 2014, a report from the European Commission highlighted various aspects of progress in the policy implementation of the internal energy market that require specific attention from Member States.

OPENNESS OF THE ENERGY MARKET

Firstly, the European energy market still lacks some degree of openness beyond national borders. There has been progress in the efficient use of existing infrastructure[e] with the implementation of reverse gas flows in Central and Eastern Europe. The reverse gas flow capability allows sending natural gas back from Western Europe to Central Europe (Poland, Slovakia, Bulgaria) and the Ukraine. Originally, long-distance gas pipelines were built to allow gas to flow only from East to West.[f] In connecting the Caspian and Middle Eastern regions to Europe via the Southern corridor, reverse flow capabilities are also valuable for countries like Italy, Switzerland, and Germany. There are however concerns related to the fact that very few gas hubs[g] have developed sufficient trading volume and liquidity.

In the power sector, the traded electricity at interconnections remained broadly stable between 2008 and 2014 according to the Agency for Coordination of Energy Regulators (ACER).

Overall, there is recognition that the electricity and gas markets do not provide a visible and efficient price signal for market participants to invest in energy infrastructures and equipment.

HARMONIZATION OF OPERATIONAL RULES

Secondly, Europe needs to progress further on setting up harmonized operational rules and network codes for infrastructure developments. Addressing this particular area of the internal market design is considered to be critically important, as it will facilitate the integration of rising shares of renewable energy sources into the energy market.

---

[d]The Energy Community includes 8 Contracting Parties—Albania, Bosnia and Herzegovina, Kosovo*, Former Yugoslav Republic of Macedonia, Moldova, Montenegro, Serbia and Ukraine.

[e]See Figure [26] of the SWD "Trends and developments in European energy markets", as annexed to this Communication, SWD (2014) 310.

[f]Preparedness for a possible disruption of supplies from the East during the fall and winter of 2014/2015 {SWD(2014) 322 final} {SWD(2014) 323 final}{SWD(2014) 324 final}{SWD(2014) 325 final}{SWD(2014) 326 final}.

[g]Frontier Economic.

FUTURE INVESTMENTS

Thirdly, the European energy market still needs significant investments in infrastructure. In 2011, it was estimated that Europe's energy system required 1 trillion Euros in investments by 2020, half of which in power generation and 210 billion Euros each for electricity and gas infrastructure. According to reports from the European Commission, these investments especially need to target the following three main areas:

1. The regional gas market in the Baltic States remains relatively isolated, and the diversification of supply in many Central-Eastern and South-Eastern Member States needs to be further improved.
2. In electricity markets, lack of physical interconnection is of concern in the market area linking Germany and the Baltic region. Further, interconnections need to be reinforced, like linking the continent's electricity grids with the Iberian Peninsula, the Baltic region, Ireland, and the United Kingdom. At the time of the report, the electricity interconnection capacity between France and Spain only covered 3% of peak demand in the Iberian Peninsula.
3. Further, the construction of an integrated offshore grid in the Northern Seas remains at project planning stage.

BIOFUELS

Fourthly, there is a lack of progress on the use of conventional and advanced biofuels in the transportation sector to achieve the 10% target by 2020. France, Italy, Germany, Spain, and the UK are the main producers and consumers of first-generation biofuels (bioethanol and biodiesel), making Europe the number 3 producer of biofuels in the world after the United States and Brazil. While EU Member States have mostly opted for mandatory blending obligations, the lack of progress in the development of second- and third-generation biofuels, produced from agricultural and forest residues or nonfood products, is limiting the advancement towards the targets. Further, also the lack of clear communication from the auto industry to consumers regarding the compatibility of biofuels with (older) car types can be considered as a factor having slowed down the adoption of biofuels for cars, as witnessed in Germany.

To conclude, although the concept of the internal market has been evolving over recent years, the progress towards the completion of the internal market is not uniform. It depends on the policy area (gas, electricity, or renewables specifically) and on intra-European regional dimensions (such as interconnections, availability of infrastructures, and liquidity of trading hubs). The internal energy market is closely related to the development and efficient use of energy infrastructures. Selected instruments to steer such investments are outlined in Sections 7.3 and 7.4, focusing on ensuring security of supply and greenhouse gas emission reductions, respectively.

7.3 THE ROLE OF ELECTRICITY CAPACITY REMUNERATION SCHEMES IN EUROPEAN ENERGY POLICY

In capacity remuneration schemes, generators are paid for holding capacity to help ensure security of supply rather than the standard model where they are paid via the energy-only market for electricity generation.

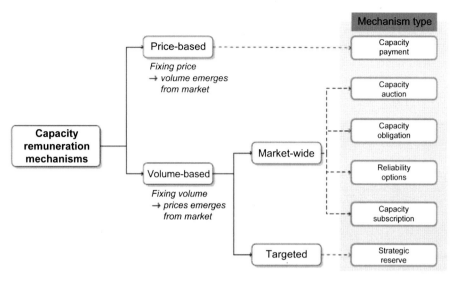

FIGURE 7.1

Categorization of capacity mechanisms.

From Hans Perter Höschle, Workshop on Fact Sheets KU Leuven. Energiestichting/Energie-Instituut (U-Wetoco), April 30, 2014.

These schemes are designed to facilitate the development of energy infrastructure towards improved energy security despite low-price environments. As opposed to other regions of the world such as Western Australia, capacity markets are not a fully fledged element of existing European energy legislation. So far, the internal energy market and the target model foresee energy trades through an energy-only market.

Capacity remuneration schemes refer to a wide variety of mechanisms that can provide a form of adjustment to prices based on marginal costs in power generation markets. This adjustment is either price or volume based (refer to Fig. 7.1). The diversity of mechanisms has made the policy debate complex.

In the European Union, capacity market discussion started in the early 2000s at the request of some large European power generators that were seeing their spreads (i.e., the difference between fuel to electricity prices) being reduced.

Nowadays, national capacity remuneration mechanisms (CRMs) have been developed in a large number of Member States in order to cope mostly with national electricity system requirements. For instance, in the framework of the Electricity Market Reform, the UK mainly needed to deal with a lack of base load capacity, while the German capacity scheme was set up to cope with large shortages of capacity during a reduced number of hours due to large renewables feed-ins.[h] Meanwhile, in France, the issue at stake is more the dependence of peak demand on weather variations. All these schemes involve the TSO and/or the National Regulatory Authority in the evaluation of security of supply concerns and the development of strategies for dealing with emergency situations.

---

[h]CEEM Working Paper 2014−8: First principles, market failures and endogenous obsolescence: the dynamic approach to capacity mechanisms, Chair European Electricity Markets, Paris Dauphine.

In November 2012, the EU Parliament's Industry, Research and Energy Committee requested the Agency for the Cooperation of the Energy Regulators (ACER) to issue an opinion on capacity markets. The response of ACER was left rather wide open to interpretation. Because of the fact that there is currently no uniform approach to capacity remuneration across Europe, ACER's opinion[i] is that in an integrated European energy market, security of supply cannot only be a national concern and should be addressed at the European, or at least regional level.

Regarding the design of capacity markets, any price-based adjustment stands as the least preferred option based on the principles of the target model. There are also question marks related to the interactions between energy-only and capacity markets, and to the risks related to having a national scheme that does not allow trading capacities across borders. In this context, Article 4.3 of the Security of Supply Directive (2005/89/EC) needs to be considered as applicable to capacity markets [3]. It states that "Member States shall not discriminate between cross-border contracts and national contracts."

In the electricity market, many aspects of electricity system and market operation need to be reconciled in the short- to mid-term horizon, while possible pan-European capacity schemes complementing the EU's "energy-only" reference model could be developed. Over the longer term, grid reliability and investment security need to be considered collectively by Member States, and not only in relation to national security concerns. To address the questions around a harmonized implementation of capacity markets, European policy makers are required to develop a pan-European definition and approach to security of supply.

7.4 THE EU EMISSION TRADING SCHEME—STEERING INVESTMENTS IN LOW-CARBON TECHNOLOGIES

The 2020 Energy Package includes the reduction of 20% of greenhouse gas emissions towards 2020 as one of its main goals. In light of greenhouse gas emission mitigation objectives, the EU Emission Trading Scheme (ETS)[j] was set up to create a pan-European market for CO_2. Initially, it was established to cover the period 2005–13, but has subsequently been prolonged to 2020. Further, it was extended to comprise a larger group of industries, including aluminum, aviation, petrochemicals, and carbon capture and storage. The ETS is founded on the underlying "polluter pays" principle. It creates a quota of CO_2 for each emitting site that can be exchanged in a pan-European quota market; a specific instrument to steer investments in low-carbon technologies.

EUROPEAN UNION EMISSION TRADING SCHEME

The European ETS applies to the 28 EU countries plus Iceland, Liechtenstein, and Norway. It sets "site-specific" limits for greenhouse gas emissions from more than 11,000 heavy energy-using installations in power generation and manufacturing industry, and to operators of flights to and from the EU, Iceland, Liechtenstein, and Norway. It covers around 45% of the EU's greenhouse gas emissions. Since 2013, auctioning is the main method for allocating allowances.

---

[i]See ACER Opinion n°05/13—February 2013 and report in July 2013.
[j]European Commission—DG Clima—EU ETS Handbook.

Since the inception of the ETS, it has been at the heart of European energy policy relating to decarbonization efforts. This was less due to the effective results delivered through the scheme, but rather due to the political support for a market-based mechanism to deliver greenhouse gas emission reductions in an economically efficient manner. So far, the European ETS suffered from over-allocation of quotas, estimated at 2 billion tonnes of CO_2 over the trading period (2013−20). As a consequence, the European price of CO_2 (€5/tonne in March 2016) stands below what it should be for sending an efficient policy signal.

In a number of European countries like the United Kingdom, Sweden, or France, the ETS scheme coexists with CO_2 taxes. The ETS even sometimes competes with national energy policies like feed-in tariffs that act in exerting downward pressure on the demand for CO_2 allowances. At the same time, these mechanisms directly affect consumer prices, as outlined in Section 7.5.

A reform of the legislation supporting the ETS is currently on-going. It considers improved rules to address carbon leakage and an accelerated reduction of the amount of allocated emission allowances during the fourth trading period from 2021 to 2030. Additionally, already from 2019 onwards, the Market Stability Reserve (MSR) will serve as a mechanism to deal with the current and potentially future over-allocation of quotas. The reserve will act according to predefined rules and restore the scarcity of allowances needed to create a more robust ETS with more consistent price signals. These prices are expected to increase by about 24% in 2030 in comparison to a case without the implementation of the reform, with first effects being perceived between 2020 and 2025.[k]

7.5 ENERGY PRICES IN EUROPE

Final energy prices to end-consumers bundle four main components: energy charges, grid-related access tariffs (to the transmission-distribution grids), retails costs, and additionally taxes and charges.

Two major trends can be observed. Firstly, taxes and charges have been rapidly rising in Europe over recent years.[l] Among these charges, the levies linked to renewables have been increasing steeply between 2012 and 2014. Secondly, price monitoring across Member States reflects that price levels for consumers (both wholesale and final) vary widely, both in the electricity and gas segments. This leads to very different price structures between countries, an issue that the ACER Monitoring Report 2015 also observes regarding the price structure between suppliers within one single Member State.

The difference in prices between countries depends on factors such as the degree of diversification of supply and the different degrees of market opening to the outside global gas market (import dependency). For example, in the first half of 2014, hub gas prices ranged from €21/MWh in the lowest-priced country to €35/MWh in the highest-priced country.

Further, there is a widening gap between wholesale and final end-consumer prices. With overcapacity in the generation market, electricity prices traded on wholesale markets have been heading

---

[k]INSIGHT_E, Hot Energy Topic 12, The market stability reserve: assessing reform needs and possible impacts on the EU ETS.
[l]"Energy prices and costs in Europe" (COM (2014) 21 final) European Commission.

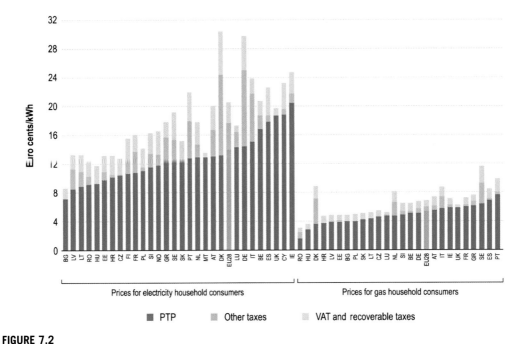

FIGURE 7.2

Electricity and gas prices for households in Europe in 2014 (in euro cents/kWh). PTP, pretax total price.

downwards, while the amount of levies (especially renewable surcharges) and taxes (such as VAT and others) have been consistently rising. This trend is acknowledged in various market monitoring reports, such as by Eurelectric [4]. Fig. 7.2 demonstrates the lack of homogeneity and coherence in prices being charged at end-user levels. When looking at both, household electricity and gas prices in the European Union, prices in the most expensive countries are about three times as high as those in the lowest-priced countries.

Both in Member States and at the European level there have been rising concerns related to affordability (refer to Section 6). This issue goes beyond the scope of energy policy only, spilling over to other policy fields such as consumer protection, industrial competitiveness, or even economic stability due to the influence of electricity prices on inflation.

REFERENCES

[1] Guidelines on State aid for environmental protection and energy 2014–2020 (2014/C 200/01). <http://ec.europa.eu/competition/sectors/energy/legislation_en.html>.
[2] Oxford Energy Comment, The EU "Target Model" for electricity markets: fit for purpose? Malcolm Keay, May 2013.
[3] Eurelectric, A reference model for European capacity markets, March 2015.
[4] Eurelectric, Analysis of European power price increase drivers, eurelectric study, May 2014.

CONCLUSIONS

Aurélie Faure-Schuyer[1], Manuel Welsch[2], and Steve Pye[3]

[1]*Institut Français des Relations Internationales (IFRI), Brussels, Belgium* [2]*KTH Royal Institute of Technology, Stockholm, Sweden* [3]*University College London (UCL), London, United Kingdom*

The European Union can certainly claim that the implementation of its energy- and climate-based policies in the field of renewables and greenhouse gas mitigation is well on track, as indicated by the level of progress towards achieving the 2020 policy targets. However, progress post 2020 will become more challenging given the more ambitious targets towards 2030 and 2050.

A review of the status of progress shows the complex situation we are facing. On one side, European energy policy needs to minimize the cost of completing the internal market. On the other side, it needs to consider strategic objectives, such as opening up new opportunities and markets through the energy transition, while ensuring affordability to final consumers, or implementing a long-term climate policy consistent with the Paris agreement.

The dimension related to energy security needs to be framed at a pan-European level, and so do the criteria of import dependency, which traditionally were (and to some extend always will be) a domain of national energy policy. Finally, in entering a new investment cycle, investors are awaiting to know to what extent wholesale markets can ensure proper investment incentives through price signals and to what extent they will be complemented by the capacity remuneration scheme. The role of distribution and transmission system operators built with the vertically integrated model of large incumbents was further reviewed with the unbundling. Still, this role, which was fitted to ensure security of supply nationally within each country, is bound to evolve.

In many European countries, new national political reforms are being implemented in order to secure a cost-efficient transition towards low-carbon energy systems (e.g., the German Energiewende and Ministerial Energy Reform, the United Kingdom Market Reform, or the France Energy Transition). This situation can be detrimental to the visibility and clarity of a European political framework if not properly coordinated.

Such national policy reforms are to some extent contrasted by the launch of the Energy Union[a] process in 2014, which was later formalized through the "Commission Strategy for an Energy Union" in 2015 (see Section 6.1). Completing the internal European energy market (the foundation of the 20−20−20 targets) is a priority for the Energy Union, which opens up a new mode of governance for energy policy.[b] The process towards achieving the Energy Union further indicates that

---

[a]"Recalling its conclusions of June 2014, the European Council endorsed further actions to reduce the EU's energy dependence and increase its energy security for both electricity and gas." European Council Conclusions, October 23/24, 2014.
[b]http://ec.europa.eu/europe2020/making-it-happen/index_en.htm

Europe's Energy Transition. DOI: http://dx.doi.org/10.1016/B978-0-12-809806-6.00008-0

more attention will need to be paid to the dimensions related to energy security and affordability in the future, while advancing further towards the long-term decarbonization of the energy system.

Both from a market integration point of view and from a regulatory perspective, European energy policy requires stronger and more focused policy action together with a dynamic mode of policy coordination. To ensure its effectiveness, European energy policy further needs to comprise a suite of harmonized and targeted strategies and instruments to address the individual components of the energy system in parallel. The following sections cover these components, from energy supply including renewable energy to its implications on markets, system reliability and flexibility, and on households, consumers, and society in general.

ENERGY SUPPLY: A CHANGING ENVIRONMENT

INTRODUCTION

Paul Deane

University College Cork (UCC), Cork, Ireland

While global energy demand increased by 38% from 2000 to 2014, EU final energy consumption decreased by approximately 6.5% during the same period (from 1133 Mtoe in 2000 to 1061 Mtoe in 2014). This is an encouraging trend towards achieving the EU policy ambitions presented in the previous section, and puts energy consumption below the indicative targets for 2020, set to 1086 Mtoe by the European Energy Efficiency Directive. However, the EU is still heavily dependent on imported fossil fuels and is the biggest importer of natural gas in the world.

Natural gas represents around a quarter of gross inland EU energy consumption. About 26% of this natural gas is used in power plants (including combined heat and power plants) and 23% is used in industry; the rest is used in the residential and commercial sectors. Gas is expected to continue to play a vital role in the EU energy system for decades to come with EU modeling showing natural gas at between 20% and 25% of primary energy consumption by 2050, even under strong decarbonization scenarios. Recent years have seen a drop in overall gas consumption in the EU with values back to mid-1990 levels. The power sector has seen a decline in gas use due to a myriad of factors including low carbon prices, increased renewables, lower demand due to the economic crisis, and cheaper coal. Despite efforts to diversify, Russia has remained as Europe's biggest gas supplier, supplying 40% of EU gas needs. In 2015 Gazprom Export supplied 159 billion cubic meters (bcm) of gas to EU Member States with Germany increasing its offtake of Russian gas in 2015 to 45 bcm.

Recent numerical modeling studies by PRIMES[a] show that EU energy production is projected to continue to decrease from around 760 Mtoe in 2015 to around 660 Mtoe in 2050, thus reinforcing the need for policy makers to encourage the exploitation of indigenous resources. At the same time, the Paris Agreement of December 2015 under the United Nations Framework Convention on Climate Change (UNFCCC) sets the goal of holding the increase in the global average temperature to well below $2°C$ above preindustrial levels, and aims to limit the increase to $1.5°C$ in order to reduce significantly the risks and impacts of climate change.

Driven by this, the EU's target of an 80% reduction in greenhouse gas emissions by 2050 (from 1990 levels) calls for a deep, rapid transformation of the energy system. In the power sector, CO_2 intensity must drop from around $350\ gCO_2/kWh$ at present, to a maximum of around $10\ gCO_2/kWh$ by 2050. While carbon pricing is often referred to as the "silver bullet" for tackling CO_2 emissions, it is clear that a policy "mix" will be needed to achieve an effective low-carbon transition in a cost-effective and feasible manner. Alongside carbon pricing, this includes

---

[a]https://ec.europa.eu/energy/en/data-analysis/energy-modelling

Europe's Energy Transition. DOI: http://dx.doi.org/10.1016/B978-0-12-809806-6.00009-2

technology-based and behavior-based instruments—forming three "pillars of policy." These instruments need to be designed to ensure a smooth transition to a low-carbon economy.

However, the exploitation of indigenous fossil resources (without carbon capture facilities) is difficult to reconcile with EU policies to mitigate climate change. Recent science tells us that to have a reasonable chance of staying below the 2°C threshold large reserves of fossil fuels must remain untouched and are thus generally termed as "unburnable fossil fuels." Chapter 10, Decarbonizing the EU Energy System, first presents the issue of these unburnable fossil fuels and the potential implications for Europe. It then looks at what existing energy and climate policies have achieved to date, and may achieve in the future.

In addition to their economics, the remaining "burnable" fossil fuels are of importance for diversifying the EU's energy supply. Questions around security of supply and exploitation of new gas sources, such as shale gas, may present challenges and opportunities for the EU that need to be carefully considered. Chapter 11, Gas Security of Supply in the European Union, highlights issues of security of supply for Europe and in particular discusses Europe's strong reliance on imported gas. Gas and geopolitics are intrinsically linked and it is shown that there is no easy answer or quick solution to Europe's reliance on imported gas. However, existing potential for new gas routes and gas storage may provide some mitigation measures for the EU. The chapter concludes with investigating the diversification of Europe's fossil fuel supply through a potential exploitation of shale gas. While highly uncertain, shale gas may provide some opportunities for Europe in the future, if managed carefully.

An alternative to a diversification of fossil fuel supplies is provided by biofuels, especially in the transport sector—the sector with the largest energy demand, consuming approximately 32% of energy in the EU. Surface transport (including rail) accounts for approximately 85% of energy demand in transport and is predominately diesel-based ($\sim 54\%$), whereas aviation accounts for under 15% of energy demand. While surface transport in the EU has benefited from renewable energy policy, biojet fuel has not. Chapter 12, Biofuels for Aviation: Policy Goals and Costs, therefore focuses on the challenges facing aviation in the EU and in particular the potential of biofuels to partly replace kerosene. Here the use of biojet fuels may assist in the transition to low-carbon aviation. However, costs remain uncertain.

Overall, the changing landscape of European energy supply is one that presents both challenges and opportunities to the EU. The levels of decarbonization required to meet Europe's emission reduction targets require a broad mix and range of both technologies and measures, as discussed further in the concluding chapter of this section (see Chapter 13: Conclusions and Outlook).

DECARBONIZING THE EU ENERGY SYSTEM

10

Paul Drummond[1], Steve Pye[1], Christophe McGlade[1], Carole Mathieu[2], Željko Jurić[3], Marko Matosović[3], and Paul Deane[4]

[1]*University College London (UCL), London, United Kingdom* [2]*Institut Français des Relations Internationales (IFRI), Paris, France* [3]*Energy Institute Hrvoje Požar (EIHP), Zagreb, Croatia* [4]*University College Cork, (UCC), Cork, Ireland*

10.1 INTRODUCTION

Climate studies [1] have demonstrated that average global temperature rises expected in the future are closely related to the cumulative emissions of greenhouse gases that are emitted over a given timeframe. Coupled with the political commitment to keep global warming below 2°C (out to 2100),[a] this has provided the concept of a remaining global "carbon budget" associated with avoiding dangerous climate change. In line with scientific findings reported by the International Panel on Climate Change (IPCC) in its fourth Assessment Report, the EU's objective, in the context of necessary reductions by developed countries as a group, is to reduce greenhouse gas emissions by 80%−95% by 2050 compared to 1990. This calls for a deep, rapid transformation of the energy system [2]. In the power sector, CO_2 intensity must drop from around 350 gCO_2/kWh at present, to a maximum of around 10 gCO_2/kWh by 2050. In parallel, increasing electrification of energy services could lead up to a 50% increase in demand, meaning a doubling of existing generation capacity.

Decarbonization and the context of a limited carbon budget are important challenges for European policy makers. Ambitious, well-designed policy instruments must drive such transformations. Additionally, policy support for "enabling" infrastructure, such as electricity grid expansion, hydrogen pipelines, and carbon capture and storage (CCS), will also be required, but are outside the scope of this chapter.

This chapter first presents the issue of a carbon budget and unburnable fossil fuel reserves. It then assesses the implications for EU Member States, energy industries, and financial markets. The research project CECILIA2050[b] was tasked with examining the existing climate policy landscape in the EU, including its impact, and proposing policy pathways to 2050. In Section 10.6 onwards some of the lessons of this project are distilled. These sections assess what carbon pricing and other policy instruments have achieved to date, and may achieve in the future.

---

[a]United Nations Framework Convention on Climate Change (UNFCC), Report of the conference of the parties on its fifteenth session part two.
[b]EU FP7 Grant No: 308680.

Europe's Energy Transition. DOI: http://dx.doi.org/10.1016/B978-0-12-809806-6.00010-9

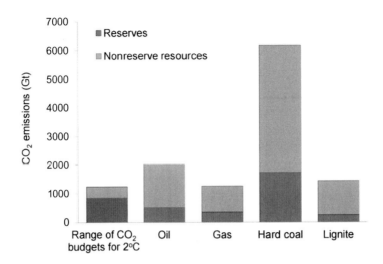

FIGURE 10.1

Aggregate CO_2 emissions from unburnable resources. First bar depicts estimated carbon budget with upper and lower estimates shown in lighter shade [6].

10.2 CARBON BUDGET AND UNBURNABLE CARBON

To have a reasonable chance of staying below the 2°C threshold, the majority of existing fossil fuel reserves must not be produced. These reserve volumes have been termed "unburnable fossil fuels." The precise range of carbon budgets associated with the 2°C threshold varies. The Intergovernmental Panel on Climate Change (IPCC) [3] recently suggested a carbon budget of around 870–1240 billion tonnes (Gt) CO_2 between 2011 and 2050. This budget would give a better-than-evens chance of avoiding a 2°C temperature rise. It has subsequently been noted that the CO_2 emissions that would result from the unabated combustion of current estimates of fossil fuels reserves are more than three times this estimated carbon budget (Fig. 10.1) [4].

There are a wide range of definitions used to report the availability of fossil fuels and in particular the precise meaning of the terms reserves and resources can vary substantially. "Reserves" are generally volumes of oil, gas, or coal that are recoverable under current economic conditions and have a specific probability of being produced; "resources" encompass a much broader estimate that includes volumes that are considered recoverable over all time with both current and future technology, irrespective of current economic conditions. In 2012 global CO_2 emissions from fuel combustion were 32 Gt CO_2, with coal accounting for 44%, oil 36%, and gas 20% [5]. Emissions have risen by over 50% since 1990, largely driven by increases in non-Annex I countries, and they are anticipated to continue to grow in the future in the absence of strong and firm mitigation commitments.

10.3 UNBURNABLE FOSSIL FUEL RESERVES

A paper published in *Nature* [6] provided the first geographic distribution of the oil, gas, and coal reserves that should stay in the ground (or be classified as "unburnable") under an economically

Table 10.1 Distribution of Reserves Unburnable Before 2050 Under a 2°C Scenario With CCS [7]

	Oil		Gas		Coal	
	Gb	%	Tcm	%	Gt	%
Africa	23	21	4.4	33	28	85
Canada	39	74	0.3	24	5.0	75
China and India	9	25	2.9	63	180	66
CSA	58	39	4.8	53	8	51
Europe	5.0	20	0.6	11	65	78
FSU	27	18	31	50	203	94
MEA	263	38	46	61	3.4	99
OECD Pacific	2.1	37	2.2	56	83	93
ODA	2.0	9	2.2	24	10	34
USA	2.8	6	0.3	4	235	92
Global	431	33	95	49	819	82

Some unconventional oil and gas reserves are included in relevant regions, e.g., 48 billion Gb oil sands in Canada.
CSA, Central and South America; FSU, the Former Soviet Union countries; Gb, billions of barrels; Gt, billions of tonnes; MEA, Middle East; ODA, other developing Asian countries; OECD, the Organisation for Economic Co-operation and Development; Tcm, trillions of cubic meters; USA, United States of America.

optimal scenario in which there is a global effort to mitigate greenhouse gas emissions that provides a 60% chance of staying below the 2°C threshold (Table 10.1).[c]

The headline figures from the study were that over 80% of current coal reserves, half of gas reserves, and a third of oil reserves globally should be classified as unburnable. However, the reserves identified as unburnable are not spread evenly around the world. For example, the overwhelming majority of the very large coal reserves in China, Russia, and the United States should remain unused, along with over 260,000 million barrels of oil reserves in the Middle East (a volume equivalent to all of the oil reserves currently held by Saudi Arabia). The Middle East should also leave over 60% of its gas reserves in the ground. It was also found that because of its expense, its relatively late date of introduction (2025), and the assumed maximum rate at which it can be built, CCS has a relatively modest effect on the overall levels of fossil fuels that can be produced before 2050.

10.4 IMPLICATIONS FOR EU MEMBER STATES

With less than 20% of existing oil and gas reserves in Europe unburnable in this 2°C scenario, overwhelmingly concentrated in the North Sea, the potential direct impact of stringent carbon constraints on Member States' oil and gas reserves could be viewed as somewhat limited.

[c]This issue was also discussed in Ref. [1].

However, the results still raise questions around how Member States reconcile their commitments to the 2°C goal with their seeking to produce all indigenous fossil fuel reserves (e.g., as in the UK[d]). The use of fiscal incentives to boost extraction or carry out research into fossil fuel extraction will also likely be increasingly questioned in a carbon-constrained world.

In addition, many Member States are actively considering the development of their potential shale gas resources[e] (see also Chapter 11: Gas Security of Supply in the European Union). Poland views shale gas as a strategic asset due to its current high reliance on gas imports, and the UK, despite recently introducing restrictions on where drilling for shale gas can take place, is continuing to permit exploration over large areas of the country. Shale gas exploration is in its infancy, and the resource potential and regulatory positions of countries are still being reviewed and developed. In this context, it can be anticipated that countries will be asked to establish how the development of new shale gas resources fits within their decarbonization obligations. Further, the development of the potential oil and gas resources in the Arctic are inconsistent with efforts to limit climate change, which will impact those countries and multinationals with stakes in the Arctic region.

Table 10.1 shows that nearly 80% or 65 Gt coal reserves in Europe should be classified as unburnable before 2050 in order to stay within the 2°C global temperature increase. The use of coal needs to diminish rapidly and significantly. This will affect those EU Member States with both large current coal production (e.g., Germany and Poland) and large consumption. In 2012, coal was particularly prevalent in the electricity sector in a number of Member States including: Poland, Greece, the Czech Republic, Bulgaria, and Germany. If the world is to stay below the 2°C limit, the use of unabated coal in power generation should decline swiftly and be replaced by lower-carbon sources. It is therefore questionable how the continued use of coal without CCS, and more generally the opening of new coal production facilities in the absence of large-scale CCS demonstration, can fit with the EU's agreed aims of almost full decarbonization of the power sector by 2050.

Finally, if Member States seek to burn their fossil fuel reserves beyond the limits shown in the economically optimal scenario or develop new resources, they put the 2°C objective at risk. Logically, other regions would need to produce less reserves than what their own limits suggest, for the world to stay within the global carbon budget. If such adjustments are made, the regions concerned could ask for financial compensation, arguing that the deviation from the economically optimal scenario created an additional shortfall of revenues for them.[f] While compensation mechanisms have been debated for long in the climate negotiations, the optimal distribution put forward by this recent *Nature* study could form a more concrete basis for the discussion.

---

[d]UK Department of Energy and Climate Change (DECC), Government response to Sir Ian Wood's UKCS: maximising economic recovery review.

[e]Many aspects of the potential for shale gas have been described in a previous INSIGHT_E paper, HET3 Shale gas prospects for Europe.

[f]Further, the global optimum and the resulting carbon budget of a country may be very different from the optimum from a nation's perspective, and bear additional costs. The sharing of any additional costs is traditionally a central and critical part of global climate change negotiations.

10.5 IMPLICATIONS FOR EUROPEAN ENERGY INDUSTRIES AND FINANCIAL MARKETS

Building on the above concept, some researchers have highlighted that the reserves of publicly listed fossil fuel companies may become stranded assets.[g] Should these companies be allocated a share of the remaining carbon budget to 2050 based on the fossil fuel reserves that they own today (25% of the total proved reserves), it can be argued that a large portion of their reserves will not provide positive cash flows. Because the share prices of fossil fuel companies are partly based on their reserves, one risk could be that these companies are currently overvalued by investors. However, the exposure of other market players to fossil fuel commodities and firms holding fossil fuel reserves is limited. For EU pension funds their estimated exposure amounts to around 5% of total assets, for EU insurance companies to 4%, and for EU banks to 1.4% [8]. Therefore, while any potential "carbon bubble" may create losses, this is unlikely to be to the point of threatening the stability of the EU financial system.

However, the conclusion that any reserves are at risk has been challenged. Some companies [9] contend that at the current rate of production, their proved reserves will be entirely produced before climate policy has an impact on fossil fuel demand (e.g., Royal Dutch Shell indicate that their current proved reserves will be fully produced in 11.5 years and similarly 16 years for ExxonMobil). It has also been argued that climate policies are most likely to be implemented gradually, leaving financial institutions and companies sufficient time to adjust their capital allocations instead of facing sudden losses [10].

Nevertheless, beyond the valuation of current reserves, the productivity of the capital invested to develop new resources (estimated at $674bn/year[h]) is also questioned as it increases the potential for future stranding over the longer term. Such expenditure means that fossil fuel companies may be viewed as increasingly risky for investors in terms of the delivery of long-term returns. Although the extent to which carbon risks will materialize is hotly debated, mitigation strategies are emerging as a key trend for investors [11]. One area of work relates to information disclosure. For investors to better measure their exposure, companies should be required to report on the carbon stocks embedded in their reserves and resource base and provide stress-testing for their business model in a carbon-constrained world.[i]

There is an increasing divestment movement focusing on fossil fuel companies. The need to reduce financial risks is strengthened by the ethical argument that companies contributing to climate change should not be funded.[j] Others consider that investors should have a constructive engagement with the fossil fuel companies[k] to incentivize them to factor carbon risk into their decision making (e.g., using theoretical CO_2 prices), to curb investments in the highest-cost and

---

[g]See in particular: Carbon Tracker and the Grantham Research Institute, LES, Unburnable carbon 2013: wasted capital and stranded assets, 2013.
[h]See Ref. [10] (CAPEX spent by the first 200 listed fossil fuel companies from August 2012 to August 2013).
[i]See for instance: Kepler Chevreux, Stranded assets, fossilized revenues, 2014.
[j]See for instance: the Fossil Free campaign, http://gofossilfree.org/the-great-deflation/
[k]See for instance: Institutional Investors group on Climate Change, Investor Expectation: Oil and Gas Company Strategy, 2014.

most carbon-intensive projects, and also to reduce their operational emissions (with investments in CCS technologies for instance).

Whatever the implications on European Member states, industries, and markets, first policy instruments will need to be designed to ensure that the concept of "unburnable fossil fuels" will not just remain a theoretical concept but actual practice.

10.6 IS CARBON PRICING CONTRIBUTING TO STAYING WITHIN OUR CARBON BUDGET?

Carbon pricing is often put forward as a panacea in the economics literature for curbing "excessive" CO_2 emissions. The principal instrument for carbon pricing in the EU is the EU ETS. The varied history of the EU ETS is well known; initial average prices of €20−25/tCO_2 were achieved in the first year of operation (2005), before decreasing to nearly zero by the end of Phase 1 (2007) in reaction to allowance oversupply and the inability to bank for compliance in future phases. Prices initially recovered to previous highs at the start of Phase 2 (2008), before slowly declining, largely in response to the global financial crisis which reduced demand for EU ETS sector outputs (and associated emissions). This led prices to stabilize at well below €10/tCO_2 from late 2011 onwards, with some volatility [12].

It is likely that EU ETS-induced abatement peaked, in line with prices, in 2005 and 2008, with evidence suggesting that CO_2 emissions from EU ETS sectors in 2008 would be 1−3% higher in most Member States in the absence of the EU ETS [13]. However, it is equally likely that very little to no abatement was induced when prices were near zero in 2007. On an EU-wide scale, it appears that the vast majority of abatement achieved by the EU ETS since its establishment has been through fuel-switching from existing coal to existing gas capacities in the power sector, particularly in Germany and the UK, rather than the installation of renewables or more efficient technologies in industry. As a result, the EU ETS has thus far produced little or no long-term infrastructure change (although some national-level carbon pricing may have had some effect).

10.7 WHAT COULD CARBON PRICING ACHIEVE IN THE FUTURE?

Multiple values and trajectories for carbon prices needed to deliver decarbonization have been produced by numerous modeling studies. From such studies, projected values commonly center between €35−75/tCO_2 in 2030 and €250/tCO_2 in 2050 [2].

From a techno-economic perspective, what could be achieved? Fig. 10.2 provides an example of changes to the levelized cost of electricity for different technologies under a €250/tCO_2 carbon price. It is clear that under the assumptions given,[1] coal becomes clearly uneconomic, whilst unabated gas remains competitive with offshore wind and solar PV, with onshore wind and nuclear as the least-cost options. However, various issues complicate this picture. The carbon price

---

[1]Projected data for a 2019 start date for carbon pricing in the UK. The derivation of these values is detailed in Ref. [2].

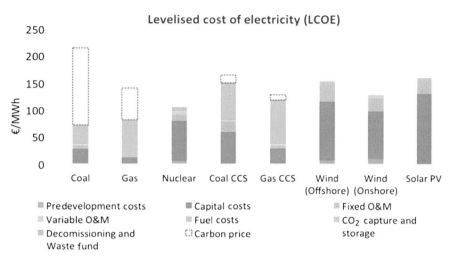

FIGURE 10.2

Levelized cost of electricity in 2050 with €250/tCO$_2$ carbon price.

illustrated is that for 2050; if an approximately linear price increase is assumed, the carbon price burden will be much less in most of the intervening time.

The modeling also assumes carbon price stability and predictability. As discussed above, this may be highly difficult to achieve, particularly under a cap-and-trade system without substantial price management mechanisms. Additionally, fuel prices fluctuate frequently (particularly coal and gas), and capital cost developments are difficult to predict far in advance (particularly for less mature technologies). These factors are also likely to vary relatively substantially across Member States. In the case of CCS, it is not clear whether the technology will in fact be available at all. Other aspects, such as electricity market design, will also play an essential role.

Taking first the example of fuel prices; weighted-average petrol and diesel prices across the EU between January 2005 and January 2015 were €1.37/L and €1.24/L, respectively. A €75/tCO$_2$ carbon price in 2030, when the transition from fossil fuels must be in full swing, would add an additional 15% to these prices [2]. Evidence suggests that in the EU changes in fuel prices influence travel demand, but have little influence in vehicle choice. Capital costs, in particular, play a much more significant role [14]. Additionally, company car taxation arrangements in many Member States allow for the fuel costs to be borne by the employer rather than the vehicle user (and be VAT-deductible), reducing or removing the incentive to purchase a more efficient vehicle, and to reduce travel demand [2].

Underlying price volatility adds further complication. Fig. 10.3 illustrates the variation in EU petrol diesel prices between 2005 and 2015. The differential between peak and trough prices over this time, largely driven by oil price variations, was large enough to have fully counteracted the addition of a carbon price at values even substantially higher than that suggested for 2030. To compound this issue, a significant proportion of fuel prices are taxes and duties (over 50% for petrol in

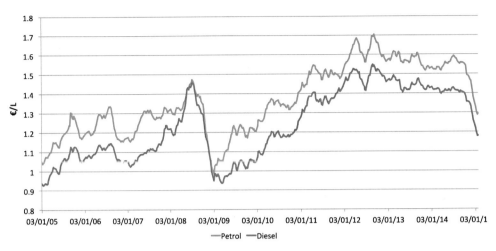

FIGURE 10.3

Weighted-average EU petrol and diesel prices (2005–15).

most Member States), much of which may be reduced in order to compensate for an added carbon price, further reducing its potential impact. In other words, a carbon price alone on fuel could have limited impact on the necessary transition of the transport sector.

Similar issues may be found in other sectors. For example, the landlord–tenant dilemma may prevent a carbon price on heating fuels from stimulating increased energy efficiency (e.g., insulation) or the use of low-carbon heating technologies (e.g., heat pumps) in buildings. This is because tenants are unable to install such items themselves, while landlords are not incentivized to invest as they usually do not pay the energy bills.

10.8 WHAT HAVE OTHER POLICY INSTRUMENTS ACHIEVED?

Alongside carbon pricing, other instruments, which may broadly be categorized as "technology-based" (regulatory) and "behavior-based", are present.

The Renewable Energy Directive, a key regulatory measure, requires that all Member States achieve a certain level of renewable energy as a proportion of their total energy consumption by 2020. Although these targets are not exclusive to electricity, all Member States (except Latvia) currently provide subsidies (in one way or another) for the deployment of renewable electricity, to achieve these targets. The evidence suggests that such subsidies are almost entirely responsible for the increase in renewable electricity across the EU over recent years [12], from around 3% in 2003 to around 15% in 2013 (excluding hydropower). Similarly, regulations on the CO_2 intensity of passenger cars, introduced in 2009 to replace a system of largely ineffective voluntary agreements, is likely the key driver behind the fleet-average reduction of the CO_2 intensity of new cars from 170 gCO_2/km in 2001 to 119 gCO_2/km in 2015—ahead of the regulatory target of 130 gCO_2/km by 2015. However, even without considering emissions manipulations such as by Volkswagen, there is a recognized gap in fuel consumption and CO_2 emissions between the real-world performance of vehicles and laboratory tests upon which regulatory compliance is based. While in 2001 the discrepancy was around 8%, by 2013 it had increased to around 31% for private cars, and as much as 45% for company cars [15].

In the buildings sector, the Ecodesign Directive is projected to have a substantial impact on the energy consumption of buildings over time. The directive implements minimum energy performance standards on energy-using and energy-related products used in buildings (from heating and cooling equipment to lighting and appliances). By 2020, it is estimated that energy consumption equivalent to 14% of 2009 residential consumption would be prevented [16]. However, a noncompliance rate of 10%−20% has been estimated, largely due to Member States failing to dedicate necessary resources to monitoring and enforcement [17].

Although Member States are required to ensure that all new buildings constructed from 2021 are "nearly-zero energy," existing minimum energy consumption standards in many Member States are already poorly enforced, with compliance often found to be relatively low [1]. Similarly, of the 17 Member States that have, or are planning to implement, an Energy Efficiency Obligation Scheme (EEOS) for compliance with Article 7 of the Energy Efficiency Directive,[m] at least eight have major credibility issues—despite analysis projecting that such instruments will achieve around 40% of the energy savings required by this directive to achieve the 20% energy efficiency target by 2020 [18].

Major behavior-focused instruments have largely centered on product labeling, particularly of buildings, energy-using products, and cars. Such labeling serves to highlight energy efficiency or CO_2 intensities, with the objective of overcoming information deficits and shifting demand to more energy- and CO_2-efficient options. Evidence suggests that while such instruments may be effective in influencing product efficiency improvements by manufacturers, they have thus far had relatively little impact in influencing consumer choice. This is for three reasons: first, under- or nonimplementation and a lack of compliance with requirements; secondly, varied or relatively ineffective design (e.g., unclear or doesn't provide the most effective information to the target audience); and thirdly, aspects such as capital costs or the availability of certain features, which may often be more important than energy or CO_2 efficiency [2].

10.9 WHAT COULD OTHER POLICY INSTRUMENTS ACHIEVE IN THE FUTURE?

Technology-based instruments could be made progressively more stringent, amended to fix existing failings where possible, and applied more widely (or in the case of subsidy instruments also more generously), to potentially induce a substantial shift to efficient, low-carbon technologies and practices across the economy. New instruments could also be introduced. For example, CO_2 intensity limits on power generation may prevent the construction of new, unabated coal-fired plants,

---

[m]Article 7 requires Member States to implement an Energy Efficiency Obligation Scheme (EEOS), in which energy suppliers must achieve average annual cumulative savings of 1.5% compared to their average total energy sales across 2009−12 (or other measures that achieve equivalent savings). Transport and EU ETS installations may be excluded.

reducing the possibility of creating new stranded assets in the future. Further, the lack of certification schemes for suppliers of energy efficiency measures in the building stock is an often-cited barrier to the introduction of such measures. Their introduction may thus help overcome information asymmetries and provide confidence to encourage uptake.

However, if instances of under- and nonimplementation and noncompliance remain at present levels (including "technical" compliance, but practical underachievement), the full potential of such instruments cannot be realized. Policy instruments should aim at reducing such issues, such as through the planned introduction of the Worldwide Harmonized Light Vehicle Test Procedure for compliance to reduce the differential between laboratory and "real-world" conditions when testing for CO_2 intensity regulation compliance for cars. However, there are practical limits to how far monitoring and enforcement can be improved at both EU and Member State levels from an administrative and resourcing perspective—particularly if certain regulations were to be expanded or new instruments to be introduced.

Additionally, regulations or subsidies that require or encourage efficiency investments that lead to reduced costs may produce a rebound effect, further reducing the absolute energy savings achieved. Alongside the introduction of effective carbon pricing, behavioral instruments such as product labeling can help to reduce this effect. Other options are also available. For example, evidence regarding the use of "nudging"[n] is largely positive in producing moderate reductions in energy consumption through altering behavioral dynamics, as recently mandated by the Energy Efficiency Directive for residential energy bills. Similarly, Personalised Travel Planning (PTP) has shown substantial promise in encouraging a shift towards public transport from private cars.

10.10 THE NEED FOR A BROAD POLICY MIX

Carbon pricing is often considered as the "silver bullet" for tackling CO_2 emissions and remaining within our carbon budgets. However, it is clear that even if a substantial, predictable and broadly applicable price could be established in the EU, real-life market dynamics and structures mean that the theoretical potential of such an instrument cannot be easily realized. As such, carbon pricing alone cannot be relied upon to deliver the level of decarbonization required. It is clear that a policy "mix" will be needed to achieve an effective low-carbon transition in a cost-effective and feasible manner. This mix needs to include technology-based and behavior-based instruments alongside carbon pricing—forming three "pillars of policy" [19]. This is recognized by the Commission's Communication on the policy framework for climate and energy for 2030 (and more recent publications).[o]

A level of political concession and negotiation is inevitable in policy making. Framing and assessing the challenge of and potential for responses to decarbonization around the three "pillars of policy" may help identify gaps in the policy landscape where significant untapped potential may exist. For example, evidence suggests the potential for informational and behavioral instruments is substantially underexploited in some sectors [20].

---

[n]Behavioral strategies to steer individuals towards adopting a more energy-efficient behavior.
[o]http://europa.eu/rapid/press-release_IP-15-5358_en.htm

This in turn may facilitate proposals for well-coordinated, complementary and dynamic policy packages, the individual components of which may otherwise be less effective or even infeasible. Additionally, concessions that may be counter-productive in the long term should to the extent possible also be reduced. This includes, for example, exemptions and derogations that may increase or encourage the risk of high-carbon "lock-in." Reducing such concessions would minimize the need for revision in the future and increase long-term stability and confidence in the long-term decarbonization ambition.

REFERENCES

[1] M. Meinshausen, et al., Greenhouse gas emission targets for limiting global warming to 2°C, Nature 458 (2009) 1158−1162.
[2] P. Drummond, Policies to Deliver a Low Carbon Energy System in Europe, University College London, London, 2015.
[3] L. Clarke, et al., Assessing transformation pathways, in: O. Edenhofer, et al. (Eds.), Climate Change 2014: Mitigation of Climate Change, Cambridge University Press, New York, 2014.
[4] M.R. Raupach, et al., Sharing a quota on cumulative carbon emissions, Nat. Clim. Change 4 (2014) 873−879.
[5] IEA Statistics, CO_2 emissions from fuel combustion, 2014.
[6] C. McGlade, P. Ekins, The geographical distribution of fossil fuels unused when limiting global warming to 2°C., Nature 517 (2015) 187−190.
[7] C. McGlade, S. Pye, Unburnable fossil fuels in a 2°C world. Insight-E Hot Energy Topic 6.
[8] Green European Foundation, The price of doing too little, too late, 2014.
[9] Shell, Letter to shareholders, May 21, 2014/ExxonMobil. Report: energy and carbon—managing the risks, 2014.
[10] CIEP, Transition, what transition? 2014.
[11] MSCI, 2015 ESG trends to watch, 2015.
[12] P. Agnolucci, P. Drummond, The Effect of Key EU Climate Policies on the EU Power Sector, University College London, London, 2014.
[13] B. Meyer, M. Meyer, Impact of the Current Economic instruments on Economic Activity, Gesellschaft für Wirtschaftliche Strukturforschung., Osnabrück, 2013.
[14] P. Drummond, Understanding the Impacts and Limitations of the Current EU Climate Policy Mix: Synthesis and Conclusion, University College London., London, 2014.
[15] ICCT, From laboratory to road: a 2014 update of official and "real-world" fuel consumption and CO_2 values for passenger cars in Europe, 2014.
[16] CSES and Oxford Research, Evaluation of the ecodesign directive (2009/125/EC) [Online], 2012. <http://ec.europa.eu/enterprise/dg/files/evaluation/cses_e.codesign_finalreport_en.pdf>.
[17] P. Drummond, Review of the Existing Instrument Mix at EU Level and in Selected Member States—The European Union, University College London., London, 2013.
[18] J. Rosenow, et al., Study Evaluating the National Policy Measures and Methodologies to Implement Article 7 of the Energy Efficiency Directive, Ricardo-AEA., Didcot, 2015.
[19] M. Grubb, J.-C. Hourcade, K. Neuhoff, Planetary Economics: Energy, Climate Change and the Three Domains of Sustainable Development, Routledge, Abingdon, 2014.
[20] P. Drummond, Policies to Deliver a Low-Carbon Energy System in Europe: Examining Different Policy Pathways, University College London., London, 2015.

GAS SECURITY OF SUPPLY IN THE EUROPEAN UNION

Marie-Claire Aoun[1], Damir Pešut[2], Marko Matosović[2], Robert Bošnjak[2], Paul Deane[3], James Glynn[3], Brian Ó. Gallachóir[3], Stanislaw Nagy[4], Thierry Badouard[5], Nathalie Desbrosses[5], Constantinos Taliotis[6], Maïté de Boncourt[1], and Kimon Keramidas[5]

[1]*Institut Français des Relations Internationales (IFRI), Paris, France* [2]*Energy Institute Hrvoje Požar (EIHP), Zagreb, Croatia* [3]*University College Cork, Cork, Ireland* [4]*AGH University, Kraków, Poland* [5]*Enerdata, Grenoble, France* [6]*KTH Royal Institute of Technology, Stockholm, Sweden*

11.1 INTRODUCTION

While Chapter 10, Decarbonizing the EU Energy System, showed that large quantities of global gas reserves need to remain untouched, the EU's energy system will remain widely dependent on gas supplies for many years to come. Ensuring gas security of supply is therefore a key criterion for energy policy design in the EU.

Since the 2009 crisis between Russia and Ukraine, the EU has adopted several legislative tools to strengthen EU gas security of supply. The third legislative package, the security of supply Regulation (EU) 994/2010 and the Energy Infrastructure package identifying Projects of Common Interest (PCI) have significantly improved the ability of the EU to face import disruptions. However, several countries remain particularly vulnerable to the occurrence of disruptions. When considering national production, storage, and the diversity of suppliers, Bulgaria, Czech Republic, Estonia, Finland, Latvia, and Lithuania seem to be at risk.[a]

In 2015, 70% of the EU's gas consumption was supplied through imports. Member States have different import profiles with divergent levels of dependency on Russian imports. Several European Member States rely heavily on Russian supplies (Greece, Austria, Poland, Romania, Hungary, Bulgaria, Czech Republic, Estonia, Finland, Latvia, Lithuania, and Slovakia), which show that the EU gas supply security needs to be examined both from an internal and international perspective.

The following sections provide an introduction to the gas infrastructure both within the EU and connecting the EU with its main current and prospective external gas suppliers. It discusses the role of liquefied natural gas (LNG) and provides an assessment of the role of shale gas for Europe, drawing on experiences in the US. In this context, costs, available resources, technologies, and environmental risks are addressed.

---

[a]Romania, Poland, and Hungary also import the bulk of their gas from Russia, but have either domestic production or significant storage capacity.

Europe's Energy Transition. DOI: http://dx.doi.org/10.1016/B978-0-12-809806-6.00011-0

11.2 **THE EU's GAS INFRASTRUCTURE**

An analysis of the implementation of the Regulation (EU) 994/2010 on security of supply shows that, in 2014, only 18 countries reported an ability to be resilient (as measured by the N−1 rule[b]) to potential gas disruptions. The Member States which did not pass the N−1 rule are Sweden, Lithuania, Luxembourg, Bulgaria, Ireland, Portugal, Slovenia, and Greece [1]. The Energy Community South-West subregion,[c] could meet the N−1 criterion on a regional level, presuming that interconnections between countries exist, all the storage projects are implemented, and at least one large supply source is built (be it an LNG terminal or gas pipeline). The use of the N−1 criterion should however be used with caution, since it accounts only for theoretical capacity of gas infrastructure and does not take into consideration available gas flows (booked capacity), nor the case of transit countries, where not all existing capacities are available to the transiting country. This criterion should be considered only as one of the indicators for security of gas supply.

The map of PCI in Fig. 11.1 shows a high density of pipeline projects in the South-East Europe (SEE) region[d] and a large number of reverse flow projects[e] in the western part of Europe. Although Western Europe is already well interconnected, west−east interconnections remain insufficient, particularly in order to facilitate flows of gas from LNG terminals in France, Spain, and Portugal to the central part of Europe. Implementation of the proposed PCI will create the basis for solidarity mechanisms and allow greater flexibility of gas flows in case of emergency. Reverse flow capacities have significantly increased since the 2009 crisis, especially in Western and Central Europe. Between 2009 and 2014, the number of bidirectional interconnection points on the European gas network increased from 24% to 40% [1].

The situation is however different in the SEE region, where there is a need to develop the transmission gas network to increase interconnections and create new supply routes. Modeling of the gas network by ENTSOG[f] shows that in the event of a disruption of the gas transit through Ukraine, countries in SEE will be severely impacted if only projects that reached Final Investment Decision (FID) were commissioned (the main countries affected would be Bulgaria, Greece, Croatia, Hungary, Romania, Serbia, and Slovenia). In case of implementation of all projects (i.e., FID and non-FID), the infrastructure resilience would however be satisfied. A similar conclusion also holds for Poland and Lithuania in case of disruption of the gas transit through Belarus, although the impact is not as severe as in SEE. The lack of approved projects relevant to the gas transit through Ukraine therefore has a wider regional dimension.

---

[b]A redundancy design criteria for ensuring the continuous operation, also in times of a failure of one major supply infrastructure element or equivalent.
[c]Croatia and six Balkan Contracting countries: Albania, Bosnia and Herzegovina, Kosovo, FYR of Macedonia, Montenegro, and Serbia.
[d]This region includes: Greece, Bulgaria, Albania, Republic of Macedonia, Kosovo, Serbia, Montenegro, Bosnia and Herzegovina, Romania, Moldova, Croatia, Slovenia, Cyprus, and Turkey.
[e]Many pipelines accommodate only unidirectional gas flows; reverse flow allow bidirectional flows.
[f]European Network of Transmission System Operators for Gas.

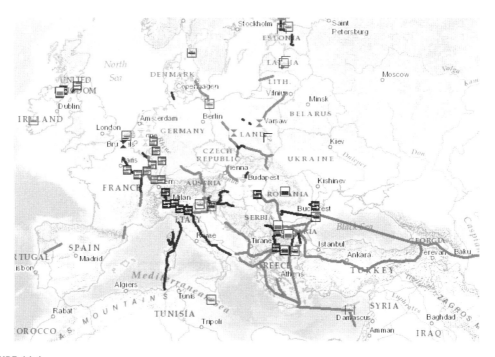

FIGURE 11.1

Map of natural gas projects of common interest.[g]

Given the lack of interconnections in the SEE region, the improvement of interconnection capacity between the countries and the integration of new supply routes should be considered as an EU priority in order to mitigate identified risks in the region.

In addition to the development of sufficient interconnection capacity, the improvement of storage infrastructure is key for EU security of supplies. Storage can allow for timely response in prolonged periods of high demand and serves as a reliable back-up supply for renewables integration. Storage can also safeguard against unexpected high-impact events and technical failures, and mitigate geopolitical risk. The EU28 has approximately 149 storage facilities with a total technical working gas volume of storage of more than 100 bcm, and a certain number of facilities in development (Fig. 11.2).

Gas storage obligations for supplying customers are issued in several Member States (Hungary, France, Italy, Slovakia, Spain, and Portugal). In all these countries, storage capacity plays an important role in supplying customers in the winter season, in particular on peak days. Furthermore, Hungary has a special security (strategic) storage unit, which is an instrument to supply gas in emergency cases exclusively to protected customers. It should provide the country with 40−45 days of autonomy, if the main import from Russia failed. A number of EU Member States do not have any gas storage facilities, such as Cyprus, Estonia, Finland, Greece, Luxembourg, Malta, and Slovenia. Among these countries, Estonia, Finland, and Lithuania have a

---

[g]Online version available at http://ec.europa.eu/energy/infrastructure/transparency_platform/map-viewer/main.html.

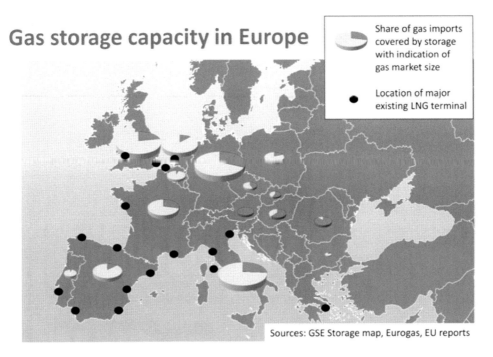

FIGURE 11.2

Gas storage facilities in the EU.

From GSE Storage map, Eurogas, EU reports.

very high reliance on Russian imports. Currently, Lithuania has a project in the planning phase (Syderiai UGS) which is expected to be commissioned in 2021.[h] A number of LNG projects are also proposed in Malta, Greece, and Finland.

For those Member States without an adequate geological structure for gas storage, policy coordination could provide some support, potentially including the lease of storage capacities in neighboring countries with adequate storage. However, a number of barriers exist for the development of new storage facilities, as they are capital-intensive with 20−25 years pay-back and long lead times (5−8 years) for construction. Thus, sustained low seasonal price spreads are putting strong economic pressure on gas storage facilities leading to facility closures.

In addition to storage, the exploitation of shale gas and biomethane would contribute to increasing the EU gas supply security through increasing domestic production. The potential of shale gas is described in more detail in Section 11.4 onwards. The European Biogas Roadmap indicates[i] that, if the necessary actions were taken, the level of biomethane production could reach 18−20 bcm in 2030, providing about 3% of the European natural gas consumption, and around 10% of total gaseous vehicle fuel consumption.

[h] < http://www.le.lt/index.php/projects-in-progress/syderiai-underground-gas-storage/535 >
[i] Available for download at http://european-biogas.eu/

11.3 **THE EXTERNAL DIMENSION OF THE EU's APPROACH**

Given the historical tensions between Russia and Ukraine, the EU is seeking to diversify its supplies through additional pipeline sources. The development of the Southern Corridor figures amongst the most debated options. Its original planned contribution was to secure 10%−20% of natural gas demand in the EU by 2020, which would total 45−90 bcm/year. The gas would come from Azerbaijan's Shah Deniz field through Georgia, Turkey, Greece, and Albania to the south of Italy. Currently, the Southern Corridor relies on the Trans Adriatic Pipeline (TAP) project, which will be operational in 2020 (with initial capacity of 10 bcm and potentially rising to 20 bcm) and the Trans-Anatolian gas pipeline (TANAP), expected by 2018 (with initial capacity of 16 bcm rising to 31 bcm in 2026).

TAP commenced construction in 2016 and is on schedule with the planned project activities. The other major project, TANAP, has awarded a 5-year contract for the supply of engineering, procurement, and construction management (EPCM) services to an Australian-based engineering company.

At the time of writing, two other projects key to the future of the Southern Corridor are the expansion of the South Caucasus Pipeline (SCP)—(1) a section of the Baku-Tbilisi-Erzurum (BTE) pipeline, which may provide an additional 16 bcm of gas per annum from the Shah Deniz 2 development in the Caspian Sea to the Georgia−Turkey border by 2018—and (2) the Trans-Caspian Pipeline (TCP) between Turkmenistan and Azerbaijan via the Caspian Sea. TCP could provide additional diversification of gas supply, but numerous risks and difficulties concerning costs and investments undermine its feasibility.

The Southern Corridor may have a significant impact on the diversification of import routes and could increase long-term security of gas supply. Although primarily focused on bringing Caspian gas to Italy, the Southern Corridor could open the possibility of connecting Albania and Croatia via the Ionian−Adriatic Pipeline, which would also add to creating an interconnected gas network in SEE. However, its success will be affected by the development of other gas markets and their rising consumption, primarily energy-hungry Asian countries. China has strong interests in the Caspian Region, especially in Turkmenistan with the additional advantage of an already existing pipeline that transports gas to China.

Other alternative pipeline projects to diversify imports are more uncertain. Israel's offshore production is still in its early stages and debates on whether to use the gas for internal purposes or exports were vivid. The Iraqi and Iranian gas potential is real: with more than 15% of global gas reserves, Iran could contribute to the EU supplies through Turkey provided the necessary investments are made. However, the development of the Iranian resources remains subject to a high geopolitical risk and to several internal obstacles such as domestic energy consumption. As for additional supplies coming from Africa, the future of the GALSI pipeline remains uncertain. The Trans-Saharan pipeline that would bring Nigerian gas (up to 30 bcm/year upon completion) to Europe through Algeria is also struggling to secure resources from the Niger delta, as well as to design a safe route north amidst terrorism threats and geopolitical tensions.

It should be however noted that several EU gas pipelines remain currently underutilized. The total EU import capacity from Russia is currently 256 bcm, while actual exports to Europe were

159 bcm in 2015. Thus, additional investments for security of supply reasons should be assessed with regards to the current overcapacity in the European transmission system.

REGIONAL CASE STUDY ON THE EASTERN MEDITERRANEAN'S GAS POTENTIAL

The Eastern Mediterranean region appeared on the new world gas map with the discovery of the Tamar field in 2009. Although the volumes of gas discovered are not a global game changer, potential resources could well boost the economies of the host countries and potentially provide respectable gas volumes to the EU—an attractive opportunity given the EU's current reliance on Russian gas. The discoveries also have the potential to promote regional stability through economic cooperation.

However, the drop in oil and gas prices since 2014, which has delayed LNG projects and oil and gas investments worldwide, is casting high doubts on the export perspectives of the region towards Europe on the medium term.

Furthermore, the evolution towards a more restrictive regulatory framework in Israel, as well as the discoveries of the Egypt gas Zohr field, has changed Israel's export prospects, as the latter were primarily intended for the Egyptian market. Alternative export destinations are now being explored, focused more on the regional scale, such as supply to the Jordanian market. Previous exploratory successes in Cyprus' Aphrodite field have not continued, which undermines the possibility of a dedicated LNG terminal on the island. In any case, Break-even needs of projects will be more demanding for projects targeting the European and Asian markets due to higher costs than those targeting regional markets, such as Egypt and Turkey. At the same time, the geopolitical environment is highly volatile in the region. The continued settlements in Israel threaten relations with its Arab neighbors and could put regional gas deals on hold, while the increasing isolation of Turkey may encourage the country to act more as a deterrent force if its gas transit role is diminished.

In addition to measures to increase security of gas supply, in its 2016 Sustainable Energy Security Package, the European Commission specifically pointed to the potential role for LNG in a resilient energy union. There are currently 23 LNG facilities in the EU (representing a total technical capacity of around 200 bcm per year) with the majority of them in Spain and Western Europe. This gives good access to potential shipments from across the Atlantic but highlights a wider issue for the EU gas network. Traditionally gas had moved east to west across Europe and the infrastructure to move gas from western LNG hubs to central Europe needs to be improved as identified by a number of the PCI. In 2015, LNG accounted for 10% of EU gas consumption. The EU LNG industry has been impacted until 2014 by higher LNG prices in Asian markets resulting in a decrease in LNG terminal utilization rates in Europe from 53% (of total installed capacity) in 2010 to just 19% in 2014 (compared with a global average of 33%). The global LNG landscape has changed since 2014, ending the high post-Fukushima tension on the LNG markets. On one hand, markets have entered an era of excess of LNG liquefaction capacity with the US and Australian projects coming on stream. On the other hand, the Asian and European prices have been converging, with the slowdown of the Asian gas demand growth. The context for Europe to increase its LNG imports and diversify its gas supplies is now more favorable, as recognized by the LNG Strategy published in February 2016. However, Europe will remain a last resort market for global LNG, as it has to compete with other more attractive markets (Asia, Latin America, etc.), and EU LNG is in competition with very low pipe gas prices, in particular Russian gas.

11.4 SHALE GAS PROSPECTS FOR EUROPE

Apart from diversifying gas imports, the exploration of shale gas presents an additional option to increase security of gas supply in Europe. Many studies have been commissioned these last few years at EU, international and national level in order to bridge the knowledge gap over shale gas resources and its extraction impact. However, the current situation in Europe is not conducive to the rapid development of shale exploitation, even in Member States where the combination of geological conditions and public opinion is the most favorable, such as Poland. Interestingly, the amount of funds necessary for the extraction of shale gas in Poland is so high that, according to the Polish Academy of Science [2], the combined resources of companies based in Poland are far from satisfactory for large-scale gas production. Given the extent of investments needed, knowing at what economic and environmental costs unconventional gas resources can be obtained is crucial. Technological developments can substantially influence this cost curve. At a macro level, the development of gas production from domestic sources could keep LNG imports at current levels (12%−15% of total gas demand up to 2050) or even bring them down to 9% in a shale boom scenario. Conversely, if there was no development of shale gas in Europe there would likely be an increase in LNG imports up to 28% by 2050 and indigenous gas production within the EU would decrease to 6% of demand in the mid-21st century [3].

At the end of 2013, the European Union held less than 1% (1.6 trillion cubic meters (tcm)) of proven gas reserves while it consumed approximately 0.4 tcm in 2013.[j] Conventional gas production in Europe is in decline and the output of EU's largest gas field "the Groningen field" in the Netherlands will continue to reduce significantly over the next years. This is in sharp contrast to the situation in the US. The success of shale gas developments in the US has led to significant benefits in terms of improved security of supply and lower energy prices. US shale gas production has increased rapidly by 645% over the period of 2007−12.[k] However, using shale gas for ensuring security of gas supply in the US requires stable prices, growing demand, internal gas pipeline infrastructure, appropriate drilling efforts, and investments in minimizing well production decline rates. The level of drilling activity in the sector is dictated by respective oil and gas prices, which in turn are dictated by the supply−demand balance as a result of economic activity and existing production capacity. The price premium between oil and gas has incentivized drilling efforts to switch to tight oil production. This led to an annual increase in the rig count of 16% to 1592 rigs with an overall 24% increase in horizontal drilling; typically for hydraulic fracturing. Surplus shale gas production had caused prices to drop below breakeven prices in some wells [4].

Past and forecast growth of shale gas production in the US (see Fig. 11.3) are positive influences in diversifying US security of gas supply. Cheap gas critically enabled timely US manufacturing competitiveness compared with EU and Asian markets through cheaper feedstocks, fuel substitution, and reduced electricity prices. This also had a complementary environmental benefit of reduced electricity carbon intensity.[l] If significant volumes of shale gas could be produced in Europe, wholesale gas prices are expected to be lower when compared to a future with

---

[j]BP statistical review 2014.
[k]International Energy Agency, IEA unconventional gas forum, http://www.iea.org/ugforum
[l]US-Energy Information Administration (EIA), Annual Energy Outlook 2014.

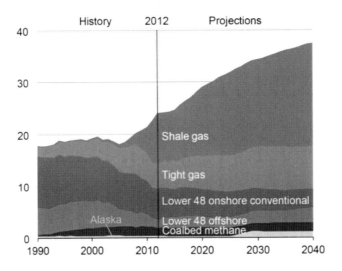

FIGURE 11.3

United States gas production history and forecast. (US-Energy Information Administration (EIA), Annual Energy Outlook 2014.)

no shale gas production. Security of supply will increase as import dependency is reduced. According to a Pöyry study, the share of Russian gas in the EU supply mix could be 50% by 2050 in a shale boom scenario, instead of 60% in a no-shale scenario [3]. Reducing import dependency and improving security of supply are two key economic benefits of EU indigenous shale gas production.

11.5 COSTS, RESOURCES, AND TECHNOLOGIES REQUIRED FOR THE EXPLOITATION OF SHALE GAS

Existing analyses show substantial geological gas resources as well as technical recoverable resources (TRR) in Europe. According to a 2014 study [5], the TRR in the EU could amount to 12.3 tcm,[m] but another analysis indicates a TRR between 13 and 26 tcm (assuming 20%−40% of recovery) with present extraction technologies.[n] This brings Europe quite close to the US, where TRR amount to 15.5 tcm [6]. However, specific geological conditions, regulatory (environmental) constraints, and a lack of drilling equipment may increase the cost of extraction in Europe compared to the situation in the US. Shale gas production in Europe could increase to a level of 30−160 billion cubic meters (bcm) in the case of substantial capital investment, while the average

---

[m]tcm, tera cubic meters = 10^{12} m^3; bcm, billion cubic meters; MMcm, million cubic meters; Mcm, thousand cubic meters. All units are given in "normal cubic meters" (Nm^3), 1 Nm^3 being the volume occupied by gas in specific conditions of pressure and temperature (respectively 1 atm and 273K).
[n]US-Energy Information Administration (EIA), Annual Energy Outlook 2013.

shale gas cost (breakeven price on well head) has been estimated by various groups and ranges from 220−260 to 380−500 USD/Mcm (thousand cubic meters). This last estimate could be reduced by 40% in 2030, with the assumption of URR of 60−120 million normal cubic meters (Nm^3) per well [7]. According to a JRC analysis [7], the possible breakeven cost in 2030 amounts to 225 USD/Mcm (including a 10% increase due to environmental protection).

Despite these specificities, shale gas production in Europe has to face the same challenges as in the US: access to transport and distribution infrastructure and high declines of gas production (up to 80% decline of gas rate in the first 3 years, while it is assumed that 70% of the TRR have been produced in the first decade). Consequently, this requires continuous drilling and stimulation activity. Based on the US experience, it may be assumed that 70% of drilling wells will produce gas in 30 years, and about 30% will be abandoned in the first 3 years. According to an analysis from the Polish development program, it may be necessary to invest 120 billion euros during the next 20 years to stimulate the industry [2]. Since it is closely dependent on the intensity of geological exploration and investments in mining, the full development of the shale gas industry cannot be expected to take place before at least 2030. The case of Poland is particularly informative. The development (including exploration) of one shale gas concession of 200 km^2 requires drilling approximately 330 wells from 26 pads, including approximately three gathering and gas treatment centers as well as a compression unit (Table 11.1).

This would cost 15−25 billion USD, with an estimated recovery of approximately 30−120 Mcm, depending on geological conditions. The average productivity could increase by 3.3% in the first 5 years, with a possibility of improving the extraction process up to 75% over the next 15 years. In parallel, the high initial CAPEX would be reduced due to lower costs of drilling, lower costs of stimulation service, and more efficient recovery. Investment costs for drilling, completion and fracking, and surface infrastructure could be lower by 48%, 19.6%, and 24%, respectively, compared to current levels.

Table 11.1 Capital and Operating Expenditure (CAPEX and OPEX) Estimates for the Development of a 200 km^2 Shale Gas Concession in Poland [8]

	Million USD	%
CAPEX Costs		
Gathering center	5.2−10.0	
LNG and LPG separation installation and compressor	16.7	
Auxiliary pipeline[a] [9]	0.55−0.76/km	
Seismic works [10]	26	
Provision (for abandoning and liquidation of wells)	−	10% of drilling cost
OPEX Costs		
Fixed costs (per pad)	3.15	
Variable costs	1.4$/1000 Nm^3	
Depreciation and amortization of pipelines	−	2.5%/year
[a]This issue was also discussed in Ref. [9].		

11.6 ASSESSMENT OF THE ENVIRONMENTAL RISKS OF SHALE GAS EXTRACTION AND TRANSPORTATION

There is no scientific confirmation that the use of hydraulic fracturing techniques leads to contamination of groundwater pollution [11]. However, accidental surface spills of fluids and wastewater, and changes in hydrology and water infiltration caused by new infrastructure may affect shallow groundwater and surface water resources. Indeed, out of the 25 major accidents tied to shale gas operations in the Marcellus Play, Pennsylvania, US, from January 2008 through August 2011 (3500 wells drilled), 19 were related to water contamination, surface spill, or gas migration in underground aquifers or substrates [12]. The risks associated with surface spills of chemicals (in particular those stored and used for drilling and stimulation of the hole [13]) could be minimized in Europe by introducing an obligation to protect the drill pad [14] (after removing the humus layer) by a special durable thick PVC layer ("geomembrane"), which allows complete isolation of soil and groundwater.

Recent experiments in Poland have shown no case of leakage of the process fluid during drilling operations and well stimulation. The development of "green chemistry" has resulted in a new generation of cleaner fracturing fluids ("CleanSuite," "CleanStim," or "OpenFrac," etc.). The potential migration of natural gas into groundwater through the cement protection mantle—considered as the greatest environmental risk [14]—can be almost completely eliminated by building a separate drilling column made from new-generation "microparticle" cement, which counteracts the formation of microcracks. These well casing and cementing technologies fully protect the aquifers from contact with drilling fluid or chemical liquids in drilling pads. With this technology, the risk of possible pot aquifer contamination by gas migration becomes negligible, if all works are performed with the best available technologies (BAT). Beyond that, the risk of drilling mud migration into aquifers is similar to normal/conventional drilling processes [15].

In spite of the development of new technologies consuming less water, the quantity of water required by hydraulic fracturing techniques remains controversial, especially in dry areas. On average, in the US, recycled water represents only between 6% and 10% [16] of the 10−20 million liters of water needed to hydraulically fracture a new well [17]. However, the situation in northern Europe is different as water supplies are reasonable [18]. Moreover, water consumption for shale gas production is 25−50 times lower than water savings from a coal-to-gas switch in the power sector [19]. New technologies also allow for the use of fracturing using salt water (instead of fresh water in its absence [15]) and the recycling of up to 90% of the backflow water (for example in the Marcellus Play). In Texas, fracturing process optimization has resulted in a reduction of up to 50% of the amount of water used for hydraulic stimulation (in Woodford Shale Play for instance), and one would also expect alternative fracturing technologies over the next 10 years to lead to an even bigger reduction of the impact on the environment.

A shale gas well may require between 1000 and 2000 one-way heavy truck trips (or 6000−9000 trips for an eight-well pad) [20], mainly to deliver water. This may lead to traffic congestion by heavy trucks, increased noise, diesel-motor emissions, and road accidents. It can also create an economic burden for local municipalities and could damage rural roads and bridges that were not built to carry heavy loads. The cost of heavy truck traffic per natural gas well in Pennsylvania is estimated to amount to between US$13,000 and US$23,000 (€10,000−17,000) in damage to state roadways (2011 data). However, the reuse of flowback wastewater can significantly reduce the road traffic.

Regulation must include strong monitoring, reporting, and enforcement measures to prevent water and soil pollution. Regulation must be based on best available practices for drilling and wastewater management. Operators should fully disclose all chemical types and quantities used to gain European citizens' trust as their perception of risks is distorted by a weak onshore oil and gas culture.

11.7 ENSURING EUROPE'S SECURITY OF GAS SUPPLY IN THE FUTURE

Key measures are necessary in order to strengthen the EU security of gas supply. In the short and medium term, there is a need to improve solidarity mechanisms among Member States, notably by enhancing the access to LNG sources and storage facilities. Priority investments need to target the projects that enhance the interconnections in the most vulnerable countries, specifically in the SEE region. The proposal of a new Regulation on security of gas supplies published by the European Commission in 2016 is aimed at increasing cooperation between Member States by applying a prescriptive regional approach and a binding last resort solidarity mechanism in case of a crisis. The challenge to these debated measures is to find the right balance between a prescriptive cooperative approach and the provision of sufficient flexibility to Member States to adapt during a crisis. Further, infrastructure investments need to support a diversification of supply options. The main challenge here is to commit to heavy and costly investments to develop infrastructures in the long term in order to diversify EU supplies, while several pipelines and LNG facilities are currently underutilized.

Fostering indigenous gas production through biomethane and shale gas are further options to increase security of gas supply. Especially shale gas production could significantly improve security of gas supply and reduce energy dependence in Europe. Although the conditions for extraction are less favorable in Europe than in the US, Europe could benefit from the technological development and learning process in the US. An enabling regulation should include enforceable principles of transparency, monitoring, and risk mitigation, and impose the use of the BAT in order to prevent water and soil pollution. It should also make sure that the accompanying infrastructure is in place before drilling starts. But above all, meaningful consultation and useful engagement with stakeholders and citizens is a prerequisite before any developments can take place.

REFERENCES

[1] Rodríguez-Gómez N., Zaccarelli N., Bolado-Lavín R. 2015; Improvement in the EU Gas Transmission Network Between 2009 and 2014; EUR 27522 EN; doi: 10.2790/708926
[2] The Statement of the Presidium of the Polish Academy of Sciences Concerning Natural Gas in Shales (Shale gas). Pol. Acad. Sci.: Mineral Resour. Manage. 30 (2) (2014) 5–14.
[3] Pöyry Consulting, Macroeconomic effects of European shale gas production, November 2013.
[4] R. Weijermars, Economic appraisal of shale gas plays in Continental Europe, Appl. Energy 106 (2013) 100–115.
[5] ICF, Mitigation of climate impacts of possible future shale gas extraction in the EU, January 2014.

[6] M. Krupa, Efficiency model of exploration and extraction of hydrocarbon from shales in Poland, PhD thesis, AGH University of Science and Technology, Krakow, 2014.

[7] I. Pearson, et al., Unconventional gas: potential energy market impacts in the European Union. JRC Scientific and Policy Reports, 2012.

[8] P. Drummond, Review of the Existing Instrument Mix at EU Level and in Selected Member States— The European Union, University College London, London, 2013.

[9] M. Meinshausen, et al., Greenhouse gas emission targets for limiting global warming to 2°C, Nature 458 (2009) 1158–1162.

[10] C. McGlade, S. Pye, Unburnable fossil fuels in a 2°C world. Insight-E Hot Energy Topic 6, February 2015.

[11] A.J. Krupnick, et al., The natural gas revolution: critical questions for a sustainable energy future, March 2014.

[12] T. Considine, et al., Environmental impacts during Marcellus shale gas drilling: causes, impacts and remedies, 2012.

[13] MIT, The future of natural gas, June 2011.

[14] Internatrional Energy Agency (IEA), Golden Rules for a Golden Age of Gas: World Energy Outlook Special Report on Unconventional Gas, OECD/IEA, Paris, 2012.

[15] G. King, Hydraulic fracturing 101: unconventional gas wells, 2012.

[16] M.E. Mantell, Produced water reuse and recycling challenges and opportunities across major shale plays. Chesapeake Energy Corporation, March 2011.

[17] NETL, Environmental impacts of unconventional natural gas development and production, May 2014.

[18] D. Buchan, Can shale gas transform Europe's energy landscape? Centre for European Reform, July 2013.

[19] B.R. Scanlon, et al., Drought and the water-energy Nexus in Texas, 2013.

[20] S. Abramzon, et al., Estimating the consumptive use costs of shale natural gas extraction on Pennsylvania roadways, J. Infrastruct. Syst. 20, (2014) 06014001.

BIOFUELS FOR AVIATION: POLICY GOALS AND COSTS

12

Paul Deane, Brian Ó. Gallachóir, and Richard O. Shea

University College Cork (UCC), Cork, Ireland

12.1 INTRODUCTION

Aviation is one of the strongest-growing transport sectors. Global airline operations consumed approximately 1.5 billion barrels of Jet A-1 fuel, producing 705 million tonnes (Mt) of CO_2 in 2013, just under 2% of the total of manmade CO_2 emissions. In the period up to 2050, worldwide aviation is expected to grow by up to 5% annually. If fuel consumption and CO_2 emissions were to grow at the same rate, CO_2 emissions by worldwide aviation in 2050 would be more than six times their current figure [1].

Europe is home to approximately 3,800 passenger aircraft and over 700 commercial airports (with more than 15,000 passenger movements per year) which supported the free movement of 842 million passengers in 2013 (as reported by Eurostat), an increase of 1.7% on 2012 levels. CO_2 emissions from aviation in 2013 in Europe were 150 Mt, representing 13% of total transport emissions. Final energy consumption in aviation in 2013 was 49 Mtoe or 14% of transport energy usage.

This chapter first presents the policy landscape up to 2050. It then continues to describe future increases in passenger activity. It discussed potential fuel savings due to technical improvements and operational improvements regarding air traffic management (ATM). A detailed overview and comparison of cost estimates for various biojet fuels is then given. The chapter further discusses feedstocks, before analyzing three scenarios to 2050 and their implications for biofuel production and CO_2 emissions.

12.2 EUROPEAN POLICY CONTEXT

A number of targets and policy instruments exist that concern biofuels (including biojet fuels). Fig. 12.1 presents a graphical overview of medium- and long-term policy targets for aviation at the EU and global levels. The EU's Renewable Energy Directive (RED) sets a binding target of 20% gross energy consumption from renewable sources by 2020 (20% RES). To achieve this, the Directive allocates individual targets to Member States ranging from 10% in Malta to 49% in Sweden. Each Member State is also required to have at least 10% of their transport fuels from renewable sources (10% RES-T) by 2020. It is anticipated that liquid biofuels in road transport will make the largest contribution to the 10% RES-T target owing to the fact that road transport accounts for 72% of transport emissions (EU-28, 2012). For both targets (RES and RES-T), only biofuels that meet specific sustainability criteria can be included. The denominator for the 20%

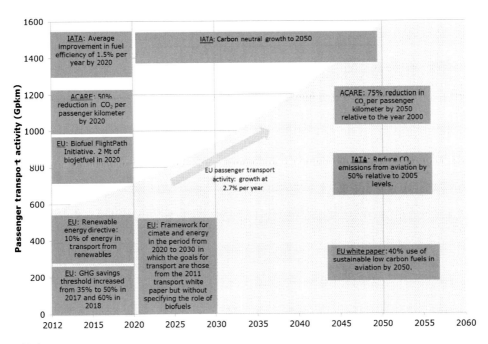

FIGURE 12.1

EU (*green*, light gray in print versions) and global (*blue*, dark gray in print versions) policy landscape to 2050.

RES target includes energy use in aviation, while the numerator includes all forms of renewable energy in all forms of transport. Therefore, in principle, biojet fuel usage can also count towards the 20% RES target.

The Fuel Quality Directive (FQD) sets a 6% target for greenhouse gas emission reductions from all energy used in road transport and non-road mobile machinery for 2020, compared with 2010. The FQD target does not apply to aviation fuel, but is expected to be a driver for increased road biofuels, alongside the RED. Under the RED the greenhouse gas savings threshold (one of the sustainability criteria) is increased for existing installations from 35% for all biofuels to 50% from January 1, 2017, and to 60% from January 1, 2018 for installations that start producing biofuels after January 1, 2017. Equally biofuels cannot be grown in areas converted from land with previously high carbon stock such as wetlands or forests, and biofuels cannot be produced from raw materials obtained from land with high biodiversity such as primary forests or highly biodiverse grasslands.

In 2011, the European Commission adopted a White Paper on Transport [2] which includes 40 initiatives to build a competitive transport system that will increase mobility, remove major barriers in key areas, and fuel growth and employment. The roadmap aims to dramatically reduce Europe's dependence on imported oil and to cut carbon emissions in transport by 60% by 2050. Also, there is an ambition of a 40% use of sustainable low-carbon fuels in aviation.

The 2013 Directive on the deployment of alternative fuels infrastructure [3] acknowledges the fact that aviation can rely only on alternative *liquid* fuels of drop-in type (and for the time being, biofuels remain the main alternative). This contrasts with other transport modes which can rely on electricity, LNG, or hydrogen. The Trans-European Network for Transport (TEN-T) guidelines recognize that alternative fuels serve, at least partly, as a substitute for fossil oil sources, contribute to the decarbonization of the transport sector and enhance its environmental performance. In its 2014 Communication,[a] the European Commission proposed a policy framework for climate and energy covering the period from 2020 to 2030, in which the goals for transport echo those from the 2011 White Paper on Transport but without specifying the role of biofuels, i.e., leaving it free for Member States to opt for other alternatives such as electric cars, etc.

The Biofuel FlightPath Initiative[b] was introduced in June 2011. As part of this initiative, the European Commission with Airbus, Air-France-KLM, British Airways, Lufthansa, and the biofuel producers Chemtex Italia, Neste Oil, Biomass Technology Group, UOP, and Swedish Biofuels are targeting an annual production of 2 Mt of fuel derived from renewable sources by 2020. This equates to approximately 1% of the total world jet fuel consumption in 2020 or 4% of EU jet fuel consumption. To put this in context, in 2013 approximately 13.1 Mt of biofuels were consumed in *all forms of transport* in Europe. Alternative jet fuels are currently produced in small quantities compared to both jet kerosene and to corn ethanol. While there are no specific figures for Europe in terms of volumes consumed, over 200 flights were operated globally in 2014 using alternative jet fuel and in the last decade over 1600 commercial flights have occurred by 21 different airlines. In 2011, Lufthansa became the first airline worldwide to use a biofuel mix in scheduled daily operations when it conducted a 6-month test run with an Airbus A321 on the Frankfurt−Hamburg route totaling over 1188 flights involving 800 tons of biojet fuel.

12.3 **AMBITION TO 2050**

There are a number of Global and European targets for emissions reductions and alternative fuel use in aviation. The goals pursued by the Advisory Council for Aviation Research and Innovation in Europe (ACARE) in terms of greenhouse gas emissions are a 50% reduction in CO_2 per passenger kilometer by 2020 (relative to year 2000 levels) and a 75% reduction by 2050 [4]. These targets are therefore independent of traffic growth.

At a global level, the International Air Transport Association (IATA) has also set ambitious targets to curb fuel consumption and mitigate emissions from aviation in its Carbon Neutral Growth initiative, according to which the aviation industry has committed to an average improvement in fuel efficiency of 1.5% per year from 2010 to 2020 and a cap on aviation CO_2 emissions from 2020 (carbon-neutral growth). By 2050, the ambition is to reduce CO_2 emissions from aviation by 50% relative to 2005 levels.

In 2013, at the 38th Session of the International Civil Aviation Organization (ICAO) Assembly, members reaffirmed ambitions towards collective global aspirational goals for the international aviation sector to improve annual fuel efficiency by 2%, and to limit CO_2 emissions at 2020 levels. The Assembly also defined a range of measures designed to help achieve these goals. This

[a]ec.europa.eu/clima/policies/2030/index_en.htm
[b]http://ec.europa.eu/energy/en/topics/biofuels/biofuels-aviation

includes: technology improvements, operational changes, alternative fuels such as biojet fuels, and market-based measures. However, it was recognized that the aspirational goal of 2% annual fuel efficiency improvement is unlikely to deliver the level of reduction necessary to stabilize, and then reduce, aviation's absolute emissions contribution to climate change, and that more ambitious goals will need to be considered to deliver a sustainable path for aviation. To date, no long-term binding targets exist.

12.4 LONG-TERM PASSENGER FORECASTS

A primary driver for emissions in aviation is passenger activity. This section briefly reviews passenger forecast figures to 2050.

World passenger traffic, expressed in terms of revenue passenger kilometers (RPK) on total scheduled services, increased by 5.2% in 2013 compared to 2012, according to ICAO preliminary figures. This represents the fourth consecutive year of positive growth for the air transport industry since 2009 and corresponds to a slightly higher increase than in 2012.

The ICAO estimates that global passenger traffic is expected to grow from 5 billion to more than 13 billion RPK over the period 2010−30, i.e., an average annual growth rate of 4.9%. Within the EU, aviation traffic is expected to grow at an average rate of 3% annually until 2050, pointing to a fuel consumption growth of 2% annually, and hence a more than doubling of CO_2 emissions by 2050 [1].

In the report *EU trends in energy and transport to 2050* [5] air transport is projected to be the highest growing of all passenger transport modes, increasing by 133% between 2010 and 2050 (2.1% p.a.), mainly due to the large increase in international trips (e.g., to emerging economies in Asia). Higher potential for air traffic growth (3.1% p.a. for 2010−50), including for international holiday trips, is expected in the EU-12 Member States due to their less mature markets and projected faster-growing GDP per capita. Aviation activity in the EU-15 is expected to increase at a lower rate compared to the EU-12 due to weaker growth of GDP per capita and the available capacity at airports.

12.5 TECHNICAL IMPROVEMENTS

Technological improvements will play an important role in emissions reduction from aviation to 2050. The ICAO Committee on Aviation Environmental Protection (CAEP) projects future environmental trends in aviation that include greenhouse gas emissions. The CAEP uses the latest input data and related assumptions to investigate the implications of technology improvements on trends related to the global climate, particularly fuel burn and CO_2 emissions. Results [6] are presented for global full-flight fuel burn for international aviation from 2005 to the year 2050. Under the scenarios investigated technological improvements to 2050 range from a 0.57% p.a. reduction in fuel burn (from 2015 to 2050) for a moderate technology improvement scenario to 1.5% p.a. (2010−50) under an optimistic improvement scenario.

12.6 AIR TRAFFIC MANAGEMENT

As the technological pillar of Europe's ambitious *Single European Sky Initiative*,[c] *SESAR*[d] is the mechanism that coordinates and concentrates all EU research and development activities in ATM. The European ATM Master [7] Plan is the agreed roadmap driving the modernization of the ATM system and connecting SESAR research and development with deployment. The roadmap includes a target of a 2.8% reduction in environmental impact per flight by 2020.

The modernization of the European ATM systems is discussed in the document *A Blueprint for the Single European Sky* [8] and is expected to deliver 300 kg fuel savings per flight, resulting in €6 billion of cost savings, and a 12 Mt reduction in CO_2 emissions for 20 million flights annually.

According to a review by the IPCC [9], improvements in ATM and other operational procedures could reduce aviation fuel burn by between 8% and 18%. It reports that the large majority (6%−12%) of these reductions comes from ATM improvements, which are anticipated to be fully implemented in the next 20 years. All engine emissions will be reduced as a consequence.

CANSO, the Civil Air Navigation Services Organisation, states in its report *ATM Global Environment Efficiency Goals for 2050* that 100% ATM fuel efficiency is not achievable as flight safety, airport capacity limitations, weather conditions, and noise abatement require deviations from the optimum flight route. They estimate the Global ATM system is already between 92% and 94% fuel-efficient. CANSO has set the ATM industry the aspirational goal of recovering all of the remaining recoverable inefficiency by 2050, resulting in a global ATM system which was between 95% and 98% efficient at that time.

12.7 COST OF BIOJET FUELS

Alternative jet fuels are currently produced batch-wise in small quantities as the demand is not yet sufficient to justify continuous production. This makes an analysis of costs challenging and the costs reviewed vary significantly. As of February 2015, the price of conventional jet fuel is 621 $/t (0.48 $/L) and in 2012 fuel costs accounted for approximately 30% of operating costs for airlines.

From 2007 to 2012, the United States military purchased approximately 7 million liters of jet fuel through its procurement agency DLA Energy (Defense Logistics Agency), which provides data regarding the actual purchase prices of biofuels. These prices are detailed in *IATA 2014 Report on Alternative Fuels* and vary from 0.99 $/L for Fischer-Tropsch (FT) jet fuel from natural gas or coal to 10.99 $/L for hydroprocessed renewable jet (i.e., hydroprocessed esters and fatty acids (HEFA)) from camelina, algal oil, used cooking oil, and tallow, and 15.59 $/L for fuel from alcohols. For commercial aviation, there are limited data available on costs of alternative fuel purchase agreements.

---

[c]eurocontrol.int/dossiers/single-european-sky
[d]http://www.sesarju.eu/

In a recent US study of the ambition of the Federal Aviation Administration's goal of 1 billion gallons of renewable jet fuel each year from 2018, Winchester et al. [10] used an economy-wide model of the US aviation industry. They found that if soybean oil is used as a feedstock for meeting the FAA aviation biofuel goal in 2020, it would require an implicit subsidy from airlines to biofuel producers of 0.71 $/L of renewable jet fuel. If the aviation goal can be met by fuel from oilseed rotation crops grown on otherwise fallow land, the implicit subsidy is 0.09 $/L of renewable jet fuel.

Pearlson [11] reviews HEFA fuel production, and estimates the gate price of fuel for several plant sizes and operating conditions. The gate price was found to range between 1.00 $/L for a 378 million liter p.a. HEFA facility, and 1.16 $/L for a smaller 116 million liter p.a. facility.

Seber et al. [12] present an environmental and economic assessment of producing hydroprocessed jet and diesel fuel from waste oils and tallow. They calculate the production costs for these fuels using a discounted cash flow rate of return model. The minimum selling price was estimated to be 0.88–1.06 $/L for yellow grease-derived HEFA, and 1.05–1.25 $/L for tallow-derived HEFA fuel.

The EU report on *A performing biofuels supply chain for EU aviation* investigates the costs of biojet fuels for a target of 2 Mt/year by 2020 [1]. To achieve this target, construction of the plants has to start soon. The deployment of the biojet fuels is foreseen in two steps (see Fig. 12.2); first the starting of operation of *first of its kind* dedicated plants by 2016, and then a steady increase in supply chains to bring more biojet fuel to the market.

According to the document, sustainable biojet kerosene currently comes at significant additional costs for airlines. In addition to the estimated 3 billion euros investment in technologies and

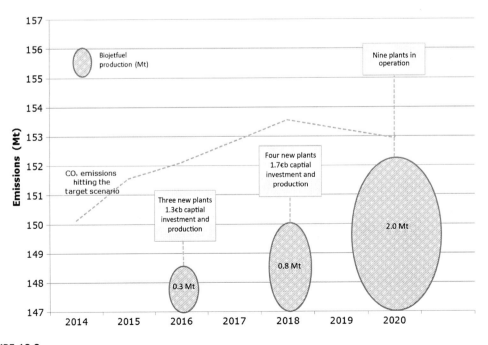

FIGURE 12.2

Projected biojet fuel production to 2020 and estimated associated EU aviation CO_2 emissions pathway.

production facilities to enable a constant production flow of biokerosene, mechanisms are also needed to address the cost increase, which is currently attached to biokerosene. This cost increase, currently calculated at €3 billion for 2 Mt (ca. 1.20 €/L), reduces the potential market uptake.

For the year 2020, analysis done by the IEA [13] assumes a cost range for FT jet fuel from 1500 to 1800 €/t (i.e., 1.20 to 1.45 €/L) and for HEFA jet fuel from 1200 to 1300 €/t (0.96 to 1.05 €/L). This analysis is based on production costs of HEFA (based on palm oil) and FT biofuel (based on forest wood).

A comparison of current and future projected kerosene prices from the EIA [14] to IEA projected biojet fuel prices in 2020 is given in Fig. 12.3. Given the EIA projected price of jet fuel in 2020 (0.54 €/L), the use of biojet fuel would lead to a cost increase of between 0.42 and 0.91 €/L based on IEA estimates, while the previously mentioned EU analysis suggests a higher additional cost of 1.20 €/L. These costs, if spread across all domestic and intra-EU-28 flights in 2020, would add between 1.20 and 4.30 €/passenger to the cost of a typical 1000-km flight, assuming the targeted biojet fuel production of 2 Mt in 2020, i.e., 4% of the estimated EU 28 jet fuel volume.

12.8 FEEDSTOCKS

A major concern with biojet fuel is the limitations of feedstock quantity and quality, since only a limited number of feedstocks meet the requirements to produce the strict physical and chemical characteristics of jet fuel. Feedstock supply is further compounded by the fact that there are competing uses for biomass, e.g., heat, electricity, and chemicals. Each crop has benefits and drawbacks in terms of costs, availability, yields, etc. Increasingly wastes have been considered a viable feedstock option as stated above.

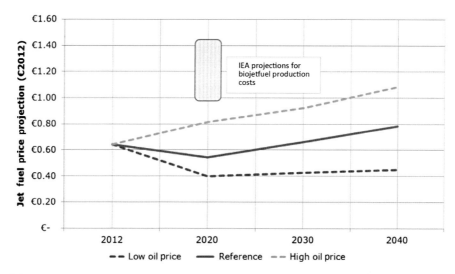

FIGURE 12.3

EIA price projections per liter for jet fuel in the United States to 2040 from the 2014 Annual Energy Outlook compared to projected IEA biojet fuel costs in 2020 (€1 to $0.85).

Algal oils could potentially replace vegetable oils in the biofuels process but these will not be commercially available within the next 5−8 years. Due to very high infrastructure costs for industrial algal cultivation it is unclear when competitiveness versus conventional plant oil or other advanced biofuels will be achieved. However, due to the fact that in principle there are no issues related to land use, algal oils have attracted significant interest from the aviation sector. Deltares [15] concludes that producing biojet fuel from algae grown in The Netherlands currently costs approximately 28 €/L, which is approximately 60 times higher than the cost of conventional jet fuel.

12.9 SCENARIO ANALYSIS

We use simple scenario analysis to compare the future quantity of biojet fuels required in European aviation under three levels of ambition to 2050.

The first scenario is *No Action* and this provides a counterfactual to the other scenarios. Growth in passenger activity to 2050 is assumed to be 2.7% p.a. with no annual fuel efficiency or ATM improvements.

The second scenario is *Hitting the Target* and assumes that EU emissions from aviation in 2050 will be 50% of the 2005 reference level, thus applying the IATA global goal at EU level. Growth in passenger activity to 2050 is again assumed to be 2.7% p.a., which is consistent with ICAO estimates. Annual fuel efficiency improvements due to technology and operational improvements are set at 1.5% p.a. to 2020, and improvements due to ATM are assumed to be 0.2% p.a. Note that these combined assumptions are more optimistic than the IATA self-commitment. It is here assumed that the Biofuel Flightpath Initiative delivers 2 Mt of biofuel production in Europe in 2020. An output of this scenario is the growth in annual biofuel production from 2020 to 2050 required to meet the emissions target (see Fig. 12.4).

The third scenario is called *Lower Growth* and assumes growth in passenger activity of 2.1% p.a. (aligned with EU estimations) with annual fuel efficiency improvements to 2020 due to technology improvements at 0.75% p.a. and improvements due to ATM at 0.1% p.a. It is assumed that the *Biofuel Flightpath Initiative* delivers 2 Mt of Biofuel production in 2020 with a growth of 5% p.a. thereafter. However, it does not assume that 2050 EU emissions from aviation will meet the IATA 50% reduction target (see Fig. 12.5).

Results of the analysis are as follows: In the absence of any action or improvements in fuel efficiency or ATM, CO_2 emissions will grow to 405 Mt (compared to 152 Mt in 2005). Results indicate that for the *Hitting the Target* scenario, an annual growth in biofuels of 13.1% is required from 2020 to meet the IATA emission reduction target. This translates into the production of 83 Mt of biofuels in 2050 representing approximately 77% of final energy demand in aviation in 2050. This clearly requires strong growth in biofuel production (as shown in Fig. 12.6), particularly in the period post 2040 where production will almost have to triple in 10 years. If biofuels are withdrawn as a mitigation option (but ATM and fuel efficiency improvements are allowed), then the resulting CO_2 emissions in 2050 are 334 Mt, breaching the IATA 50% reduction target of 75 Mt by approximately 258 Mt (shown in Fig. 12.4).

A final sensitivity was done on this scenario where annual fuel efficiency improvements due to technology are set at 1.5% p.a. to 2050. This reduces the amount of biofuels required to meet the target from 83 to 43.6 Mt or by 64% of the energy content of the biofuels.

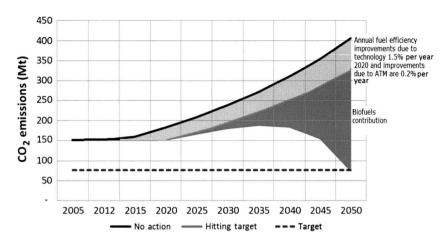

FIGURE 12.4

Schematic of the *Hitting the Target* scenario with contributions from efficiency, ATM, and biofuels outlined.

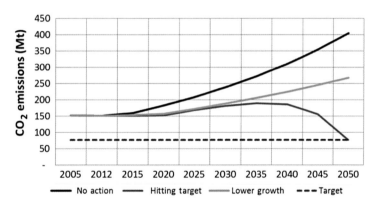

FIGURE 12.5

EU CO_2 emissions from aviation under three investigated scenarios.

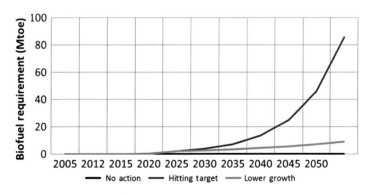

FIGURE 12.6

Biofuel requirement under three investigated scenarios.

In the *Lower Growth* scenario CO_2 emissions in 2050 grow to 267 Mt, therefore breaching the IATA 50% reduction target by 191 Mt. Biofuel production is assumed to grow by 5% p.a. and this leads to a contribution of 8.8 Mt of biofuels in 2050 or 9% of energy in aviation. In the absence of any contribution for biofuels for this scenario CO_2 emissions would grow to 294 Mt.

12.10 CONCLUSION

It is widely acknowledged that (in the absence of fuel switching) improved efficiency through technological progress, combined with better ATM, will not be sufficient to reach the IATA 2050 target. Aviation biofuels will have an important role to play. The main obstacle to the widespread uptake of biofuels is not due to technical constraints but rather economic in nature. For large-scale deployment of biofuels, as detailed in the *Hitting the Target* scenario, it will be imperative that significant volumes of biojet fuel are produced and utilized. Increasing the volume and the availability invariably decreases prices but will not happen without sufficient support mechanisms.

REFERENCES

[1]   EC, A performing biofuels supply chain for EU aviation. 2 million tons per year, 2013.
[2]   EC, Roadmap to a single European transport area—towards a competitive and resource efficient transport system, 2011.
[3]   EC, Directive (2014)/94/EU of the European parliament and of the council on the deployment of alternative fuels infrastructure, 2014.
[4]   EC, Flightpath 2050 Europe's vision for aviation report of the high-level group on aviation research, 2011.
[5]   EC, EU energy, transport and GHG emissions trends to 2050 reference scenario, 2013.
[6]   ICAO, ICAO environment report, 2014.
[7]   SESAR, The roadmap for sustainable air traffic management updated with SESAR's first developments European Union European ATM Master Plan, 2013.
[8]   IATA, ATA, ERA, A blueprint for the single European sky, 2013.
[9]   IPCC, Special report aviation and the global atmosphere, 1999.
[10] N. Winchester, et al., Economic and emissions impacts of renewable fuel goals for aviation in the US, 2013.
[11] M. Pearlson, et al., A techno-economic review of hydroprocessed renewable esters and fatty acids for jet fuel production, 2013.
[12] G. Seber, et al., Environmental and economic assessment of producing hydroprocessed jet and diesel fuel from waste oils and tallow, 2014.
[13] IEA Bioenergy, The potential and role of biofuels in commercial air transport-biojetfuel, 2012.
[14] EIA, Annual energy outlook (2014), 2014.
[15] Deltares, Algae as a source of fuel for the Dutch aviation sector, 2011.

CONCLUSIONS AND OUTLOOK

Paul Deane

University College Cork (UCC), Cork, Ireland

There are no silver bullets to the EU reliance on imported energy but progressive policy measures can encourage greater exploitation of indigenous resources, diversification of external supplies, and greater deployment of energy efficiency. The EU is widely dependent on gas imports and needs to mitigate the impacts of any potential supply interruptions. Therefore, in the short to medium term improvement of gas interconnection capacities between Member States and the integration of new supply routes should be considered as an EU priority. In addition to the development of gas interconnection capacity, improved gas storage infrastructure would improve security of gas supply for the EU. Gas storage can safeguard against unexpected events and potentially mitigate geopolitical risk.

The transition to a low-carbon economy is an important challenge for European society and policy makers. We highlight the role of well-formulated policy instruments which are needed to drive such an ambitious transformation. In the area of technology-based instruments, we suggest that these could be improved by making them progressively more stringent over time and amended to fix existing failings where possible. For example, CO_2 intensity limits on power plants may prevent the construction of new, unabated coal-fired capacity, thus reducing the possibility of creating new stranded assets in the future. Further, the lack of certification schemes for suppliers of energy efficiency measures in the building stock is often cited as a barrier to the rollout of new measures. A properly introduced scheme may help overcome information asymmetries and encourage greater uptake of energy efficiency measures.

Policy makers must also remain cognizant of the challenges set by the concepts of carbon budgets and unburnable carbon, and strategies to exploit fossil fuels must be balanced with the EU's long-term decarbonization objectives. While shale gas production could significantly improve security of gas supply and reduce energy dependence in Europe, the actual resource is highly uncertain and conditions of extraction are expected to be less favorable in Europe than in the US. However, if managed correctly and carefully, Europe could benefit from shale gas exploitation and should aim to learn from lessons and best practice in the US. An enabling regulation should include enforceable principles of transparency, monitoring, and risk mitigation, and impose the use of the best available technologies in order to minimize the risk of water and soil pollution. Above all, meaningful consultation and useful engagement with stakeholders and citizens is a prerequisite before any developments take place.

Transport is the largest energy-consuming sector in Europe, and thus plays a key role in a transition towards an energy system that stays within its carbon budget. However, in most areas of

Europe's Energy Transition. DOI: http://dx.doi.org/10.1016/B978-0-12-809806-6.00013-4

transport, emission reductions are generally expensive. While surface transport profited from EU renewable energy policy, which led to the development of a biodiesel industry, biojet fuel has not benefited from this uplift. The key hurdle for widespread use of biofuels as part of Europe's energy system is not that technologies are not mature, but that costs are unfavorable. For large-scale deployment of biofuels, it will be imperative that significant volumes of biojet fuel are produced and utilized in a sustainable manner. Increasing the volume and the availability invariably decreases price but will not happen without sufficient policy support mechanisms.

While part of this section focused on the supply of biofuels, in particular for aviation, the following section further explores the role of renewable energy for decarbonizing the energy system of the European Union. It investigates specifically the related impacts on market operation and design.

IMPACT OF RENEWABLE ENERGIES ON MARKET OPERATION AND DESIGN

IV

INTRODUCTION

14

Dogan Keles

Karlsruhe Institute of Technology (KIT), Karlsruhe, Germany

In accordance with the Kyoto Protocol and subsequent international climate deals such as the Paris Agreement, an important target of the European Union (EU) Member States and other partners is limiting the global temperature change to no more than 2°C above preindustrial levels. To achieve this goal, a suite of measures is required. Some focus specifically on energy supply and related market-based instruments (such as the EU-ETS emission trading system), as discussed in the previous section. Other approaches focus on the demand side, including the expansion of energy efficiency measures in end-use energy applications.

The focus in this section is on those that target renewables specifically, and their implications on market operation and design. Due to the 2020 targets [1], the EU Member States have committed themselves to achieve a share of 20% of RES within their primary energy consumption. The expansion of RES is achieved by different political instruments such as fixed quotas or feed-in tariffs. Fig. 14.1 gives an overview over the promotion strategies for renewable energies.

Indeed, electricity production from RES has increased in most European Member States over the past 10−15 years. However, the expansion of RES in the electricity sector has not only lowered greenhouse gases, as RES electricity can be produced almost without emissions. The RES expansion also causes new challenges for the electricity grid and the market infrastructure. As the electricity production from RES is not always located close to demand centers, it has to be transported in large scale over long distances, e.g., in Germany from the north to the south. In times of peak RES production, the grid can be congested and the entire production might not be transmitted to regions with high electricity demand. If the RES electricity production exceeds the grid capacity, some parts of the production have to be curtailed to avoid damage or outages in the grid infrastructure. The numbers for curtailed renewable energy production have reached considerable levels and count for some 100 GWh in large electricity markets with high shares of variable RES production, such as Germany or Italy. The challenges and future prospects to address them are discussed in detail in Chapter 15, Curtailment: An Option for Cost-Efficient Integration of Variable Renewable Generation?

The merit-order effect entailing a lower wholesale electricity price level is another challenge to be addressed to reach a successful system integration of RES. In many countries parts of RES electricity is funded by fixed feed-in tariffs or a market premium, so that these energy amounts are bid into the market with a price of 0 €/MWh or even with negative prices. The reason for this is, inter alia, that electricity from wind and PV is produced with marginal costs of nearly zero and unlike, e.g., hydro power connected to reservoirs, needs to be dispatched in the moment it generates electricity. Therefore, the availability of PV and wind power significantly lowers the equilibrium

Europe's Energy Transition. DOI: http://dx.doi.org/10.1016/B978-0-12-809806-6.00014-6

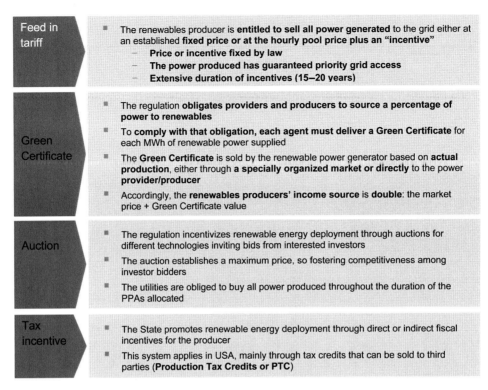

FIGURE 14.1

Policy instruments to promote RES.

From C. Klessmann, C. Nabe, K. Burges, Pros and cons of exposing renewables to electricity market risks—a comparison of the market integration approaches in Germany, Spain, and the UK, Energy Policy 36 (10) (2008) 3646–3661 [2].

market price in times with large production from these sources. This price reduction effect is called the "merit order effect." The importance and the expected height of the merit order effect throughout Europe are discussed in Chapter 16, Impact on Electricity Markets: Merit Order Effect of Renewable Energies.

The merit order effect is assumed to increase the missing-money problem [3] for peak load power plants, as with higher shares of RES electricity production price peaks as well as full load hours are strongly reduced. Hence the question arises, whether power plant investments can be refinanced in an energy-only market or if an adaptation of market design in electricity markets is necessary [4]. Chapter 17, Market Design Options for Promoting Low-Carbon Technologies, discusses selected market design options that could be introduced to integrate high shares of renewables and to refinance necessary investments via the electricity market without any promotion schemes. The introduced market design options are selected from the literature and are evaluated, amongst others, regarding their complexity or the goals that could be achieved with the particular design option.

Besides the qualitative evaluation of design options for low-carbon electricity markets, design options can be also evaluated with market simulation models to analyze their cost-efficiency and effectivity to guarantee generation adequacy. The analysis can shed light on possible development paths of a real-world implementation of specific design options. In Chapter 18, Case Study: Design Options for the German Electricity Market, a case study on the German electricity market is carried out making use of an agent-based simulation model. The current market design in Germany, i.e., an energy-only market, is compared with a capacity market as an additional market segment that allows power plant operators and investors to earn additional income. This may prove necessary if the energy-only market concept reveals an inability to provide sufficient earnings to cover the fixed and investment-related costs of power plants. In energy-only markets with sufficient liquidity, power plants bid with marginal costs and ask for a scarcity rent in peak load times to gain contribution margins to investment-related costs. The agent-based simulation applied in the case study is suited to analyze whether sufficient scarcity rents can be earned in future under the assumption of high shares of RES. If the earnings in the energy-only market are not sufficient to cover the investments, less and less investments will be carried out, so that other design options become inevitable in order to maintain generation adequacy.

After the analysis of design options based on the German case, this section concludes in Chapter 19, Conclusions and Outlook, with a summary of the main findings and with highlighting future research needs, especially with regard to the effects of a fast expansion of RES in the electricity sector and necessary adaptations of market design.

REFERENCES

[1] European Commission, Directive 2009/28/EC of the European Parliament and of the Council of 23 April 2009 on the promotion of the use of energy from renewable sources and amending and subsequently repealing Directives 2001/77/EC and 2003/30/EC, Off. J. Eur. Union (2009).
[2] C. Klessmann, C. Nabe, K. Burges, Pros and cons of exposing renewables to electricity market risks—a comparison of the market integration approaches in Germany, Spain, and the UK, Energy Policy 36 (10) (2008) 3646–3661.
[3] P. Joskow, Capacity payments in imperfect electricity markets: need and design, Util. Policy 16 (3) (2008) 159–170.
[4] P. Cramton, S. Stoft, The convergence of market designs for adequate generating capacity, 2006.

CURTAILMENT: AN OPTION FOR COST-EFFICIENT INTEGRATION OF VARIABLE RENEWABLE GENERATION?

Martin Steurer[1], Ulrich Fahl[1], Alfred Voß[1], and Paul Deane[2]

[1]*University of Stuttgart, Stuttgart, Germany* [2]*University College Cork (UCC), Cork, Ireland*

15.1 INTRODUCTION

According to the European Directive 2009/28/EC, renewable energy systems (RES) enjoy preferential treatment in the electricity grid as far as the secure operation of the power system is not compromised. However, there will be times when it is not possible to accommodate all priority dispatch generation such as variable renewable generation (VRG) sources, like wind and solar, while maintaining the safe operation of the power system. Security-based limits have to be imposed, due to both local network and system-wide security issues. Therefore, it is necessary to reduce the output of variable renewable generators below their maximum available level on occasions when these security limits are reached. This reduction of VRG is referred to as "curtailment."

In the directive, Member States are explicitly requested to minimize the use of curtailment. Simultaneously, ambitious targets for the development of RES are set. In some countries this leads to a remarkable increase in the production of electricity from variable renewable sources, such as wind and solar. Beside the supply security issue, the question of cost-efficient integration of this rapidly growing source of generation is also crucial from an economy and social acceptance viewpoint. Jacobsen and Schröder [1] argue that the curtailment of a small percentage of VRG feed-in may be optimal from a power systems operation and cost-efficient perspective.

This chapter gives a brief overview of the current situation and future prospects concerning variable renewable curtailment in the EU. Furthermore, it suggests a closer look at the potential risks and benefits of curtailment.

15.2 STATUS QUO IN SELECTED MEMBER STATES

Fig. 15.1 displays the share of wind, photovoltaics, and their sum in electricity consumption in EU Member States in 2012 and 2020 according to the National Renewable Energy Action Plan (NREAP)[a] targets.

---

[a]Individual EU countries have different available resources and their own unique energy markets. This means that they will have to follow distinctive paths when it comes to meeting their obligations under the Renewable Energy Directive, including their legally binding 2020 targets. In their national action plans, they explain how they intend to do this.

Europe's Energy Transition. DOI: http://dx.doi.org/10.1016/B978-0-12-809806-6.00015-8

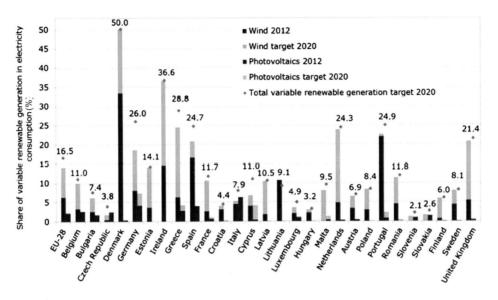

FIGURE 15.1

Share of variable RES in electricity consumption in 2012 and 2020 (according to National Renewable Energy Action Plan targets) (Eurostat and National Renewable Energy Action Plans).

The graph illustrates the disparity between the different Member States concerning the actual and future role of VRG in their electricity mix. The distinctions can be explained by the specific RES targets of the individual Member States and the different availability of other RES sources like hydro power or biomass. The figure demonstrates that the integration of VRG is currently an eminent issue in countries such as Denmark, Germany, Ireland, Spain, Italy, and Portugal. Therefore, the situation in these countries is analyzed in the following concerning the occurrence of VRG curtailment. Nevertheless, according to their NREAP targets, other Member States like Greece, the Netherlands, and the United Kingdom will also need to deal with a considerably variable wind and solar feed-in in the years to come.

The existing renewable capacities have led to the following amount of curtailed VRG feed-in in the EU in the period 2009–12 (see in Table 15.1)[2].

Motives for curtailing differ in the concerned Member States as further outlined in the following.

DENMARK

An interesting situation concerning VRG curtailment is occurring in Denmark. Even though wind feed-in exceeded demand for 848 hours or nearly 10% of the time in the western Danish electricity system in 2012, curtailment was close to zero. This is due to strong interconnection with Germany and Norway and the availability of hydro resources in Nordic countries. If spot market prices fall below a minimum price floor, which is currently −500 €/MWh, selling bids beyond this limit

Table 15.1 Curtailed VRG in EU Member States in GWh and as Percentage of Total VRG Feed-In [2][a,b,c,d]				
	Curtailed VRG Feed-In[e] (GWh)			
	2009	**2010**	**2011**	**2012**
Germany	74 (0.2%)	127 (0.3%)	421 (0.6%)	385 (0.5%)
Ireland	n.a.	26 (1.0%)	106 (2.4%)	103 (2.5%)
Spain	40 (0.1%)	320 (0.6%)	202 (0.4%)	148 (0.3%)
Italy	700 (9.7%)	527 (4.8%)	264 (1.3%)	166 (0.5%)

[a]*Bundesnetzagentur (Bundeskartellamt): Monitoringbericht gemäß § 63 Abs. 3 i. V. m. § 35 EnWG und § 48 Abs. 3 i. V. m. § 53 Abs. 3 GWB. Bonn, 2013.*
[b]*EirGrid: 2011 Curtailment Report. 2011.*
[c]*EirGrid: 2012 Curtailment Report. 2012.*
[d]*Red Eléctrica de España (REE). Available from: http://www.ree.es.*
[e]*No considerable amounts of VRG feed-in have been curtailed in Denmark and Portugal.*

would be curtailed. This happens very rarely even though negative prices occur about 0.5% of the time in the Nord Pool Spot market.[b]

GERMANY

In Germany, congestion in the distribution system is the main driver for VRG curtailment. To date 98% of the curtailed energy in 2012 was caused by scaling back on the distribution grid level, while only the remaining 2% was curtailed on the transmission grid level. Also in 2012, 93% of the curtailed VRG was from wind power, which is concentrated in northern Germany and a cause of congestion. However, in 2012 for the first time, southern Germany's distribution grids were also affected by curtailment as the growing PV share strained the distribution grid. However, PV accounts for only 4% of the curtailed VRG with the remaining 3% coming from other RES.[c]

A situation where VRG exceeds demand hasn't yet been observed in Germany, but negative electricity prices occur even more often than in Denmark. This can be attributed to a relatively high base of conventional must-run capacity. A current study by Götz et al. [3] states that if this must-run capacity (due to contractual obligations) doesn't decrease by 2022, the number of hours with negative prices could exceed 1000.

To date, negative electricity prices have been allowed in the countries covered by the European Power Exchange (EPEX), i.e., France, Germany, Austria, and Switzerland, in the countries covered by Nord Pool, i.e., Denmark, Estonia, Finland, Latvia, Lithuania, Norway, and Sweden, as well as in Belgium and the Netherlands. Electricity markets with particularly frequent occurrences of negative prices are Germany and Denmark. Situations with extremely low prices were observed,

[b]Nord Pool Spot. Available from: http://www.nordpoolspot.com
[c]Bundesnetzagentur (Bundeskartellamt): Monitoringbericht gemäß § 63 Abs. 3 i. V. m. § 35 EnWG und § 48 Abs. 3 i. V. m. § 53 Abs. 3 GWB. Bonn, 2013.

for example in October 2009 in Germany reaching -500 €/MWh or at Christmas 2012 in Germany and Denmark reaching -200 €/MWh.[d]

IRELAND

The situation in Ireland requires special attention as the power system currently faces challenges concerning the integration of VRG that may face larger systems in the future. Real-time instantaneous penetration of wind power plants of 50% poses operational challenges to the power system operation. The fundamental issues which give rise to curtailment in Ireland are being addressed by the DS3 program.[e] This program has been specifically designed to securely and efficiently increase the level of system nonsynchronous penetration (SNSP) which can be accommodated in the system and also address other system-wide limitations. The definition of SNSP is given in Eq. (15.1).

$$\text{SNSP} = \frac{\text{Wind generation} + \text{HVDC imports}}{\text{System demand} + \text{HVDC exports}} \tag{15.1}$$

Studies from the DS3 program indicate that it would not be prudent to operate the power system above aggregate levels of SNSP of 50% without addressing a number of important issues. Specifically, the main limitations are in the frequency response of the system following the loss of the largest in-feed which could result in rates of change of frequency (RoCoF) greater than 0.5 Hz/s. This could lead to the cascade tripping of all generators on the system as they are not currently obliged under the grid code to withstand such a rate of change. In addition, protection settings on distribution connected units, which use RoCoF protection to manage islanding situations, would also be a factor. It is likely that, even by addressing these issues, it would not be prudent to operate the power system above SNSP levels of 75% [4]. While mitigation measures can be employed, it will be necessary, in order to operate a secure power system, to curtail VRG output at times.

A study for the 2020 Irish electricity system [5] shows potential levels of grid security-based curtailment in the years to come. It indicates that wind curtailment levels of 7% could exist if a SNSP level of 75% was tolerated.

Fig. 15.2 presents results from an hourly production cost model for the Irish system in the year 2020 with over 6000 MWel of wind power plants assumed to be connected. Sensitivities with respect to SNSP limits from 60% to 100% are modeled as well as varying levels of HVDC exports. The maximum allowable SNSP level has a direct impact on the annual curtailment of wind power plants. In particular, the higher the maximum allowable SNSP the lower the curtailment levels of wind power in all cases. This has a direct effect on the annual percentage of electricity from renewable energy and ultimately the efficacy of the investment in wind power plants.

The level of VRG curtailment in Ireland is affected by a number of factors which vary from year to year. The amount of wind installed on the system and the capacity factor of the wind generation will have an impact on the levels of curtailment. The level of demand is another important factor which can change between the years. The testing and commissioning of new wind power plants can lead to increased levels of curtailment as new units are offered priority during this commissioning process. Generally, curtailment typically occurs during periods of low demand most

---

[d]European Power Exchange (EPEX Spot). Available from: https://www.epexspot.com
[e]EirGrid (DS3 Programme). Available from: http://www.eirgridgroup.com/how-the-grid-works/ds3-programme/

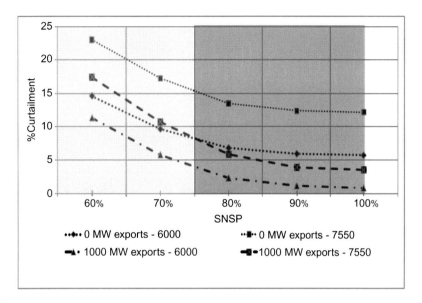

FIGURE 15.2

Curtailment levels on wind power plants with respect to maximum allowable SNSP operational limit [4].

often overnight and in the morning, when the minimum generation levels of conventional plants are imposed.

SPAIN

Throughout most of 2009, VRG curtailment in Spain was primarily due to inadequate transmission and distribution system capacity. Since the end of 2009, however, a growing share of wind energy is also curtailed due to limited demand. As Fig. 15.3 illustrates, the limited transmission capacity of the Iberian Peninsula to France is a bottleneck.

Fig. 15.3 details the electricity import capacities of the Member States in relation to the respective generation capacities in 2011 and according to the ENTSO-E Ten Year Network Development Plan for 2020 [6].

The Spanish system operator Red Eléctrica de España in consequence expects to curtail 1.6 TWh or 2.2% of variable RES by 2016. For 2020, it is estimated that 3.6% of wind and solar generation may be curtailed.

ITALY

As the majority of wind power plants in Italy are connected to the transmission grid and located in southern Italy, transmission grid congestion is a very important reason for curtailment. In the past years, network upgrades and extensions have improved the situation considerably. From a 10% share of VRG feed-in curtailed in 2009, the figure went down to less than 1% in 3 years (see Table 15.1).

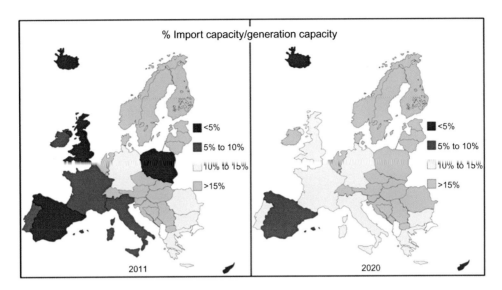

FIGURE 15.3

Proportion between import capacity and generation capacity in 2011 and 2020 [6].

PORTUGAL

In Portugal, legislation allows curtailment of renewable energy generation only for contracts signed after 2007, and then only for technical reasons. Several instances of wind and other nondispatchable sources of generation exceeding demand have already occurred.

15.3 FUTURE PROSPECTS

As the foregoing analysis showed, curtailment of VRG feed-in in the EU to date is driven by technical grid security reasons and not by economic reasons. Negative residual loads (i.e., if the load minus the variable generation is negative) are not yet occurring often and only in a few regions of the EU. If the targets concerning the share of RES in electricity consumption are met, this will heavily reshape the residual load curves in a number of Member States.

POSSIBLE DEVELOPMENT OF THE RESIDUAL LOAD AND POSSIBLE IMPACTS

As an example, Fig. 15.4 highlights possible patterns of the residual load duration curve in Germany with an RES share of 50%, 80%, and 100%, illustrating the expected magnitude of surplus energy and power in the years to come.

European regulation requests Member States to take appropriate grid- and market-related operational measures in order to minimize curtailment. In consequence, the current energy infrastructure in the concerned regions and countries has to be strengthened to be able to accommodate

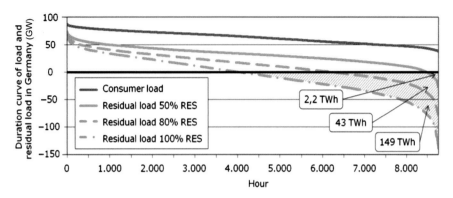

FIGURE 15.4

Possible development of the German residual load curve at different shares of renewable energy systems (own calculations).

the distributed and temporal unsteady feed-in of high shares of VRG. If innovative approaches like demand-side integration, power-to-heat or power-to gas remain out of consideration, this implies major investments in grid infrastructure and storage. Beside their environmental implications, these investments are potentially highly inefficient from a micro- and macroeconomic point of view as their capacity utilization might be very low. This is due to the fact that local and system-wide peaks in renewable feed-in occur only in a small number of hours a year. Thus, the current regulation in place could potentially lead to a future electricity system that is not cost-efficient and to increasing electricity retail prices and decreasing social acceptance for RES.

POSSIBLE ECONOMIC EFFECTS OF CURTAILMENT

The use of VRG curtailment not only for grid security but also for economic reasons can potentially contribute to a significant reduction of investment needs in both grid and storage extension. For that purpose, the power output of VRG plants would have to be limited in some hours of the year, but their energy production over the year would only decrease by a small percentage.

Krzikalla et al. [7] analyzed historic feed-in curves for Germany and concluded that the reduction of the generation from wind power plants to 70% of their maximum power output would decrease their total energy output by only 1.3% in the year 2011. A power limitation to 80% would have led to an energy output reduction of 0.5%. For PV a limitation to 70% of the maximum power would have caused a loss of 2% of the energy output in 2012. With a limitation to 80% this figure would have been 0.5%.

A current study by the German Energy Agency [8] indicates that the costs for distribution grid extension in Germany to the year 2030 could decrease by 30% if limitation of VRG plants to 70% of their maximum power output was allowed.

A study by Jacobsen and Schröder [1] states that curtailment of VRG may not only lead to avoided investment costs in energy infrastructure but also to avoided operational costs for systems reserve procurement and regulating energy. This is due to the reduction of possible forecast errors for VRG feed-in influencing the necessary reserve provision. The economic importance of this effect depends on the future development of the forecast accuracy and of market coupling effects on the reserve procurement need.

However, there is also an effect of curtailment on the systems operation costs that goes in the opposite direction. Curtailment reduces the share of the consumer load covered by renewable energies. When curtailment occurs because of network congestion, the "missing" electricity production must be met elsewhere by conventional capacities. When curtailment occurs because of excess power supply, the curtailed energy cannot be brought back into the system later when the residual load is positive. Consequently, curtailment increases fuel use and generation-related emissions of the conventional power plants. This has negative implications on the systems operation costs and the external costs that aren't covered by the EU Emissions Trading System, such as NOx emissions.

REFERENCES

[1] H.K. Jacobsen, S. Schröder, Curtailment of renewable generation: economic optimality and incentives, Energy Policy 49 (2012) 663−675.

[2] D. Lew, et al., Wind and Solar Curtailment, National Renewable Energy Laboratory (NREL), Golden, CO, 2013.

[3] P. Götz, et al., Negative Electricity Prices: Causes and Effects, Agora Energiewende, Berlin, 2014.

[4] J. O'Sullivan, et al., Achieving the highest levels of wind integration—a system operator perspective, IEEE Trans. Sustain. Energy 3 (4) (2012) 819−826.

[5] E. McGarrigle, J. Deane, P. Leahy, How much wind energy will be curtailed on the 2020 Irish power system? Renew. Energy 55 (2013) 544−553.

[6] ENTSO-E, Ten-year network development plan 2012, 2012.

[7] N. Krzikalla, S. Achner, S. Brühl, Möglichkeiten zum usgleich fluktuierender Einspeisungen aus Erneuerbaren Energien, 2013.

[8] Deutsche Energie-Agentur (German Energy Agency), dena Smart-Meter-Studie—Analyse von Rolloutszenarien und ihrer regulatorischen Implikationen, Berlin, 2014.

IMPACT ON ELECTRICITY MARKETS: MERIT ORDER EFFECT OF RENEWABLE ENERGIES

16

Paul Deane[1], Seán Collins[1], Brian Ó. Gallachóir[1], Cherrelle Eid[2],
Rupert Hartel[3], Dogan Keles[3], and Wolf Fichtner[3]

[1]*University College Cork (UCC), Cork, Ireland* [2]*Institut Français des Relations Internationales (IFRI), Paris, France*
[3]*Karlsruhe Institute of Technology (KIT), Karlsruhe, Germany*

16.1 INTRODUCTION

The influence of renewable energy sources (RES) on the energy system is growing with the increasing share of renewable electricity deployed. However, this growing share has not only a strong impact on the grid infrastructure, e.g., the curtailment of RES electricity as introduced in Chapter 15, Curtailment: An Option for Cost-Efficient Integration of Variable Renewable Generation?, but also on the market results, especially on electricity prices. This is due to the mechanism that determines spot prices as a function of supply and demand. The supply curve, the so-called merit order, is derived by ordering the supplier bids according to ascending marginal cost. The intersection of the demand curve with the merit order defines the market clearing price, i.e., the electricity spot market price. The feed-in of RES with low or near zero marginal cost results in a shift to the right of the merit order. This shift moves the intersection of the demand curve and the merit order to a lower marginal price level and thus the electricity price on the spot market is reduced (see Fig. 16.1). This reduction in price is called merit order effect.

In the following, a brief review of ex post analyses about the merit order effect is presented looking at its current impacts and ahead to 2030 and 2050 and carrying out an ex ante analysis of the merit order effect of energy scenarios defined by the EU 2030 Climate and Energy Policy Framework [2].

16.2 REVIEW OF EX POST ANALYSES OF THE MERIT ORDER EFFECT

There is a significant amount of analysis of the merit order effect, the bulk of which are referred to in Refs. [3] and [4]. These studies can in general be categorized as model-based or statistics-based studies.

In this chapter, we present a statistical analysis of the merit order effect using the example of wind power in Germany. The merit order effect can be shown by analyzing historical market prices from the European Electricity Exchange (EEX). A linear regression analysis of market prices and wind power feed-in shows an average price reduction of €1.47/MWh for every additional GW of wind power. This average effect cannot explain extreme price events. "Thus, the correlation of

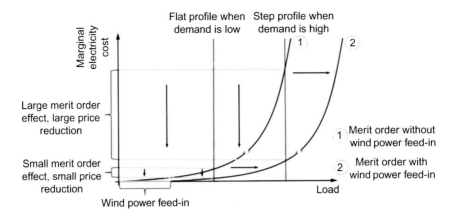

FIGURE 16.1

Right shift of the merit order and the supply curve particularly due to wind power feed-in.

From D. Keles, et al., A combined modeling approach for wind power feed-in and electricity spot prices,
Energy Policy 59 (2013) 213–225 [1].

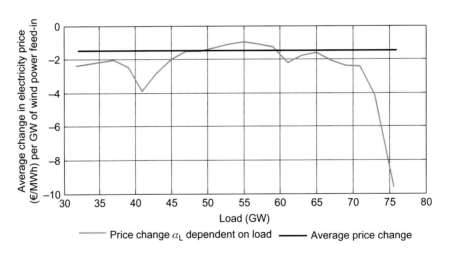

FIGURE 16.2

Average change of the deseasonalized electricity price per GW wind power depending on load interval.

From D. Keles, et al., A combined modeling approach for wind power feed-in and electricity spot prices,
Energy Policy 59 (2013) 213–225.

electricity price and wind power feed-in might depend on point of time and is presumably nonlinear" according to Keles et al. [1]. To further analyze the price reduction effect the current power plant mix as well as the demand situation are taken into account. Therefore, hourly records of electricity price, wind power feed-in, and demand (load) are formed and sorted ascending by the load. With a linear regression the price change α_L as a function of the load can be shown in Fig. 16.2.

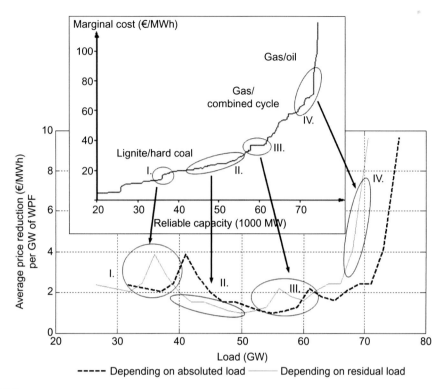

FIGURE 16.3

Price reduction per GW wind power feed-in depending on the load level and the German merit order curve.

From D. Keles, et al., A combined modeling approach for wind power feed-in and electricity spot prices,
Energy Policy 59 (2013) 213–225.

The negative values indicate that the wind power feed-in leads to lower electricity prices. Furthermore, it can be obtained that the price reduction effect highly depends on the load situation and can be significantly higher than the average reduction of €1.47/MWh (see Fig. 16.2). This is in line with the findings of Hirth [5]. Hirth [5] further shows that this price reduction also affects the market value of variable renewables and is also dependent on the penetration of renewable energies. The market value[a] of wind power falls from 110% of the average power price to 50%−80% with an increase of wind power penetration from 0% to 30% of total electricity production [5].

A further comparison of price reductions in the German merit order curve is shown in Fig. 16.3. There are four significant changes in the curve according to Keles et al. [1]. These changes

[a]The market value is calculated as the average value of each energy unit from wind power earned at wholesale markets. The wind power produced in each hour is priced with the electricity price of that hour. Finally, the average is calculated for each MWh.

can in general be linked to technology switches in the merit order. In area "I," a local peak is evident, representing the change from lignite- to coal-fired power plants. In general, the price reduction effect is higher when lignite-fired power plants are the price setting units instead of coal (area "II"). A similar peak can be obtained in area "III," where a switch from coal- to gas-fired power plants occurs in the merit order, although the price reduction effect in area "I" is higher than in area "III." The occurrence of negative prices is high in this area because plant operators try to avoid shut-down and ramp-up costs and accept negative electricity prices to stay online. Other restrictions like reserve requirements and, in the case of gas-fired power plants, heat delivery, cause plant operators to be online, which can lead to an excess electricity supply and thus to negative prices. Area "IV" represents the peak load power plants (oil- or gas-fired), which are the most expensive power plants due to their low efficiency and high fuel costs. In this area the price reduction effect is very high, if their utilization is avoided.

The merit order effect outlined here is dependent on the German market design. However, other market designs would lead to a similar merit order effect according to Keles et al. [1].

Traditionally, electricity demand does not respond to price level changes that occur on spot or balancing markets. The traditional perspective of "generation follows the demand" is however expected to change in a situation where the demand responds to electricity price levels and consumers are able to benefit financially from shifting consumption.

Demand response (DR) is regarded as the modification of electricity consumption in response to the price of electricity generation and state of the electricity system reliability [6]. The communication of price levels to electricity consumers could lead to an electricity system where increasingly the "demand follows generation." Within Europe, there are some standing arrangements to involve energy-intensive industrial customers in DR. This is mostly done through critical peak pricing or time of use pricing and some system operators make use of large avoided loads as part of their system balancing services [7]. However, this is still not applied in many European countries; DR is only commercially active as a flexibility resource in France, Ireland, the United Kingdom, Belgium, Switzerland, and Finland [8]. Countries with large penetration of RES, such as Germany, currently use demand flexibility to maintain system-wide reliability [9].

DR could reduce the required capacity of peaking electricity units, could increase load factors of existing generation units, and furthermore can have positive effects on electricity network capacity utilization. Furthermore, DR could be used to provide balancing capacity to complement the variability of renewable sources.

DR is anticipated to play a role in Europe in order to reach the 2020 targets and beyond. In particular, the Energy Efficiency Directive (EED), art. 15, explicitly urges EU national regulatory authorities to encourage demand-side resources, including DR, "to participate alongside supply in wholesale and retail markets," and also to provide balancing and ancillary services to network operators in a nondiscriminatory manner [10]. The European Commission states that the potential in Europe for DR in electricity markets is believed to be high but is currently still underutilized [11] due to the concentration on industrial users primarily. Residential users are in the future also expected to become involved in DR provision, but still some technical, regulatory, and economic barriers exist [8]. In the following, the impact of DR on total system costs is quantified at an EU-wide level in 2030 and 2050, after analyzing the ex ante merit order effect for the same years.

16.3 **EX ANTE ANALYSIS OF MERIT ORDER EFFECT—METHODOLOGY**

Looking ahead, we analyze the merit order effect in two distinct power plant portfolios in 2030 and 2050, using a power systems model-based approach. These portfolios are developed based on scenario analysis results carried out with the PRIMES model that were used to inform the EU 2030 Framework for climate and energy policies. In our analysis, the merit order effect is assessed by looking at the difference in prices between two scenarios, a Reference and a Mitigation Scenario. A brief description of these scenarios is provided in the following.

The Reference Scenario corresponds to the EU Reference Scenario 2013 [12], which explores the consequences of current trends including the full implementation of policies adopted by late spring 2012. The Reference scenario has been developed through modeling with PRIMES, GAINS, and other related models and benefited from the comments of Member State experts. It provides an energy system pathway up to 2050, taking into account already agreed upon policies. The Mitigation Scenario by contrast investigates GHG reductions of 40% and 80% in 2030 and 2050, respectively, met through economy-wide equal carbon prices. Aggregate portfolio capacities in each Member State for the Reference Scenario for 2030 and 2050 are shown in Figs. 16.4 and 16.5 respectively.

FIGURE 16.4

2030 Reference Scenario capacities.

FIGURE 16.5

2050 Reference Scenario capacities.

MODEL DESCRIPTION

A model-based technique is employed to investigate the electricity price difference between the reference and mitigation scenario. The software used to model the electricity market is the PLEXOS Integrated Energy Model. PLEXOS is a modeling tool used for electricity and gas market modeling and planning. In this analysis, the focus is on the merit order effect and the modeling is limited to the electricity system, i.e., gas infrastructure and delivery is ignored in these simulations. The model optimizes the power plant dispatch considering pumped storage options and subject to operational and technical constraints at hourly resolution. The objective function is to minimize total costs over the year across the full system. This includes operational costs, consisting of fuel, carbon, and start-up costs. Model equations can be found in Refs. [13] and [14]. In these simulations a perfect market is assumed across the EU (i.e., no market power or bidding behavior and power plants bid their short run marginal cost). A power plant portfolio is constructed for each Member State for each scenario (Reference and Mitigation) and each year (2030 and 2050). In all, approximately 2220 individual thermal power plants are included in the model. Power plant capacities, efficiencies, and fuel types are based on the PRIMES model.

The model seeks to minimize the overall generation cost across the EU to meet demand subject to generator technical characteristics. The resulting market price is defined as the marginal price at Member State level (often called the shadow price of electricity) and does not include any extra revenues from potential balancing, reserve, or capacity markets or costs such as grid infrastructure cost, capital costs, or taxes. These additional revenues or costs are not considered in this study.

To determine the impact of increased levels of variable renewable generation, annual carbon prices (equivalent to the prices set by the European emission trading system EU-ETS) are set at €40/t CO_2 in 2030 and €100/t CO_2 in 2050 for both scenarios. In the Reference Scenario, electricity demand rises 12% between 2010 and 2030, increasing further to +32% in 2050 (compared to 2010). Driving forces for this include greater penetration of appliances following economic growth, which mitigate the effects of eco-design standards on new products, increasing use of heat pumps and electro-mobility. The share of electricity in final energy consumption rises from 21% in 2010 to reach 24% in 2030 and 28% in 2050. In the year 2030, the demand for electricity at EU28 level is 5% lower in the Mitigation Scenario than in the Reference Scenario, whereas in 2050 demand for electricity is 16% higher in the Mitigation Scenario, due to further electrification of transport and heat.

Interconnection between Member States is modeled as net transfer capacities and no interregional transmission is considered. The electricity network expansion is aligned with the latest 10 Year Development Plan from ENTSO-E, without making any judgment on the likelihood of certain projects materializing. Fuel prices are also consistent across scenarios for each year and are shown in Table 16.1.

RESULTS FOR 2030

Results for the year 2030 for each Member State are show in Fig. 16.6 in terms of the absolute reduction in annual wholesale electricity price in the Mitigation scenario relative to the Reference scenario. Results are driven by differences between the power plant portfolios in the two scenarios and also by differences in demand. Across the EU the general trend is for variable renewable generation to increase in the Mitigation Scenario with resulting reductions in market prices. In the majority of central European Member States these reductions are relatively benign at less than €1.5/MWh with an overall average of €1.6/MWh.

The greatest impact is seen in the UK and Ireland. In the UK two elements are driving a strong reduction in wholesale price between the Reference and Mitigation Scenario. Firstly, the demand in the Mitigation Scenario is approximately 5% lower than in the Reference Scenario. Secondly, there is

Table 16.1 Fuel Prices Used in Study [2]

Fuel Prices	2030	2050
Oil (in €2010/boe)	93	110
Gas (in €2010/boe)	65	63
Coal (in €2010/boe)	24	31

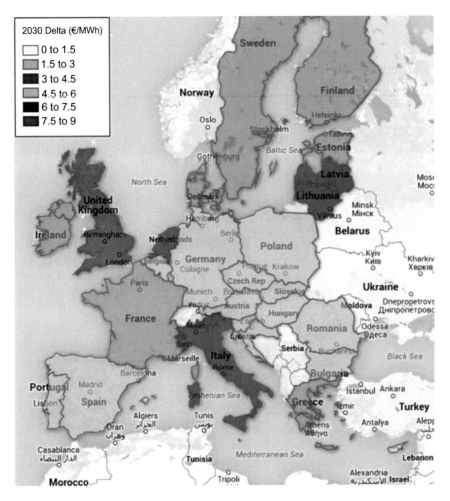

FIGURE 16.6

Reduction in price (€/MWh) in the Mitigation Scenario for 2030, as compared to the Reference Scenario.

a strong increase in installed renewable capacity with almost a third of the EU total offshore wind capacity installed in the UK. This has a strong seasonal impact and tends to reduce prices in the winter months when wind speeds are high and demand is also highest. This reduces the need for higher marginal cost generators to meet peak demand. Similarly Ireland sees a strong reduction in prices between the two scenarios. This is primarily driven by an increase in onshore wind capacity.

In contrast to the UK and Ireland, Italy sees a large increase in PV. This has a big impact on wholesale electricity prices in summer months with negligible differences in prices in winter. Results for The Netherlands show a 4% drop in wholesale market price between the Reference and Mitigation Scenario driven in part by a drop in demand of almost 9% and increases in both onshore and offshore wind energy. In the Baltic region, an increase in biomass waste-fired generation capacity in Latvia and Lithuania coupled with an increase in onshore wind capacity in Estonia contribute to average price reductions of 3%−4%.

On the Iberian Peninsula, both Spain and Portugal have already high levels of renewables in the Reference Scenario. Demand drops by approximately 6% in both Member States in the Mitigation Scenario. In the Mitigation Scenario the installed capacity of wind and solar energy reduces in Portugal compared to the Reference Scenario. Both Member States experience only a minor reduction in prices. France is the Member State with the largest absolute reduction in demand. France also sees a strong increase in biomass waste capacity and associated generation in the mitigation scenario.

Turning to price volatility, a number of Member States exhibit strong variations in monthly prices as shown in Fig. 16.7. In particular, Ireland and the UK show strong fluctuations in monthly prices, which are primarily driven by high levels of variable renewables. Both Member States need to curtail variable renewables at 7% and 1%, respectively. It should be noted that operational constraints which currently limit the instantaneous penetration of variable renewables (as highlighted in Chapter 15: Curtailment: An Option for Cost-Efficient Integration of Variable Renewable Generation?, on wind energy curtailment) are not considered in this modeling exercise. Inclusion of these limits would increase curtailment in this region.

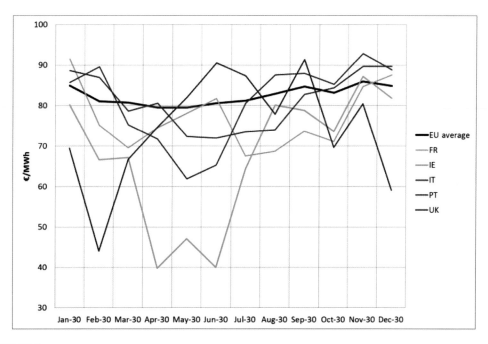

FIGURE 16.7

Monthly 2030 prices for select Member States for Mitigation Scenario. EU average is also shown in black.

The large growth in renewable capacity, changes in demand, and differences in power plant portfolios between the scenarios impact the utilization of thermal power plants in 2030. Natural gas-fired plants are particularly affected. The EU-wide average cost of generation for natural gas in 2030 is approximately €72/MWh, compared with €41/MWh for coal. The Mitigation Scenario has higher ambitions in terms of emissions reductions and has approximately 8% less installed natural gas capacity. In the Reference Scenario these plants are operating at a 25% capacity factor EU-wide compared with 18% in the Mitigation Scenario. Greece experiences the largest reduction of the capacity factor from 48% down to 27%, with natural gas generation being replaced by onshore wind and other renewables. Germany too sees a significant reduction in natural gas generation with annual capacity factors reducing from 40% to 35%.

RESULTS FOR 2050

For the year 2050, installed capacities of wind and solar power increase from 45% in the Reference Scenario to 52% in the Mitigation Scenario. The 2050 portfolios are also characterized by significant emissions captured with CCS (carbon capture and storage), particularly in Poland and Italy. In contrast to 2030 with its overall reduction in electricity demand, 2050 sees a 16% increase in demand in the Mitigation Scenario over the Reference Scenario, with a number of Member States having more than a 25% increase in demand in the Mitigation Scenario (see Fig. 16.8).

Across the EU, the increase in installed capacity of variable renewable generation has strong implications on electricity prices. Overall, there is a reduction in average wholesale prices of approximately €4.2/MWh. For example, Greece sees a modest increase in demand, but a large relative increase in the installed capacity of variable renewables and hydro power. This leads to significantly lower wholesale electricity prices. This effect is particular pronounced during summer months when solar generation is high. In addition, other low-carbon options, such as nuclear power, may strongly impact prices: Romania experiences an increased installed capacity of nuclear power in the Mitigation Scenario. Coupled with increases in variable renewable generation this contributes to a strong reduction in price.

A number of Member States, however, see an increase in prices from the Reference to the Mitigation Scenario. For example, the price increase in Poland is caused by an overall reduction in installed capacity coupled with an increase in demand. Belgium also sees higher prices in the Mitigation Scenario. There, demand increases by 22% while overall installed capacity grows by only 12%, with a significant portion of this growth in variable renewables. Balancing these variable renewables requires greater imports and also gas-fired generation within the country, leading to overall higher wholesale prices.

It is important to remember that the carbon price for the Mitigation Scenario is held at €100/t.[b] This carbon price level would lead to significantly higher prices in the Mitigation Scenario for all Member States.

---

[b]In the EU 2030 Framework for climate and energy policies Impact Assessment Document [12] the carbon price in the Mitigation Scenario is estimated at €264/t. However, in this study this price is limited to the value mentioned above.

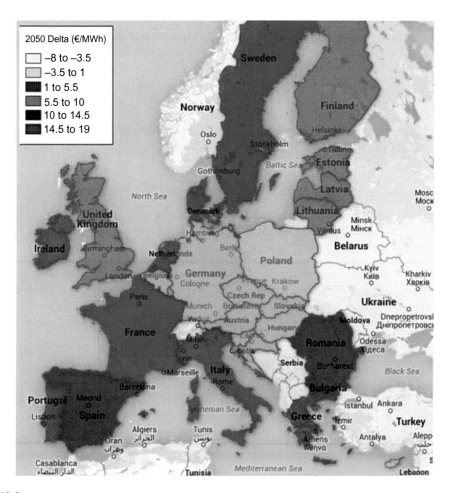

FIGURE 16.8

Reductions in price (€/MWh) in the Mitigation Scenario for 2050, as compared to the Reference Scenario.

IMPACT OF DEMAND RESPONSE

DR can have a significant impact on the power plant dispatch. In this study the main type of DR that is considered is load shifting, meaning that the electricity demand has been shifted from peaking moments to off-peaking moments in time. To examine the impact of DR simulations were undertaken for the Reference Scenarios where 10% and 15% of each Member State peak demand was made available for DR in 2030 and 2050, respectively. Replacing this peak demand in off-peak moments leaves the electricity demand equal for each year. DR consequently reduces the need for expensive peaking plants to operate and decreases the marginal price while it increases load factors of the baseload units. DR units are modeled as virtual pumped storage units with 100%

efficiency. The optimizer's objective function is to minimize total system costs, whereas a customer using DR will aim to reduce their overall electricity bill. This is a relatively simple method to simulate DR and will not reflect full system implications as it does not directly include a price response component (which is important with high levels of variable renewable generation), but provides a useful starting point in gauging its impact from a system-wide perspective.

From an EU-wide perspective, the introduction of DR in 2030 reduces total system generations costs (i.e., variable cost of generation and start-up costs of generators) by €2.0bn or approximately €0.5/MWh. For the year 2050 the impact is slightly bigger at a total reduction in system costs of €2.8bn or approximately €0.6/MWh. Impacts are not shown at individual Member State level as the simplified technique used here is appropriate for assessing the reduction in system costs but not for assessing the impact on prices.

16.4 COMMENTS AND DISCUSSIONS

This chapter quantifies the merit order effect in 2030 and 2050 in European electricity wholesale markets by comparing a Reference and Mitigation Scenario for both years. It is important to note that these estimates do not reflect the total costs of electricity as they exclude subsidies and other costs. It has been shown that for the scenarios examined the inclusion of variable renewables can put downward pressure on wholesale electricity prices with the greatest impacts seen in Member States with high levels of variable renewable penetration. While the inclusion of variable renewables has a primary impact, this chapter also highlights the impact of demand for electricity and portfolio changes on wholesale market prices. These changes and impacts differ for each Member State but pronounced impacts are seen in Member States where these conditions are met. It is also interesting to note that in general the merit order effect as analyzed here is lower in Member States with a higher number of interconnection points, particular in central Europe, while peripheral Member States have a more pronounced impact. Increased interconnection has not been analyzed in this report, but would make an interesting future study.

While a detailed economic analysis of the impact of wholesale prices on generator revenues is beyond the scope of this analysis, some points can be taken from the current analysis. Within the power sector in Europe today, current market prices are not sufficient to cover investment and yearly fixed costs of all plants operating in the system. This situation is expected to become more critical in particular due to the current overcapacity induced by the economic slowdown in recent years and the penetration of renewables, which predominantly have investment-related costs and O&M costs. The low capacity factors for natural gas-fired plant, particularly in 2030, suggest that natural gas-fired plants may still struggle to achieve sufficient financial remuneration in an energy-only market in some Member States.

Like all modeling exercises the results in this study have to be interpreted in the context of modeling assumptions which have important implications for the understanding of results. Firstly, it is important to bear in mind that only one set of deterministic scenarios has been examined and results are therefore representative for these inputs. One year of wind and solar profiles has been examined and therefore interannual variations in generation output have not been captured. Equally one set of maintenance and forced outages for thermal plant has been used and no sensitivity to results of these outages was presented. More specifically the modeling technique used in this exercise employs perfect foresight, whereby the model has full knowledge of all input variables such as demand and variable renewable generation output. It is well understood that power systems with high penetration levels of variable renewable electricity will be more challenging to operate in the absence of perfect foresight. Finally, the modeling assumptions assume a perfect market where Member States can easily transport power throughout the EU network.

Independently of the modeling limitations, this chapter could show that the integration of variable renewables can lead to a decrease in wholesale electricity prices, especially in Member States with high levels of variable renewable penetration. Therefore, new regulative measures, such as changes in the market design, become more and more inevitable to establish a more investment-friendly environment. This environment is necessary to ensure that not only flexible power plants, but also RES technologies, can earn their capital and fixed costs. In Chapter 17, Market Design Options for Promoting Low-Carbon Technologies, different market design options are discussed, focusing on their ability to integrate also low-carbon technologies into the electricity market.

REFERENCES

[1] D. Keles, et al., A combined modeling approach for wind power feed-in and electricity spot prices, Energy Policy 59 (2013) 213–225.

[2] European Commission, A policy framework for climate and energy in the period from 2020 to 2030. Communication from the Commission to the European Parliament, the Council, the European Economic and Social Committee and the Committee of the Regions. Brussels, 2014.

[3] D. Azofra, et al., Wind power merit-order and feed-intariffs effect: a variability analysis of the Spanish electricity market, Energy Convers. Manage. 83 (2014) 19–27.

[4] S. Ray, et al., Wind energy and electricity prices: exploring the merit order effect. A literature review by Pöyry for the European Wind Energy Association, EWEA, 2010.

[5] L. Hirth, The market value of variable renewables: the effect of solar wind power variability on their relative price, Energy Econ. 38 (2013) 218–236.

[6] U.S. Department of Energy (DOE), Benefits of demand response in electricity markets and recommendations for achieving them. A report to the United States Congress Pursuant to Section 1252 of the Energy Policy Act of 2005, 2006.

[7] J. Torriti, M. Hassan, M. Leach, Demand response experience in Europe: policies, programmes and implementation, Energy 35 (4) (2010) 1575–1583.

[8] Smart Energy Demand Coalition (SEDC), Mapping Demand Response in Europe. Tracking Compliance with Article 15.8 of the Energy Efficiency Directive. Brussels, 2014.

[9] E. Koliou, et al., Demand response in liberalized electricity markets: analysis of aggregated load participation in the German balancing mechanism, Energy 71 (2014) 245–254.

[10] European Commission, Directive 2012/27/EU of the European Parliament and of the Council of 25 October 2012 on energy efficiency, amending Directives 2009/125/EC and 2010/30/EU and repealing directives 2004/8/EC and 2006/32/EC, Off. J. Eur. Union (2012).

[11] European Commission, Delivering the internal electricity market and making the most of public intervention. Communication from the Commission (Draft), 2013.

[12] European Commission, EU energy, transport and GHG emissions trends to 2050: Reference Scenario 2013, Luxemburg, 2013.

[13] J.P. Deane, G. Drayton, B.P. Ó Gallachóir, The impact of sub-hourly modelling in power systems with significant levels of renewable generation, Appl. Energy 113 (2014) 152–158.

[14] PLEXOS Integrated Energy Model Help Files. Available from: <http://www.energyexemplar.com/> (accessed May 2016).

MARKET DESIGN OPTIONS FOR PROMOTING LOW-CARBON TECHNOLOGIES

Rupert Hartel, Dogan Keles, and Wolf Fichtner

Karlsruhe Institute of Technology (KIT), Karlsruhe, Germany

17.1 INTRODUCTION

The different promotion schemes in the EU have led to an increasing share of renewable energy, especially wind and solar power. Due to the increasing feed-in of electricity from variable renewables, the number of operating hours of conventional power plants has decreased in recent years and their revenue situation has gotten progressively worse. As large amounts of electricity from RES, such as wind and solar power, are fed into the energy-only market (EOM), prices tend to decrease, since these technologies have marginal costs of zero (merit order effect). Only during periods when the demand is covered at least partly by conventional generating capacity will the price be set by the marginal costs of fossil-fuel generators. In summary, higher prices are set by fossil-fuel generators, if variable RES are covering only a small part of the full load. Therefore, these RES are partly gaining profits from high prices occurring in the EOM.

Additionally, the overall target of reducing GHG emissions is not directly considered in the EOM. Instead, the price for the GHG emission allowances is reflected within the marginal costs of conventional electricity generation. However, as mentioned above, variable RES would only benefit from higher electricity prices due to the European emission trading system (EU-ETS) when prices are being set by conventional electricity generation.

It is expected that prices will continue to decrease as the shares of electricity feed-in from RES increase, as outlined in Chapter 16, Impact on Electricity Markets: Merit Order Effect of Renewable Energies. However, assuming that the promotion of renewable energy is phased out in the near future, the question is whether investments in RES will be still carried out or not. The related key question is whether there is a "missing-money-problem" for new investments in low-carbon technologies, such as renewables, and if yes, how this can be mitigated by altering the electricity market design.

17.2 IS THERE A "MISSING-MONEY-PROBLEM" FOR LOW-CARBON TECHNOLOGIES?

The increasing RES capacity in the system has been driven by political promotion strategies to date, guaranteeing sufficient revenue streams for these technologies. The presence of these

Europe's Energy Transition. DOI: http://dx.doi.org/10.1016/B978-0-12-809806-6.00017-1

strategies indicates that RES technologies are not able to refinance themselves on the EOM due to their high investment costs. What is evident is that these schemes have led to decreasing material cost and an improvement of the efficiency of RES technologies, which in turn have reduced the associated investment costs and therefore the levelized costs of electricity (LCOE).

Fig. 17.1 shows a comparison of the levelized costs for different production technologies. While RES technologies still have higher costs than conventional generators, in some cases, notably solar photovoltaic (PV) and onshore wind, the costs are in the same range. This leads to the question of whether RES are competitive in an EOM, if the promotion strategies are phased out, or if there is a "missing-money-problem."

As previously mentioned, RES with low or zero variable costs tend to decrease the electricity price in an EOM based on marginal costs. The price reduction effect is increasing with an increasing RES capacity [2]. Due to this price reduction effect, RES are probably not able to recover their capital investment under the current market design, leading to a "missing-money–problem". An analysis by Kopp [2] shows that variable RES cannot refinance their costs in EOMs in the long

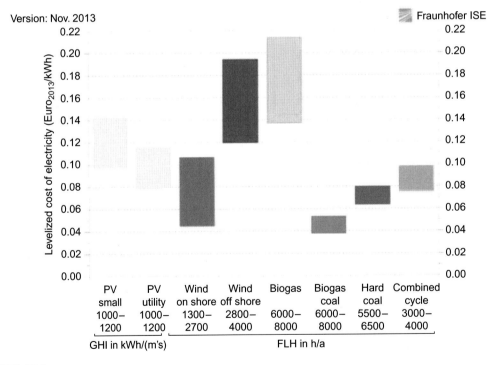

FIGURE 17.1

LCOE of renewable energy technologies and conventional power plants in Germany in 2013.

From C. Kost, et al., Studie: Stromgestehungskosten Erneuerbare Energien, Fraunhofer-Institut für Solare Energiesysteme ISE, Freiburg, 2013 [1].

Table 17.1 Overview of Possible Market Design Options		
No.	**Possible Market Designs**	**Aim**
1	Greater carbon price certainty	Promote low-carbon technologies [6,7]
2	Support low-carbon investments in current markets	
3	Regulate to limit high-carbon generation	
4	Separate low-carbon market for electricity	
5	Single buyer agency	
6	Capacity obligations on suppliers	
7	Capacity obligations on system operator	
8	Change the pricing system to pay-as-bid	Develop a market for a completely renewable electricity system [8]
9	Dispatch based on marginal costs and pricing on LCOE	
10	Market premium	
11	Technology-specific auctions	
12	Capacity market	Promote renewable energies [9,10]
13	Competitive premium system	

run, even if their LCOE falls below the LCOE of conventional power plants. This is also the case in scenarios where a high CO_2 price and increasing fuel prices are assumed.[a]

The price reduction effect of RES, often called the merit order effect (refer to Chapter 16: Impact on Electricity Markets: Merit Order Effect of Renewable Energies), is also reducing the revenue streams for conventional power plants as well as for other low-carbon generators, like nuclear. With an increasing share of RES it is likely that there will be a "missing-money-problem" for all low-carbon technologies.

In Section 17.3, we provide an overview of possible market designs that address this issue. We focus on the studies by Baker et al. [6] and HM Treasury [7] to analyze possible market designs for low-carbon generators in general, and Winkler and Altmann [8], Öko-Institut [9], and Kopp et al. [10] regarding market designs for renewable energy sources.

17.3 POSSIBLE MARKET DESIGNS

Table 17.1 gives an overview of the market design options that are considered in this chapter. Some of the presented options are quite similar, but are presented in the literature in a different context. Therefore the options can be distinguished by their aim. Options 1−7 focus on a market

---

[a]However, different literature sources state that this is strongly dependent on the development of the market framework. In a model-based analysis, Ref. [3] shows that a capacity scarcity or an increasing demand can lead to investment incentives in new capacities in an EOM. For further studies on the market value of RES, see Refs. [4] and [5].

design for low-carbon technologies, while options 8−11 evaluate market design options for a completely renewable energy system. Finally, options 12 and 13 focus on the promotion of RES. These options are explained in more detail in the following.

PROMOTING LOW-CARBON TECHNOLOGIES

Based on the example of the United Kingdom, Baker et al. [6] state that there is the following consensus: the existing market design is unlikely to provide the necessary investment incentives in low-carbon technologies to satisfy the UK's climate change goals. The Energy Market Assessment (EMA) by the HM Treasury/DECC [7], which is the basis for the analysis carried out by Baker et al. [6], discusses the five possible models for altering the current design of the UK electricity market (as shown in Fig. 17.2).

1. *Greater carbon price certainty alone* (Option A in Fig. 17.2): The basis of this concept is a competitive market framework, where all generators sell their electricity in a wholesale market. The support schemes for RES would remain in place. The government would increase the certainty on future carbon prices to encourage investments in low-carbon technologies. This could be conducted, for example, with an additional payment, paid by the government to low-carbon generators as soon as the carbon price falls below a certain level.

2. *Support low-carbon investments in current markets* (Option B in Fig. 17.2): In this concept a competitive wholesale market for all technologies is again the basis. The government would intervene by giving additional payments to low-carbon generators beside the additional payments mentioned in option A, if the electricity price falls below a certain level. This could be done by obligations, feed-in tariffs, and additional payments. This approach provides for higher and more certain revenues.

3. *Regulate to limit high-carbon generation* (Option C in Fig. 17.2): Another option is to achieve the climate change goals via regulatory intervention. The government would by law limit the amount of high-carbon generation units that can be built and/or limit the full load operation hours of existing plants [7].

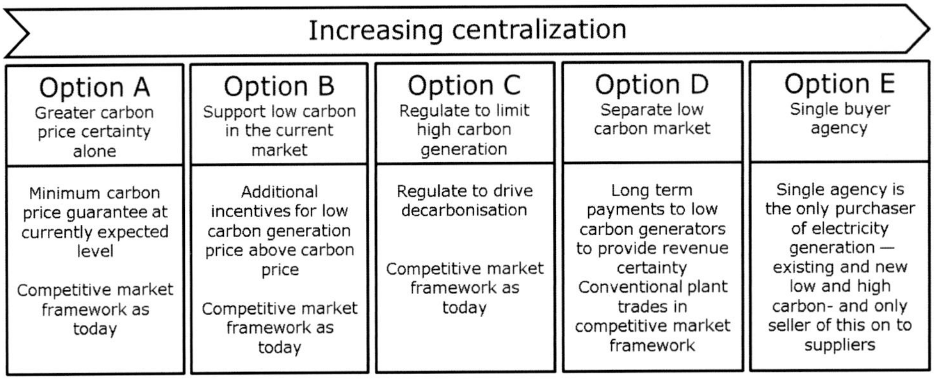

Increasing centralization				
Option A Greater carbon price certainty alone	**Option B** Support low carbon in the current market	**Option C** Regulate to limit high carbon generation	**Option D** Separate low carbon market	**Option E** Single buyer agency
Minimum carbon price guarantee at currently expected level Competitive market framework as today	Additional incentives for low carbon generation price above carbon price Competitive market framework as today	Regulate to drive decarbonisation Competitive market framework as today	Long term payments to low carbon generators to provide revenue certainty Conventional plant trades in competitive market framework	Single agency is the only purchaser of electricity generation — existing and new low and high carbon- and only seller of this on to suppliers

FIGURE 17.2

EMA market reform options (Ref. [6] based on Ref. [7]).

From P.E. Baker, C. Mitchell, B. Woodman, Electricity market design for a low-carbon future, The UK Energy Research Centre, 2010 [6].

4. *Separate low-carbon market for electricity* (Option D in Fig. 17.2): This option guarantees a revenue stream which is separated from the existing wholesale market. The price could be determined by competitive tendering, being set by the government or by the regulation of an appropriate return.

5. *Single buyer agency* (Option E in Fig. 17.2): In this model a central agency needs to be established and acts as the only buyer of electricity from the utilities. The agency would identify the need for low-carbon technologies based on the GHG emission reduction goal. If the generating capacity was procured on the basis of levelized costs and not on variable costs, the single buyer model could transform the nature of the electricity market [6]. Due to their high levelized costs, there would be no reason to dispatch low-carbon emission capacities on the basis of submitted bids via a spot market. Therefore, the dispatch is instead determined on the basis of a carbon emission hierarchy and between plant technologies on the basis of marginal cost. This approach will improve the investment climate by providing investors with confidence through guaranteed income streams. Furthermore, this will lead to a reduction of capital costs since the price uncertainty and volatility are decreasing [6].

   In addition Baker et al. [6] discuss two capacity-based market options:

6. *Capacity obligations on suppliers*: The underlying idea is to concentrate on low-carbon capacity rather than on the output. Several examples exist where obligations are placed on suppliers to procure sufficient generation capacity [6]. These obligations mainly focus on the security of supply. To support low-carbon technologies these obligations need to be defined as technology-specific ones. In general, it would be possible to achieve investments in low-carbon technologies and security of supply. This could be conducted in terms of capacity certificates. Suppliers would need to purchase these certificates, with the proceeds distributed to the certificate holders. These certificates need to consider the carbon intensity of different technologies by premium payments for low-carbon technologies. Another possibility is a bid system on the basis of carbon intensity and bid price [11].

7. *Capacity obligations on the system operator*: Another option is to place an obligation on the system operator rather than on the supplier. Again, several systems already exist with the focus of establishing a generation capacity requirement. These capacity markets are technology-neutral and are focusing only on the security of supply. However, there is no reason why a capacity market could not be designed in a way that the carbon intensity of generation is considered. So both could be achieved—security of supply and carbon emission reduction goals [6]. The system operator is to be preferred as the obligated party, because of his ability to anticipate further system needs, such as the optimization of the generation portfolio. However, it is unclear how a nonmarket-based requirement could coexist with investments on a commercial basis [6].

DEVELOP A MARKET FOR A COMPLETELY RENEWABLE ELECTRICITY SYSTEM

Winkler and Altmann [8] further analyze market design options, particularly for a completely renewable power sector in Germany. The study differentiates between changes applied to the power system and to the market design. The changes applied to the market design can be distinguished in three ways; changes to the current market design, add-ons to the current market design, and more radical market changes. They analyze how the market rules can be changed to address the challenges of generating investment incentives and cost recovery.

8. *Change the pricing system to pay-as-bid*: The change of the current pricing system to a pay-as-bid pricing is one proposal analyzed. Auction winners would get paid their bid price instead of the most expensive bid price that is accepted. It is to assume that market participants would bid with their fixed operation costs and variable costs to assure cost recovery. This is not necessarily the case, since plant operators need to dispatch more often to at least partly recover costs. In particular, plants with high capital costs and low marginal costs will try to dispatch as often as possible.

9. *Dispatch based on marginal costs and pricing on LCOE*: Another way of changing the pricing in the electricity spot market is by allowing more complex bids. The system operator would be informed of the marginal as well as the average production costs of the market participants. The dispatch of the plants would be organized according to rising marginal costs, whereas payments would be based on the average production costs. This approach could lead to different problems. "The information asymmetry between the generators and the market operator can be used for influencing the prices" according to Winkler and Altmann [8].[b] This complex bidding system could also lead to an inefficient plant dispatch and a disproportional increase of technologies with low marginal costs.

10. *Market premium*: A further add-on to the market design could be the introduction of a market premium. In a completely renewable electricity system a market premium can support variable RES and reduce investment uncertainty by using a "cap and floor" system. Similar to fixed feed-in tariffs, the government or the system operator is challenged to set the right level for the market premium to ensure sufficient investments and to avoid windfall profits for generators.

11. *Technology-specific auctions*: Technology-specific auctions and long-term contracts could also be possible changes to the market design. An example of such a system can be found in Brazil. Similar to capacity markets the generator is paid a price for the capacity, but in addition variable generation sources are paid a long-term payment for electricity generated, similar to feed-in tariffs. The prices for the payments are determined via an auction. Such a system would solve the problem of cost recovery and investment incentives, but incorporates other potential drawbacks. A central instance needs to define the capacity need for each technology, which can lead to technology lock-in or disregard for alternative technologies.[c]

PROMOTE RENEWABLE ENERGIES

Similar to the capacity obligations discussed by Baker et al. [6] under option 7, Öko-Institut [9] proposes a market model for reform of the German EOM. It particularly addresses the need for RES, but recognizes that the technologies will probably not be able to refinance themselves on the actual EOM. This proposal is more detailed than the analysis carried out by Baker et al. [6] and is therefore included here within a separate subsection.

---

[b]Plant operators could bid with lower marginal cost to get a guaranteed dispatch while at the same time bid with higher LCOE than they actually have.

[c]Germany and other European countries are about to introduce systems that are based on auctions for RES.

12. *Capacity market*: The new proposed model is a combination of EOM and capacity market. In general all new capacities (conventional and renewable) are facing the electricity price signals of the EOM. The standard option for this is the mandatory direct sale introduced with the 2014 amendment of the German EEG.[d] In addition to the achieved revenues from the EOM, all new capacities are rewarded with capacity payments. This payment is determined ex ante and is fixed long term. For variable electricity producers, the capacity payment is made on the basis of a reference capacity credit that is compatible with the needs of the future electricity system and is determined by the mean feed-in for the middle eight deciles of the hours of a year. Dispatchable capacity, renewable as well as conventional, is priced by its nominal capacity. This approach guarantees a fixed revenue stream and reduces price uncertainty. In addition to the capacity payments, a risk margin mechanism accompanies the model to account for unexpected high revenues. If the revenues for each technology group exceed a strike price, the plant operator must pay a corresponding cash settlement. This payment is set off against the capacity payment. To achieve special targets this model foresees additional payments. Fig. 17.3 illustrates the proposed mechanism.

Another possible market design to promote RES is proposed by Kopp et al. [10] and is similar to the market premium (option 10) proposed by Winkler and Altmann [8].

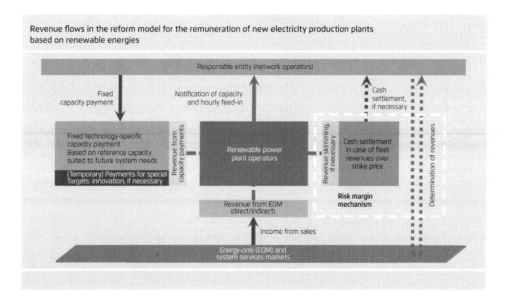

FIGURE 17.3

Market model proposed by Öko-Institut, described in option 12 [9].

Öko-Institut, Erneuerbare-Energien-Gesetz 3.0 (Langfassung). Studie im Auftrag von Agora Energiewende, 2014 [9].

[d]Renewable Energy Act in Germany ("Erneuerbare Energien Gesetz").

Kopp et al. [10] identify six possible options to promote renewable energies. Three options are based on feed-in tariffs and premiums and would be guided by the government. The remaining three options are dependent on a competitive market design. Three out of the six options are combined in option 13 to form a single new market design.

13. *Competitive premium system*: This concept is based on two revenue streams for RES:
   a. Revenues from decentralized trading of the produced electricity on the EOM.
   b. An additional long-term payment of a fixed premium over a period of 15–20 years. The level of the premium is determined through an auction.

The direct trading on the EOM guarantees that the electricity production from RES reacts on market signals and therefore will lead to an efficient plant operation [10]. The additional premium makes it possible for plant operators to recover their capital costs.

In an auction the government defines a financing budget for RES. Auction participants would apply for a part of this budget by indicating their full costs over the contract duration, e.g., 20 years. Alternatively they could bid for support needed (difference between market price in the hours they produce and their full costs), which would better reflect the different market value of the different technologies. The lowest bids are awarded first with the level of their bid (pay-as-bid). This is carried on in an ascending order until the budget is exhausted. The bids can either refer to capacity (MW) or to production (MWh) with a limited number of full load hours. The auction can be technology unspecific, meaning one budget for all renewable technologies applying, or technology specific, where the budget for each technology is set individually.

17.4 ASSESSMENT OF THE MARKET DESIGNS PRESENTED

Based on the market designs reviewed there are different options to modify the electricity market design. The options presented differ regarding their focus, complexity, the degree of change to the wholesale market, and the instruments that are used to achieve the goal of the market design reform. Table 17.2 evaluates the market designs according to the above-mentioned characteristics. Guaranteeing higher certainty over future carbon prices will probably not solve the problem for RES to refinance on a market, based on marginal cost, according to Kopp et al. [2].

Assumed small changes, like changing the pricing mechanism of an electricity market, as presented by Winkler and Altmann [8] to a pay-as-bid auction may not solve the problem of achieving investment incentives for low-carbon generators. Greater changes to the pricing mechanism based on average production costs would imply a higher degree of complexity. This change would also mean a re-ordering of the plant dispatch.

A further inclusion of the carbon intensity into the dispatch as proposed by Baker et al. [6] would mean an integration of environmental features into the market design. However, it is unclear how to implement a concrete GHG emissions reduction goal in such a mechanism and therefore the degree of complexity will probably further increase.

Add-ons to the current market, like capacity mechanisms or feed-in premiums, which are already applied in some countries, could be a further option. Öko-Institut [9] presents how such a system could be implemented in the German electricity market. The focus of the system is on RES and therefore it is not promoting all low-carbon technologies. The question remains whether such systems could be extended to include low-carbon generators in general. Baker et al. [6] states that

Table 17.2 Evaluation of the Characteristics of the Presented Market Design Options

No.	Focus	Complexity	Changes to EOM	Instrument	Goal
1	Low carbon	Low	None	Payments	Price certainty
2	Low carbon	Low	None	Payments	Price certainty
3	Low carbon	Medium	None	Regulation	Limit GHG emission
4	Low carbon	Medium	None	Payments	Revenue certainty
5	Low carbon	High	Pricing/dispatch	Market change	Limit GHG emission
6/7	Low carbon	Medium	None	Capacity payments	Revenue certainty
8	RES	Low	Pricing	None	Revenue certainty
9	RES	Medium	Pricing/dispatch	Market change	Revenue certainty
10	RES	Medium	none	Payments	Revenue certainty
12	Conventional/RES	Medium	None	Capacity payments	Revenue certainty
11/13	RES	Medium	None	Auction	Revenue certainty

the carbon intensity could be considered in capacity mechanisms to promote low-carbon generation in general. However, this again will increase the complexity of an already complex system.

The assessment further shows that there are three main tendencies of market design reforms:

1. Keeping the existing EOM, but with market add-ons for low-carbon technologies;
2. The establishment of a separate market for low-carbon technologies;
3. An overall single market based on LCOE production and plant dispatch based on marginal costs or carbon intensity.

In Table 17.3 we make our own assessment of each option to one of the three main tendencies. Additionally, each option is evaluated regarding whether it provides investment incentives and if the system is dependent on additional payments.

Market design options which are based on additional payments would probably lead to a higher investment incentive for market participants. The overall single market is the option that does not include additional payments for low-carbon technologies. This market design option might lead to investments in inefficient technologies. A pricing system centered on LCOE can provide investment incentives but as long as the dispatch is based on marginal cost or carbon intensity there will be no incentive for technologies with low marginal cost and zero CO_2 emissions to improve the efficiency of the market, since their dispatch is guaranteed.

17.5 FINAL REMARKS

The cost recovery of RES in an EOM is a controversial question. There are indications that fixed cost coverage on an electricity market, which is based on marginal cost, is unlikely for renewable energy sources at this point in time [2]. With an increasing share of RES and due to the merit order

Table 17.3 Assessment of the 14 Market Design Options

	Greater Carbon Price Certainty	Support Low-Carbon Investment in Current Market	Regulate to Limit High-Carbon Generation	Separate Low-Carbon Market for Electricity	Single Buyer Agency	Capacity Obligations on Suppliers	Capacity Obligations on the System Operator
Focus of study	Low carbon	Low carbon	Low carbon	Low carbon	Low carbon	Low carbon	Low carbon
Provide investment incentives	Unlikely	Unlikely	Unlikely	Likely	Inefficient investment	Likely	Likely
Separate market for low-carbon	No	No	No	Yes	No	No	No
Market with add-ons	Yes	Yes	No	No	No	Yes	Yes
Overall single market	No	No	Yes	No	Yes	No	No
Additional payments	Yes	Yes	No	Yes	No	Yes	Yes

	Change the Pricing System to Pay-as-Bid	Dispatch Based on Marginal Costs and Pricing on LCOE	Market Premium	Technology-Specific Auctions	EOM and Capacity Market		Competitive Premium System
Focus of study	RES	RES	RES	RES	RES	RES	RES
Provide investment incentives	Inefficient investment	Inefficient investment	Likely	Likely	Likely	Likely	Likely
Separate market for low-carbon	No	No	No	No	No	No	No
Market with add-ons	No	No	Yes	Yes	Yes	Yes	Yes
Overall single market	Yes	Yes	No	No	No	No	No
Additional payments	No	No	Yes	Yes	Yes	Yes	Yes

effect, this is also likely for other low-carbon technologies, which have high capital and high variable costs. Therefore, it is likely that there will be a "missing-money-problem" for low-carbon technologies. This leads to the question how the market design could be transformed to promote low-carbon technologies.

The presented options for altering the market design to promote low-carbon technologies have up- and downsides and differ in their degree of complexity. A future market design should be as simple as possible, as an increasing degree of complexity could also lead to higher uncertainty for market participants, besides the uncertainty that would arise due to the market change. For example, the introduction of a market premium instead of feed-in tariffs or auctions for RES which are recommended in the EU guidelines [12], could help to bring renewable energy technologies closer to the market, while keeping the changes to the market to a minimum. This will improve the understanding on how renewable energy technologies will participate in the market. However, it is unclear in which way these instruments need to be transformed to include low-carbon technologies in general.

A change in the pricing system from marginal cost to LCOE and a changed dispatch would mean a restructuring of the market design. Different aspects need to be considered to guarantee a level playing field for the different technologies. But the question remains how a completely new system can be implemented and it is questionable if it is even necessary at this point.

The assessment further shows that there seem to be three main tendencies for altering the market design to promote low carbon (existing EOM with market add-ons for low-carbon technologies, a separate market for low-carbon technologies or an overall single market based on levelized costs). The establishment of a separate market for low-carbon technologies or a change in the pricing system is a complex instrument and an implementation seems unrealistic. However, further research based on quantitative modeling is needed to identify which of the tendencies is suitable to satisfy the needs of the future electricity system. A quantitative approach is applied in the following, to evaluate the effectivity of design options in the German electricity market.

REFERENCES

[1] C. Kost, et al., Studie: Stromgestehungskosten Erneuerbare Energien, Fraunhofer-Institut für Solare Energiesysteme ISE, Freiburg, 2013.

[2] O. Kopp, A. Eßer-Frey, T. Engelhorn, Können sich erneuerbare Energien langfristig auf wettbewerblich organisierten Strommärkten finanzieren, Z. Energiewirtsch. 36 (2012) 243–255.

[3] H. Höfling, Investitionsanreize für neue Erzeugungskapazität unter wachsendem Einfluss erneuerbarer Stromerzeugung. Eine modellbasierte Szenarioanalyse des deutschen Strommarktes. Eine modellbasierte Szenarioanalyse des deutschen. Zentrum für Sonnenenergie- und Wasserstoff-Forschung Baden-Württemberg (ZSW), 2013.

[4] L. Hirth, The market value of variable renewables: the effect of solar wind power variability on their relative price, Energy Economics 38 (2013) 218–236.

[5] M. Nicolosi, The economics of renewable electricity market integration. An empirical and model-based analysis of regulatory frameworks and their impacts on the power market. PhD thesis, University of Cologne, 2012.

[6] P.E. Baker, C. Mitchell, B. Woodman, Electricity market design for a low-carbon future, The UK Energy Research Centre, 2010.

[7] HM Treasury, Energy Market Assessment, Department of Energy & Climate Change, London, 2010.

[8] J. Winkler, M. Altmann, Market designs for a completely renewable power sector, Z. Energiewirtsch. 36 (2012) 77−92.

[9] Öko-Institut, Erneuerbare-Energien-Gesetz 3.0 (Langfassung). Studie im Auftrag von Agora Energiewende, 2014.

[10] O. Kopp, et al., Wege in ein wettbewerbliches Strommarktdesign für erneuerbare Energien, 2013.

[11] S. Gottstein, The role of forward capacity markets in increasing demand-side and other low carbon resources: experiences and prospects, 2010.

[12] European Commission, Guidelines on State aid for environmental protection and energy 2014-2020, 2014/C 200/01, 2014.

CASE STUDY: DESIGN OPTIONS FOR THE GERMAN ELECTRICITY MARKET

18

Lea Renz[1], Rupert Hartel[1], Dogan Keles[1], Wolf Fichtner[1], and Hrvoje Keko[2]

[1]Karlsruhe Institute of Technology (KIT), Karlsruhe, Germany [2]Energy Institute Hrvoje Požar (EIHP), Zagreb, Croatia

18.1 INTRODUCTION

Currently, there is an intensive discussion in some EU countries, such as Germany, about the optimal design for electricity markets with a high share of renewable energy production. The reason for this discussion is doubts whether the energy-only market (EOM), which is the current market design in the German electricity sector, can provide sufficient investment incentives to ensure security of supply in the long term. In the EOM, only electricity is paid and not the provision of electricity generating capacity. The market price is determined by the marginal cost of the most expensive power plant which is still needed to cover the current demand.

Due to the increasing feed-in of volatile renewable electricity into the grid, the number of operating hours of conventional power plants is decreasing, which reduces the revenues of utilities. However, a significant amount of "back-up" capacity[a] has to be implemented, as the capacity credit[b] of newly built fluctuating renewable energy units is relatively low. This "back-up" capacity may consist of flexible conventional power plants such as gas turbines and of conventional hydro power connected to reservoirs, but also of demand-side measures.

But only a part of the required flexible conventional capacity will be in operation, assuming that fluctuating renewable power plants (like wind turbines) achieve a certain level of full load hours. In that case, scarcity prices occur in only a few hours of the year and generating facilities may not be able to earn sufficient revenues to cover their fixed costs. Thus, by increasing the share of renewable electricity production, the "missing-money" problem tends to be exacerbated and can only be compensated by higher price spikes (near the Value of Lost Load (VoLL), refer to Chapter 24: Need for Reliability and Measuring its Cost) during the few hours of scarcity in the EOM. However, at the moment it is difficult to assess the political and social acceptance of higher price spikes in European countries.

---

[a]Note that the often used term back-up capacity may be misleading, as it may be interpreted as if all the installed fluctuating renewable energy capacity will require back-up capacity. In reality, all generation technologies are to a varying extent unavailable at certain points in time. The overall supply security has to be maintained at the power systems level, with technologies backing-up each other mutually.

[b]Capacity credit is a measure that indicates to what extent other generation capacity could be replaced by a renewable plant, so that security of supply can still be guaranteed. It is typically expressed as percentage of the available capacity of a conventional power plant.

Europe's Energy Transition. DOI: http://dx.doi.org/10.1016/B978-0-12-809806-6.00018-3

Overall, this raises the question whether the marginal cost-based EOM provides enough incentives for investments in new power plant capacity (both renewable as well as conventional) or if a new market design including a capacity market should be introduced to guarantee returns on investment while ensuring system adequacy.

18.2 MODELING DESIGN OPTIONS FOR THE GERMAN ELECTRICITY MARKET

In order to investigate the consequences of different market design options on the German electricity market, several modeling approaches can be used, e.g., optimization models or agent-based models. Optimization models calculate the cost-optimal solution of an equation system. Thereby the optimization is performed from the perspective of a central planner neglecting the perspective of the different involved players. However, these are playing a crucial role in taking investment decisions and thus also in assuring security of supply. Agent-based models are capable of modeling single players as agents with individual strategies and different restrictions, both technical and economic. Further, the agent-based approach is capable of integrating different types of markets like the day-ahead market or capacity markets [1]. Thus, agent-based models are well fitting for the requirements of the problem to be investigated. While most of the studies analyzing future market designs use energy system models based on optimization approaches [2,3], this contribution uses the agent-based approach. The electricity market is modeled as a market with imperfect competition and the agents do not have perfect foresight assessing investment decisions.

MODELING OF THE ENERGY-ONLY MARKET

The analyses following in this chapter are based on an existing agent-based model (PowerACE), which has already been used to conduct several energy economic analyses [4,5]. The model depicts the central players (energy supply companies, system operators, regulators, consumers) and the most important markets, like the day-ahead market, the electricity balancing market, and the futures market. Energy supply companies are represented by agents taking both short-term and long-term decisions, like scheduling of power plants and new construction or dismantling of power plants. Thus, interactions and feedback effects between short- and long-term strategies can be investigated. Further, demand side management (DSM) measures, in particular interruptible loads, are modeled by demand-reducing bids that are placed if price peaks are estimated. In order to investigate rare events, which are just occurring under specific parameter combinations, the model simulates the agents' decisions with an hourly resolution. Fig. 18.1 provides an overview of the central elements of the model.

Once per year, the agents who are responsible for the investment planning of energy supply options are given the opportunity to enhance the power plant portfolio. Several investment options are given endogenously to the agents. The economic value of these options is determined by a net present value approach under consideration of expected future demand and future national power plant capacities. If an agent identifies a need for expanding his future portfolio and if the investment option has a positive net present value, the decision to construct a new power plant is taken. Afterwards, the next

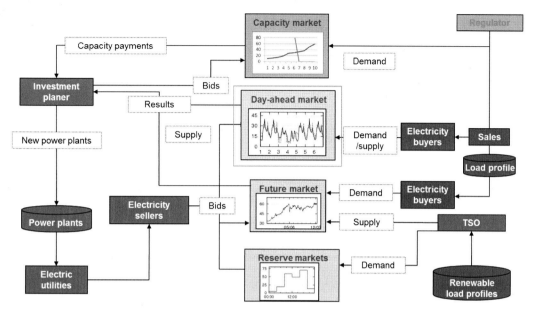

FIGURE 18.1

Schematic illustration of the agent-based model.

agent undertakes his investment planning. The investment decisions previously taken by other agents are thereby considered as public information and are included into the investment decision. Refs. [5−7] provide more detailed information about the single elements of the model.

To model the electricity market as exact as possible, further data are required, which is (if available) taken from official sources. For instance, each power plant in Germany with a capacity higher than 5 MW is modeled based on the list of power plants provided by the Federal Grid Agency (Bundesnetzagentur).[c] Further, the database for the simulation consists of input parameters from sources such as the Energy Roadmap 2050 of the European Commission. Historical hourly values for the feed-in of photovoltaic and wind are provided by the European Energy Exchange.[d]

MODELING CAPACITY MECHANISMS

Several capacity mechanisms are currently discussed for the German electricity market. This contribution focuses on the assessment of a capacity reserve and a centralized capacity market. The implementation of a capacity reserve is currently preferred by the Federal Ministry for Economic Affairs and Energy (BMWi) as a solution to ensure the security of supply during a transition phase

---

[c]Bundesnetzagentur für Elektrizität Gas Telekommunikation Post und Eisenbahnen (BNetzA): Kraftwerksliste, 2014.
[d]European Energy Exchange (EEX). Available from: www.eex.com

of the electricity market to a renewable-based one and will therefore probably be implemented shortly [8]. The centralized capacity market is based on the "forward capacity market" from New England and is similar to a proposal to implement a "market for security of supply contracts" as presented in Ref. [9].

Capacity Reserve

The capacity reserve is modeled as a single price auction, which takes place once per year and is tendered by the transmission system operators. The volume of the reserve amounts to 5 GW over-all. The highest permitted price for the capacity reserve amounts to 55.700 €/MW.[e] Only power plants that are available within 10 hours are allowed to participate in the tender since the operation of the capacity reserve is scheduled daily. Power plants that are contracted in the capacity reserve are not allowed to operate in the spot market. The system operator operates these power plants at the maximum system price of 3000 €/MWh[f] only in cases where not enough capacity is available on the spot market to supply the demand. As a consequence, the spot market price also rises to the maximum price.

In the years 2017−20 the planned climate reserve is considered and therefore not the whole size of the capacity reserve will be tendered for this period. The climate reserve consists of different lignite power plants that are not allowed to participate in other markets anymore and are only generating energy in times of peak load, for which the plant owners are compensated. This measure is implemented to reduce national CO_2 emissions.

Just as power plants in the climate reserve, power plants that are part of the capacity reserve or have been part of it in the past are not allowed to participate in other markets. A power plant there-fore has to cover all costs with the capacity reserve. Therefore, the agents of each power plant k, which meets the technical requirements of the reserve, submits a bid $b(k)$ that considers the fixed costs c_{fix} and the opportunity costs c_{opp}:

$$b(k) = \max\{c_{fix}(k), c_{opp}(k)\}$$

The opportunity costs consist of the expected revenues on the other markets m during the time when the power plant is in the capacity reserve and the value of the option to be allowed to partici-pate in other markets in the future after this period. If a power plant switches to the capacity reserve, due to the political proposal, it is not allowed to operate at regular energy markets. Hence, it is loses its option to earn money in the regular energy markets after being at the capacity reserve. Therefore, this option value has to considered within the bids submitted to the capacity reserve auction.

$$c_{opp}(k) = \sum_m \text{return}(m, k) + \text{option value}(k)$$

Considering that mainly power plants with short remaining lifetime are contracted to the capac-ity reserve, an option value of "0" is assumed.

---

[e]The maximum price is determined by the annuity of a gas turbine: specific investment of 400 €/kW, annual fixed cost of 9 €/kW, planning horizon of 15 years and interest rate of 8%.
[f]According to the maximum price at the EPEX day-ahead spot market.

Centralized Capacity Market

The capacity market integrated in the model is comparable to the "forward capacity market," which is currently implemented in the market area of the North American system operator ISO New England. In the first step the regulator determines the reserve margin R for a year t and thus the amount of required secured conventional capacity ConCap to assure an appropriate security of supply level:

$$\mathrm{ConCap}_t = (1 + R_t)(D_{\mathrm{peak},t} - RE_t - \mathrm{Imp}_t),$$

where as $D_{\mathrm{peak},t}$ is the load, RE_t is the secured feed-in of renewables and Imp_t is the secured import of electricity at the time of annual peak load.

In the second step the regulator determines the required amount of capacity obligations for each supplier. For this purpose, the share of the supplier in the annual peak load is calculated and multiplied by the required secured capacity ConCap. Each energy supplier can fulfill his capacity obligations either with his existing conventional capacities, with new capacities, or with capacity options, which are traded on the capacity market. After determining the input parameters the energy suppliers offer their capacities on the market, whereas various types of offers are differentiated: Existing capacities have to offer at a price of "0 €/MW" or of their operational fixed costs—otherwise they could be pushed out of the market, while new power plants offer at a price between a minimum price and the starting price of the auction.[g]

New power plants receive their offer price for a guaranteed period of time of typically several years and afterwards the capacity price resulting on the market. In order to calculate the offer price for new power plants in a first step each supplier calculates the investment option with the highest net present value K^- without any additional revenues from the capacity market. In a second step, the offer price is determined so that the net present value K^+, which includes revenues from all market including capacity market, is equal to "0."

18.3 MAIN RESULTS OF THE MARKET DESIGN ANALYSIS

To provide decision makers with new insights into the question whether the EOM provides sufficient investment signals for a decarbonization of the electricity mix, the agent-based simulation model PowerACE is applied [6]. Different capacity mechanisms are implemented in addition to the EOM in the model. Thus, different market designs were analyzed under various parameter settings regarding the investment behavior of the agents as well as the development of generation capacity, electricity prices, carbon dioxide emissions, and costs. Furthermore, it is possible to examine whether an undersupply of demand occurs in different scenarios and parameter settings.

The model also allows the implementation of demand flexibility. Thus, on the one hand demand response can prevent market failure in the EOM by setting the price in scarcity hours and on the other hand demand resources can take part in capacity markets, earning additional revenues.

---

[g]The modeled auction is a descending clock auction, where the auctioneer starts with a high price and lowers the price in the following bidding rounds until the offered capacity is reduced to the level of the capacity demand.

The analyzed period covers the years 2010–50. The expansion path of renewable energy is consistent with the objective of the German federal government of reaching a share of 80% of electricity supply by 2050.

Simulation results for the EOM and for an energy market design with a centralized capacity market based on capacity options are briefly summarized and compared in the following. The following figures show the development of installed power plant capacities in the German EOM (Fig. 18.2) and for the case with a centralized capacity market (Fig. 18.3). The investment activity in the EOM is fluctuating over the time, which can be explained by a high level of prices on the wholesale market during scarcity periods. High price periods incentivize new investments, so that a period of nonscarcity follows until decommissioning of power plants causes a new scarcity triggering a new investment period.

In the simulation with a centralized capacity market, however, the investments are carried out earlier, more evenly and up to a higher total installed capacity. The level of security of supply is thus significantly higher in the case of a capacity market than in the EOM. Besides, the results indicate that the introduction of a capacity market promotes the construction of natural gas capacities. This comes along with the need of restructuring the power sector to more low-carbon technologies, as gas power plants are emitting less carbon dioxide than coal power plants and are very flexible to balance fluctuations of renewables.

Regarding the trend of the yearly average wholesale electricity prices, the results indicate that in years of capacity shortage prices increase in the EOM considerably stronger than with a

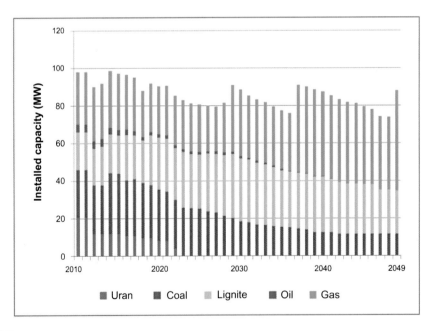

FIGURE 18.2

Installed conventional capacity in the EOM.

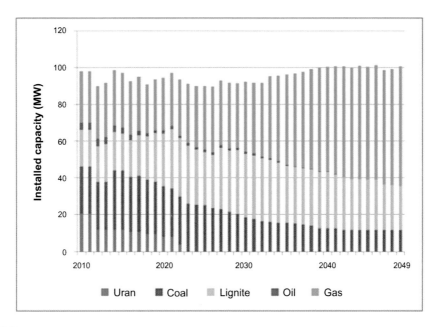

FIGURE 18.3

Installed conventional capacity in a market design with a centralized capacity market.

capacity market. Even the total expenditures of consumers (for electricity and for capacities) in the simulation with a capacity market are lower than the electricity expenditures in the EOM in years affected by scarcity. However, it can be stated, that in years with sufficient generation capacity, the consumers have to pay more for purchasing electricity in the case with a capacity market compared to the EOM. Over the whole modeling period, the costs of both market designs seem to be at the same level, if the capacity market is well parameterized. Higher expenditures for consumers, resulting from the higher investment activity in a capacity market, would occur if the capacity market offers too much incentive and creates excess capacity. It can be concluded that the major challenge of a capacity market is an adequate parameterization to avoid capacity excess. For example, the required reserve margin should on the one hand be sufficient to ensure security of supply, but on the other hand it should be as low as possible to keep the capacity costs for consumers reasonable.

The lower investment activity in the EOM raises also the question of whether situations occur in which the demand cannot be met. Agent-based simulation models allow the examination of a shortfall in demand. In the simulation with a capacity market, due to its objective and with adequate parameter setting, shortage of demand can be prevented. However, in the EOM this situation occurs during several hours of the year when accounting for demand response in terms of shedable load.

The evaluation of an energy market design with a decentralized capacity market based on capacity certificates still requires further research. Nevertheless, a preliminary analysis indicates that the investment activity is, on the one hand, strongly influenced by assumptions about the risk attitude of the single market players and, on the other hand, by the regulatory penalty given for a shortfall of capacity certificates. These considerations emphasize the importance of an adequate and reasonable parameterization of capacity markets.

In summary, the modeling results for the EOM could serve as an indication for future investment activities carried out in an EOM whose potential is not yet fully tapped. Beside the load shedding potential, which is implemented in the model, other measures exist for improving the efficiency of the EOM. These include the implementation and analysis of the load shifting potential as well as the future potential of electricity storage technologies or virtual power plants. In fact, capacity markets do have the potential to ensure security of supply, but an adequate parameterization is difficult. Many changes, which have been made to existent capacity markets, e.g., in the capacity markets of ISO New England or PJM in the US, emphasize this fact. Before introducing new market segments like capacity markets, the impacts of the suggested measures on the efficiency of the EOM, on prices and on the investment behavior should be reviewed. If the improvements do not lead to sufficient investment activity, especially in the long term, the introduction of new market segments will become unavoidable.

18.4 POLICY RECOMMENDATIONS

Changes in the electricity market design can unsettle investors and lead to additional risk premiums and transaction costs. For the short term, in particular to handle already occurring regional congestions, the introduction of a strategic reserve could be sufficient to guarantee security of supply. Instead of performing major changes in the electricity market design, it is recommended to improve the functioning of the EOM, e.g., by raising price caps, so that prices near the VoLL are possible. In addition, measures that lead to a more flexible demand and that advance electricity storage technologies should be implemented, and intraday and balancing markets should be intensified and reinforced as well. These measures would allow a better integration of renewable energies (e.g., by allowing to adjust to forecast errors on day-ahead markets) and individual demand segments. Furthermore, European cross-border trade should be enhanced by expanding the European grid. This would strengthen the European electricity market and diversify the overall capacity mix.

In the long term (2025 and beyond), if the EOM still does not set investment signals, but new capacity is needed due to decommissioning of old capacity, capacity markets could be introduced. These would allow handling the missing-money problem, which is expected to worsen as the shares of renewable energies increase and in absence of capacity markets. In order to achieve a better market integration, it is important that renewable energy technologies also take part in capacity markets according to their capacity credit, as they are also affected by the missing-money problem as pointed out in Section 17.2.

REFERENCES

[1] L. Tesfatsion, Agent-based computational economics: growing economies from the bottom up, Artif. Life 8 (1) (2002) 55–82.

[2] Research to Business Energy Consulting (r2b), Endbericht Leitstudie Strommarkt—Arbeitspaket Funktionsfähigkeit EOM & Impact-Analyse Kapazitätsmechanismen, Köln, 2014.

[3] Frontier Economics and Formaet Services GmbH, Strommarkt in Deutschland—Gewährleistet das derzeitige Marktdesign Versorgungssicherheit? Bericht für das Bundesministerium für Wirtschaft und Energie (BMWi), London, 2014.

[4] F. Sensfuß, M. Ragwitz, M. Genoese, The merit-order effect: a detailed analysis of the price effect of renewable electricity generation on spot market prices in Germany, Energy Policy 36 (8) (2008) 3086–3094.

[5] A. Bublitz, et al., Agent-based simulation of the German and French wholesale electricity markets—recent extensions of the PowerACE model with exemplary applications. In: Proceedings of the Sixth International Conference on Agents and Artificial Intelligence, pp. 40–49, 2014.

[6] M. Genoese, Energiewirtschaftliche Analysen des deutschen Strommarkts mit agentenbasierter Simulation, Nomos Verlag, Baden-Baden, 2010.

[7] A. Bublitz, et al., An assessment of the newly proposed strategic reserve. In: 2015 12th International Conference on the European, 2015.

[8] Bundesministerium für Wirtschaft und Energie (BMWi), Ein Strommarkt für die Energiewende—Diskussionspapier des Bundesministeriums für Wirtschaft und Energie (Weißbuch), 2015.

[9] Energiewirtschaftliche Institut an der Universität zu Köln (EWI), Untersuchungen zu einem zukunftsfähigen Strommarktdesign, 2012.

CONCLUSIONS AND OUTLOOK 19

Dogan Keles

Karlsruhe Institute of Technology (KIT), Karlsruhe, Germany

The strong increase of electricity production from renewable energy sources (RES) leads to new challenges for the network infrastructure and market regulation. To handle pressure on electricity networks, the curtailment of RES electricity production gains in importance, if network extension lags behind. The amount of curtailed electricity has reached several hundred GWh in major national energy markets, such as in Italy and Germany.

Our analyses presented in Chapter 15, Curtailment: An Option for Cost-Efficient Integration of Variable Renewable Generation?, have shown that limiting the output of wind power plants in Germany to 70% of their maximum capacity would reduce their electricity production by only 1.3% in the year 2011. A limitation to 80% would reduce the energy output by 0.5%. For PV, a similar effect could be observed by the same production limitation. However, the 70% limitation of wind and PV production plants can decrease the costs for grid extension in Germany by almost 30%. Other studies have shown that beside the grid investment expenses also operational costs can decrease as, e.g., the grid operators could reduce the system reserve capacities. A drawback of such a limitation measure is that the curtailed electricity would be produced by conventional and carbon dioxide-emitting power plants. However, as the share of curtailed electricity is very low, the impact on carbon emissions would be marginal.

Curtailment of fluctuant RES electricity production is not the only effect of a strong RES expansion. The so-called merit order effect is the major factor regarding the market influence of RES. In Chapter 16, Impact on Electricity Markets: Merit Order Effect of Renewable Energies, it was shown that the integration of variable renewables leads to a significant decrease of wholesale electricity prices, especially in Member States with high levels of variable renewable power production. This in turn means that today's power market in Europe does not produce market prices that are sufficient to cover the fixed costs of all power plants that are necessary to maintain generation adequacy. This situation becomes even more critical, as the current overcapacity in some EU countries caused by the utilities from the preliberalization era and by the expansion of renewables depresses wholesale prices. The low utilization rate of gas-fired plants with increasing shares of PV and wind energy output makes the financial remuneration of gas power plants more difficult in an energy-only market (EOM) in some Member States. Therefore, new regulative measures, such as changes in the market design, are expected to be inevitable in the future.

The regulative changes, especially the changes of market design, should promote the integration of low-carbon technologies into the electricity market. The design options presented in Chapter 17, Market Design Options for Promoting Low-Carbon Technologies, have advantages and disadvantages for different production technologies and they differ in their degree of complexity. On the one side, well-designed electricity markets should not discriminate low-carbon technologies, especially RES technologies, on the other side they should not be overly complex, as complexity could lead to higher uncertainty for market participants. A market design based on levelized costs of energy (LCOE) dispatch of power plants instead of marginal costs would mean a disruptive change of the market design and seems difficult to realize, as it is challenging to determine the LCOE of each power plant, especially for RES plants at different production sites. Therefore, the question remains how a completely new system can be implemented and whether a new system could be effective in promoting low-carbon technologies.

The assessment of the design options highlighted that there seem to be three main tendencies for a new market design. These tendencies are changes in the existing EOM design with some add-ons for low-carbon technologies, a separate market (also capacity market) for low-carbon technologies, especially RES, and a market based on LCOE. As the establishment of a separate market and the change in the pricing system to being LCOE based are complex measures, their implementation seems currently unrealistic. However, further research based on quantitative modeling and simulation can provide insights on how major changes may affect the electricity market.

Finally, Chapter 18, Case Study: Design Options for the German Electricity Market, presented a model-based analysis for the German electricity market, which was carried out to obtain quantitative insights about the impacts of different market design options on generation adequacy. Based on these results it is recommended to improve the current EOM design, e.g., by raising price caps, so that prices close to the value of lost load (VoLL) are possible. In addition, measures promoting flexible demand, such as dynamic tariffs for households, should be implemented to lower peak demand and reduce the need for new investments. These changes are less disruptive and could be implemented more easily than redesigning markets beyond the current EOM design. In the long term (2025 and beyond), however, if the EOM does not set investment signals and guarantees generation adequacy while old power plants are being retired, capacity remuneration mechanisms could be necessary to handle the missing-money problem. This missing-money problem is expected to worsen with an increasing share of RES electricity production. Still, to mitigate climate change it remains important that low-carbon technologies such as RES are allowed to take part or are even favored by a new market design.

The analyses undertaken are to be extended to gain further findings about the impact of RES electricity production in the future. Such analyses are needed to help determine the most effective and efficient regulative measures and market design options to facilitate the further integration of RES. These analyses have to be carried out in the context of European market integration, which is pushed by the so-called "Price Coupling of Regions" (PCR) mechanism and the "Energy Union" concept. The analysis of market design options in the coupled European market area could focus on impacts of the uncoordinated introduction of market regulations in different countries, as is currently taking place in several EU countries (France, UK, and Germany have introduced differing capacity mechanisms).

However, to find more efficient solutions, the model-based analyses should also cover alternative approaches, such as coordinated design options, in which the principles of the internal European market with equal competition would not be restrained. Such a market design has to be developed and evaluated with regard to its capability to introduce and value flexibility within the energy market. A strong penetration of flexible technologies is essential for a successful RES integration, and thus for the attainment of climate goals. However, their establishment in the energy market is still challenging and requires strong efforts of different actors and new concepts, as described in the following section.

In this context it can be stated that there is a need not only for the development of new market concepts, but also for a quantitative analysis of the effectiveness of these concepts.

RELIABLE AND FLEXIBLE ENERGY SYSTEMS

INTRODUCTION

Abhishek Shivakumar

KTH Royal Institute of Technology, Stockholm, Sweden

Reliable and affordable electricity supply is critical for any economy to function efficiently. While Europe has enjoyed a high degree of supply security over the last few decades, the utility industry has identified "liberalization and privatization" (which largely took place in the 1990s) and "renewable capacity expansion" (which forms an essential option for sustainable energy systems) as the two major trends that increase the risk of power outages [1,2]. The EU, which pursues a policy of increasing the share of renewable energy sources (RES) in national and regional generation mixes, must make additional efforts in order to maintain current levels of supply reliability.

The previous section on the impact of renewable energies on markets suggested that European regulation requests Member States to take appropriate grid- and market-related operational measures in order to maintain security of electricity supply. These may include grid adaptations as in the case of Germany [3] or performance-based regulation (PBR) for distribution system operators (DSOs) in the UK [4]. On the technical side, grid adaptations ensure that increasing amounts of variable RES can be absorbed by the power system. PBR represents a policy measure that creates an incentive for electrical utilities to improve their reliability levels.

Whatever measures are being taken, the current energy infrastructure in the concerned regions and countries will have to be strengthened to be able to accommodate growing shares of variable RES. In this section, we further expand on this topic by assessing how to define the appropriate level of security of supply and how system flexibility can contribute to achieving this level, as outlined in the following.

For a secure energy system, it is critical to maintain continuous service in the face of rapid and large swings in supply or demand. This ability is defined as "flexibility" in the context of the electricity system, and is the "extent to which a power system can adjust the balance of electricity production and consumption in response to variability, expected or otherwise."[a] Traditionally, power system flexibility was provided almost exclusively by controlling the supply side. In systems with increasing shares of variable RES, additional flexibility is needed to maintain system reliability. This is because they displace traditional, more flexible supply-side options and thus reduce the available flexibility within the system. In addition, their inherent stochastic nature simultaneously increases the need for flexibility. This has created a "flexibility gap." Chapter 21, Need for Flexibility and Potential Solutions, proposes flexibility options and associated business models in order to address this flexibility gap.

One of the most promising options to provide flexibility to the energy system is energy storage. It has increasingly come into focus as a key enabling technology in the energy system. Battery

---

[a]"Renewables Grid Integration and Variability", IEA, 2014.

Europe's Energy Transition. DOI: http://dx.doi.org/10.1016/B978-0-12-809806-6.00020-1

storage, for instance, could become a game-changer in the electricity industry. In recent years, there has been a significant shift towards the Li-ion battery technology for grid applications, not only for small-scale storage but also for large-scale application. Chapter 22, Storage Solutions and Their Value, investigates the role of storage in the energy system of the past, present, and future. Further, it seeks to identify the framework conditions likely to influence technology development, in particular the regulatory hurdles, market conditions, and environmental risks.

In the medium to long term, stationary fuel cell and hydrogen (FCH) technologies and applications are considered as potentially significant elements in energy systems with a high share of RES. Frequently discussed topics include the contribution of fuel cells and hydrogen to low-carbon heat and power generation, hydrogen production from variable renewables for seasonal or daily energy storage (power-to-hydrogen), and ancillary services from fuel cells and hydrogen for the electricity grid. Besides the gain in flexibility for the energy system, FCH technologies are associated with the mitigation of greenhouse gas emissions and local air pollution, high energy efficiency, reduction of fossil fuel dependency, and promotion of technology exports. Chapter 23, The Role of Fuel Cells and Hydrogen in Stationary Applications, evaluates the merits and the potential of stationary FCH applications on a technology as well as on an energy system level.

The level of flexibility required is closely linked to the level of reliability demanded from the power system. Currently, (future) power system design is often based on "traditional" approaches that are based on rules of thumb derived from experiences with the current system. These may be quantified by defining an acceptable loss of load probability (LOLP), which specifies the share of time when a generation shortfall may occur. Other design criteria are redundancy measures to ensure the system can cope with an outage in essential supply infrastructure (e.g., N−1 rule). Both approaches have in common that they do not build on quantifications of the impacts of interruptions on individual consumers or consumer categories. Thus, both approaches will not result in a socially optimal level of interruptions. A clear understanding of the socioeconomic costs of interruptions across the EU would be an important step to decide on such an optimal level. Chapter 24, Need for Reliability and Measuring its Cost, provides guidance on how to value the consequences of supply interruptions for consumers and thus determine the demand for electricity system reliability.

This section concludes with Chapter 25, providing a summary of the main findings and highlighting future research needs. It emphasizes the need to develop innovative business models that incentivize approaches like power-to-heat or power-to-gas and storage technologies.

REFERENCES

[1] M. Heddenhausen, Privatisations in Europe's liberalised electricity markets—the cases of the United Kingdom, Sweden, Germany, and France. Berlin, 2007.
[2] J. Percebois, Electricity liberalization in the European Union: balancing benefits and risks, Energy J. 29 (2008) 1−20.
[3] S. Pye, et al., Energy poverty and vulnerable consumers in the energy sector across the EU: analysis of policies and measures, INSIGHT_E, 2015.
[4] U.S. Energy Information Administration (EIA), Today in energy, March 4, 2013. Available from: <http://www.eia.gov/todayinenergy/detail.cfm?id = 10211>.

NEED FOR FLEXIBILITY AND POTENTIAL SOLUTIONS

Abhishek Shivakumar[1], Constantinos Taliotis[1], Paul Deane[2], Johann Gottschling[3], Rajesh Pattupara[4], Ramachandran Kannan[4], Dražen Jakšić[5], Karmen Stupin[5], Rudolf V. Hemert[5], Bo Normark[6], and Aurélie Faure-Schuyer[7]

[1]*KTH Royal Institute of Technology, Stockholm, Sweden* [2]*University College Cork (UCC), Cork, Ireland* [3]*University of Stuttgart, Stuttgart, Germany* [4]*Paul Scherrer Institute, Villigen, Switzerland* [5]*Energy Institute Hrvoje Požar (EIHP), Zagreb, Croatia* [6]*InnoEnergy Scandinavia, Stockholm, Sweden* [7]*Institut Français des Relations Internationales (IFRI), Brussels, Belgium*

A flexible system would be able to, among other things, absorb high shares of renewable energies, allow for power produced by end-users to be fed into the grid, reliably adjust to sudden changes in load, and maintain affordable prices for end-users. This chapter explores the challenges that the EC faces in its transition to a more flexible energy system and proposes potential solutions. The solutions include an analysis of mechanisms (policy or market-based) that can support such a transition. In this chapter, we highlight the importance of quantifying, valuing, and appropriately incentivizing flexibility options. In light of past and current experiences, we review the future need for flexibility (amount of energy, power needed, time scales) in the future, at a time horizon out to 2030 and 2050. This aspect of the chapter based its analyses on modeling exercises, and considers potential solutions. We supplement our modeling study with an analysis of current regulation around flexibility and storage through national case studies.

21.1 TRADITIONAL ENERGY SYSTEM REQUIREMENTS: A FOCUS ON TIMES BEFORE MARKET LIBERALIZATION

Prior to the liberalization process of Europe's energy markets, which began in the early 1990s, national electricity supplies were mostly provided by a few, often vertically integrated, companies holding a legal monopoly on the entire value chain. Hence, the production, transmission, and distribution of electricity were granted to single companies. According to the predominant view in most EU Member States, it was evident that competition was not suitable due to the macroeconomic importance, the technical complexity, and the capital-intensive nature of facilities in the electricity sector [1]. Electricity tariffs were generally fixed and revisited by the governments to enable cost recovery of investments in and operation of the grid and power plant portfolio[a] [3].

---

[a]However, even today the liberalization process is far from being complete in a number of Member States. Ref. [2] captures an overview of the current situation in Europe. The report indicates that in 2013, 19 out of the 28 Member States back then (including the UK) had begun the liberalization process in the electricity market, while 20 Member States had begun liberalization in the gas market.

Europe's Energy Transition. DOI: http://dx.doi.org/10.1016/B978-0-12-809806-6.00021-3

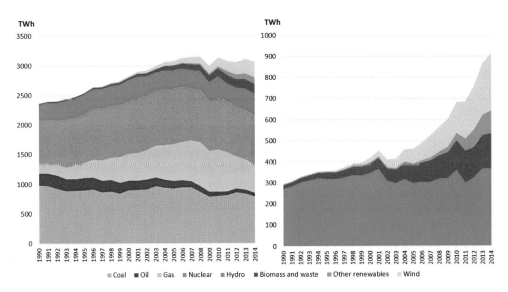

FIGURE 21.1

Gross electricity generation by fuel in the EU 1990−2008. The figure on the right represents an enlargement of only the renewable sources from the figure presented on the left.

In view of the above, power suppliers invested in power plant portfolios to meet the demand anticipated for all consumers in the supply region both securely and economically, taking into consideration legal and technical restrictions and the availability of fuels. According to Fig. 21.1, the demand for electricity in Europe in the early 1990s was predominantly met by coal (including lignite) and nuclear power plants. Electricity generation from renewables was almost exclusively provided by hydro power plants.

Since the share of volatile feed-in from renewables was negligible, the need for flexibility[b] was mainly related to the typical load patterns of residential, commercial, and/or industrial power consumers. In this regard, fluctuations over the day, during the week, and on a seasonal basis are observable within an electrical power system. Peak demand usually occurs during day-time and off-peak demand during the night-time, when domestic or commercial consumption is lower. Irregular events such as televised events or extreme weather can also lead to irregular changes in demand. During the week, the demand on weekdays generally exceeds the demand on weekends due to the share of commercial activities. Seasonal variations occur due to a generally higher demand in Europe in winter than in summer.

As indicated by Fig. 21.2, the residential, commercial, and industrial sectors show different consumption patterns. The largest variations in consumption can be observed in the residential sector with the highest share of electricity used for cooling and heating purposes compared with the other

---

[b]"Flexibility is the ability of a power system to maintain continuous service in the face of rapid and large swings in supply or demand [4]."

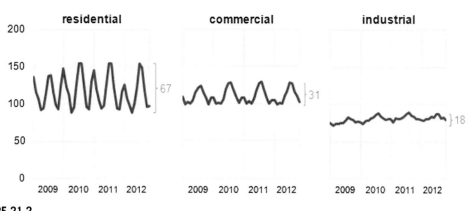

FIGURE 21.2

Retail sales of electricity by end-use sector in billion kilowatt-hours in the US [5].

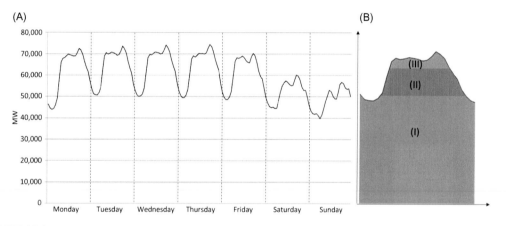

FIGURE 21.3

(A) Hourly load curve of a sample European country during 1 week in winter. (B) Example of a hourly load curve on a weekday: base load (I), intermediate load (II), peak load (III).

From (A) Data provided by ENTSO-E and (B) diagram by author.

sectors. The industrial sector experiences little variability in electricity use. Within industry, economic variables as well as technical operating conditions of heavy industries affect industrial energy use more than weather-related factors [6].

Regardless of the season, there is a surge in demand in the morning when domestic consumers start using electrical appliances or industrial companies begin operation (see Fig. 21.3). In the course of the morning demand stabilizes when shops open and electrical equipment, such as computers, is powered. Later in the day another surge occurs when the working day is over and people start to return home and switch on electrical equipment. In the course of the evening demand decreases to a minimum as people begin to retire to bed.

Table 21.1 Flexibility of Conventional Power-Generating Technologies [7]

	NPP	HC	LIGN	CCG	PS
Start-up time "cold"	~40 h	~6 h	~10 h	<2 h	~0,1 h
Start-up time "warm"	~40 h	~3 h	~6 h	<1,5 h	~0,1 h
Load gradient ↗ "nominal output"	~5%/M	~2%/M	~2%/M	~4%/M	>40%/M
Load gradient ↘ "nominal output"	~5%/M	~2%/M	~2%/M	~4%/M	>40%/M
Minimal possible load	50%	40%	40%	<50%	~15%

Power generators endeavor to balance the load plus losses throughout the grid and schedule the operation of all units in their power plant portfolio at any time in order to minimize the overall cost of electricity generation. Following the schematic representation in Fig. 21.3B three types of power plants can be considered according to their flexibility and cost-optimal dispatch: base load, intermediate, and peak load power plants.

Table 21.1 presents an overview of the flexibility of the following conventional power-generating technologies: nuclear (NPP), hard coal (HC), lignite (LIGN), combined cycle gas (CCG), and pumped hydro storage (PS).

BASE LOAD

Base load units are designed to operate for long periods of time at or near full load, as they have low operation costs due to their use of low-cost fuels. They supply the basic demand in the network. This plant type is not designed to respond to major shifts in output. A shutdown is only executed in case of forced outages and maintenance. For example, lignite, run-of-river, or nuclear power plants are usually operated as base load power plants. Although technically suitable to perform load-following operations (as indicated in Table 21.1), the start-up times of lignite and nuclear power plants are prohibitive to a more flexible operation, as they may take from several hours up to nearly 2 days [5].

As shown in Fig. 21.4, the EU's electricity (base load) generation in 1990 was largely based on nuclear power plants and lignite power plants, subject to fuel availability. For example, the annual full load hours of nuclear power plants ranged from nearly 5200 in the UK up to almost 7800 in Belgium. Power generation from lignite was considerable, particularly in Germany, reaching more than 6600 full load hours [8].

INTERMEDIATE LOAD

Demand in excess of the base load requires the use of further and more flexible capacities. Power plants in the range of intermediate load start up in the morning to meet the surge in demand and shut down in the evening when demand begins to fall again to the base load level [9]. Usually HC and CCG units are used to meet the intermediate load. These power plant types are designed for frequent partial-load operations and daily start up and shutdown routines [10].

As shown in Table 21.1, HC and CCG units can be brought online more quickly and can additionally quickly dispose of loads at gradients of up to 2%/min. As illustrated by Fig. 21.4, HC power was of high importance for intermediate load generation, particularly in Denmark and the

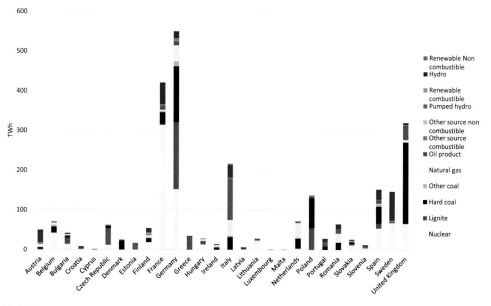

FIGURE 21.4

Gross electricity generation by fuel in 1990 in the EU-28.

From authors' own representation based on data from Eurostat.

UK, amounting to annual capacity factors of 49% and 59%, respectively [8]. The generation from HC in Denmark in 1990 accounted for more than 90% of total power generation, indicating that HC power plants were also deployed for base load generation [7].

PEAK LOAD

Peak load units are necessary to cover sudden peaks in demand that occur at specific, generally predictable hours of a given period (i.e., the peak load in the evening, when consumers simultaneously switch on electrical equipment). In addition, peak load units provide ancillary services[c] and flexibility to the power system in case of forced power plant outages or sudden and unexpected rises in demand. Gas- and oil-fired turbines, reciprocating engines, and storage units comprise the majority of peak load power plants, as they are able to start up from a cold condition within minutes and show higher responsiveness than intermediate load power plants [5].

As shown by Fig. 21.4 almost every country in the EU-28 operated gas- and/or oil-fired generation plants in 1990, providing peak power and flexibility to the power system. For example, electricity generation from natural gas accounted for more than 50% in the Netherlands. Natural gas

---

[c]"Ancillary services" is used to refer to a variety of operations beyond generation and transmission that are required to maintain grid stability and security. These services generally include frequency control, spinning reserves, and operating reserves.

power stations ran on average nearly 3500 full load hours in 1990. As with coal in Denmark, the high share of oil-based power generation in many countries in 1990 (Cyprus: 100%; Estonia: 94%; Italy: 47%) indicates that oil was also used for intermediate load generation [7,8].

21.2 INCREASING PENETRATION OF VARIABLE RENEWABLES IN THE EU

Since then, the liberalization of European electricity markets resulted in a changing operational environment, requiring a more flexible operation also from traditional base load plants, such as nuclear power. This is especially due to new regulatory policies for electricity generation from renewable energy sources (RES), which appeared on the political agenda in most EU Member States as well as on the EU level. In particular, the European Commission has strongly encouraged ambitious targets and support schemes for large-scale market penetration of renewable energies [11].

Between 1990 and 2013, total electricity generation from RES increased by 177%. The most significant growth has been in distributed variable RES (primarily generation from solar and wind). In 2013, electricity generation from RES in the EU-28 reached 854 TWh, 37% of which was from wind and solar power. The quantity of electricity generated from wind turbines has more than tripled in the period between 2005 and 2013. Solar power generation has grown considerably and increased 55-fold in the same period. As illustrated by Fig. 21.5, significant amounts of wind and solar generation needed to be integrated into Europe's electricity system, especially in Germany, Spain, Italy, and the UK.

Due to uncertain weather conditions, the amount of wind and solar power in the system cannot be predicted with certainty. In fact, the generation is subject to daily and seasonal fluctuations.

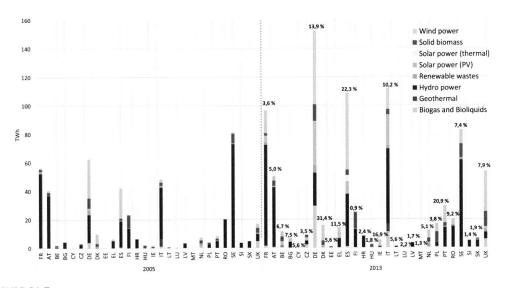

FIGURE 21.5

Gross electricity generation from renewable sources in the EU-28 by country and share of variable generation (solar and wind) in gross electricity consumption.

From authors' own representation on the basis of data from [12].

Consequently, in addition to demand-driven fluctuations due to consumer behavior the growing amount of variable RES has led to generation-driven fluctuations. This increases the challenge of keeping the electricity system in constant balance and thus the need for adequate infrastructure to integrate the varying outputs. As long as the share of variable RES in a power system is low the system can operate as usual [13]: When the share of variable RES is lower than 15%−20% of the overall electricity consumption, the grid operators can usually compensate the variability introduced by renewables without any additional investments. However, the large growth of RES has led to a situation where the generation share exceeds 20%−25% at times, a situation that some European countries are facing today, such as Denmark, Spain, and Germany [14].

Fig. 21.6 illustrates such a situation, presenting hourly load and renewable generation in Germany from March to April 2015. The share of wind and solar generation in total electricity consumption exceeded at least 30% in 442 hours and 50% in 92 hours during that time period. At times, a share above 65% was reached. In contrast, for more than 100 hours, wind and solar generation contributed less than 5%, requiring the remainder of the power generation portfolio to meet the demand. As a result, the residual load (the difference between load and variable RES feed-in) was subject to considerable fluctuations. The maximum increase in hourly load from 1 hour to another during the considered period was 18%, which was reasonably foreseeable due to a regular surge in demand. However, the morning fluctuations of the hourly residual load were significantly higher due to less accurately predicted feed-in from wind turbines and PV systems. A maximum value of more than 35% was reached, corresponding to a power request of nearly 10 GW within 1 hour. As shown in Table 21.2

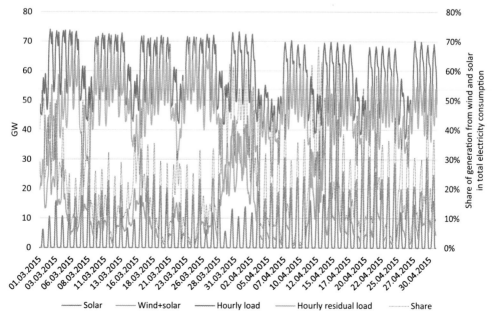

FIGURE 21.6

Hourly load, wind and solar generation in Germany.

From authors' own representation based on data from [15−19].

Table 21.2 Short-Term Variations of Large-Scale Regional Wind Power, as Percent of Installed Wind Power Capacity, for Different Time Scales and Regions [20]

Region	Region Size (km²)	Number of Sites	10–15 min		1 h		4 h		12 h	
			Max Decrease (%)	Max Increase (%)	Max Decrease (%)	Max Increase (%)	Max Decrease (%)	Max Increase (%)	Max Decrease (%)	Max Increase (%)
Denmark West	300 × 300	>100			−23	+20	−62	+53	−74	+79
Denmark East	200 × 200	>100			−26	+20	−70	+57	−74	+84
Denmark	200 × 200	>100			−25	+36	−65	+72	−74	+72
Ireland	280 × 480	11	−12	+12	−30	+30	−50	+50	−70	+70
Portugal	300 × 800	29	−12	+12	−16	+13	−34	+23	−52	+43
Germany	400 × 400	>100	−6	+6	−17	+12	−40	+27		
Finland	400 × 900	30			−16	+16	−41	+40	−66	+59
Sweden	400 × 900	56			−17	+19	−40	+40		

other countries in Europe are facing similar challenges; regional fluctuations from wind power can reach considerable sizes, especially in Denmark and Ireland.

Generally, the coincidence of increasing generation from variable RES and reducing demand, for example at the beginning of a weekend, and the opposite at the beginning of the week, can lead to extreme power ramps. This imposes new requirements for dispatchable generation [13]. It underlines that in addition to continual improvements of the accuracy of forecasts, more flexibility and back-up resources are necessary to cope with an increasing share of nondispatchable RES in the EU energy mix. All flexibility sources need to be assessed in terms of their ability to integrate RES volatility and optimize the energy system with regard to security of supply and affordability. The role of storage and flexible generation must be reconsidered in this context.

21.3 TECHNOLOGY OPTIONS TO PROVIDE FLEXIBILITY

At present, a range of flexibility options are available to regulators and system operators. These options can be classified as operational (e.g., cycling thermal fleets, forecast integration), institutional (e.g., new market designs, integration of demand response), or physical (e.g., storage, transmission). Figs. 21.7 and 21.8 together give a schematic overview of available technology options – both physical and operational - to meet the growing need for flexibility in electricity markets. A comprehensive summary of other flexibility options is provided by NREL [REFERENCE: J. Cochran, M. Miller, O. Zinaman, M. Milligan, D. Arent, B. Palmintier, M. O'Malley, S. Mueller,

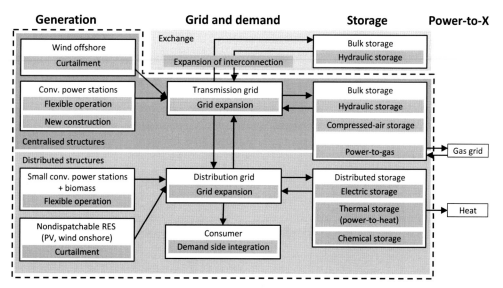

FIGURE 21.7

Flexibility options in the electricity market [37].

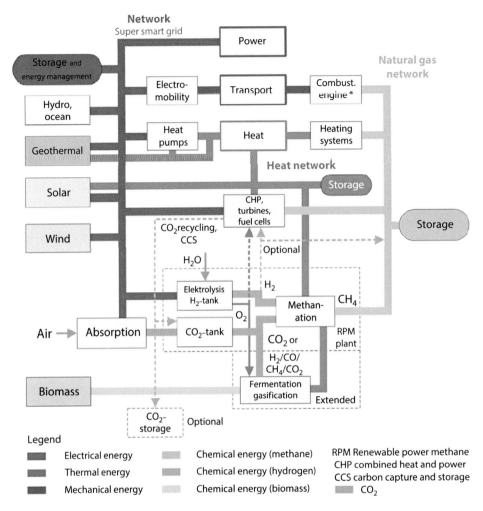

FIGURE 21.8

Conceivable design of an integrated energy network system. From Sterner, Bioenergy and renewable power methane in integrated 100% renewable energy systems, Dissertation, University of Kassel, 2009 [38]; L. Brodecki, J. Tomaschek, U. Fahl, Synergies in the integration of energy networks for electricity, gas, heating and cooling. INSIGHT_E Rapid Response Energy Brief, 2014 [39].

E. Lannoye, A. Tuohy, B. Kujala, M. Sommer, H. Holttinen, J. Kiviluoma and S. Soonee, "Flexibility in 21st Century Power Systems," National Renewable Energy Laboratory, 2014].

Flexibility options in power supply include dispatchable centralized and distributed power generation, but also variable RES, as controlled curtailment plays a role in meeting power system flexibility. Further, consumers willing to shift their power demand in favor of network requirements can provide additional flexibility, taking advantage of new applications in communication and control that enable two-way communication. In addition to the suitability of energy storage facilities to provide peak energy and balancing to the grid, energy storage helps to remove electricity from the system in times of oversupply from variable RES. This electricity is then available for subsequent use in periods of undersupply (temporal compensation).

The expansion and modernization of power transmission and distribution networks are "key enablers of flexibility" in the system. They allow for the compensation of over- and undersupply between regions, thereby alleviating local network congestion (spatial compensation). Furthermore, increasing the capacity of network lines can provide access to spatially distributed flexibility resources [4]. In addition, cross-sectoral storage is a further option to deal with fluctuating input by using power-to-X technologies—for example by coupling the electricity and heating sectors in the form of heat accumulators (power-to-heat). Accordingly, further cross-sectoral technologies such as power-to-gas and power-to-mobility (electric vehicles) in the transport and chemical sectors could in the future enable additional flexibility for the electricity system [21].

The preferable flexibility options depend on he considered operational timeframe. Fig. 21.9 gives a summary of the suitability of different flexibility options, highlighting the major constraints

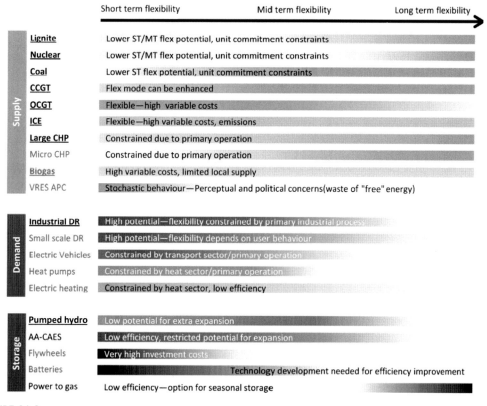

FIGURE 21.9

Comparative assessment of the characteristics of flexibility options in different operational timeframes (*Red* (light gray in print versions): small-scale distributed technologies; Bold, underlined: mature technologies) [4].

for their deployment subject to operational timeframes: *short-term* flexibility (up to 1 hour), *mid-term* flexibility (up to days), and *long-term* flexibility (seasonal variations).

The most mature options are on the supply side. Particularly open cycle gas turbines (OCGT) and internal combustion engines (ICE) can provide short-term flexibility. Cold start times and ramping capabilities are limiting factors to the suitability of other plant types (see Table 21.1). The main options for mid-term flexibility on the supply side are flexible coal, gas-fired (OCGT and CCGT), and ICE plants.

In the short term, electricity storage, or more specifically pumped hydro storage facilities, fill the generation gap in times when wind and solar power decreases and other plants are just being ramped up [14]. As shown in Fig. 21.11, Germany, together with Spain and Italy, operate pumped-storage facilities exceeding 5000 MW. Further flexible capacities amounting to 3 GW come from Luxembourg and Austria, but are directly connected to the German transmission network [23]. Besides Germany, seven countries in Europe have obtained licenses to build new pumped storage power plants. Altogether, additional storage capacities of 1700 MW are planned in the EU, while additional capacities of 194 MW are in an early planning stage (no license yet) [24].

On the demand side, large-scale industrial demand response (DR) is a mature option to provide short- and mid-term flexibility. Small-scale applications would require a suitable IT infrastructure and need to address the associated challenges regarding data management.

21.4 CASE STUDIES
GERMANY

The spread between the maximum and minimum values of the residual load is one indicator for the flexibility needed in a power system. The gradient of the hourly load change is another. In Germany, the residual load varied between 18 and 77 GW in 2013. In the same year hourly load changes of up to +15 GW and −10 GW occurred [25].

Despite recent expansions of the interconnection capacities between Germany and its neighboring countries, load adjustments via exports and imports of electricity are only possible to a limited extent. This is due to the similar characteristics of variable RES production and consumption behavior within the neighboring countries.

The flexibility needed in the German power system is currently provided widely by the domestic power generation portfolio. Since many of the existing thermal power plants were constructed in the 1980s and 1990s before variable generation from wind and solar became significant, measures had to be taken to improve their flexibility. Today, base load power plants incapable of flexible operation are barely represented in the overall electricity generation mix, and recently built power plants are designed from the onset for flexible operation. Fig. 21.10 illustrates a situation in the recent past where due to a regular surge in demand in the morning and a simultaneous decrease of wind supply a large requirement for additional dispatchable capacity occurred, amounting to 45 GW within 8 hours. The gap was almost completely closed by coal (including lignite) and gas power plants. Lignite and coal power plants provided nearly 75% of the flexibility needed. Nuclear

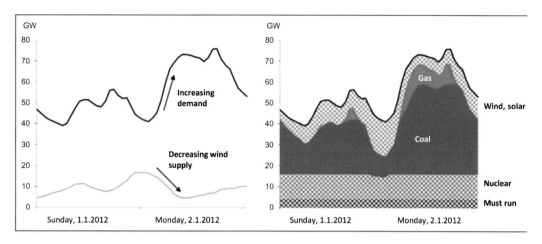

FIGURE 21.10

Electricity demand, wind supply, and unit commitment in Germany on January 1, 2012 [22].

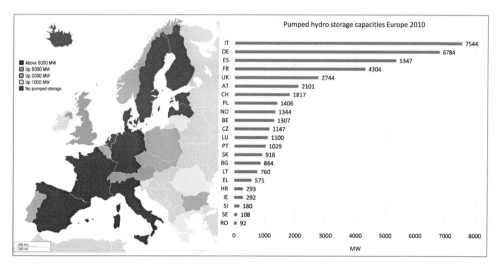

FIGURE 21.11

Pumped hydro storage capacity in Europe in 2010 [26].

From authors' own representation based on data from [27].

power plants can also operate flexibly within certain limits (see Table 21.1), but are ramped only if flexibility reserves from fossil fuel generation are already exploited [22].

SCANDINAVIA

Sweden, Norway, Finland, and Denmark are integrated in a well-functioning electricity market (Nord Pool) and also have well-established cross-border cooperation mechanisms between TSOs. More than half of the annual power generation is from hydro power, 20% from nuclear, 15% from fossil fuel-fired generation, and the rest from other sources. In addition to the pumped storage capacities available in Norway (refer to Fig. 21.11), Scandinavia has considerable reservoir storage capacities at its disposal—more than one-third of the annual generation capability. The largest share of those is situated in Norway and Sweden (85 TWh in Norway and 34 TWh in Sweden). They are designed to balance seasonal imbalances of the hydro inflow (which can vary substantially between years) and the load, and provide a large flexibility up to long timescales.

Supported by a few pumped hydro storage facilities, balancing needs are currently fulfilled by the existing hydro plants enabling both downward and upward regulating capacity. Short-term deviations are balanced via energy trade taking advantage of the interconnections in Scandinavia and to other countries.

In 2014, a 240-km cable was installed across the Skagerrak Strait separating southern Norway and northern Denmark. Skagerrak 4 (as it is called) uses high-voltage direct current (HVDC) converters at either end of the cable to transform AC into high-voltage DC and vice versa. This cable represents the starting point for more ambitious projects from Norway to other Member States—especially those with significant amounts of wind power—such as Germany and the United Kingdom. With some modifications, existing hydropower reservoirs in Norway could transfer, bidirectionally, about 25 GW of stored energy without significant environmental implications—that is five times current levels. This can be done by installing pumps to shift water between neighboring reservoirs.

The existing Skagerrak 4 cable demonstrates the synergy between wind power in Denmark and hydropower storage in Norway. This is evidenced by the fact that Denmark is able to absorb the world's highest levels of wind power penetration in recent years—41.2% of Denmark's electricity demand in the first half of 2014.[d] At times wind power production is even surplus to the country's domestic electricity demand.

Due to these various flexibility options along with a large flexible generation fleet, the Nordic system is capable of withstanding large demand- and generation-driven fluctuations and sudden disturbances in both transmission and generating units [13].

CYPRUS

Cyprus operates an isolated power system and relies fully on imported fuels for electricity generation. Up to 2010 the electricity generation portfolio included three conventional power plants with a total capacity of 1438 MW, fired mainly by heavy fuel oils (92% of the energy mix) and gasoil [28]. Power supply from RES was not significant (PV: 6 MW; biomass: 7 MW [28]), until the

---

[d]Source: http://spectrum.ieee.org/green-tech/wind/norway-wants-to-be-europes-battery

installation of the first wind farm in 2010 with a capacity of 82 MW. Meanwhile, the installed capacity increased up to 147 MW in 2014.[e]

In contrast to large interconnected power systems, frequency control in isolated systems is a significant concern in daily operation. Large frequency deviations due to sudden changes in variable generation and/or transmission outages must be balanced immediately to preserve security of supply. With the influence of variable feed-in from RES, the requirements in this regard have increased [29].

As Cyprus currently neither has energy storage nor demand-side flexibility options, all flexibility must be provided by conventional generation and RES curtailment [30]. However, a case study for Cyprus' power system revealed that the currently available reserve is not capable of balancing the real-time fluctuation of wind, leading to frequent curtailment. Higher shares of variable energy would further constrain the ramping capability of the conventional power plants due to part loading of generators [31]. Consequently, the system will not be able to integrate wind power without high levels of real-time wind curtailment or demand shedding [32], and compensating larger outages may be beyond the systems capability (refer to Section 24.4 on the outage occurring in July 2011).

However, although Cyprus currently operates no energy storage, future pumped storage capacities have already been licenced, and additional projects are at an early planning stage (no license yet). These additional projects combine a total installed capacity of 190 MW, which is planned to be able to operate 11 hours at full load [24].

21.5 FUTURE NEED FOR FLEXIBILITY

To assess the role of electricity storage in the medium and long term, a set of long-term, low-carbon electricity supply options were analyzed for Europe. A multiregional cost-optimization model was used to generate insights on future electricity supply options under given policy constraints. The model, called European Swiss TIMES[f] Electricity Model[g] (EUSTEM), has 11 regions encompassing 20 of the EU-28 countries (plus Switzerland and Norway, see Fig. 21.12). The EUSTEM model covers 96% of the total electricity generation and 90% of the total installed capacity of the EU-28 + Switzerland and Norway in 2014 [33]. It should be noted that EUSTEM is an electricity system model, i.e., there is no representation of heating or transport sectors. As such, the focus of this analysis is to generate insights on the need for electricity storage.

EUSTEM identifies the "least-cost" combination of technologies and fuel mixes to satisfy exogenously given electricity demands under a given set of constraints and based on the operational characteristics of these technologies. The framework allows for prospective analysis over

---

[e]Source: http://www.thewindpower.net

[f]The Integrated MARKAL/EFOM System (TIMES) framework is a perfect foresight, technology-rich, cost optimization modeling framework (Loulou, 2005).

[g]It is worth noting that EUSTEM is an extension to the existing five regions Cross border Swiss TIMES electricity model (CROSSTEM) (see Ref. [36]).

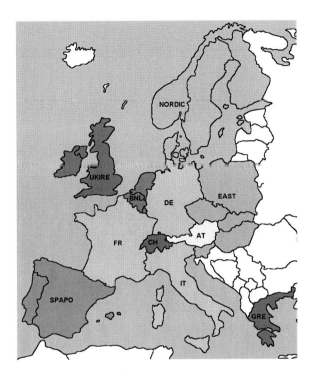

FIGURE 21.12

EUSTEM regions.

a long model horizon (70 + years) while at the same time being able to represent a high level of intra-annual detail in demand and supply (e.g., electricity load curves). It also has an enhanced storage algorithm, enabling the modeling of electricity storage systems [34]. It should be noted that DR management and electricity efficiency improvements are not explicitly represented, with demand-side measures expected to be captured in the assumed electricity demand growth rate.

EUSTEM is used to generate insights on possible electricity supply pathways to decarbonize the EU electricity sector by 2050, similar to the EU Roadmap to 2050 [35]. The model identifies the long-term capacity expansion plans to meet the given policy targets.

SCENARIOS

Two scenarios have been analyzed. The first scenario represents a least-cost electricity supply option, which is used as a baseline for comparison. The focus of the assessment is however on a decarbonization scenario of the EU electricity system, which highlights the importance of electricity storage in a highly renewables-based electricity generation system.

Least-Cost Scenario (LC)

This scenario presents a least-cost electricity supply pathway without reflecting foreseeable market changes due to climate change mitigation policies or renewable targets. In this scenario, no specific constraints on technologies are included, except the existing national policies on phasing out nuclear power. Technology growth constraints have been applied on certain technologies such as coal, wind, and solar PV based on historical trends to reflect practical limits to the deployment. This was done to prevent unrealistic penetrations of these technologies. A CO_2 price is implemented based on the EU ETS prices from the "New Energy Policy" scenario of the IEA World Energy Outlook [37]. The CO_2 price varies between 11 $€_{2010}$/t-CO_2 in 2010 and 44 $€_{2010}$/t-CO_2 in 2050 and is very close to the assumptions in the reference scenario of the EU Energy Roadmap [20]. There are no market incentive tools (such as feed-in tariffs) applied for the case study. No particular market or interconnector constraints are applied on electricity imports and exports between regions, i.e., the model has full freedom to trade electricity and expand the cross-border interconnector capacities.

Decarbonization Scenario (CO_2)

The decarbonization scenario has the same boundary conditions as the *least-cost* scenario, with an additional CO_2 emissions cap to decarbonize the EU electricity sector by 2050. The total CO_2 emissions from the power sector across the regions are reduced by 61% of the 1990 levels by 2030, and 95% by 2050. These emission caps are in line with the CO_2 emissions targets in the EU energy roadmap to 2050 [20].

RESULTS

In this section, results are presented for Germany, France, and Italy. France and Italy have substantial flexible hydro systems which can be used to balance and store electricity. Germany on the other hand has limited pumped hydro storage potential, thereby enabling a contrasting outlook compared to France and Italy.

The model generates a wide range of outputs such as installed capacity, generation mix, hourly long-run marginal cost, capital cost, etc. In this section, we limit the discussion of results to the costs of the capacity expansions and the installed capacities. These are inputs to our dispatch model that was used in Section 22.5 for an evaluation of the value of storage systems.

Capacity Expansion

Fig. 21.13 shows the total installed capacity of Germany in the decarbonization scenario for the period 2030−50, as well as for the base year 2010. Results from the least-cost scenario are also shown to illustrate the technology preferences of the model in the absence of any climate change mitigation targets. Although such a least-cost scenario is highly unlikely, it is presented as a basis to understand the cost-optimization framework.

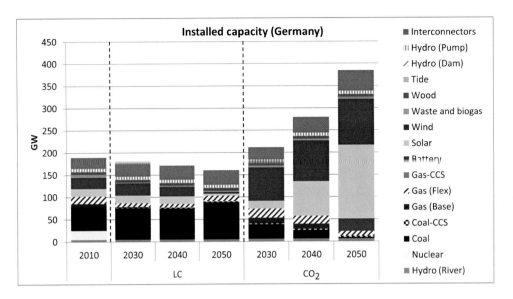

FIGURE 21.13

Electricity capacity expansion (Germany).

Results from the least-cost scenario show that in the absence of nuclear-based generation and any long-term renewable incentive schemes (like feed-in tariffs), coal power plants (especially using the lignite available in Germany) would become the most cost-effective option, performing better than renewable technologies such as wind and solar PV. This can be seen by the phase-out of existing wind and solar PV technologies by 2050.

Although wind and solar PV technologies become much cheaper towards 2050, there are several other factors that lead to this generation mix. In this scenario, for example, Germany invests considerably in cheap lignite technology and exports excess base-load electricity to neighboring countries that lack the availability of such baseload options (e.g., in the year 2050, around 50 TWh of electricity is exported by Germany to neighboring regions, mainly Switzerland and BENELUX (see Fig. 21.12 for EUSTEM regions)). Such a situation may seem unrealistic, but from a purely cost-optimal point of view, in a single market model, there would be no reason for Germany to invest in renewables to meet its electricity demand if it can export excess baseload electricity and generate more revenue, thereby decreasing its overall system costs.

However, the total share of renewables for all of the EUSTEM regions increases from 13% of the total demand in 2010 to 27% in 2050. This can either be due to other constraints preventing the investments in fossil-fuel technologies (see Fig. 21.14 for the situation in France, where growth constraints on nuclear and coal-fired power plants were applied) or due to better performances of renewables depending on geographical locations (see solar PV investments in Fig. 21.15 for the situation in Italy). The large base-load generation from coal plants within the overall EUSTEM regions is supplemented by dispatchable gas and hydro plants to provide sufficient flexibility for the system.

In the decarbonization scenario (CO_2), coal-based generation in Germany is gradually replaced by wind and solar PV, supplemented by flexible gas and electricity imports. The share of renewable

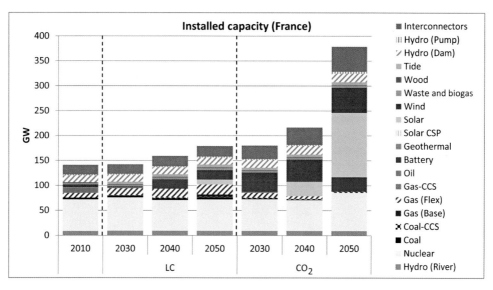

FIGURE 21.14

Electricity capacity expansion (France).

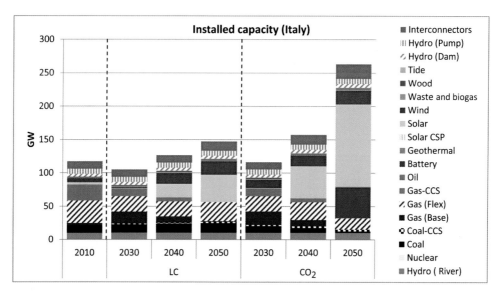

FIGURE 21.15

Electricity capacity expansion (Italy).

capacities increases from 35% in 2010 to 76% by 2050. In order to balance the variable generation from renewables, around 27 GW of battery storage is invested in by 2050 in addition to the existing 7 GW of pumped hydro storage available in Germany. This installed storage capacity amounts to around 9% of the total installed capacity. Additional flexibility is provided by dispatchable gas plants, which account for approximately 3% of the total installed capacity. Finally, there is a large expansion in interconnector capacities, which increases by around 84% between 2010 and 2050. The majority of the expansion occurs between the NORDIC and BENELUX regions due to their high renewable and carbon capture and storage (CCS) potentials. Results indicate that in order to meet stringent CO_2 emissions targets, it would be cost-optimal for Germany to become a net importer of electricity (around 20% of the final electricity demand is imported in 2050).

Fig. 21.14 shows the installed capacity in France. It was assumed that France keeps its nuclear generation at today's level (in energy terms[h]). In the least-cost scenario, a steady increase in wind and solar PV technologies can be observed, especially by 2040 and 2050. This is attributed to the growth constraints applied on nuclear and coal expansion. Hence, in order to meet the increasing electricity demand, renewable generation is competitive compared to gas-based generation, although some investments in flexible gas plants are still made to add flexibility to the electricity system. This is an apt example of an external constraint (i.e., the growth constraints on nuclear and coal) influencing decisions in a cost-optimization model (in contrast to the German case discussed previously).

In the decarbonization scenario, France has a slightly higher nuclear capacity by 2050. This higher capacity is used at lowered annual load factors to account for seasonal variabilities introduced by the high share of renewables. Solar PV and wind capacities expand considerably by 2050 and account for around 48% of the total installed capacity. The stringent CO_2 emissions cap makes investments in gas and coal plants unattractive in this scenario, thereby resulting in these higher penetrations of renewable technologies. Battery and pumped hydro storage account for almost 9% of the total installed capacity (as was the case with Germany), despite the availability of dam hydro power (5% of the total installed capacity), which also provides flexible generation. Interconnectors are also significantly expanded (from 20 GW to almost 50 GW), primarily to facilitate low-carbon nuclear electricity exports to Italy, Switzerland, Germany, and the UK.

Fig. 21.15 shows the installed capacity of Italy. In the least-cost scenario, solar PV and wind technologies already occupy a share of 46% of the total installed capacity by 2050. In this case, base-load electricity is obtained from coal-based generation and electricity imports from EAST (see Fig. 21.12 for EUSTEM regions) and France. The model prefers solar PV technologies, whose profile follows the electricity peak load at noon (see load curve diagram in Ref. [31]), with flexible gas and hydro power plants filling any gaps. This is in strong contrast with France, where renewable investments were made due to the inability to expand its baseload option; and Germany, where renewable technologies were phased-out by 2050 in favor of coal-based baseload generation.

For Italy, results for the decarbonization scenario (CO_2) closely resemble its least-cost solution (*LC*) until the year 2040. Afterwards, there is a significant increase in solar PV installations, making up almost 47% of the total installed capacity (which rises to 55% when including wind).

---

[h]Based on France's announcement to restrict production from nuclear power to 50% of the total electricity generation by 2025. Commonly, energy policies rather focus on limitations on investments in new capacities, which is also a component of the French policy.

Battery and pumped storage account for more than 20% of the total capacity, significantly higher than in France and Germany. This is explained by the much higher share of solar power in the generation mix of Italy compared to Germany, where wind-power dominates over solar PV generation. Interconnectors with neighboring regions are almost doubled, with Italy still remaining a net importer of electricity (around 14% of the demand in 2050 is covered by electricity imports, primarily from France).

Based on the results discussed above, the penetration of new storage technologies, such as batteries, occurs only towards the end of the time horizon, i.e., by the year 2050. This is attributed to two main reasons, namely the increasing share of variable renewables and the cost reduction of storage technologies. For example, in Italy, the share of solar PV and wind power is around 27% of the total electricity generation in the year 2040, which increases to 55% by 2050. Concurrently, the share of flexible generation technologies such as gas plants, which help in balancing the system, is reduced from 36% in 2040 to 18% in 2050, mainly due to the stringent CO_2 emissions cap. Hence the increasing share of variable generation and decrease in flexible backup technologies coupled with the reduction in technology costs makes investments in battery technologies cost effective by the year 2050. This conclusion is valid for the other regions as well, where similar trends are observed.

Cost of Capacity Expansion

One of the key outputs of EUSTEM is the total system costs and the composition of capital investment costs. Fig. 21.16 shows the capital investments required in Germany. The cumulative investment required in the least-cost scenario between 2018 and 2050 is around €232 billion.[i] On the other hand, the investment costs in the decarbonization scenario for the period 2046−55 alone are close to €350 billion. In total, the cost of decarbonizing the electricity system of Germany incurs an additional capital cost of almost €450 billion between 2018 and 2050. The cost of investing in battery storage, which primarily occurs during 2046−55, is approximately €40 billion, i.e., €4 billion per year in that period. The revenue generated by battery electricity storage must be able to cover these investment costs. Investment costs for France and Italy are summarized in Table 21.3.

21.6 CONCLUDING THOUGHTS

In this chapter, we discussed the growing importance of flexibility in the EU energy system. At present, there exist several technology options to provide this flexibility, from storage to demand-side management. We highlight the importance of quantifying, valuing, and appropriately incentivizing these flexibility options. The analysis of the present situation highlighted that EU energy policy is mostly based on characteristics of existing generation assets (fossil fuel, nuclear, and hydro), their ramping dynamics, and start-up costs. So far, flexibility has been provided from the generation supply side, and not the demand side. Accordingly, systems are designed to provide sufficient flexibility to supply the highest demand (peak demand) on the grid—within reliability limits. However,

---

[i]Currency conversion: 1 €2010 = 1.32 CHF2010 (XE (2014)), Current and Historical Rate Tables, http://www.xe.com/currencytables/

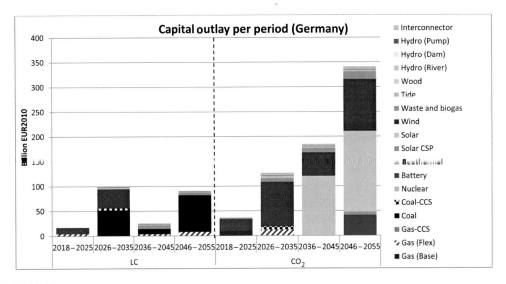

FIGURE 21.16

Investment costs per period (Germany).

Table 21.3 Capital Cost Comparison

Key Cost Parameters (billion EUR2010)	Germany	France	Italy
Total cumulative cost 2018–50 (least cost)	232	383	211
Total cumulative cost 2018–50 (CO_2)	684	798	447
Cost of decarbonizing electricity sector	450	415	236
Cost of battery storage (for period 2046–55) (CO_2)	40	43	68

building on the Energy Efficiency Directive, a future integration of demand-side storage options into the grid may enable a diversion from such previous design criteria. It may allow drawing on the most efficient flexibility options across the entire system, from demand to supply.

Chapter 22 on "Storage Solutions and Their Value" considers the benefits of storage in the energy system, including the provision of flexibility. It provides a techno-economic perspective on different storage technologies and their potential role in the EU energy system.

REFERENCES

[1] M. Heddenhausen, Privatisations in Europe's liberalised electricity markets—the cases of the United Kingdom, Sweden, Germany, and France, Berlin, 2007.

[2] S. Pye, A. Dobbins, C. Baffert, J. Brajković, I. Grgurev, R. Miglio, et al., Energy poverty and vulnerable consumers in the energy sector across the EU: analysis of policies and measures. INSIGHT_E, 2015.

[3] J. Percebois, Electricity liberalization in the European Union: balancing benefits and risks, Energy J. 29 (2008) 1−20.

[4] G. Papaefthymiou, K. Grave, K. Dragoon, Flexibility options in electricity systems, Berlin, 2010.

[5] F. Delea, J. Casazza, Understanding Electric Power Systems: An Overview of the Technology, the Marketplace, and Government Regulation, John Wiley & Sons, New York, 2010.

[6] U.S. Energy Information Administration (EIA), Today in energy, March 4, 2013 [Online]. Available from: <http://www.eia.gov/todayinenergy/detail.cfm?id = 10211>.

[7] Eurostat, http://ec.europa.eu/eurostat/home [Online]. Available from: <http://appsso.eurostat.ec.europa.eu/nui/show.do?dataset = nrg_105a&lang = en> (accessed 30.06.15).

[8] Eurelectric, Power statistics and trends 2012—full report, Brussels, 2012.

[9] P. Breeze, Power Generation Technologies, Newnes, Oxford, 2005.

[10] K. Strauss, Kraftwerkstechnik zur Nutzung fossiler, nuklearer und regenerativer Energiequellen, Springer, Berlin, 2009.

[11] I. Kühn, New competition-based support schemes for electricity generation from renewable energy sources. In: First Austrian-Czech-German Conference on Energy Market Liberalization in Central and Eastern Europe, Prague, 1990.

[12] Eurostat, http://ec.europa.eu [Online]. Available from: <http://ec.europa.eu/eurostat/de/data/database> (accessed 25.06.15).

[13] Eurelectric, Flexible generation: backing up renewables, Brussels, 2011.

[14] European Commission, The future role and challenges of energy storage. DG ENER Working Paper, 2013.

[15] European Network for Transmission System Operators for Electricity (ENTSO-E), https://www.entsoe.eu/ [Online]. Available from: <https://www.entsoe.eu/db-query/consumption/mhlv-a-specific-country-for-a-specific-month> (accessed 30.06.15).

[16] Tennet TSO GmbH, www.tennet.eu/de/home.html [Online]. Available from: <http://www.tennettso.de/site/Transparenz/veroeffentlichungen/netzkennzahlen> (accessed 30.06.15).

[17] Amprion GmbH, www.amprion.net/ [Online]. Available from: <http://www.amprion.net/netzkennzahlen> (accessed 30.06.15).

[18] 50Hertz Transmission GmbH, www.50hertz.com [Online]. Available from: <http://www.50hertz.com/de/Kennzahlen> (accessed 30.06.15).

[19] TransnetBW GmbH, https://www.transnetbw.de [Online]. Available from: <https://www.transnetbw.de/de/kennzahlen> (accessed 30.06.15).

[20] European Wind Energy Association (EWEA), Powering Europe: wind energy and the electricity grid, Brussels, 2010.

[21] Agora Energiewende, Electricity Storage in the German Energy Transition—analysis of the storage required in the power market, ancillary services market and the distribution grid, Berlin, 2014.

[22] J. Lambertz, H.-W. Schiffer, I. Serdarusic, H. Voß, Flexibilität von Kohle- und Gaskraftwerken zum Ausgleich von Nachfrage- und Einspeiseschwankungen, Energiewirtschaftliche Tagesfragen 7 (2012) 16−20.

[23] W.-P. Schill, J. Diekmann, A. Zerrahn, Power storage: an important option for the German energy transition, DIW Econ. Bull. (2015) 137−147.

[24] Eurelectric, Hydro in Europe: Powering Renewables, Brussels, 2011.

[25] Agora Energiewende, The European Power System in 2030: Flexibility Challenges and Integration Benefits, Berlin, 2015.

[26] M. Zuber, http://www.hydroworld.com/, January 7, 2011 [Online]. Available from: <http://www.hydro-world.com/articles/print/volume-19/issue-3/articles/new-development/renaissance-for-pumped-storage-in-europe.html> (accessed 28.07.15).

[27] Eurostat, Infrastructure—electricity—annual data (nrg_113a), 2010 [Online]. Available from: <http://ec.europa.eu/eurostat/data/database> (accessed 15.07.12).

[28] A. Poullikkas, S. Papadouris, G. Kourtis, I. Hadjipaschalis, Storage solutions for power quality problems in Cyprus' electricity distribution network, 2014.

[29] A.G. Petoussis, S. Stavrinos, DEMSEE 2010: Fifth International Conference on Deregulated Electricity Market Issues in South-Eastern Europe. In: *Modeling of the Dynamic Behavior of the Island Power System of Cyprus*, Sitia, Crete, Greece, 2010.

[30] A.I. Nikolaidis, C.A. Charalambous, Action Steps for Refining the Cyprus National Action Plan on RES Penetration for Electricity Generation—should we reconsider?, 2013.

[31] J.P.S. Catalao, Smart and Sustainable Power Systems—Operations, Planning, and Economics of Insular Electricity Grids, CRC Press, Boca Raton, FL, 2015.

[32] K.D. Vos, A.G. Petoussis, J. Driesen, R. Belmans, Revision of reserve requirements following wind power integration in island power systems, Renew. Energy 50 (2013) 268−279.

[33] ENTSO-E, Consumption data, 2014 [Online]. Available from: <https://www.entsoe.eu/data/data-portal/consumption/Pages/default.aspx>.

[34] Loulou, R., Remme, U., Kanudia, A., Lehtila, A., Goldstein, G., 2005. Documentation for the TIMES Model - PART I, 1−78.

[35] European Commission, Energy roadmap 2050, 2011 [Online]. Available from: <http://ec.europa.eu/energy/energy2020/roadmap/doc/com_2011_8852_en.pdf>.

[36] S. Maire, R. Pattupara, R. Kannan, M. Vielle, F. Vöhringer (2015). Electricity Markets and Trade in Switzerland and Its Neighbouring Countries (ELECTRA); Building a Coupled Techno-Economic Modeling Framework − Schlussbericht. Final Report to Swiss Federal Office of Energy, Bern.

[37] International Energy Agency, World Energy Outlook 2010, International Energy Agency, Paris, 2010.

[38] K. Hufendiek, Elements of a new target model for European electricity markets towards a sustainable division of labour between regulation and market coordination, 8−9 July 2015. In: A Cost Effective Mix of Flexibility Options for Integrating a High Share of Variable Renewables, Paris, 2015.

[39] Sterner, Bioenergy and renewable power methane in integrated 100% renewable energy systems, Dissertation, University of Kassel, 2009.

[40] L. Brodecki, J. Tomaschek, U. Fahl, Synergies in the integration of energy networks for electricity, gas, heating and cooling. INSIGHT_E Rapid Response Energy Brief, 2014.

STORAGE SOLUTIONS AND THEIR VALUE

22

Bo Normark[1], Aurélie Faure-Schuyer[2], Abhishek Shivakumar[3], Constantinos Taliotis[3], Paul Deane[4], Johann Gottschling[5], Rajesh Pattupara[6], Ramachandran Kannan[6], Dražen Jakšić[7], Karmen Stupin[7], and Rudolf V. Hemert[7]

[1]*InnoEnergy Scandinavia, Stockholm, Sweden* [2]*Institut Français des Relations Internationales (IFRI), Brussels, Belgium* [3]*KTH Royal Institute of Technology, Stockholm, Sweden* [4]*University College Cork (UCC), Cork, Ireland* [5]*University of Stuttgart, Stuttgart, Germany* [6]*Paul Scherrer Institute, Villigen, Switzerland* [7]*Energy Institute Hrvoje Požar (EIHP), Zagreb, Croatia*

Energy storage has increasingly come into focus as a key enabling technology in the energy system. This is driven by several factors, including: (1) the increased electrification of the energy system and the associated changes in demand patterns, driven by new loads such as electric vehicles and heat pumps; (2) the decarbonization of the power system and the associated increases in the penetration of variable renewable electricity production, and related security of supply concerns.

Against a backdrop of the discrepancy between electricity demand patterns (with peak and off-peak periods) and the ramping capabilities of supply technologies, electric energy storage (EES) systems provide system flexibility and allow electricity production to be uncoupled from its supply to consumers.

This chapter assesses the cost competitiveness of storage technologies in providing flexibility services as described in Chapter 21, Need for Flexibility and Potential Solutions. Barriers in the current market structure are identified and alternative designs suggested.

22.1 GENERATION

Traditionally, pumped storage hydropower plants are operated to compensate overproduction of conventional plants during off-peak periods. The stored electricity is then released to provide peaking power, resulting in lower peak production costs and a more uniform load factor for generation, transmission, and distribution systems. Base load power plants operating near full capacity for economic reasons are prevented from ramping (thereby improving efficiency of the overall generation and reducing emissions).

Similarly, benefits can be obtained by operating storage technologies when the carrying capacity of the transmission and distribution system is likely to overload temporarily. Instead of having to add extra grid capacity, energy storage can help meet the peak load and lower the load in the transmission and distribution system.

Europe's Energy Transition. DOI: http://dx.doi.org/10.1016/B978-0-12-809806-6.00022-5

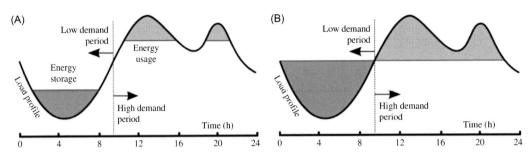

FIGURE 22.1

Load profile of a large-scale electricity storage system. (A) EES in peak shaving; (B) EES in load leveling [1].

Additionally, EES can participate in load-following operation and can be considered as a standby and spinning reserve in case of power supply outages. Due to their "black start"[a] capability, EES can also contribute to restoring power system operation after an outage.

EES can further contribute to reducing generation capacity requirements for meeting peak demand. As illustrated in Fig. 22.1, sufficient capacities of EES would enable thermal generating capacities to only meet average demand rather than peak demand. This requires the electricity price spread between peak and off-peak times to be sufficiently high to be able to economically efficiently operate the EES.[b]

Since the frequency within a power network must be kept within tight tolerance bounds, frequency regulation is an important service in order to maintain security of power supply. Historically, frequency regulation was mainly provided by ramping of generation units. However, also EES are able to adapt the charging and discharging process in order to contribute to frequency control.

As with frequency, the voltage in a power system must be kept within tolerances. More precisely, reactive power needs to be balanced to prevent voltages to rise and drop across the power network. As an alternative to thermal generation units, EES can also provide voltage control.

22.2 STORAGE SOLUTIONS

As shown in Fig. 22.2, different types of electrical energy storage systems can be distinguished according to the energy form used: mechanical, electrochemical, chemical, electrical, and thermal. However, some technologies in the figure are still under development or a long way from market maturity. For a brief description of specific technologies see Ref. [2]. In Fig. 22.2B the technology options are compared by their rated power, energy content, and nominal discharge time, covering a wide spectrum from seconds to month. This includes applications ranging from larger-scale generation- and transmission-related systems, to those "beyond the meter" and into the customer/end-user site, including portable devices, transport vehicles, and stationary energy resources.

[a] **A black start** is the process of restoring an electric power station or a part of an electric grid to operation without relying on the external transmission network. Normally, the electric power used within the plant is provided from the station's own generators.
[b] Note that this is not the case for reservoir storage, where rather the future water value determines when to operate it.

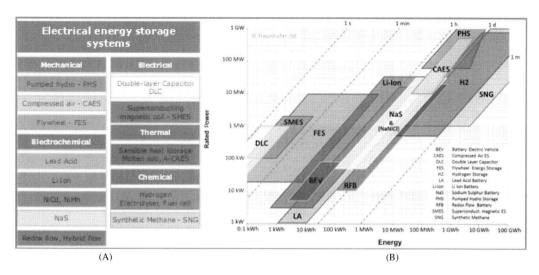

FIGURE 22.2

Classification of electrical energy storage systems according to energy form (A); comparison of rated power, energy content, and discharge time of different EES technologies (B). [3].

Besides power plant and power network operators, end-users also contribute to the provision of power storage. In many EU Member States, customers have opted for a retail tariff that incentivizes electricity consumption during off-peak periods due to lower electricity prices. For example, with electric night storage heaters as one early form of demand-side management in the residential sector, demand for electricity is shifted to off-peak times to be released as heat in peak times, thereby reducing the need for power plants to balance load profiles.

From all of the storage options mentioned above, hydropower storage is the only large-scale storage technology available to date, providing the most efficient and economical way to store potential electricity. Pumped hydro storage (PHS) usually offers a short- to medium-term storage capacity, depending on the size of the reservoir, while conventional storage hydropower plants with a natural inflow are capable of offering significant long-term storage capacities [3]. The operation of pumped hydropower storage has been essential in the past, when Europe's networks were mainly composed of a large number of regional grids with very weak interconnections [3]. Apart from hydropower, other storage technologies—such as larger-scale battery and flywheel storage—are very rare and not efficient due to either inappropriate infrastructure or economic reasons [5].

22.3 PUMPED HYDRO STORAGE

PHS is currently the only commercially proven, large-scale, economically viable (>100 MW) energy storage technology. The fundamental principle of this storage type is to store electric energy

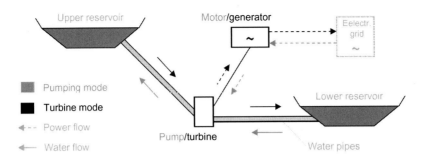

FIGURE 22.3

Simplified schematic of PHS system.

From http://www.store-project.eu.

in the form of hydraulic potential energy. Water stored in an upper reservoir is processed in a turbine to recover its potential energy in the form of mechanical (kinetic) energy.

Fig. 22.3 shows a simplified schematic of a PHS system, but many different subtypes exist. For example, seawater PHS uses the ocean as a lower reservoir (one system currently exists in Japan), or underground PHS uses deep mining structures for one or both reservoirs. However, underground PHS systems are still at a conceptual stage and are not commercially widely available.

Generally, two main types of PHS are distinguished, namely pure PHS and pump-back PHS [1]. Pure PHS plants rely entirely on water that has been pumped to an upper reservoir from a lower reservoir, a river or the sea. Pure PHS systems are also known as "closed-loop" or "off-stream." Pump-back PHS use a combination of pumped water and natural inflow to generate electricity similar to a conventional hydroelectric power plant. Pump-back PHS may be located on rivers or valleys with glacial or hydro inflow.

PHS systems are among the oldest and most widely used energy storage options and therefore fully commercialized. Some of the earliest PHS plants were built in the alpine regions of Switzerland and Austria, regions that have a rich hydro resource and a natural complimentary topography for PHS. PHS development on a European level is closely correlated to nuclear power development, as it allowed nuclear power plants to run as base load plants at their maximum rated capacity. However, countries such as Austria with no nuclear power, but a rich hydro resource, developed PHS to primarily enhance the operation and efficiency of large-scale hydro power plants.

The chronological development of PHS in many countries shows that the majority of plants were built from the 1960s to the late 1980s (Fig. 22.4). This was in part due to a rush for energy security and nuclear energy after the oil crises in the early 1970s. Fewer facilities were developed during the 1990s due to a natural saturation of the best available (and most cost-effective) locations and a decline in the growth of nuclear power.

The hydraulic, mechanical, and electrical efficiencies of pumped storage determine the overall cycle efficiency, ranging from 65% to 85%. If the upstream pumping reservoir is also used as a traditional reservoir, the inflow from the watershed may balance out the energy loss caused by pumping. If not, net losses lead to pumped hydropower being a net energy consumer. Power ratings of PHS systems range from several MW up to 2 GW with discharge times up to 100 hours depending on the storage volume of the reservoirs (see Fig. 22.2B). Pumping and generating in PHS systems generally follow a daily cycle but weekly or even seasonal cycling is also possible with larger PHS plants.

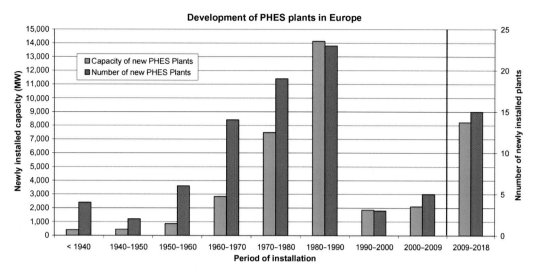

FIGURE 22.4

Chronological development of PHS (or PHES) in MW capacity and plant number in the EU for existing and proposed PHS.

Reproduced with permission from Zach K., Auer H. Lettner G., Report Summarizing the Current Status, Role and Costs of Energy Storage Technologies, 2012, <http://www.store-project.eu> [19].

CURRENT STATUS OF PHS

Pumped hydro is the primary mature storage technology to provide short- and mid-term flexibility. More recently there has been a renewed interest in the technology as an integrator for variable wind power. Currently there are more than 90 GW of PHS systems (with power rating >100 MW) installed worldwide, representing approximately 3% of global generation capacity. In Europe, most of the PHS capacity is located in mountainous areas (Alps, Pyrenees, Scottish Highlands, Ardennes, and Carpathians). Germany has the largest number of PHS plants with 23 operational plants ranging in capacity from 62.5 to 1060 MW. Germany is second only to Spain in terms of installed MW capacity. Over 6000 MW of PHS is installed on the Iberian Peninsula. Spain has 14 PHS plants with sizes ranging from 65 to 745 MW, the largest plant being the Iberdrola-owned Villarino plant. Portugal has five major PHS plants with an average capacity of 160 MW. PHS in Portugal and Spain are predominantly of the pump-back type, operating on major rivers or as part of larger hydro complexes or cascades. These types of facilities often have an important function in addition to electricity storage, such as for irrigation or flood control.

The largest PHS plant in the EU is the 1800 MW EDF-owned "Grand Maison" facility in the French Alps opened in 1987. Before the construction of the "Grand Maison" facility, the 1728 MW Dinorwig plant in the UK was the largest PHS plant in Europe. Dinorwig can achieve full load from a spinning state in less than 20 seconds.

On the worldwide scale the USA and Japan have the highest total installed capacities of PHS. In the USA, this capacity amounts to approximately 22 GW, accounting for approximately 2.1% of total installed generating capacity. Like the USA, Japan developed PHS to complement nuclear power facilities, providing peak power in the evenings and storing nuclear power when demand is low.

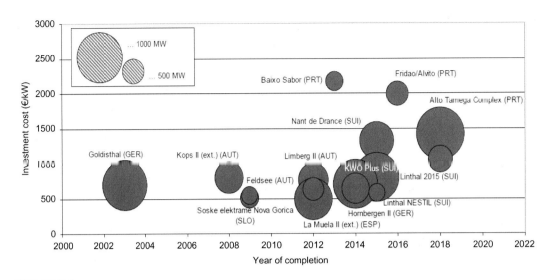

FIGURE 22.5

Comparison of the specific investment cost for selected PHS systems.

DRIVERS FOR NEW PHS DEVELOPMENT

Drivers for new PHS development are region- or country-specific, but generally renewable energy targets are often seen as drivers for new development. Targets for increasing renewable energy are stimulating wind energy and solar power developments in many countries. Increased variable generation is seen to drive the demand for system reserve and increase the value of PHS to provide ancillary services. In addition to renewable energy targets, reducing the volatility or increasing the efficiency of current hydroelectric assets is also a prime driver for developers.

PHS plants are characterized by a long asset life (typically 50–100 years), high capital cost, low operation and maintenance cost, and round-trip efficiencies of 60%–85%. There are, however, limited siting possibilities for new PHS. The large-scale deployment of PHS projects has associated environmental impacts that should not be overlooked. PHS in particular—even for new facilities and designs—has a significant land and water footprint, and GHG (CH_4) emissions are released at the reservoir surface.

Project costs for PHS are very site-specific and do not only depend on the installed power, but also on the energy storage at any given site. Fig. 22.5 details the published capital costs and installed capacities for a number of proposed PHS plants, the majority of which are in Europe. A general linear trend is observed in the relationship between installed capacity and capital cost. Capital costs per MW for select proposed PHS are between €470/kW and €2170/kW.

PHS projects may be remunerated in liberalized electricity markets through ancillary services payments, capacity payment, and electricity trading. Generally, electricity trading is the major source of revenue for PHS as operators may take advantage of energy arbitrage[c] opportunities.

---

[c]Buying electricity at off-peak prices and selling at peak prices.

Table 22.1 Pumped Hydro Energy Storage Market Studies in the JRC Report

Market Region	Year	Arbitrage	Reserve	Author and Year
Belgium (BE)	2007	Yes	Yes	He et al. (2011) [7]
Germany (DE)	2002–10	Yes		Steffen (2011) [8]
Germany (DE), France (F)	2010–30	Yes	Yes	Loisel et al. (2010) [9]
Spain (ES), Italy (I)	2008–11	Yes		Rangoni (2012) [10]

For arbitrage to be economic, the pumping price has to be at least 25%–30% lower than the selling price to compensate for energy losses, and significant volatility (not necessarily high energy prices) must be present in the wholesale price of electricity to earn revenues. Increased wind generation in many countries naturally lends itself to increase the price volatility in the wholesale market.

Current trends for new PHS plants show that developers operating in liberalized markets tend to repower or enhance projects, or build "pump-back" PHS rather than traditional "pure pumped storage" plants. This is partly driven by a lack of economically attractive new sites. An advantage with "pump-back" facilities is that energy storage is generally much greater, allowing plants to store large amounts of cheap electricity. This is because they are usually situated in mountainous topographies, whose valleys allow building dams with rather large reservoirs. Plants with significant inflow may also operate as conventional hydroelectric generation units during times of excess inflow, thus increasing the economic competitiveness of these plants.

Repowering or enhancement of existing projects is also attractive as large savings are made on the capital expenditure of the project by using existing infrastructure (usually reservoirs), thus also reducing environmental and planning issues. Repowered plants benefit from improvements in technology and design and usually use more efficient and larger turbines/pumps. From an investor standpoint the internal rate of return for repower projects is on average higher than that of new plants.

VALUE OF PHS

The value of pumped storage in electricity markets is highly dependent on the makeup of the system in terms of thermal generation portfolio, renewables penetration and type, market structure, and interconnection. A number of existing studies have aimed to quantify the value of pumped storage in diverse systems. These studies are well summarized in an EU JRC report (Table 22.1) [5]. This section is based on information and text from this report.

Fig. 22.6 shows a review of profitability figures from the JRC report for EU projects. The graph bars represent the ranges of annual gross margins. Gross margin is the difference between storage revenue and variable plus fixed O&M costs per kW of installed (turbine) capacity.[d]

---

[d]If a specific study did not explicitly state annual storage revenues, these are calculated from other data published. For [8], annual gross margins were recalculated from the net present value, applying the interest rate, economic lifetime, and inflation rates provided. In the case of [6] the figures obtained from the simulation of 1 week of storage dispatch optimization were extrapolated in the report to an entire year, simply multiplying results for 52 weeks. All currency units are normalized to €2012, applying exchange rates and inflation figures according to Eurostat. Arbitrage-only figures are presented for all studies except for [6] and [8], which also include revenues from reserve and other markets.

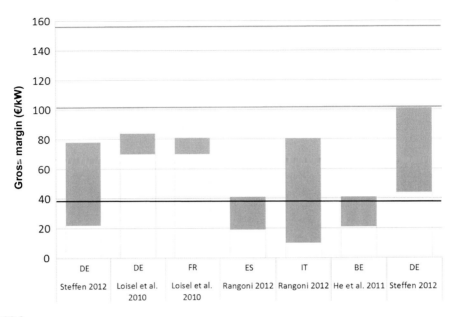

FIGURE 22.6

Annual gross margin (€/kW) for pumped storage for a number of study regions. Information on the chart is taken from JRC Report; black lines: low CAPEX; *red* (gray in print versions) lines: high CAPEX; respective lower lines: low WACC; upper lines: high WACC. (The ranges shown in this figure are given by the following variation of the input parameters. Historical energy prices taken from different years [10]. Prices are generated by a market model making different assumptions on the storage penetration [9].)

The report highlights that as authors make different assumptions on the investment level and weighted average costs of capital (WACC), the profitability estimates are usually not comparable. Therefore, a total of four possible cases are shown by combining two different values for the WACC (6% and 10%) with two different levels of specific capital expenditures (CAPEX) (500—1500 €/kW), taken from the Technology Map of the European Strategic Energy Technology Plan. The different WACC levels represent typical values for a regulated and a deregulated business. An investment life time of 35 years is assumed for both cases. The break-even points for investments in a generic PHS are shown as straight lines in Fig. 22.6. Profitability is reached if gross revenues exceed these lines. The black lines represent low CAPEX cases (500 €/kW), while the red lines represent high CAPEX (1500 €/kW), each with WACC of 6% (lower line) and 10% (upper line).

The possible storage gross margin of a PHS seen in all scenario/studies varies by about one order of magnitude (10—110 €/kW/year). Arbitrage-only operation allows the repayment of a low CAPEX (500 €/kW) investment in some cases, but does not provide sufficient revenues for a high CAPEX (1500 €/kW) investment in any of the cases considered. Repayment of a high CAPEX/low WACC combination seems feasible if reserve markets (and other services) are included. In none of the studies do gross revenues allow repayment in a high WACC and high CAPEX scenario.

The profitability for Italy was calculated on the basis of the average national power price (PUN, *prezzo unico nazionale*), which results from the zonal prices weighted with exchanged volumes for

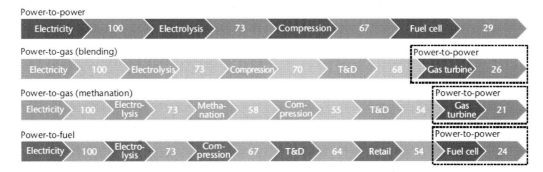

FIGURE 22.7

Current conversion efficiencies of various hydrogen-based renewable energy integration pathways [20].

Reproduced with permission from OECD/IEA 2015 Technology Roadmap: Hydrogen and Fuel Cells, IEA Publishing. Licence,
<http://www.iea.org/t&c> [20].

each Italian price zone [6]. Spreads may be higher within zones, providing a further upside potential. Publications on hybrid systems of PHS and wind on non-interconnected islands were not included in the JRC review.

22.4 OTHER STORAGE TECHNOLOGIES

Other mechanical storage systems have not yet significantly penetrated the energy market. Experience with compressed air energy storage (CAES) is limited. Diabatic[e] and advanced adiabatic CAES (A-CAES) can be distinguished. Worldwide only two diabatic CAES utilities are operated to date, of which the first was built in 1978 in Germany, with a capacity of 290 MW (Huntorf). Adiabatic systems promising higher efficiencies and zero direct CO_2 emissions are not available [10]. The main drawback of CAES storage is the need for suitable geological structures. The construction of artificial caverns for storage would involve high cost [11].

Although flywheel storage is a mature technology and fully introduced in the industrial market (i.e., motion smoothing, ride-through power for power disturbances), it is not competitive at higher power ratings.[f] High maintenance requirements and installations regarding safety lead to increased costs [12].

Electrochemical storage, such as battery energy storage (BES), has not yet been able to compete with PHS or CAES at larger scales. This is due to their limited lifetime and low storage capacities as well as their higher maintenance requirements. Furthermore, concerns existed about negative environmental impacts caused by batteries due to toxic materials [12].

Chemical storage via hydrogen is expected to be suitable for daily and seasonal energy storage in the medium to long term. Due to the low round-trip efficiencies for power-to-power pathways (Fig. 22.7), hydrogen generation for energy storage is mainly envisaged based on the use of excess

---

[e]In a diabatic CAES, air is cooled before compression and reheated before expansion in a gas turbine. In an adiabatic CAES, the air's heat energy is stored separately and recovered before expansion [11].

[f]The first flywheel energy storage plant is expected to launch commercially in 2017 [18].

renewable electricity in electrolysis. The merits of fuel cell and hydrogen pathways for heat and power generation in future energy systems are evaluated in more detail in Chapter 23, The Role of Fuel Cells and Hydrogen in Stationary Applications [12].

Supercapacitors (double-layer capacitors (DLC)) and superconducting magnetic energy storage (SMES) as new options for electrical energy storage are not yet at a stage of development for market introduction [12].

Thermal storage has been in use since the 1960s in terms of night storage heaters in order to utilize surplus power generation at night. With the growth of nuclear energy, storage heaters became popular in the 1970s [13]. Night storage heaters were predominant in the UK, Germany, and France. In the UK 8% of households used storage heaters. During the period 1995–2000, 22% of households in France used central heating, of which 20% was supplied by storage heaters [14]. For heaters powered by electricity, thermal storage still constitutes an effective and cheap way of providing system flexibility. Further, new developments in thermal storage technologies are being rapidly developed across Europe. An instance of such thermal storage systems is underground thermal energy storage (UTES), currently deployed in the Netherlands, Sweden, and Germany and the "1000 MWh molten salt storage" technology which enhances the dispatchability of power generation from concentrating solar power (CSP) [15].

22.5 VALUE OF STORAGE

Storage options and physically and operationally well-interconnected market can help to cope well with the increased requirements for flexibility due to variable RES [16]. Energy storage can potentially provide a wide range of services including energy arbitrage, peak shaving, and system services. It is clear that bundling of services will increase the value of storage, but also increases the complexity and the need for new business models and reformed regulation.

A comprehensive study on the value of storage has been done by the authors, focusing on Austria, France, Germany, and Italy. This study involved the modeling of two scenarios, a least-cost and a decarbonization scenario with a much more ambitious deployment of renewable generation. Two types of storage have been considered, pumped storage and battery storage. The key benefit of the simulation is that it allows comparing the value of storage to the potential revenue generation.

The study has been limited to assessing the value of energy arbitrage in single years to keep the modeling at reasonable levels. If, for instance, the value of peak shaving is to be fully considered, the highest benefit is typically in the deferment of grid infrastructure investments. Assessing this benefit in detail requires a complex analysis, considering both, a detailed operational analysis within a year and capacity expansion analysis across longer timeframes, which was beyond the scope of this study. Further, it focuses specifically on the value of centralized storage.

Within this study the wholesale market prices are derived for two specific years (2030 and 2050) using a model-based approach. A power plant portfolio is constructed for each Member State for two scenarios (least cost and CO_2 mitigation/decarbonization) and 2 years (2030 and 2050). In all, approximately 3000 individual thermal power plants are included in the model. Power plant capacities, efficiencies, and fuel types are based on outputs from the EUSTEM model described in Section 21.5. The model minimizes overall generation costs to meet demand subject to the technical characteristics of the power plants. The resulting market price is defined as the marginal price at Member State level (often called the shadow price of electricity) and does not include any extra revenues from potential balancing, reserve or capacity markets, or costs such as grid infrastructure costs, capital costs, or taxes. Results of these simulations for 2030 and 2050 are shown in Tables 22.2 and 22.3.

The study verifies findings from other studies that multiple benefits are required to justify battery storage. It confirms that there is a clear correlation between the degree of the penetration of renewables and the value of storage. Under current estimations of battery prices, there is no business case for battery storage up to 2030, which are therefore not listed in Table 22.2. Battery storage becomes however attractive in selected markets in 2050. Moreover, there are large variations between the countries which were investigated. The main reason is the significant difference in their production mix and infrastructure.

22.6 FACILITATING STORAGE DEPLOYMENT

At a European level the *STORE-Project.eu*[g] has made a number of recommendations to assist the deployment of storage projects. The project recommends that if a need for energy storage is identified, then this should be clearly expressed in energy policy, and that discernible objectives are formulated at EU and Member State levels. For PHS, it recommends that physically viable sites are identified and tested (subject to environmental assessment) at a strategic level during the development of related plans and programs. It further recommends that clear guidelines for sustainable project development, best practice guidelines, and guidelines for planning are established to further the sustainable development of bulk energy storage. Finally, it suggests the establishment of appropriate mechanisms to improve the efficiency and speed with which bulk electricity storage projects are considered during the planning and approval stages.

22.7 MAIN CHALLENGES AHEAD

With the increasing penetration of variable energy production, energy storage is now widely expected to play a significant role in the EU energy system. It can potentially provide a wide range of energy services including energy arbitrage and peak shaving as well as balancing services. The conditions across EU Member States, however, are very different from one another. The main objective of this chapter was to analyze how different conditions lead to a better or worse case for storage.

We found that significant legislative barriers still need to be overcome. In existing legislation and regulations throughout the EU, pumped hydro storage (PHS) has mostly been defined as a "generation" technology. Essentially, PHS are deemed to complement and store base load production of nuclear and hydro power through energy arbitrage. However, PHS fitted with variable or adjustable speed turbines are well-suited to provide balancing services to TSOs and DSOs, outside of the intraday market. This is in addition to the provision of other grid services such as frequency regulation. In these markets, PHS may act in combination with other flexible-generation power plants.

---

[g]Source: http://www.store-project.eu/

Table 22.2 Summary of Wholesale Prices from Modeling Results for 2030

Property	Units	Austria Pumped Storage — Least Cost (LC) Scenario	Austria Pumped Storage — CO$_2$ Scenario	France Pumped Storage — Least Cost (LC) Scenario	France Pumped Storage — CO$_2$ Scenario	Germany Pumped Storage — Least Cost (LC) Scenario	Germany Pumped Storage — CO$_2$ Scenario	Italy Pumped Storage — Least Cost (LC) Scenario	Italy Pumped Storage — CO$_2$ Scenario
Market price	$/MWh	465	728	408	1,583	4,922	5,482	6,053	5,360
Generation	GWh	377	505	580	2,201	5,488	5,303	7,459	6,291
Units started		25,921	25,609	408	1,583	4,922	5,482	6,053	5,360
Dispatchable energy	GWh	25,455	24,881	—	—	—	—	—	—
Undispatched energy	GWh	681	764	291	1,250	1,309	1,845	2,347	2,140
Hours of operation	h	2	3	3	10	8	6	9	8
Capacity factor	%	341,833	489,318	209,943	796,967	1,662,965	1,212,719	2,282,521	1,924,901
Ramp up	MW	31,500	32,280	10,740	45,720	44,760	44,940	91,080	83,100
Minutes of ramp up	min	341,833	489,318	209,943	796,967	1,662,965	1,212,719	2,282,521	1,925,211
Ramp down	MW	32,460	33,660	11,280	46,620	44,460	46,980	82,440	76,620
Minutes of ramp down	min	1,794	2,879	348	1,326	1,501	1,128	1,663	1,759
Hours of pump operation	h	42,834	71,439	37,678	46,420	442,723	15,946	616,567	559,886
Pump cost	$000	100	105	98	51	93	9	103	106
Price received	$/MWh	46,357	76,074	39,939	80,706	455,546	36,646	624,323	566,229
Pool revenue	$000	3,523	4,635	2,261	34,286	12,823	20,700	7,756	6,343
Net revenue	$000	3,030	3,030	1,810	1,810	6,666	6,666	7,650	7,650
Installed capacity	MW	465	728	408	1,583	4,922	5,482	6,053	5,360

Market price (€/MWh), average load-weighted price for region over the year; dispatchable energy (GWh), total energy available for dispatch over the year; undispatched energy (GWh), energy not dispatched over the year; ramp up (MW), total megawatt ramping up; minutes of ramp up (min), total minutes spent ramping up; cost of purchased energy = pump load (or recharge load) * price for each hour; average price received for energy sold (€/MWh), average of hourly price when energy is sold back to market; gross revenue = generation * average price received for energy sold for each hour; net revenue = gross revenue − cost of purchased energy.

Table 22.3 Summary of Wholesale Prices from Modeling Results for 2050

Property	Units	Austria Pumped Storage LC	Austria Pumped Storage CO₂	Austria Batteries LC	Austria Batteries CO₂	France Pumped Storage LC	France Pumped Storage CO₂	France Batteries LC	France Batteries CO₂	Germany Pumped Storage LC	Germany Pumped Storage CO₂	Germany Batteries LC	Germany Batteries CO₂	Italy Pumped Storage LC	Italy Pumped Storage CO₂	Italy Batteries LC	Italy Batteries CO₂
Market price	$/MWh	102.36	94.56	102.36	94.56	98.91	20.61	98.91	20.61	96.30	103.46	103.60	103.60	102.63	89.33	102.63	89.33
Annual generation	GWh	593	696	–	2,377	671	3,336	–	24,684	5,098	9,063	–	48,065	7,017	11,589	–	57,610
Number of starts	–	423	330	–	963	881	3,746	–	269	6,254	11,061	–	722	8,464	10,035	–	535
Dispatchable energy	GWh	25,801	25,680	–	3,476	671	3,336	–	24,684	5,098	9,063	–	129,294	7,017	11,589	–	256,272
Undispatched energy	GWh	25,208	24,984	–	1,100	–	–	–	–	–	–	–	81,229	–	–	–	198,662
Hours of operation	h	636	868	–	2,154	436	1,585	–	2,977	1,214	1,615	–	3,132	1,520	1,662	–	4,277
Capacity factor	%	2	3	–	19	4	10	–	10	9	16	–	14	11	17	–	14
Ramp up	MW	468,421	521,408	–	1,101,860	318,838	2,831,958	–	7,399,185	1,895,015	3,351,426	–	13,488,610	2,589,922	3,070,772	–	14,395,746
Minutes of ramp up	min	30,420	40,080	–	72,720	13,920	78,960	–	102,840	42,060	43,140	–	103,320	53,400	32,760	–	127,500
Ramp down	MW	468,421	522,056	–	1,101,860	318,838	2,831,958	–	7,387,491	1,895,015	3,351,426	–	13,488,610	2,589,922	3,070,772	–	14,395,746
Minutes of ramp down	min	28,560	40,740	–	73,680	14,340	80,280	–	108,480	40,740	45,000	–	126,060	53,880	33,420	–	162,240
Hours of pump operation	h	2,322	2,647	–	2,386	584	1,437	–	2,024	1,547	1,722	–	2,541	1,907	1,921	–	2,690
Cost of purchased energy	$000	64,123	27,231	–	150,773	73,404	1,009	–	410,277	531,889	302,315	–	2,750,066	783,213	285,471	–	2,989,015
Average price received for energy sold	$/MWh	116	95	–	109	115	3	–	21	107	99	–	109	114	92	–	93
Gross revenue	$000	68,696	66,249	–	258,542	77,412	8,393	–	526,708	545,944	899,630	–	5,250,889	803,075	1,063,400	–	5,374,391
Net revenue	$000	4,573	39,018	–	107,769	4,007	7,385	–	116,426	14,055	597,315	–	2,500,813	19,862	777,929	–	2,385,365
Installed capacity	MW	3,030	3,030	–	1,400	1,810	3,780	–	29,078	6,666	6,666	–	39,600	7,650	7,650	–	45,600

Further, there is no EU legislation specifying the definition of storage facilities and TSOs treat storage as they deem fit for their local/national circumstances. The different approaches across national markets may create distortions which have an impact on access and related costs for storage energy in neighboring markets.

Finally, the issue of storage ownership remains significant. Ownership of storage facilities has to be assessed in relation to flexibility requirements of the system over the short, mid, and long term. For this reason, the regulatory framework for storage needs to provide clear rules and responsibilities concerning the status (legal ownership and technical) of energy storage facilities. It should guarantee a level playing field with other sources of generation, and exploit the flexibility of storage options to stabilize the grid and facilitate the integration of renewable energy supply. The regulatory framework should therefore be technology neutral, in order to allow fair competition between different technological solutions.

The regulatory as well as the economic boundary conditions are also decisive for the implementation of energy storage in the form of hydrogen, and the use of hydrogen in stationary fuel cells and hydrogen applications. Situations in which these technologies can provide benefits to the energy system (e.g., due to increased flexibility to cope with variable renewable generation) are assessed in more detail in Chapter 23, The Role of Fuel Cells and Hydrogen in Stationary Applications.

REFERENCES

[1] S. Sabihuddin, A.E. Kiprakis, M. Mueller, A numerical and graphical review of energy storage technologies, Energies 8 (1) (2015) 172−216.

[2] International Eletrotechnical Commission (IEC), Electrical energy storage white paper, Genva, 2011.

[3] J.M. Pedraza, Electrical Energy Generation in Europe: The Current Situation and Perspectives in the Use of Renewable Energy Sources and Nuclear Power for Regional Electricity Generation, Springer, Cham, Heidelberg, New York, Dordrecht, London, 2015.

[4] European Commission, The future role and challenges of Energy Storage. DG ENER Working Paper, 2013. < http://ecnphlgnajanjnkcmbpancdjoidceilk/content/web/viewer.html?file = https%3A%2F %2Fec.europa.eu%2Fenergy%2Fsites%2Fener%2Ffiles%2Fenergy_storage.pdf > .

[5] C. Levillain, E. Serres, D. Chantelou, C. Bonety, A. Marquet, Energy storage in power grids—applications and opportunities, 1999.

[6] A. Zucker, T. Hinchliffe, A. Spisto, Assessing storage value in energy markets—a JRC scientific and policy report, JRC, 2013.

[7] X. He, E. Delarue, W. D'haeseleer, J.-M. Glachant, A novel business model for aggregating the values of electricity storage, Energy Policy 39 (2011) 1575−1585.

[8] B. Steffen, Prospects for pumped-hydro storage in Germany, 2011.

[9] R. Loisel, A. Mercier, C. Gatzen, N. Elm, P. Hvroje, Valuation framework for large scale electricity storage in acase with wind curtailment, Energy Policy 38 (2010) 7323−7337.

[10] B. Rangoni, A contribution on electricity storage: the case of hydro-pumped storage appraisal and commissioning in Italy and Spain, Util. Policy 23 (2012) 31−39.

[11] D. Swider, Compressed air energy storage in an electricity system with significant wind power generation, IEEE Trans. Energy Convers. 22 (1) (2007) 95−102.

[12] European Association for Storage of Energy (EASE); European Energy Research Alliance (EERA), Joint EASE/EERA recommendations for a European Energy Storage Technology Development Roadmap towards 2030, 2013.

[13] S. Cole, D.V. Hertem, L. Meeus, R. Belmans, Energy storage on production and transmission level: a SWOT analysis. Heverlee-Leuven.

[14] European Commission, SAVE II Labelling & other measures for heating systems in dwellings. Final report January 2002; Appendix 4—Stock model of residential heating systems. Delft, Netherlands, 2002.

[15] European Commission, SAVE II Labelling & other measures for heating systems in dwellings. Final report January 2002; Appendix 1—Characterisation of heating systems and their markets, Milano, 2002.

[16] European Association for Storage of Energy (EASE), European Energy Research Alliance (EERA), European energy storage technology development roadmap towards 2030, 2015.

[17] Eurelectric, Flexible generation: backing up renewables, Brussels, 2011.

[18] J. Gallagher, First Hybrid Flywheel Energy Storage Plant in Europe announced in Midlands, March 26, 2015 [Online]. Available from: <https://www.djei.ie/en/News-And-Events/Department-News/2015/March/First-Hybrid-Flywheel-Energy-Storage-Plant-in-Europe-announced-in-Midlands-html>.

[19] Zach K., Auer H. Lettner G., Report Summarizing the Current Status, Role and Costs of Energy Storage Technologies, 2012, <http://www.store-project.eu>, <www.store-project.eu>.

[20] OECD/IEA 2015 Technology Roadmap: Hydrogen and Fuel Cells, IEA Publishing. Licence, <http://www.iea.org/t&c>, <www.iea.org/t&c>.

THE ROLE OF FUEL CELLS AND HYDROGEN IN STATIONARY APPLICATIONS

23

Kathrin Volkart[1], Martin Densing[1], Rocco De Miglio[2], Thierry Priem[3], Steve Pye[4], and Brian Cox[1]

[1]PSI, Villigen, Switzerland [2]E4SMA, Turin, Italy [3]CEA, Grenoble, France
[4]University College London (UCL), London, United Kingdom

This chapter evaluates the role of fuel cells and hydrogen (FCH) technologies in the future energy sector. However, the first FCH applications date well back in time. One of the first applications was in space missions: From the 1960s to nowadays, hydrogen has been used in fuel cells to provide electricity for space ships, e.g., during the GEMINI and APOLLO space programs and in the space shuttles [1]. Only recently, FCH technologies and applications have started to be developed for the energy sector, and several countries now focus on research and development projects for innovative FCH technologies and applications: Japan, South Korea, the USA, and Germany are leaders in demonstration projects and the commercialization of FCH technologies due to proactive national incentives and funding. They see FCH technologies, processes, and applications as potentially relevant elements in a low-carbon energy system in the medium to long term.[a] Expected benefits include the mitigation of greenhouse gas emissions and local air pollution, their high energy efficiency, the reduction of fossil fuel dependency, and promotion of exports.

Hydrogen is an energy carrier with very high gravimetric energy density (142 MJ/kg), but low volumetric energy density (5.6 MJ/L at 700 bar), e.g., in comparison with gasoline (46 MJ/kg, 34 MJ/L). Hydrogen can be produced from various hydrocarbons or water, and it can be further converted into other energy carriers such as methane (via methanation). Today, hydrogen is mostly used as industrial feedstock, e.g., in petrochemistry for refining, in ammonia production for fertilizers, and in methanol production [2]. In the energy sector, fuel cells allow for its conversion into electricity. Because this process is based on electro-chemistry, it is not limited by the Carnot efficiency and thus has the potential to operate with an electrical efficiency of up to 60% and an overall theoretical efficiency of over 80% (including both heat and electricity) [3]. The simultaneous production of heat and electricity allows for the use of fuel cells as combined heat and power (CHP) applications.

Stationary FCH solutions are expected to be deployed in the future energy system, e.g., for energy storage (seasonal or diurnal, with optional re-electrification), for ancillary services to stabilize the power grid, and for residential heating with micro combined heat and power (micro-CHP) plants using fuel cells. In comparison with FCH applications for mobility (e.g., fuel cell cars), stationary FCH facilities have several advantages: a lower power and energy density is required, lower ramping rates are needed, less vibrations are to be withstood, co-generation with

---

[a]The strengths and weaknesses of different world regions regarding FCH technologies were assessed by the INSIGHT_E consortium in Ref. [14].

Europe's Energy Transition. DOI: http://dx.doi.org/10.1016/B978-0-12-809806-6.00023-7

heat as valuable co-product is possible, no buffer battery is needed (exception: back-up systems), less stringent tank safety is obligated, and no precautionary measures for traffic accidents are required.

Thus, this chapter specifically focuses on the evaluation of merits and potential roles of stationary FCH technologies in the short to mid term (2020−30) as well as mid to long term (2040−50), also given that mobile FCH applications are extensively investigated in many studies elsewhere. The description of the FCH technologies and pathways is followed by a merit assessment of individual FCH pathways, as illustrated through four case studies. The role of stationary FCH technologies is then assessed more broadly based on the role they can play within the overall energy system and including interactions with the mobility sector and industrial use. The chapter concludes with policy recommendations.

23.1 FCH TECHNOLOGIES AND PATHWAYS

There is a large range of possible FCH energy technologies available: After hydrogen generation, for example from natural gas or via electrolysis, the energy carrier must be stored and then transported to FCH applications such as fuel cell CHP plants or hydrogen boilers. The FCH technologies and applications can thus be concatenated to FCH pathways starting from energy sources and ending in energy services as illustrated in Fig. 23.1. Each FCH pathway consists of a set of technologies for hydrogen generation, hydrogen storage, hydrogen transport, and FCH application. These steps and the corresponding technologies are described in the following subsections, before their merits are assessed in more detail in Section 23.2.

HYDROGEN GENERATION

The first step of each FCH pathway is the hydrogen production from an energy source. Today, approximately 96% of global hydrogen production stem from fossil-fueled thermochemical processes, while only 4% stem from electrolytic or byproduct processes [4]. About 60 million tons (Mt) of hydrogen are produced every year; thereof the European contribution is 8.8 Mt [5]. The main actors in the global hydrogen market are large gas manufacturers.

With the growing deployment of renewable energy generation, water electrolysis has become a promising solution for hydrogen generation. Alkaline electrolysis is the most mature and widely developed technology in industry. Nowadays, several companies provide their customers with high-power units of several megawatts allowing hydrogen production of up to 1400 Nm^3 H_2/h with a single electrolyzer stack [6]. Polymer electrolyte membrane electrolysis is less mature than alkaline electrolysis and allows for lower power ranges up to approximately 1 MW rated stack capacity using a single electrolyzer stack [6]. On the other hand, polymer electrolyte membrane electrolysis is more suited for coupling with variable renewable energies due to its flexibility with respect to power input.

Based on the EU policy which aims at the expansion of renewable energies, the assessment in Section 23.2 focuses on electricity and biomass as energy sources. As reference, and because

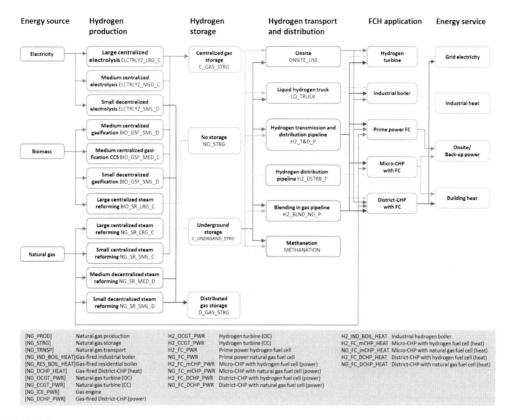

FIGURE 23.1

Overview of FCH technologies and applications (including abbreviations) which are addressed in the merit assessment in Section 23.2.

hydrogen is currently mainly produced from natural gas, this energy source is also included. Further, the consideration of biomass gasification with carbon capture and storage (CCS) allows exploring the merits of a carbon-negative option.

HYDROGEN STORAGE

The second step of each pathway is hydrogen storage in centralized or decentralized gaseous storage tanks, or underground (bulk) storage. Underground storage in salt caverns and aquifer structures, which enables handling the variations in hydrogen demand over a whole year, is envisioned in scenarios with large-scale deployment of hydrogen technologies. Energy-intensive storage in insulated liquid tanks seems not to be cost-effective for stationary applications. Hence, such tanks as well as likely future storage technologies such as metal hydrides, carbon, or other nanostructures are not considered.

HYDROGEN TRANSPORT

Hydrogen transport and distribution (T&D) is required as the third step of each pathway to deliver hydrogen from its production site to end-use. It includes gaseous hydrogen in dedicated hydrogen or natural gas pipelines, liquid hydrogen on trucks, and (as an emerging option) methanation.

Hydrogen can be compressed up to 350–700 bar and transported in steel or composite storage tanks on trucks. Railcars, ships, and barges are currently uneconomic for gaseous hydrogen transport.[b] Liquid hydrogen transport is more economic than gaseous hydrogen transport for long distances in the absence of pipelines due to the larger amount of hydrogen which can be transported. For liquid transport, gaseous hydrogen is cooled to $-253°C$ in liquefaction plants. Significant energy losses occur during liquefaction (more than 30% of the energy content of hydrogen) and evaporation is a potential issue (boil-off), particularly for small tanks.

For long distances and large volumes, pipelines for gaseous hydrogen are cost-efficient. As of 2016, 1500 km of hydrogen pipelines exist in Europe and 1150 km in the USA. The technology is very similar to the one for natural gas, but duplicating (even partially) the gas network is expected to be very expensive. Thus, retrofitting natural gas pipelines for hydrogen is envisaged as a long-term option. Nevertheless, converting existing gas pipelines into hydrogen pipelines may require substantial modifications, as the polymer pipelines are not suitable for pure hydrogen due to the high permeation. Also, present domestic appliances are not designed to be fed with pure hydrogen instead of methane. On the other hand, low blending of hydrogen up to 15% by volume in natural gas pipelines is expected to require only modest modifications [7]. Today, 5% by volume has already been allowed in German natural gas pipelines [8].

FCH APPLICATIONS

FCH applications can be categorized into industrial applications, on- and off-grid electricity generation, and building heat generation. Industrial applications include the use of hydrogen in low-temperature boilers as well as for feedstock in ammonia production, refining, and novel iron and steel production processes. Hydrogen gas turbines and prime power[c] fuel cells are applications for electricity generation, whereas fuel cell micro-CHP and district CHP plants provide electricity as well as heat for buildings. Apart from the use of hydrogen as non-energy industrial feedstock, all stationary applications mentioned are addressed in the subsequent merit assessment.

---

[b]This situation may change due to the recent development of tanks which can carry large volumes of highly pressurized hydrogen and which have been certified by the International Organization for Standardization (ISO tanks).
[c]As opposed to fuel cells in CHP applications which are usually heat-driven, prime power fuel cells are operated in accordance with a given power demand while the heat production is of minor interest. Such applications include, for example, remote telecom antennas and back-up power systems.

23.2 MERIT ASSESSMENT OF STATIONARY FCH TECHNOLOGIES AND PATHWAYS

MERITS AND KEY PARAMETERS

The FCH technologies described in the previous section are evaluated based on a set of merits, which reflect the characteristics of the technologies as well as their sustainability, i.e. their implications on economy, society, and environment. The chosen merits can be quantified for all FCH technologies as well as for their concatenation in pathways (where appropriate):

- Technology
  - Flexibility (potential to avoid curtailment of variable renewable power generation);
  - Maturity (Technology Readiness Level—TRL[d]);
  - Regulatory coverage.
- Economy
  - Levelized costs;
  - Marginal CO_2 abatement costs.
- Society
  - Public acceptability.
- Environment
  - CO_2 emissions.

To take into account different expectations and uncertainties with respect to the development of the merits and the deployment of the technologies, a set of key parameters including corresponding default values and value ranges was defined for the merit assessment (Table 23.1). The assessment was then implemented in the form of a spreadsheet tool, and a merit ranking tool was developed which can be downloaded from the website of INSIGHT_E.[e] The tool allows users to specify key parameter values themselves, according to their expectations or case studies they would like to analyze. The selection of the key parameters directly changes the merit values on the one hand and the available FCH technologies and pathways[f] on the other hand. For more details on key parameters, merit definitions, and merit values the reader is referred to the corresponding INSIGHT_E policy report [11].

EVALUATION OF FOUR CASE STUDIES

The capabilities of the merit assessment tool for FCH pathways are demonstrated with four case studies. These case studies are based on a narrative which is translated into a set of key parameter assumptions (Table 23.1), which then yields specific merit values for each case study. Fig. 23.2

---

[d]The European Technology Readiness Level (TRL) scale is a metric for describing the maturity of a technology. The scale consists of nine levels. Each level characterizes the progress in the development of a technology, from the idea (level 1) to the full deployment of the product in the marketplace (level 9).
[e]www.insightenergy.org.
[f]For example, novel FCH technologies are only available if the TRL is high enough and large-scale FCH technologies are only available if hydrogen is also used in the transport sector.

Table 23.1 Key Parameters and Case Study Assumptions

Key Parameter	Default Value	Value Range	Case Study 1	Case Study 2	Case Study 3	Case Study 4
Time period	2020–30	2040–50	2020–30	2020–30	2020–30/ 2040–50	2020–30
Interest rate (%)	6	0–6	6	6	6/6	6
Electricity price	45 ($€_{2014}$/MWh$_e$)	20–70	45	45	20/45	70
Natural gas price	30 ($€_{2014}$/GJ$_{th}$)	10–50	30	10	10/30	10
Biomass price	3 ($€_{2014}$/GJ$_{th}$)	2–0	5	0	0	8
Hydrogen price	35 ($€_{2014}$/GJ$_{th}$)	5–65	35	35	35	65
CO$_2$ price[a]	35 ($€_{2014}$/tCO$_2$)	10–60	35	35	60	10
Electricity mix CO$_2$ intensity[b]	50 (gCO$_2$/kWh$_e$)	0–1000	50	100	500/50	500
Hydrogen use in other sectors	High	Low	High	Low	Low/high	Low
TRL threshold	8	6–9	7	7	7/9	9
Public acceptability	Medium	Low, high	Medium	Medium	High	Low
Variable renewable energy share over the system peak demand (%)	40	20–60	40	30	40	20

[a]On February 25, 2016, the certificate price was below 5 €/tCO$_2$ [9].
[b]In 2011, the CO$_2$ intensity per kWh generated (gCO$_2$/kWh$_e$) was 375 (Denmark), 71 (France), 672 (Germany), 411 (Italy), 343 (Spain), 23 (Sweden), and 509 (UK) [10].

displays the result for the merit "levelized cost" for Case Study 1. The results for the other merits and the other case studies are presented in the policy report [11]. The abbreviations used in Fig. 23.2 are explained in Fig. 23.1.

Case Study 1: Off-Grid Power Generation for Islands

This case study explores pathways through which FCH can play a role in the short term for electricity generation on European islands with limited interconnections with the mainland. Sustainable power generation in island territories is a key challenge for the coming decades, because their power supply currently depends largely on fossil energy sources. Further, the small size of their power grids results in a rather high black-out probability, and larger shares of variable renewable resources are difficult to introduce. A hydrogen chain from renewable energy sources (wind, solar) up to fuel-cell end-use applications is a possible solution for islands to help reduce their carbon footprint and to strengthen the reliability of the grid by a better management of peak demand.

Such a FCH pathway (*green* (gray in print versions) box in Fig. 23.2) for the power supply in remote areas has promising merits in terms of levelized costs (Fig. 23.2), CO$_2$ emissions, and flexibility. Polymer electrolyte membrane and alkaline electrolyzers can both be used for hydrogen generation. The hydrogen storage in gas tanks and subsequent onsite consumption allows for handling varying energy demand (daily and even seasonal variations in case of relatively large

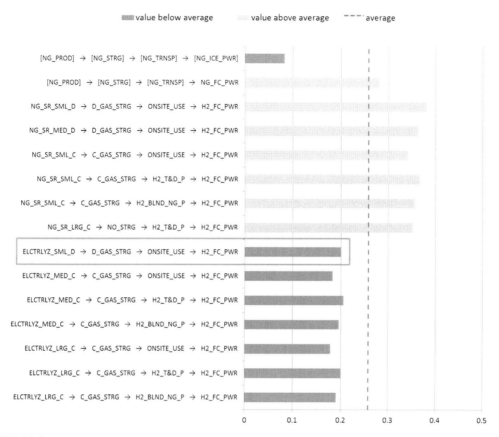

FIGURE 23.2

Levelized costs of all possible pathways for power generation in Case Study 1, in €2014/kWh$_e$ (see Fig. 23.1 for abbreviations). The *green* (gray in print versions) box indicates the pathway Case Study 1 focuses on.

energy demand). The hydrogen fuel cell not only allows for efficient electricity generation, but also for efficient heat production in colder areas where space heating is required. On larger islands, the flexibility can be increased by either increasing the size of variable power supply and hydrogen storage, or by changing to a larger electrolyzer at the expense of higher capital and operation costs.

Under the assumptions of the case study (Table 23.1), the FCH pathway under consideration is cost-competitive to the evaluated natural gas-based fuel cell pathways already in 2020−30. Thus, no policy support is required except for early adopters, because of the presently high capital costs of electrolyzers and fuel cell plants. Competing non-FCH technologies, such as the storage of electricity from variable renewables in batteries and (partial) grid connection with the mainland (for islands located close to the mainland), are not quantitatively included in the present study.

Case Study 2: Power Generation for Southern European Countries

This case study explores the role of FCH pathways in the short term for small but densely populated national systems located in the south of Europe with limited cross-border interconnections. National real income and income per capita are both expected to increase, so that the demand for electricity is projected to grow accordingly. The willingness to invest in very advanced technologies is limited due to market barriers, lack of awareness, and high interest rates for such investments. Moreover, the international market conditions are expected to keep natural gas prices low and the correlated electricity price is medium for the 2020−30 period. Nevertheless, the interest towards alternative energy sources and renewable energies in particular in the power sector is mature enough for targeted commitments, so that the country expects to then cover a significant fraction of its future electricity demand with variable renewables sources. The use of domestic biomass as an energy source is limited and generally expensive. Due to the low willingness to invest, only mature technologies with medium to high readiness levels are taken into consideration, while the public acceptability is not expected to be a strong barrier to the deployment of FCH technologies.

Under the assumption of the case study (Table 23.1) described above, we find small decentralized electrolysis with decentralized hydrogen gas tanks and the onsite use of the produced hydrogen in fuel cell district CHP plants to be particularly promising for producing electricity. This pathway offers benefits regarding flexibility, costs, CO_2 emissions, and regulatory coverage compared to the other possible FCH pathways. Hydrogen production via electrolysis is of particular interest for this case study due to its flexibility and low CO_2 emissions. On the other hand, when compared with natural gas-based pathways, FCH pathways generally suffer from lower regulatory coverage, lower public acceptance, and higher costs. To support power generation from FCH pathways in southern Europe their costs must be reduced, further R&D is required, standards and regulations are needed, and public acceptance must be enhanced.

Case Study 3: Strategic Push for Hydrogen in the Residential and Commercial Sector

This case study evaluates the situation of a group of EU Member States in northwest Europe, strongly reliant on natural gas, which determine that they will look to push towards a hydrogen economy, encompassing the transport, industry, and buildings sectors. This is driven in the post-Paris Agreement era by a more radical thinking about what is required for a successful transition, and a prevailing view that electrification of end-use services is not adequate in itself for full decarbonization. Hydrogen will need to play a prominent role, building on an ambition to re-purpose the existing gas distribution system to deliver hydrogen, in addition to a whole range of other mitigation actions. This means that in the mid-term period (2020−30) these countries experience a strong push for the commercialization of FCH applications and plan re-orientation of their gas infrastructure. In the longer term (2040−50), we see the roll out of large-scale distribution systems, effectively allowing for an extensive penetration of hydrogen into the transport and buildings sectors. The case study further illustrates the implications of a push towards several favorable conditions for the deployment of FCH technologies and applications in the residential and commercial sector (onsite power and building heat generation). The strategic push consists of higher natural gas prices, higher CO_2 prices, higher technology readiness (i.e., R&D investments), and more renewable power in the electricity supply mix in 2040−50 compared to 2020−30 (Table 23.1).

These assumptions lead to cost-competitiveness and lower CO_2 emissions of biomass- and electrolyzer-based hydrogen pathways in the long term (2040−50) compared with conventional pathways for prime power fuel cells for onsite power and micro-CHP plants for supplying heat for buildings. Natural gas-fueled micro-CHP plants are another option in the residential and commercial sector. They can rely on the existing gas network and are therefore available in the short and medium term. While still too expensive in 2020−30, they become cost-competitive in 2040−50 compared to the conventional natural gas technologies. Regarding CO_2 emissions, natural gas-fueled fuel cell pathways have only medium ranks in the long term: they are worse than renewable hydrogen pathways and better than natural gas-based hydrogen pathways.

Case Study 4: Delayed Climate Action Scenario

This case study explores the FCH pathways under a delayed climate action scenario. Low public and political interest in climate change and in new energy technologies leads to high interest rates for new projects and small investments in R&D. Mainly mature technologies will be deployed. Due to the public disinterest, the political will to reach the "2030 climate and energy framework" goal of a minimum cut of 40% in GHG emissions (from 1990 levels) in the EU is missing. There are no individual binding targets for Member States on certain energy sectors or for reforming and strengthening the ETS (EU emissions trading system, see Section II). Hence, the CO_2 price remains low. The expansion of renewable energies is neglected, resulting in a low share of renewable energies in the electricity mix. The shale gas boom in the USA has passed, which results in more demand for coal. This allows natural gas to increase in importance in the European electricity mix. One reason for the negligence of the renewable power generation is the low natural gas price caused by new pipeline projects in the North Sea and the Middle East. Declining subsidies for renewable energies paired with increasing electricity demand result in comparably high electricity prices. With no significant CO_2 price signal, the use of hydrogen in the transport sector remains small. Hydrogen thus stems from small and medium production facilities only and is expensive.

Under the assumption of delayed climate action in this case study (Table 23.1), only a limited subset of all the possible FCH pathways is available, because the use of hydrogen in other sectors is low and the TRLs stay relatively low, too. Hence, such a scenario does not favor FCH technologies and pathways. Nevertheless, they are still a possible option for all energy services (except grid electricity). The case study shows that FCH technologies and pathways are marginalized under delayed climate action. Conventional (natural gas-based) pathways are found to be more cost-competitive and may be selected for industry and building applications. The CO_2 emissions of different FCH pathways for onsite power and building heat in 2040−50 have to be scrutinized individually; they can be above or below the conventional use of natural gas.

SELECTED FINDINGS FOR FCH TECHNOLOGIES AND APPLICATIONS

Storage of Excess Electricity and Ancillary Services

Electrolyzers can be used to store electricity in the form of hydrogen. They are best suited in electricity grids supplied with a high share of variable renewable energies. Such low-carbon electricity supply is also crucial for a low-carbon footprint of electrolysis. In our ranking results, electrolysis is usually cost-competitive with other hydrogen generation technologies. Nevertheless, the comparison depends on the assumed prices of natural gas, electricity, CO_2, and biomass. Regulatory coverage, maturity, and public acceptability are found to be high for electrolysis.

Methanation, the process for the production of methane from hydrogen, is found to have medium regulatory coverage and public acceptance. The costs are comparatively high and the TRL is quite low. More R&D is thus needed to improve its technology readiness. The cost-competitiveness and the business case of the entire methanation pathways are not yet proven.

Re-Electrification of Grid Electricity Stored in the Form of Gas

Re-electrification of hydrogen is possible with gas turbines, district CHP plants, or prime power fuel cells. Hydrogen turbines are a relatively expensive, only partially regulated and immature solution. This is also true for hydrogen-fueled district CHP plants but at lower costs. Prime power fuel cells are mature and covered by standards, but still comparably expensive (in the range of hydrogen turbines). All three technologies do not emit CO_2 during operation.

The re-electrification of methane from methanation can be carried out by gas turbines, gas engines, district CHP plants (with and without fuel cell), and by prime power fuel cells. The regulatory coverage and the maturity of all these technologies are high. The public acceptability of novel fuel cell technologies is slightly lower that of conventional gas technologies. Gas engines and prime power fuel cells are found to be more expensive solutions than the alternatives. All these technologies emit CO_2 during operation. District CHP plants with fuel cell and natural gas combined-cycle plants have the lowest emissions.

As displayed in Fig. 22.7, conversion efficiencies of power-to-power pathways are quite low. This leads to comparably high costs over the whole pathway. Instead, CO_2 emissions can be very low, namely if hydrogen is produced from low-carbon electricity.

Blending of Hydrogen in Natural Gas Pipelines

Blending of hydrogen in natural gas pipelines is expected to require only small modifications of the gas grid (see sub-chapter on hydrogen transport in Section 23.1). Nevertheless, the hydrogen concentration and gas ratio must be controlled to avoid damage to the equipment running on the gas mixture. Compared with the other considered hydrogen transmission and distribution options, hydrogen blending in natural gas pipelines (up to 15% by volume) has high public acceptability, high regulatory coverage, and low costs. The major barrier is the medium maturity (TRL 7 in 2020–30), which can be improved by further R&D on the impact of the gas mixture on the gas grid and applications.

Micro-CHP Plants with Fuel Cells

Micro-CHP plants have a relatively high maturity and high public acceptability, and are fully covered by regulations. If fueled with natural gas, the CO_2 emissions are comparable to conventional natural gas technologies. The levelized costs are found to be comparatively high for heat generation and in the range of conventional technologies for power generation, but these results also depend on natural gas and hydrogen prices.

23.3 **ENERGY SYSTEM PERSPECTIVE**

The merit assessment in the previous section allows for evaluations on a technology and pathway level but not on the energy system level. Energy system modeling and scenario studies can provide a complementary view on the interactions of FCH technologies and pathways with the rest of the energy system. In particular, energy system scenario studies allow for the analysis of the services stationary FCH technologies and applications can provide to the energy system, their deployment and potential under different boundary conditions, and the identification of synergies between stationary and mobile applications. In the following, three exemplary scenario studies are analyzed to describe the potential role of stationary FCH applications in the future energy system.

GLOBAL PERSPECTIVE

The global perspective is represented by a study of the World Energy Council and the Paul Scherrer Institute (WEC/PSI) [12]. Two world energy scenarios represent a consumer-driven, market-oriented (JAZZ), and a voter-driven, regulation-oriented future (SYMPHONY). JAZZ and SYMPHONY are not normative, but likely scenarios which explore feasible outcomes. The hydrogen sector is modeled in great detail, offering all major current and conceived future options for hydrogen production and transport. For example, the hydrogen production technologies also include CCS options for natural gas reforming and coal gasification as well as different nuclear generation technologies. In both scenarios, hydrogen enters the energy system in 2020. After relapsing during the following decade, its use increases again towards 2050.

The intermediate peak of hydrogen use in the 2020 period is mainly caused by the car sector: hydrogen produced by natural gas steam reforming in combination with hydrogen hybrid cars are temporarily found to be cost-competitive mainly in China and the USA. However, the share of hydrogen in the total final consumption is marginal: for JAZZ it increases from 0.1% in 2025 to 0.3% in 2050. For SYMPHONY, the shares are slightly higher with 0.2% in 2025 and 0.5% in 2050. The share of hydrogen in electricity generation is zero in 2025 in both scenarios. Its contribution increases to 0.1% and 0.3% in 2050 for JAZZ and SYMPHONY, respectively. In both scenarios, the hydrogen production is initially dominated by natural gas steam reforming and to a lower extent by coal gasification (Fig. 23.3). In the later time periods, natural gas steam reforming stays in the mix, coal gasification is extended and nuclear hydrogen technologies are deployed. Biomass gasification plays a minor role in both scenarios.

In JAZZ, the hydrogen deployment starts in the car sector and (on a very low level) in decentralized FCH applications. From 2040, also central FCH applications are used. Nevertheless, the decentralized applications continue to dominate the stationary sector. In SYMPHONY, the hydrogen sector is dominated by the car sector. The stationary sector includes first more decentralized applications whose share is then surpassed by the centralized applications. The split between decentralized and centralized applications in the two scenarios implies synergies of central applications with a more developed passenger car sector due to the economies of scale and technology learning in production and distribution of hydrogen. Overall, the size of the stationary hydrogen sector is the same in both scenarios, independent of the difference in the CO_2 price.

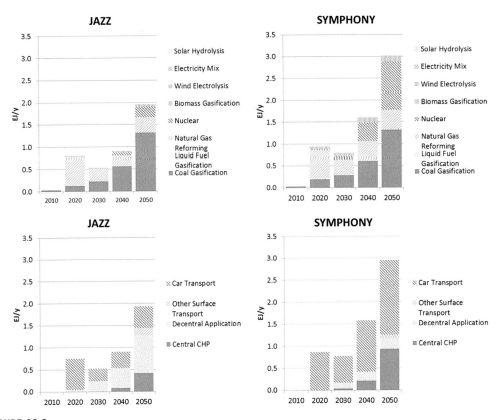

FIGURE 23.3

Hydrogen production (upper two figures) and use (lower two figures) in the WEC/PSI scenarios JAZZ and SYMPHONY. (Electricity mix refers to hydrogen production from the electricity mix of the respective year as derived from the applied model.)

EUROPEAN PERSPECTIVE

The Joint Research Centre of the European Union (JRC) conducted a scenario study on the European level [7]. Two scenarios according to EU policy trends were evaluated: Current Policy Initiative (CPI) and Stringent Decarbonization (CAP). In CPI, the 20−20−20 targets of the EU are considered for the year 2020 and later, that is 20% less CO_2 emissions compared to 1990, 20% final energy consumption supplied by renewables, and a 20% increase in energy efficiency. In addition, the scenario assumes a 27% lower total primary energy supply in 2030. The scenario results in a renewable electricity share of approximately 60% in 2050 (35% of which by PV, wind, and ocean power). In CAP, the policy assumptions are as in the CPI scenario, but with a more stringent decarbonization target of 80% less CO_2 emissions in 2050 compared to 1990. The scenario results also in a renewable electricity share of approximately 60% in 2050 (again with 35% by PV, wind, and ocean power).

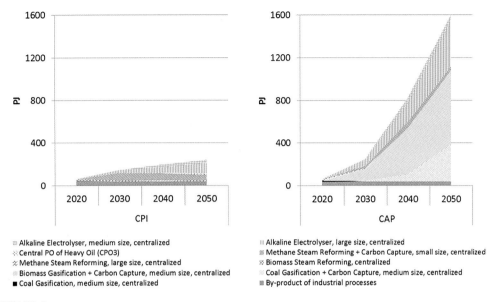

FIGURE 23.4

Hydrogen production technologies in the EU under the JRC scenarios CPI and CAP.

The modeling shows a relatively early deployment of hydrogen technologies starting in the period 2020−30. The amounts of hydrogen production relative to final energy consumption are small. In the CAP scenario with a more stringent climate policy, hydrogen provides merely 4% of the total final energy demand in the year 2050 and below 1% in 2030. In the CPI scenario, the amounts are even smaller. In the year 2050, 1% and 6% of industrial energy demand is met by hydrogen in the CPI and CAP scenario, respectively. Similarly, 1% and 5% of the transport energy demand in the year 2050 is satisfied by hydrogen in the CPI and CAP scenario, respectively, whereas it is basically 0% in 2030 in both scenarios. The most significant use is not in fuel cell cars (0%/6% of person-km in 2050 in CPI/CAP) but in public buses (3%/40% of person-km in CPI/CAP).

Apart from fossil sources (partially with CCS), a large amount of hydrogen is produced from centralized electrolyzers and from biomass (Fig. 23.4). Generation from biomass profits when used in conjunction with CCS, because this technology has negative CO_2 emissions. Synthetic fuel production is also a major application for hydrogen, e.g., for kerosene. Most of the hydrogen is consumed in industry (70% in the CAP scenario), where it is mainly used for the reduction of iron and other related processes (50% of the respective process energy demands are covered by hydrogen). The dedicated stationary use of hydrogen for heat and power is small. The major applications in both scenarios are stationary fuel cells for electricity generation.

A NATIONAL PERSPECTIVE

A typical example of a national level study is the UK scenario study by E4TECH and University College London (UCL) [13]. Two scenarios are explored that meet UK climate reduction goals of

80% greenhouse gas emission reductions in 2050 relative to 1990: The Critical Path scenario, in which the use of hydrogen in end-uses is seen to be strategically important, and the Full Contribution scenario, which models aggressive hydrogen uptake based on an early, consistent and long-term commitment to the extensive use of hydrogen across the economy.

In the Critical Path scenario, there are no expansive infrastructure investments and developments pre-2030. Key model results show that hydrogen provides 1% of final energy by 2040 in the industrial sectors. This expands to a modest extent by 2050—but strong uptake is not seen due to more cost-effective options. Hydrogen in gas turbines as a peaking technology provides 30 GW of capacity (out of a total power sector capacity of 120 GW). As the supply system expands, centralized hydrogen production via natural gas steam reforming becomes the dominant production type. The scenario shows strong uptake of hydrogen in the road transport sector by 2050, with no explicit role for hydrogen for residential or commercial heating.

The Full Contribution scenario sees a strategic push for hydrogen across all sectors. A key feature of the scenario is the replacement of gas by hydrogen across the existing gas pipeline network. However, strong penetration, due to network repurposing limits, would only be observed after 2025. Hydrogen also accounts for nearly 50% of energy consumption in industry, displacing natural gas (Fig. 23.5). As per the earlier scenario, hydrogen is also used in the power sector to provide both peak and mid-merit generation in open- and closed-cycle gas turbine power plants. The main sector that drives production and supply prior to 2050 is the transport sector. In buildings, hydrogen accounts for about 20% of residential and service sector heat demand (in both hydrogen boilers or from hydrogen-fueled district heating). In total, hydrogen production is

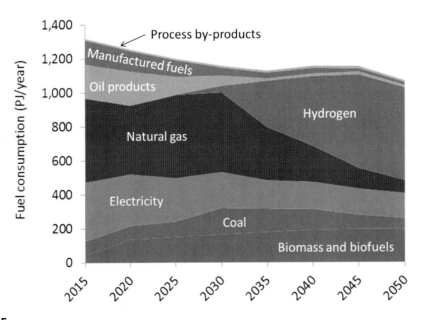

FIGURE 23.5

UK industrial fuel consumption under E4TECH/UCL Full Contribution scenario.

around six times higher than in the previous scenario, with production focused on natural gas steam reforming.

A key message from the analysis is that even with a strong strategic, more centralized push, the role for hydrogen use in end-use sectors is limited in the medium term by how quickly supply systems can be scaled. It also highlights that the pre-2030 uptake of hydrogen applications is highly contingent on a strategic vision for hydrogen in the longer term, and a strong set of actions in the very near term.

INSIGHTS FROM THE SCENARIO STUDIES

The goal of the evaluation of the scenario studies was to gain insights into the role of stationary FCH technologies and pathways within the whole energy system, i.e., including interactions with the mobility sector and industrial uses. Significant deployment of hydrogen ($>10\%$ of energy consumption) almost surely occurs only in the post-2025 period (if it happens at all), even with an immediate strategic focus on developing a hydrogen economy. Some of the obstacles are the large infrastructure requirements for developing a widespread system, and the technology readiness of specific applications. Before 2025, hydrogen is only used in niche applications. Nevertheless, this short-term period is still critical for R&D, strategic planning, and market capacity development if hydrogen is viewed as a crucial energy carrier for a low-carbon energy-system transition.

The scenarios that show a large deployment of hydrogen have two features: A strong uptake in the transportation sectors and a high carbon price. If the carbon price signal is not strong enough, as for example in the WEC/PSI scenarios, the hydrogen penetration is relatively low and hydrogen stays a niche energy vector. A strategic positioning towards hydrogen is needed for larger deployment, as illustrated in the UK-based Full Contribution scenario. This reflects the need to focus R&D on specific sectors, to consider infrastructure development, and to develop the necessary policy incentives. The (un)availability of CCS influences the use of hydrogen in any case: In the EU scenarios, limited deployment of CCS leads to a strong deployment of hydrogen via electrolysis. However, in the UK scenario, the stronger availability of CCS allows for hydrogen production via natural gas steam reforming.

23.4 CONCLUSIONS AND POLICY RECOMMENDATIONS

The potential role of FCH technologies in the energy system and their particular benefits depend decisively on the boundary conditions: With low natural gas prices, low carbon prices, low shares of renewable power generation, low R&D investments, and without particular (financial, regulatory, and political) support schemes for FCH technologies, stationary FCH applications will stay marginal and unfavorable. Benefits of FCH technologies in terms of CO_2 emissions and flexibility occur only with high carbon prices and with a large share of renewable power generation.

The current policy in the EU aims at stringent greenhouse gas emission targets which should be achieved via an increasing carbon price and, thus, the deployment of more renewable energies. Under such boundary conditions, stationary FCH applications can provide benefits to the energy system in terms of a low-carbon energy supply and increased flexibility to cope with variable renewable energies. Based on the assessments presented in this chapter, a strategic push of EU energy policies into the following directions seems to be necessary to realize these benefits.

Establishing a High Carbon Price

High carbon prices are found to be a major driver for the deployment of FCH technologies in the merit assessment as well as in the scenario studies. With higher CO_2 prices, the share of renewable hydrogen and power generation is expected to increase, while natural gas-based technologies and pathways lose competitiveness.

Supporting Renewable Energies

In case CO_2 prices stay low, direct support of renewable technologies may be considered. The effect of more renewable energies in the energy system is found to be twofold: (1) The CO_2 intensity of the electricity mix is lowered, which makes hydrogen production from electrolysis more attractive. (2) The higher share of variable power supply enables electrolysis to play to its strength regarding the flexibility it provides to the system.

Investing in Research & Development

The TRL of many FCH technologies is currently low. While a set of technologies is expected to reach maturity in the period from 2020 to 2030, many other technologies such as methanation and hydrogen generation from biomass will only be available in the long term. Investment in R&D can enable an earlier maturity of such technologies and enlarge the range of possible FCH technology investments with their associated benefits. Regarding competitiveness with Asia and North America, it is important for the EU to invest as soon as possible in research and development to allow for cost reductions by improving performance and durability.

Supporting FCH Infrastructure

Hydrogen-based pathways require new infrastructure. The development of the infrastructure requires financial, public, and regulatory support. Based on the insights gained from the scenario studies, a strategic political planning of the required infrastructure developments is needed to enable earlier and stronger deployment of FCH technologies and pathways.

Establishing Codes and Standards

The regulatory coverage of many FCH technologies has been found to be incomplete in the merit assessment. Establishing codes and standards for all FCH technologies is a key element that encourages investments in the development and demonstration of new technologies up to market readiness.

Enhancing Communication with the Public

The merit assessment showed that public acceptability of many FCH technologies is low, which can hinder their implementation. Information of the public regarding the benefits and risks of FCH technologies is expected to help in realizing FCH projects.

This chapter discussed stationary FCH technologies as solutions for dealing with increasing shares of variable renewable power generation. Such solutions are required to ensure the reliability of power supply in Europe, the value of which is discussed in more detail in Chapter 24, Need for Reliability and Measuring its Cost.

REFERENCES

[1] J.M. Andújar, F. Segura, Fuel cells: history and updating. A walk along two centuries, Renew. Sustain. Energy Rev. 13 (9) (2009) 2309–2322.

[2] Center for Energy, Environmental, and Economic Systems Analysis (CEEESA), Assessing current, near-term, and long-term U.S. Hydrogen Markets, 2016 [Online]. Available from: <http://ceeesa.es.anl.gov/news/HydrogenMarkets.html>.

[3] R.M. Dell, P.T. Moseley, D.A.J. Rand, Hydrogen, fuel cells and fuel cell vehicles, Towards Sustainable Road Transport, Academic Press, Oxford, 2014.

[4] B. Suresh, R. Gubler, X. He, Y. Yamag, Chemical Economics Handbook, IHS Chemical, Englewood, CO, 2015.

[5] AFHYPAC, Production et Consommation d'Hydrogene Aujourd'hui, Mémento de l'Hydrogène, FICHE 1.3, 2016.

[6] Siemens, SILYZER 200: high-pressure efficiency in the megawatt range, 2016 [Online]. Available from: <http://www.industry.siemens.com/topics/global/en/pem-electrolyzer/silyzer/Documents/broucher-silyzer-en.pdf>.

[7] A. Sgobbi, W. Nijs, R. De Miglio, A. Chiodi, M. Gargiulo, C. Thiel, How far away is hydrogen? Its role in the medium and long-term decarbonisation of the European energy system, Int. J. Hydrogen Energy 41 (1) (2015) 19–35.

[8] Deutscher Verein des Gas- und Wasserfachs, Arbeitsblatt G 260—Gasbeschaffenheit, 2013.

[9] EEX, European emission allowances, 2016 [Online]. Available from: <https://www.eex.com/en/market-data/emission-allowances/spot-market/european-emission-allowances#!/2016/02/25>.

[10] econometrica, Technical paper—electricity-specific emission factors for grid electricity, 2011. <http://economietrica.com/assets/Electricity-specific-emission-factors-for-grid-electricity.pdf>.

[11] K. Volkart, B. Cox, M. Densing, R. De Miglio, T. Priem, S. Pye, Assessments of the merit of hydrogen and fuel cell pathways for energy applications. INSIGHT_E Policy Report No.6, 2016.

[12] WEC/PSI, World Energy Scenarios – Composing Energy Futures to 2050, World Energy Council, London, 2013.

[13] D. Hart, J. Howes, F. Lehner, P.E. Dodds, N. Hughes, B. Fais, et al., Scenarios for deployment of hydrogen in contributing to meeting carbon budgets and the 2050 target. Report to the Committee on Climate Change, 2015.

[14] I. Drmač, D. Jakšić, N. Karadža, R. Kunze, J. Dehler, R. De Miglio, et al., Exploring the strengths and weaknesses of European innovation capacity within the Strategic Energy Technologies (SET) Plan, 2015.

NEED FOR RELIABILITY AND MEASURING ITS COST

Abhishek Shivakumar[1], Manuel Welsch[1], Constantinos Taliotis[1], Dražen Jakšić[2], Tomislav Baričević[2], and Mark Howells[1]

[1]KTH Royal Institute of Technology, Stockholm, Sweden [2]Energy Institute Hrvoje Požar (EIHP), Zagreb, Croatia

Power supply in the EU is characterized by a relatively high reliability. However, the reliability we experience today should not be taken for granted given the increasing shares of variable electricity generation, but also new opportunities to engage consumers through Smart Grids—and interrupt their supply as needed. Choosing the ideal level of reliability to aim for requires a thorough understanding of the socioeconomic costs of electricity supply interruptions, which may be very different depending on timing and type of consumer. For example, while a household may not notice an interruption during office hours, a company unable to electronically submit a tender in time might potentially lose millions.[a]

Estimating the socioeconomic costs is a nontrivial task, yet is required to determine socially optimal levels of interruptions. Such levels would ensure that investments to increase the system's reliability are balanced with the associated financial benefits, i.e., the reduced costs due to fewer and shorter interruptions. However, most reliability studies focus on suppliers. The value that society places on reliability is not clearly known across the EU. Also, the current distribution of costs between stakeholders lacks a causal link between those in charge of ensuring the power system's reliability and those having to bear the consequences of an outage.

In this chapter, we first discuss the characterization of interruptions based on different factors. Before discussing the quantification of interruption costs, we first briefly discuss the composition of interruption costs. Following this, we explore methods to quantify the costs associated with interruptions, highlighting the merits and demerits of each method. We present specific case studies to illustrate the heterogeneity of interruptions, both in their causes and effects. Further, we look at the integration of renewables through smart grids and the implications on system reliability. Finally, we point out the importance of managing electricity supply based on the provision of energy services rather than pure kilowatt hours.

24.1 CHARACTERIZING INTERRUPTIONS

Prior to estimating the costs of interruptions, it is useful to understand the reasons why the consequences of supply interruptions differ from one to another:

---

[a]However, the actual damage to society might just be less than the additional cost for a more expensive, but potentially also better tender.

Europe's Energy Transition. DOI: http://dx.doi.org/10.1016/B978-0-12-809806-6.00024-9

Firstly, there are different *types of end-users* in the electricity system. An interruption in a hospital has very different consequences to one in an industrial plant or household. Another important aspect is the *time of occurrence of the interruption*. The type of activity that is interrupted is dependent on the time of day, week, and season. For example, for a household, an interruption at 8 p.m. may interfere with recreation (e.g., television, internet), while at 3 a.m. an interruption typically has much smaller effects.

In addition to the time of occurrence, the *duration of an interruption* also significantly influences its impact. Certain types of damage, such as the loss of computer files, occur instantaneously. Others, such as the loss of working hours and the spoilage of food, are proportional to the length of the interruption and may only occur after a certain delay.

Advance notification of an electricity interruption also helps in mitigating its negative implications. For example, if one is made aware of an electricity interruption, they may avoid using an elevator. Further, if electricity supply is interrupted on a regular basis, people may prepare for it even without advance notification. While this may reduce the cost per interruption, the overall impact of electricity supply interruptions will be larger (e.g., less confidence of industry in the reliability of the system).

This relates as well to the *perceived reliability level*: the higher the perceived reliability in the affected area, the less firms and households are inclined to take precautionary measures (e.g., invest in backup facilities), and the greater the damage caused by an interruption (known as the "vulnerability conflict").

Also of importance is the *source of the outage*: an outage caused by a failure in the network may have smaller price effects than an outage caused by a shortage in generation, due to a higher redundancy in the grid.

Resulting electricity price increases can lead to large transfers of wealth from users to suppliers. While these transfers of wealth are not necessarily a social cost, they must be considered in policy making [1].

24.2 COMPOSITION OF COSTS

Typically, cost information can be inferred from a market. However, currently consumers have no option to choose the tariff they pay depending on the level of reliability they receive. Thus, grid operators lack information on the value of reliability improvements and, in unbundled markets, utilities lack balanced incentives to engage in related investments.

In the absence of market mechanisms, assessments of the costs of interruptions are required. Various types of costs need to be considered, including direct infrastructure costs and indirect costs, such as production outages. In addition, macroeconomic long-term costs related to market adjustments may occur, e.g., due to changes in the choice of business locations or investments in back-up generation.

Households: For households, only a part of the costs can be directly related to the household expenses, e.g., to replace spoiled food. Indirect, immaterial costs equally require consideration. These may include fear (e.g., to walk in an unlit neighborhood), inconvenience (e.g., freezing), and the loss of leisure time (e.g., missing the championship's final). To assess the customer's desire for security of supply commonly the willingness-to-pay (WTP) is being quantified, as further outlined later in this chapter.

Industries and commercial services: There are primarily four sources of indirect costs of power outages in industries and commercial services [2]. First, their output will be affected leading to a loss of profits. Second, power outages can result in a loss of productivity during the outage and when restarting production/operations after an interruption (e.g., recovering unsaved computer files). Third, materials and/or equipment can be damaged by an electricity outage (e.g., dyeing in the textile industry, aluminum smelting). Fourth, there may be costs of labor required after a power outage. For instance, additional labor is sometimes required to restart production for which overtime bonuses may have to be paid. Long-term costs like a loss in reputation due to production delays are often neglected.

24.3 QUANTIFYING COSTS

Several methods are available to quantitatively evaluate the effects of a supply interruption [3,4]. These include the following:

1. *Surveys/interviews (stated preferences)*: In general, the costs of interruptions may be measured by estimating the value of lost load (VoLL). One method to determine this value is to ask people how much damage they have suffered due to supply interruptions, how much they are willing to pay (WTP) for a given reduction in interruptions, the minimum amount of money they are willing-to-accept (WTA) as compensation for an increase in interruptions, or which combination of electricity price and number, duration and timing of interruptions they prefer (conjoint analysis) [5,6]. The latter may also be referred to as a choice experiment. When carried out in Sweden, such a study showed that the marginal WTP of households to reduce power outages increases with duration, and is higher during weekends and winter months [7]. This is confirmed by a study in Austria, which found that the WTP is 33% higher in winter than in summer [8]. On a yearly average, values ranged from €1.4 to avoid a 1-hour power cut to €17.3 to avoid a 24-hour interruption.

Table 24.1 summarizes and compares the VoLL for households from past survey-based studies in different countries.

The VoLLs for different countries vary due to factors such as the method used to value lost leisure time (e.g., nonpaid time, during weekends) and the time or season of occurrence. In

Table 24.1 Comparison of Outage Cost Studies for Residential Consumers (VoLL)

Reference	Country	VoLL (€/kWh)
Baarsma and Hop [9]	Netherlands	3.66
Bertazzi et al. [10]	Italy	10.89
Bliem [11]	Austria	5.3
Kjølle et al. [12]	Norway	1.08
Lawton et al. [13]	USA	7.8

developed countries with more severe winters, the total electricity consumed on a winter evening may be relatively high. Since the electricity consumed is in the denominator of calculating the VoLL, a higher electricity consumption may result in a lower VoLL (although the price of electricity itself during this period may remain high).

2. *Production-function approach*: This approach aims to estimate the welfare costs of a power-supply interruption across different sectors, durations, and times of occurrence in a week (weekday during the day, weekday evenings, and weekends), based on macroeconomic indicators. Welfare costs can be quantified through assessing the lost production for the commercial sector and lost convenience (or leisure time) for households. Within the production-function approach, quantitative statistical information is used to determine the costs in relation to a given supply interruption [14]. The lost production in each sector during an outage can be estimated directly and then aggregated to a macroeconomic total. Interactions between sectors can also be evaluated through input–output tables [15].

3. *Market behavior (revealed preferences)*: Another method to estimate how the industrial, commercial and household sectors value supply interruptions is through information on their expenditures on backup facilities, interruptible contracts, and interruption insurances. The level of expenditure on backup facilities indicates how much businesses, industry, and households are willing to pay for a higher level of supply security [16]. Past studies advocating this method were applied to cases with an average of 10 hours of interruptions per year [17]. For most of the EU, this value is larger than the cumulative duration of interruptions in a year (see Fig. 24.1 [18]) and backup generators would only have to be used for short periods of time. This would mean that the

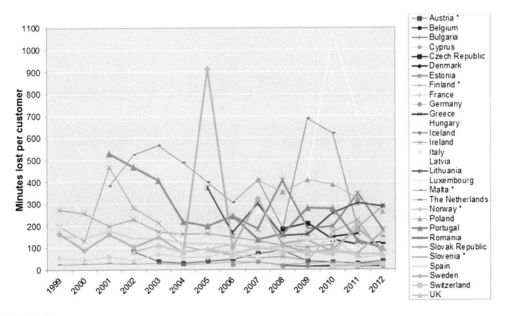

FIGURE 24.1

Unplanned interruptions > 3 minutes.

cost of capital per minute of operation is often too high for businesses or households to invest in backup technology (exceptions include hospitals and banks). This is in contrast to the US, where 22% of the peak demand equaling 170 GW is available in the form of consumer backup generators. This includes generators of up to 60 MW, but 98% of them are smaller than 100 kW [19]. In the case of Europe, the market for diesel generators has shown signs of steady growth in the past few years [20]. However, a figure of the currently present total backup generator capacity in the EU could not be identified.

4. *Case studies*: There are two main approaches to using case studies to estimate the cost of supply interruptions. In one method, effects of an actual supply interruption are first listed and these are then monetized [21]. Another approach is to undertake direct surveys after an interruption [22]. An advantage of case studies is that an actual rather than a hypothetical interruption is studied. Also, the interruption studied can be representative of other interruptions in similar circumstances (geographical location, time of occurrence, and duration of interruption), and may be used to draw some general conclusions. Some studies have shown that revealed preferences (market behavior) provides a more objective basis than subjective valuation (surveys) for estimating the cost of power outages, as it reflects "what people do rather than what they say." In the following sections, selected case studies are presented to highlight differences between supply interruptions based on factors such as geographical location, associated level of grid interconnections, duration, and time of occurrence.

24.4 ISOLATED AND VULNERABLE: CASE STUDY OF CYPRUS (2011)

As an island state and due to the absence of any interconnections, the grid network of Cyprus is currently isolated. Therefore, vulnerability due to sudden variations in generation from variable renewables or due to outages is quite high. One such occurrence of great magnitude occurred on July 11, 2011, when 98 containers of ammunitions and other material exploded at a naval base in close proximity to the biggest power plant of the island. The Vasilikos facility, which was severely damaged as a result, had an installed capacity of 648 MW, which corresponded to 53% of the generating capacity of the Electricity Authority of Cyprus (EAC) [23], the sole utility on the island.

Since this incident took place during a high-demand season, rolling blackouts subsequently followed, affecting the ability of commercial services and industry to operate. At the time, there was a decision to protect hospitals, police stations, the tourism sector, and large industrial users from these blackouts [24]. In order for the island to address the major loss in generating infrastructure, the Israeli Government provided 15 MW of standby generators, the Greek Government supplied temporary generating units of 71.6, and 120 MW were secured from a power company operating in Northern Cyprus (until February 2012). During the summer of 2012 an additional 120 MW of temporary generating units were installed in order to meet the high power demand of the season.

As a consequence of the use of less cost-efficient generation options to cover electricity demand, Eurostat reports an electricity price increase of 36% for average households between the first half of 2011 and 2012 and an increase of 26% for industrial consumers [25] (Table 24.2). Additionally, the restoration of the Vasilikos facility (completed during 2013 [23]) was estimated at a cost of €220 million [26].

Table 24.2 Electricity Prices for Medium-Sized Households and Industry

Households			Industry		
2011	2011	2012	2011	2011	2012
Q 1 2	Q 3–4	Q 1–2	Q 1–2	Q 3–4	Q 1–2
0.205	0.241	0.278	0.167	0.211	0.211

The case of Cyprus is particularly interesting within the context of long-term interruptions in electricity supply. In a situation of an island lacking interconnection with other grid networks, ensuring uninterruptible supply of energy services is critical and requires careful planning. Extreme events such as the one experienced in Vasilikos are very challenging to manage and political decisions are required to prioritize which customers should be protected and which services should remain unaffected.

24.5 TIMING MATTERS: CASE STUDY OF ITALY (2003)

One of the most reported and researched power outages occurred in Italy on September 28, 2003. At about 3 a.m., power coming from Switzerland to Italy was cut off as two key transmission lines across the border were damaged in a storm. As a result, all of Italy (except the islands of Sardinia and Elba) remained without power for up to 12 hours. Affecting a total of 56 million people, it was the largest blackout in Italy in 70 years. In the immediate aftermath of the blackout, 110 trains were canceled, with 30,000 people stranded on trains across Italy.

The root causes of the failure of the transmission line and the subsequent power outage have been extensively studied [27–29]. The case of the power outage in Italy is of special significance as it underscores the importance of considering the time of occurrence while estimating the costs of interruption.

The night of September 27, 2003 was the annual overnight festivities, Nuit Blanche (White Night) in Rome. As a result, many people were on the streets and all public transportation was still operating around the time of the blackout, despite the fact that it was very late at night. Several hundred people were trapped in underground trains. Coupled with heavy rain at the time, many people spent the night sleeping in train stations and on streets in Rome. While it was reported that emergency services coped well with the situation, several traffic accidents were said to have been caused as a result of the failure of traffic signals [30].

In recent years, only a limited number of studies took into consideration the specific circumstances of the time of occurrence of interruptions. Yet, information on the services interrupted and their correlation to the time of occurrence can be used to operate the power system more effectively from a societal perspective. For instance, electricity producers, transmission system operators (TSOs), and local network operators can make decisions about maintenance that influence the probability of a supply interruption.

Case studies such as those presented on Cyprus and Italy provide important insights to understanding the implications of outages in existing power systems. The situation may however change as power systems accommodate higher shares of variable renewable energy sources.

24.6 INTEGRATING RENEWABLES THROUGH SMARTER GRIDS: TRADEOFFS AND SYNERGIES

Ensuring a cleaner supply of energy drawing on locally available renewable energy resources has become a key policy objective of European governments. The growing reliance on renewable power sources may result in significant instantaneous shares of their generation. Balancing their often variable output requires a high degree of flexibility in the power system, i.e., changes in generation or demand must be counterbalanced quickly enough to avoid supply interruptions.

Distributed renewables and storage: When solely looking at the probability of interruptions to occur, a system with and without renewables may be designed with the same reliability. Yet, from an operational point of view, the systems may not be directly comparable. Renewable generation often involves distributed generation by households or municipalities. For example, some small hydro power plants which were built in response to Austria's feed-in tariffs are capable of black-start and isolated operation. As such, the local municipality may still be supplied with electricity even if a major outage in the transmission system occurs. (Note that such decisions taken by local municipalities were rather political than technical, to avoid complaints by their respective constituencies in case of outages.)

Similarly, household PV and solar thermal systems may also provide energy services when outages occur. Germany, for example, launched a support program for PV storage systems, providing a mix of low-interest loans and subsidies for up to a maximum of 30% of the investment cost [31]. The advantages to society are twofold. The PV storage system would increase the supply security of the connected households in the case of outages. Further, pressure on local grids is reduced by lowering the peak production of the PV systems that is fed into the grid.

Decentralized generation has a clear potential to reduce the costs of intermittency by reducing the number of consumers affected, e.g., by an outage in a main transmission line. However, the distribution of the costs for accessing the grid do require consideration. If added as a surcharge to the electricity consumption, such households or municipalities may not pay their fair share due to their low consumption. The share of the grid costs per capacity connected and per electricity generated may need to be revisited to ensure costs and benefits are adequately attributed to the various consumer groups.

Unlike distributed storage options, larger wind farms are commonly built in a more concentrated fashion in areas with favorable wind conditions. Similar to large hydro power plants, they require medium to large voltage grid connections to be established. Depending on the size of the power plant, an outage in such a line may therefore have an effect similar to an outage in a connection to a thermal power plant.

Smart Grids: Increasing shares of (distributed) renewables call for a more flexible power system controlled through smarter grid management techniques. Smart Grids build on a significant increase in the level of communication, automation, and control based on a two-way flow of information and electricity, from supplier to consumer.

One characteristic of Smart Grids is their ability to be self-healing, i.e., to reduce the extent of interruptions and restore the system's operation when outages do occur. Smart Grids further enable the integration of sources of flexibility which were largely untouched before. This is especially important as increasing the share of variable electricity generation will require a more flexible system based on parallel investments in balancing mechanisms. Conventionally, this would be provided by power plants which can quickly ramp up or down their generation, such as gas turbines. With the advent of Smart Grids, more accessible and cost-efficient options will be available to minimize the extent and costs of interruptions to customers. These may include demand-side options as well as more flexible management and operation of grid infrastructure.

Demand-side management and prioritization of loads: Smart Grids may minimize the cost of interruptions by ensuring near perfect reliability and quality of supply for high-priority demand types, while reducing the requirements for demand types which are less sensitive to these needs [32]. Loads may be prioritized according to demand types such as emergency services, financial institutions, industries, and consumers.

Such a prioritization may not be limited to consumer groups, but may also apply to demand types within one consumer group. For example, approximately half of private household demand does not need to be met instantly and can be shifted flexibly [33]. Examples include dishwashing, washing of clothes, air conditioning, and heating. In the transport sector, electric vehicles may provide this flexibility. In industry, related examples include electric boilers or process heat requirements. So, instead of having to cut off several consumer groups completely, Smart Grids may allow to interrupt specific demands, thus ensuring the supply to more high-value energy services and reducing the cost of interruption. An example of a deconstructed demand profile based on different priorities and flexibilities is provided in Fig. 24.2 [34].

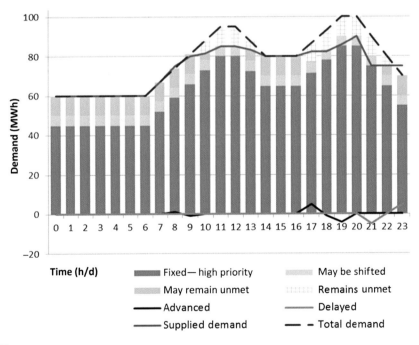

FIGURE 24.2

Supply analysis to meet demand types with different prioritizations and flexibilities.

According to ACER's estimates, currently only 10% of demand response resources are being utilized within the EU. Pricing schemes would need to ensure that the flexibility provided by consumers is rewarded accordingly. Supportive regulation is needed, not least to ensure cyber security and to protect consumers from data misuse.

Regulation: Present regulation often rewards utilities for delivering network primary assets rather than improving performance through more sophisticated grid management and consumer integration. Thus, regulation can hinder developments that do not focus on investments in network assets. Most current network design and operation practices center on variations of the historic deterministic N−1 approach that were developed in the late 1950s. A system which adheres to the N−1 rule maintains reliable operation even if a major element fails, e.g., a transmission line. This approach has broadly helped deliver secure and reliable electricity services, alongside various other traditionally applied redundancy measures. It can, however, impose major barriers for innovation in network operation and for the implementation of solutions that enhance the utilization of grid assets. Moving away from such historically developed power quality and reliability standards will help balancing asset- and performance-based options, particularly those that involve responsive demand and advanced network management techniques facilitated through Smart Grids.

According to a recent study on demand response measures, few of the EU 28 Member States were found to have created satisfactory regulatory and contractual structures that support aggregated demand response (Fig. 24.3 [35]). Some Member States are in the stage of reviewing their regulatory framework (such as Austria, the UK, Ireland, Germany, and France), while most Member States are lagging in regulatory and institutional terms. This hinders consumer participation in energy markets and system services such as balancing and the provision of reserve.

Increasing generation from variable renewables requires an increase in power system flexibility to ensure current reliability standards are met. The increased flexibility requirements may trigger investments in a set of smart technologies, which may ultimately allow decreasing the costs of intermittency. This may be achieved by shifting the current focus on the provision of electricity to a focus on the provision of services.

24.7 SERVICES, NOT kWh: EXPANDING THE APPROACH

Previously we have highlighted the need to differentiate between various consumer groups. Going one step further, it may be useful to differentiate between the values of specific energy services in order to assess the socioeconomic implications of interruptions.

From the point of view of the economy, almost no activity or production can take place without an "energy service." Activities and products command different market values. Thus, energy-services have different values. For example, for a European household heating a home might be more valuable than keeping the television on. Similarly, the energy-service of keeping a company's servers running might be more valuable than the energy service of cooling drinks for the company's employees. If there is a power cut there would be much greater damage incurred if the servers are affected than the vending machine. Yet, unless some local backup power is available, there is no differentiation between these different values for services during a power cut. That results in blanket cuts across all services, valuable or not, when there is an interruption.

FIGURE 24.3

Overview of progress of European countries relevant to deployment of demand response.

To limit damage, it would require a shift to manage electricity use at the level of services rather than by consumer or "consumer group." Herein there are strong synergies with Smart Grid developments, where the use of electricity by devices can increasingly be remotely controlled. If interruptions can be limited to lower-value uses of electricity their damage might be powerfully limited. This could be facilitated by (1) incentive programs to encourage network operators to support a more active role of consumer engagement and by (2) enforcing automatic individual customer compensations for power supply interruptions according to the occurred damage.

The next section of this book places further emphasis on the role of society and consumers as part of the energy system.

REFERENCES

[1] M. de Nooij, C. Koopmans, Bijvoet, Carlijn, The value of supply security: the costs of power interruptions: economic input for damage reduction and investment in networks, Energy Econ. 29 (2007) 277–295.

[2]   A. Tishler, Optimal production with uncertain interruptions in the supply of electricity: estimation of electricity outage costs, Eur. Econ. Rev. 37 (1993) 1259−1274.

[3]   R. Billinton, G. Tollefson, G. Wacker, Assessment of electric service reliability worth, Electr. Power Energy Syst. 15 (2) (1993) 95−100.

[4]   V. Ajodhia, M. van Gemert, R. Hakvoort, Electricity Outage Cost Valuation: A Survey, DTe, Den Haag, 2002.

[5]   W. Day, A. Reese, Service Interruptions: The Customers' Views, Pacific Gas & Electric Company, San Francisco, CA, 1992.

[6]   M. Beenstock, G. Ephraim, H. Yoel, Response bias in a conjoint analysis of power outages, Energy Econ. 20 (1998) 135−156.

[7]   Elforsk, Does it matter when a power outage occurs—a choice experiment study on the willingness to pay to avoid power outages, 2005.

[8]   J. Reichl, M. Schmidthaler, F. Schneider, The value of supply security: the costs of power outages to Austrian households, firms and the public sector, Energy Econ. 36 (2012) 256−261.

[9]   B. Baarsma, J. Hop, Pricing power outages in the Netherlands, Energy 34 (9) (2009) 1378−1386.

[10]   A. Bertazzi, E. Fumagalli, L. Lo Schiavo, The use of customer outage cost surveys in policy decision-making: the Italian experience in regulating quality of electricity supply, CIRED, 2005.

[11]   M. Bliem, Ökonomische Bewertung der Versorgungsqualität im österreichischen Stromnetz und Entwicklung eines Modells für ein Qualitäts-Anreizsystem, Klagenfurt, Alpen-Adria-Universität Klagenfurt, 2008.

[12]   G.H. Kjølle, K. Samdal, B. Singh, O.A. Kvitastein, Customer costs related to interruptions and voltage problems: methodology and results, IEEE Trans. Power Syst. 23 (3) (2008) 1030−1038.

[13]   L. Lawton, M. Sullivan, K. Van Liere, A. Katz, A framework and review of customer outage costs: integration and analysis of electric utility outage cost surveys, B. Lab. Environmental Energy Technologies Division, Berkeley, 2003.

[14]   M. Munasinghe, M. Gellerson, Economic criteria for optimizing power system reliability levels, Bell Econ. J. 10 (1) (1979) 353−365.

[15]   C.-Y. Chen, A. Vella, Estimating the economic costs of electricity shortages using input − output analysis: the case of Taiwan, Appl. Econ. 26 (1994) 1061−1069.

[16]   D.W. Caves, J.A. Herriges, R.J. Windle, The cost of electric power interruptions in the industrial sector: estimates derived from interruptible service programs, Land Econ. 68 (1) (1992) 49−61.

[17]   A. Sanghvi, Economic costs of electricity supply interruptions: US and foreign experience, Energy Econ. 4 (3) (1982) 180−198.

[18]   CEER, CEER Benchmarking Report 5.1 on the Continuity of Electricity Supply, Council of European Energy Regulators, 2014.

[19]   National Energy Technology Laboratory, Backup Generators (BUGS): The Next Smart Grid Peak Resource, 2010.

[20]   K. Deubel, Central and Eastern European Diesel Generator Set Market, Frost & Sullivan, Mountain View, CA, 2013.

[21]   J. Corwin, W. Miles, Impact Assessment of the 1977 New York City Blackout, US Department of Energy, Washington, DC, 1978.

[22]   P. Serra, G. Fierro, Outage cost in Chilean industry, Energy Econ. 19 (1997) 417−434.

[23]   EAC, Annual report 2012, Electricity Authority of Cyprus, 2013.

[24]   S. Orphanides, P. Tugwell, Cyprus blast kills 12, injures 62, reduces power by 50%, Bloomberg, July 11, 2011 [Online]. Available from: <http://www.bloomberg.com/news/2011-07-11/cyprus-fire-that-killed-eight-spread-from-power-station-to-munitions-store.html> (accessed 10.10.14).

[25]   Eurostat, Electricity and natural gas prices: 2012 semester 1, European Commission, 2013.

[26] EAC, Annual report 2011, Electricity Authority of Cyprus, 2012.

[27] UCTE, Final report of the Investigation Committee on the 28 September 2003 blackout in Italy, Union for the Coordination of Electricity Transmission, April 2004.

[28] SFOE, Report on the blackout in Italy on 28 September 2003, Swiss Federal Office of Energy, 2003.

[29] C.W. Johnson, Analysing the causes of the Italian and Swiss blackout, 28th September 2003, in: Proceedings of the 12th Australian Workshop on Safety Critical Systems and Software and Safety-Related Programmable Systems, 2007.

[30] BBC, Huge blackout cripples Italy, September 28, 2003 [Online]. Available from: <http://news.bbc.co.uk/2/hi/3146136.stm> (accessed 10.10.14).

[31] W. Schweickhardt, KfW and Federal Environment Ministry launch programme to promote use of energy storage in solar PV installations, KfW, 2013 [Online]. Available from: <https://www.kfw.de/KfW-Group/Newsroom/Aktuelles/Pressemitteilungen/Pressemitteilungen-Details_107136.html> (accessed 15.10.14).

[32] IEA, Energy Technology Perspectives 2010: scenarios and strategies to 2050, International Energy Agency, 2010.

[33] C. Block, D. Neumann, C. Weinhardt, A market mechanism for energy allocation in micro-CHP grids, in: Proceedings of the 41st Hawaii International Conference on System Sciences, 2008.

[34] M. Welsch, M. Howells, M. Bazilian, J. DeCarolis, S. Hermann, H. Rogner, Modelling elements of smart grids – enhancing the OSeMOSYS (open source energy modelling system) code, Energy 46 (1) (2012) 337–350.

[35] Smart Energy Demand Coalition, Mapping demand response in Europe today, 2014.

CONCLUSIONS

25

Abhishek Shivakumar

KTH Royal Institute of Technology, Stockholm, Sweden

This chapter draws on the conclusions of the preceding chapters. It provides a set of recommendations, pertaining to the broad topics discussed in this section: the need for flexibility and potential solutions; the need for reliability and measuring its cost; and the role of storage in this context.

The future of storage and flexibility in the EU will depend on the evolution of market designs. It will be important to elaborate guidelines for capacity market developments that support the remuneration of investments in storage and flexible production technologies. Together with physically and operationally interconnected markets and a closer integration of demand-side options, this can help provide the flexibility required to allow for increased penetration of variable renewable energy sources.

A modeling study performed by the authors confirmed findings from previous studies that multiple benefits are required to justify investment in storage technologies. Under current estimations of battery prices, there is no business case for supply-side battery storage up to 2030. It only becomes attractive in selected markets in 2050. However, variations between the countries which were investigated were large due to significant differences in their production mix and infrastructure.

Stationary fuel cells and hydrogen technologies and applications can provide benefits in terms of increased flexibility that facilitates the integration of larger shares of variable renewable generation into the energy system. Whether investments in these technologies and the associated benefits materialize decisively depends on the boundary conditions. These are more favorable the higher natural gas and carbon prices, related R&D investments, and shares of variable renewable generation are. Further, targeted support schemes are of importance. The energy system scenario studies analyzed by the authors show significant deployment of fuel cells and hydrogen technologies only past 2025, as this is when hydrogen becomes more relevant in the mobility sector. A strategic push of EU energy policies to support infrastructure development and R&D seems to be necessary to realize the benefits of fuel cells and hydrogen technologies and applications.

The scale of investments in flexibility options depends on the liquidity of the market and would require a certain level of competition among the main players and investment options. A level playing field is required to ensure a fair competition in energy markets. In order to achieve this, future market designs should adequately value the multiple benefits of storage options—in conjunction with other Smart Grid solutions—in providing system reliability and flexibility. These benefits clearly increase with the level of renewable energy penetration.

Large-scale storage facilities should be generally understood as a semiregulated activity, with the primary goals of ensuring flexibility in the system while affording security of supply. Given its semi-regulated nature, storage facilities could be operated by a separate body, such as a "storage system operator", in line with the unbundling rules of the Third Energy Package (refer to Chapter 21 on "Need for Flexibility and Potential Solutions"). Extensive research needs to be done to determine the needs and obligations of storage facilities in order for them to fulfill their foreseen role in a European electricity market. Further, secure communication between the "storage system operators" and the grid system operators (TSOs and DSOs) will need to be established.

Home storage, particularly for increased self-consumption, offers a significant market that has become economically viable without support in several countries in recent years. A key recommendation is that the EC needs to consolidate regulation around ancillary services and encourage Member States to establish environments that are favorable to investments in storage devices for prosumers.ᵃ Consequently, it is important to develop regulatory measures to stimulate self-consumption and reduction in power consumption, especially to address peak-load considerations.

Finally, in order to calculate economically optimal reliability levels, it is essential to know its actual value to society. A first step would be to replace current reliability standards—that in most Member States are still based on past engineering practices and rules of thumb—with a more technology-neutral and market-based approach. This could be achieved by comparing the damage to society with the costs of new investments to increase system reliability. This would require putting a price tag on interrupting various forms of energy services, based on the duration of the interruptions and the consumers' willingness to pay. One may argue that even an initial estimate is better and allows for a more market-based approach than not having any such value. The alternative, e.g., to define an LOLP and design the system accordingly, may be more arbitrary. While better information may be available for industries, estimations of the willingness to pay for sectors without adequate data may be improved as further information becomes available, e.g., from smart home systems.

In this section, we alluded to the importance of consumers in the EU's energy transition. The next section on society and consumer demands focuses on societal aspects of the energy system. Among other topics, it will dive deeper into future energy trends in households, the socioeconomic significance of district heating, and the protection of vulnerable consumers from energy poverty.

ᵃProsumer is a portmanteau made of "professional" and "consumer." In the electricity context, it refers to a consumer producing his own electricity, most of the time from PV panels, and storing it to consume it himself.

SOCIETY AND CONSUMER DEMANDS

INTRODUCTION

Audrey Dobbins
University of Stuttgart, Stuttgart, Germany

According to the Energy Union vision (refer to Section 6.1), European households and businesses (the consumers of energy) are at the heart of the energy system. Households in particular are envisaged to be at the core of the energy system. They are expected to benefit from a fully integrated EU-wide energy system through increased levels of self-consumption from renewables (and being able to feed these into the grid), reduced energy bills through the use of smart technology, and better energy security.

The role of consumers is rapidly becoming more relevant as it gets clearer that without their active participation, the ambitious energy and climate change objectives of the European energy transition may not be achievable. While the previous section highlighted the potential and costs of energy system reliability and flexibility and its implications for consumers, this section explicitly shifts the focus further towards society and consumer demands. It examines the role of consumers, the Commission, and different technologies on Europe's energy transition and attempts to answer questions such as: How can households actively participate and how significant is the contribution from this sector? Which options show promise? How can vulnerable consumers be protected and included in the quickly changing energy system?

With regard to empowering households to actively participate in the energy transition, facilitating self-consumption from renewables is an important measure that may readily increase the market integration of renewable energy sources. Yet, despite this potential, it is unclear to which extent self-consumption can play a significant role due to political, economic, social, and technical barriers. The interplay between current retail electricity prices, renewable energy support schemes, and technological developments to improve storage and demand response will influence the uptake of this key area, leading to passive consumers becoming active prosumers. The potential and limitations of self-consumption are assessed in Chapter 27, Self-Consumption of Electricity from Renewable Sources. It highlights the need for a balance between support mechanisms to encourage such self-consumption, but also the exploration of better business models to ensure a fair distribution of costs.

While alternating current has been the primary means of supplying households with electricity, direct current has re-emerged as a possible contender. This is due to its ability to facilitate self-consumption by directly integrating the ever-increasing amount of renewable energy produced at household level. While direct current offers the potential to decrease the energy consumption (and thereby ongoing costs) of households, the dearth of standards for direct current means large-scale adoption is stalled. Chapter 28, DC Power Production and Consumption in Households, explores the

Europe's Energy Transition. DOI: http://dx.doi.org/10.1016/B978-0-12-809806-6.00026-2

223

technical and economic feasibility of direct current networks and the role they can play in reducing electricity consumption by households while increasing the share of renewables consumed.

In addition to electricity consumption, household heat supply offers a significant potential to harness renewable energy. This is because heating makes up the largest share of energy consumption for the majority of European households. District heating and cooling therefore presents a significant opportunity to integrate renewable energy and contribute to European energy and climate targets while concurrently meeting the large heat demand. Chapter 29, District Heating in Europe: Opportunities for Energy Savings, Business, and Jobs, investigates the state of the art of district heating (and cooling) in Europe as well as the technologies, measures, and projects that could contribute to increasing its share.

The success of the European energy transition is contingent on the active participation of consumers. However, in some instances consumers require protection to ensure their continued access and participation in the energy system. This is especially the case for vulnerable households that require this protection to take advantage of upcoming technological advancements which offer the benefits of reducing overall energy consumption and therewith energy bills. In terms of energy poverty and vulnerable consumers, particular policies and measures across the Member States are reviewed in Chapter 30, Energy Poverty Across the EU: Analysis of Policies and Measures. The review highlights vast differences in comprehension and approaches to addressing the issue across Member States. This fragmented response shows the crucial role the European Commission can play to enhance and foster understanding as well as ensuring an exchange of experiences. This will facilitate the development of a comprehensive European strategy to improve the energy welfare of the most vulnerable.

This section concludes in Chapter 31, Conclusions, with a summary of the main findings. That chapter further highlights the role for the Commission to best utilize the potential consumers offer as an active part of Europe's energy transition.

SELF-CONSUMPTION OF ELECTRICITY FROM RENEWABLE SOURCES

27

Joris Dehler[1], Dogan Keles[1], Thomas Telsnig[2], Benjamin Fleischer[2], Manuel Baumann[1], David Fraboulet[3], Aurélie Faure-Schuyer[4], and Wolf Fichtner[1]

[1]Karlsruhe Institute of Technology (KIT), Karlsruhe, Germany [2]University of Stuttgart, Stuttgart, Germany [3]EIT-IE/Commissariat à l'énergie atomique et aux énergies alternatives (CEA), Grenoble, France [4]Institut Français des Relations Internationales (IFRI), Brussels, Belgium

27.1 INTRODUCTION

In Europe, a transition in support schemes for renewable energy sources (RES) for electricity production is expected to take place. This transition is characterized by a move from schemes that directly support RES towards a more indirect support to market environments that facilitate the integration of RES through market forces. Self-consumption of RES can play its part: it offers benefits to political and economic stakeholders, but is not broadly implemented yet due to the unclear profitability of self-consumption and costs of associated technologies.

In the context of this chapter, self-consumption of renewable energies is defined as electricity that is produced from RES, not injected to the distribution or transmission grid or instantaneously withdrawn from the grid,[a] and consumed by the owner of the power production unit or by associates directly contracted to the producer. To date, the technology with the highest share in distributed power generation is photovoltaics (PV). Therefore, the focus of this chapter is on this technology.

One of the major challenges to self-consumption in households is the disparity between power generation from PV and the actual demand. Most of the power production takes place when residents are not at home, pursuing their profession or other activities of daily life. Consequently, the estimated self-consumption potential without storage or demand response measures varies between 17% and 44%, depending on household size and irradiation exposure [1].

Demand response represents the practice of managing electricity demand in a way that peak energy use is shifted to off-peak periods, enabling higher rates of self-consumption or, more technically, the adaption of demand to grid operation requirements. With electricity storage and demand response, rates of self-consumption can be raised and benefits can be achieved in terms of mitigating increased network costs due to the integration of PV. There is still necessity for further research on the real potential of demand response and dedicated storage as figures differ largely between studies [1]. Fig. 27.1 provides a schematic overview of self-consumption issues and measures: load shifting can alter the electricity usage, while energy storage adapts PV production to the demand.

Compared to households, commercial enterprises can generally achieve higher rates of self-consumption, depending on the type of enterprise. This is due to the alignment of working hours

---

[a]Such as a real-time net metering scheme that has no offset between consumption and production.

Europe's Energy Transition. DOI: http://dx.doi.org/10.1016/B978-0-12-809806-6.00027-4

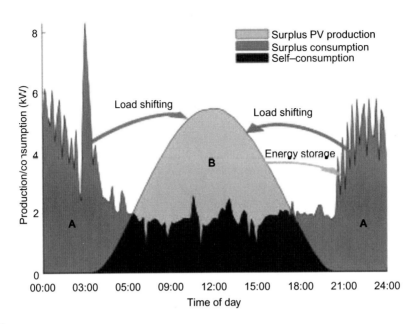

FIGURE 27.1

Schematic outline of daily net load (A + C), net generation (B + C), and absolute self-consumption (C) in a building with on-site PV.

From R. Luthander, J. Widén, D. Nilsson, J. Palm, Photovoltaic self-consumption in buildings: a review, Appl. Energy 142 (2015) 80–94.

with power production from PV. Thus enterprises can profit largely from self-consumption if the installation costs are low enough.

This chapter will address the political and economic benefits of self-consumption before arising challenges are discussed together with possible policy measures. The issue of sharing costs of the electricity network and the distribution of taxes and different levies will be summarized. Further, different options to reorganize the collection of network charges are discussed.

27.2 BENEFITS

ENABLING A TRANSITION FROM RES SUPPORT SCHEMES (FEED-IN TARIFFS, QUOTAS) TO AN INTEGRATION THROUGH MARKET FORCES

In most EU Member States policy measures are in place to support the market uptake of RES, as PV will hardly be able to compete against electricity wholesale prices in the short to medium term [2]. However, self-consumption is already competing with electricity retail prices in some EU countries, where parity between retail prices and the costs of PV generation is reached or will be reached soon. This includes, for example, Germany and Belgium, where decreasing costs of PV enable unit owners to profit from savings compared to the rather high retail prices. Such a business case could therefore foster the development of PV penetration without the support of feed-in tariffs (FiT) or premiums, even in the short and medium term. Hence, supporting self-consumption can be means to smoothen the transition from previous policy-driven support schemes to the integration of RES through market forces.

EMPOWERING CONSUMERS AND MOBILIZING NEW FINANCIAL RESOURCES FOR RES

Self-consumption can add to an efficient usage of energy by enabling consumers to take responsibility for their energy consumption and production. As it can lead to a greater awareness among consumers regarding their energy usage, it may encourage them to actively adjust their energy consumption habits. It may thus lead to a reduction in usage and to efforts to shift loads to times of high production.

The energy transition from conventional production to an RES-oriented energy system requires substantial investments regarding networks and power production. By investing into small-scale RES and technical solutions to facilitate self-consumption, citizens and commercial enterprises can contribute to the high investment needs of the energy transition and profit from the avoidance of high electricity bills.

GRID RELIEF AND COSTS OF ELECTRICITY PRODUCTION

Managed in the right way, self-consumption of RES can lower the pressure on the electricity grid arising from the feed-in of electricity from RES. This is shown, for example, for scenarios with a very high share of renewables in a case study on the power market in Germany.[b] The exploitation of RES leads to high peaks in production and a low residual load during times of high wind speeds or intense sunshine hours. At other periods there may be little contribution of RES to cover electricity demand due to low wind speeds or cloudy days. In this context, studies demonstrates that self-consumption extended by storage and demand response measures can reduce the additional integration costs[c] for PV at high penetration levels (18% of total electricity production) by an average of around 20% over all countries that were considered in the [3]. When taking grid extension on the distribution and transmission level into account, the overall additional integration costs were estimated to decline from an average of 2.6 c€/kWh without demand response and storage to 2.15 c€/kWh with these measures in place.

However, the additional integration costs of PV vary from country to country, being lower in southern Europe due to a better correspondence of demand and PV production profiles. Further, the quoted study does not take the costs into account that arise for consumers who have to invest into technological solutions as well to facilitate their self-consumption.

---

[b]For an assessment of the grid-relief through self-consumption please refer to the corresponding sub-chapter in Section 27.3.
[c]Consisting of costs for: grid extension, balancing services, and higher operating reserve requirements, lower plant factors for conventional production capacities, and losses attributed to PV.

27.3 CHALLENGES OF SELF-CONSUMPTION AND POLICY OPTIONS
SOCIOECONOMIC LIMITATIONS AND TECHNOLOGICAL SOLUTIONS

The main challenge for self-consumption, particularly with PV generation, is the diverging profiles of demand and production of electricity. While the production of electricity from PV obeys the course of the sun, demand peaks are particularly high in morning and evening hours when feed-in of PV power is low. Thus, the potential for self-consumption is limited for residential buildings and depends on the size of the installation and individual factors, if additional technological measures are not taken [1].

Increasing self-consumption by behavioral change can only partially harness the full potential of self-consumption. Further, it is unclear whether and to what extent prosumers will adapt to the production rhythm of PV electricity in the absence of strong (financial) incentives for doing so. On the positive side, system integration of mere self-consumption without any technical enhancements is straightforward. Power self-consumed does not change the residual load, since it is neither obtained from the grid nor fed-in. Therefore, integration costs of self-consumption may remain low.

However, no change in the residual load also means that the full potential benefits of self-consumption are not unleashed, such as reducing the integration costs of PV. To exploit these full potential benefits to the distribution and transmission networks, technical adaptation measures are necessary.

The measures to address disparities in PV generation and demand profiles, and to achieve a high share of self-consumption are demand response and storage of electricity. This can be described as adapting the energy demand to production periods of PV or mitigating the energy output to peak demand by storing it until needed. Both technologies carry economical and technical issues to be overcome.

GRID INTEGRATION ISSUES OF ELECTRICITY STORAGE

Maximizing self-consumption through load shifting via batteries does not necessarily entail advantages for the electricity system in case of increasing capacities of distributed generation (DG): Direct battery-charging strategies enable high self-consumption rates. However, simple direct charging strategies can cause unpredictable DG production peaks as batteries at different sites are fully charged and the surplus is abruptly fed to the grid in an uncoordinated manner.

It is possible to increase self-consumption rates and to decrease the impact of DG on distribution grids in parallel by using proper battery-charging algorithms. Linear delayed charging, for example, is based on presetting a maximum state of charge increasing linearly over the day. In this case, not all electricity generated is used to charge the battery, but some is used either for self-consumption or fed into the grid. This strategy provides a possibility of reducing DG production peaks [4]. Such grid optimized charge modes can help to improve local power quality and defer investments in transmission and distribution grid upgrades in case of high local DG penetration.

ELECTRICITY STORAGE FOR SELF-CONSUMPTION: FINANCIAL ISSUES

As investments in storage capacities and demand response measures have to be made by consumers, the affordability, and ultimately, the profitability of storage solutions is a major challenge to higher rates of self-consumption.

There are several battery storage technologies with different properties available. Some of the most important technologies are inter alia lithium-ion batteries with different electrode combinations (lithium iron phosphate - LFP, lithium nickel manganese cobalt oxide - NMC, etc.), lead acid batteries, redox-flow batteries (zinc-bromide, all-vanadium, etc.), and high-temperature batteries (sodium nickel chloride - NaNiCl, sodium sulfur - NaS) [5]. Remaining challenges for most existing battery technologies are cyclic and calendric life time, safety, and environmental concerns (e.g., heavy metals) [6]. Yet the main problem of most available technologies is the high initial costs leading to long amortization times. In combination with the lack of business models, this can be seen as the main barrier for further diffusion of battery storage from an economic perspective [7].

This effect can be seen more precisely when looking at the levelized costs of electricity (LCOE—cost of generating electricity, including initial capital cost, discount rates, operation, and maintenance cost). For example, a German domestic PV rooftop system without storage has a typical LCOE of $9-12$ c€/kWh [8,9]. In combination with lead acid battery systems this can lead to a range of total LCOE from 22 to over 44 c€/kWh, and with Li-iron-phosphate battery systems from 23 up to 47 c€/kWh [10].

In this case grid parity is difficult to achieve. But new developments in battery chemistry and economies of scale driven through the development of electric vehicles can help to overcome some obstacles by the use of more effective materials and production strategies. Applying learning curves to different Li-ion technologies based on battery market predictions show that, e.g., cell prices could fall from present ~ 300 €/kWh [10] to 200 €/kWh in 2020 and to 150 €/kWh in 2030 [11, 9]. Nowadays, complete Li-ion systems including inverters, battery management system, protective enclosure and other components have a high cost bandwidth of $870-3.200$ €/kWh [12]. It is expected that total system cost will also decrease due to learning effects of named system components [13]. At the same time spreads between rising electricity retail and falling PV self-consumption prices are increasing, making self-consumption through PV in combination with batteries more competitive in the future [14].

Case study: impact of storage on wholesale prices on the German power market

A valuation of the impact of self-consumption on wholesale prices in Germany with different load management regimes was conducted. To quantify the effect on the wholesale market, four different PV configurations were considered as described in Table 27.1 and Fig. 27.2. A 35% share of domestic prosumers (which corresponds to 4.8 million households) was assumed in Germany in 2030, corresponding to the total number of households with PV systems installed. The scenarios were evaluated using an optimising modelling approach for the German wholesale market.

Table 27.1 Scenarios Assessing the Impact of Storage on Wholesale Prices	
REF:	A reference PV system without storage and no self-consumption feeding the produced electricity into the grid
SC:	A PV system without storage covering the electricity demand (self-consumption) during daytime. The surplus energy is fed into the grid. No change of user-behavior is assumed
SC-CC:	A PV system with a storage system and a chronological charging strategy at times of demand exceeding generation. The surplus energy is fed into the grid
SC-GR:	A PV system with storage operating in grid-relief mode. The surplus energy is fed into the grid

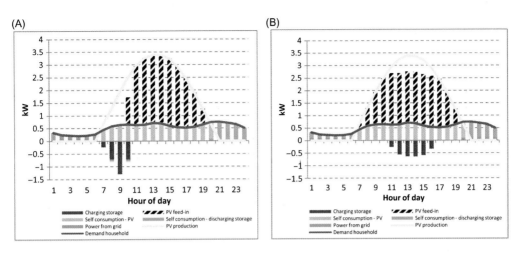

FIGURE 27.2

Different storage operation strategies in the SC-CC and SC-GR scenarios on a typical summer day in 2030. (A) Chronological charging strategy (SC-CC) and (B) Grid-relief charging strategy (SC-GR).

Table 27.2 Impacts of Self-Consumption and Total System Costs in the German Power Supply Sector for 2030

Scenario 2030		REF	SC	SC-CC	SC-GR
Deviation of system costs from REF					
System costs	(€/a 10^6)	0.00	0.00	−151.86	−326.72
Annual storage costs	(€/a 10^6)	0.00	0.00	420.96	420.96
Deviation of total costs	(€/a 10^6)	0.00	0.00	269.10	94.24

System costs of the REF and the SC scenario are the same in the electricity market calculations since there is no change of the residual load and consequently no deviation in unit commitment. In the SC-CC and SC-GR scenarios, the annual cost of the small-scale households storage systems of 421 million Euros have to be added to the result from the market model. In both scenarios considering storage, the total system savings could not cover the additional spendings on the storage units. The savings in the SC-GR scenario are about 175 million Euros beyond the savings in the SC-CC scenario. Table 27.2 shows cost deviations between the scenarios.

The analysis considered only the effects of different self-consumption strategies on the wholesale market. An additional cost saving potential can be expected at electricity grid level, which is not covered in the current analysis. Moreover, the household electricity demand structure was derived from an aggregated synthetic load profile. Detailed modeling of different household consumption patterns should be considered in further studies.

DEMAND RESPONSE ISSUES FOR SELF-CONSUMPTION

Demand response promotes better usage of energy and can reduce emissions by smoothening load curves or peaks and valleys of energy use and by better matching consumption with intermittent DG, such as with PV [15]. As mentioned previously, the potential for manual demand response is limited. Other than energy storage systems, e.g., dedicated batteries or electric vehicles, there is potential for active demand-side management of applications like heat pumps, washing machines, or electric water heaters [15]. Running cycles of these technologies can be adapted to peak power production or to needs of the electricity grid—provided that there is the necessary feedback from grid operators to consumers.

Especially electric vehicles offer high load shifting potentials [14]. A 10% market share of electric vehicles in Germany, e.g., with 50% of them simultaneously connected to the grid via typical 3.6 kW-household sockets offers a peak power/load of 7.6 GW and about 22 GWh/d for load shifting (based on daily trips and a mid-sized battery electric vehicle with a 25 kWh battery) [16]. Relevant technologies for demand response are smart metering, load limiters, or direct load control [17]. Demand-side management can also be combined with energy storage technologies in order to further increase self-consumption. Currently, the low penetration of smart meters and load control devices is hindering the development of self-consumption, as well as the management of self-consumption beneficial to the electricity grid [17].

SUBSIDIES FOR STORAGE AND TECHNICAL SOLUTIONS

To support the market uptake of storage and demand management solutions, thereby contributing to self-consumption indirectly, support may be provided for investments of prosumers in storage technologies. Similar to the fast development of PV cells, such an incentive might accelerate the development of storage and demand management, until these technologies become financially attractive even without subsidies in the long run. Germany, for example, supports storage installations with low-interest loans investment subsidies.

To make sure that the benefits of self-consumption get realized, a subsidy scheme for storage should ensure that peak load is managed in a way that the electricity network benefits. As we have argued, uncoordinated charging of batteries can have a negative effect on grid balancing. Electricity storage can fulfill balancing tasks for the grid, if regulations allow battery owners to provide such energy flows [18]. This might extend the current business models of DG.

Another option is to indirectly push the progress of self-consumption by supporting research and development activities for storage and demand management. By creating enabling environments for companies and research facilities to explore and invent new technologies, prices for applications may reduce, making such solutions more attractive to prosumers.

DIRECT SUPPORT BY PREMIUMS ON SELF-CONSUMPTION

Supporting self-consumption directly, a premium on every self-consumed kilowatt hour is a straightforward possibility to reward consumer engagement in load shifting measures. Such a premium promotes the management of consumption according to production. This might also include the purchase of storage or demand management solutions, if they appear to be an economic feasible step towards higher self-consumption. For example, Germany made use of this option until PV reached grid parity in 2012. The UK has a feed-in tariff scheme also remunerating generated and self-consumed electricity. In an attempt to exploit emerging market opportunities from the UK support scheme, major companies have been launching PV storage solutions in the UK market from 2015 on [19].

A premium on every self-consumed kilowatt hour may however compromise energy efficiency measures, due to the remuneration of the consumption of electricity. Further, support schemes should be designed to facilitate the adaptation of charging cycles of batteries to the needs of the grid.

SUPPORT MEASURES ON THE GRID-SIDE: PROMOTE ICT TO ACCELERATE DEVELOPMENT

As the development of a high share of self-consumption depends on the evolution of information and communications technology (ICT) in connection with the electricity grid, another measure is to support the fast implementation of "smart" meters and network management solutions. This way, batteries and home applications of prosumers can react flexibly to management issues of the grid, thereby lowering grid integration costs of RES contributing to a flattened demand and supply curve. An example may be the promotion of early warnings from a prosumer to the grid operator about its future power request or injection to the network in order to enable the operator to take precursory measures.

REDUCE THE AMOUNT OF ELECTRICITY ALLOWED TO BE FED INTO THE GRID OR COMPENSATED BY FEED-IN TARIFFS

In order to reinforce measures taken by a prosumer, there is the option to limit the amount of electricity that is allowed to be fed into the grid. This could be a general limit to fed-in electricity or the flexible possibility to lower input from specific prosumers by the DSOs. Such a limit may encourage the discipline of prosumers to self-consume the produced energy.

A prerequisite for production units larger than 100 kWp in Germany is that they are controllable by the DSOs. However, in Germany, the possibility to take PV units off the grid is not meant to be an incentive for self-consumption, as curtailed energy gets remunerated.

27.4 SHARING GRID COSTS, LEVIES, AND TAXES
THE STRUCTURE OF ELECTRICITY RETAIL PRICES

Generally, retail prices for electricity are on the rise and expected to increase further in the future. The retail price can be divided into three major portions. For the average household prices in Europe the component of energy and supply costs decreased (from 8.1 c€/kWh in 2008 to 7.7 c€/kWh in 2012), while the component of taxes and levies increased (5.1−6.7 c€/kWh) and so did the share of the network (4.65−5.1 c€/kWh) (see also Fig. 27.3) [20]. End-user prices vary largely between the Member States, being the lowest in Bulgaria (2012: 8.26 c€/kWh) and highest in Denmark (29.97 c€/kWh) [21].

Estimated additional integration costs of PV consist largely of additional conventional capacity costs [3]. At high PV penetration levels, additional capacity costs vary between 1.6 c€/kWh in Portugal and 0.9 c€/kWh in Greece. Those costs can be mitigated or lowered by self-consumption [3].

DISTRIBUTION OF GRID COSTS

Network charges in Europe are mainly covered depending on the volume of the electricity demand of the respective end-user. An advantage lies in the incentive sent to reduce the electricity demand. However, they do not account for the actual cost structure of DSOs and TSOs, which mainly depends on the maximal load that is obtained at once [22]. In addition, those costs are avoided by self-consumers. Thus, there is concern that intensified self-consumption will lead to an unfair distribution of grid costs because self-consumers still need the grid infrastructure, but obtain less energy from the grid, thus not paying their fair share of grid fees.

Pudjianto et al. [3] performed a modeling exercise to estimate the share of the necessary additional transmission grid extension and operating costs in order to facilitate high PV penetration levels. These additional costs appears to be rather small, even at the high penetration levels considered (<0.05 c€/kWh by 2020, 0.28 c€/kWh by 2030). The distribution network costs vary by Member State, being the highest in Belgium (0.9 c€/kWh). Additional costs can be reduced by demand response and storage (e.g., to 0.6 c€/kWh for distribution network costs in Belgium) [3].

A factor that was not considered in the study of Pudjianto et al. [3] is that systems with increased shares of self-consumption may also profit from the "smartening" of the power grid. However, the smart meters and communication devices required to increase the shares of self-consumption also create costs. Ultimately, the profitability of self-consumption for consumers depends on how these costs get allocated. If these costs get paid by adding them to the electricity bill by volume, then they get allocated to a large portion to customers that do not profit from self-consumption [23].

DISTRIBUTION OF OTHER LEVIES AND TAXES

The growing share of taxes and levies included in retail prices contributes to the profitability of self-consumption, as those additional costs are avoided when consuming the electricity self-produced. Therefore, levies for PV support can be lowered, if units eligible for a feed-in tariff support don't fully make use of this tariff, as they self-consume the produced electricity instead of feeding it into the grid.

On the other hand, self-consumption can lead to an altered or even unfair distribution of those charges. Levies for combined heat and power (CHP) and other policy support costs make up for a portion of the electricity retail price for households and industrial customers [20]. So while self-consumers may profit from these policies, they may not contribute their fair share. Further, taxes on electricity could also be avoided, thereby lowering public revenues.

The structure of retail prices of energy might be a source of insecurity for long-term investments into measures for self-consumption. Since a large portion of the retail price of electricity are taxes and levies and the profitability of self-consumption depends largely on the retail price, changes to policies and taxes endanger investments to storage or demand-side management (DSM) solutions. Ref. [24] provides an example from Germany that illustrates how significantly the net present value of a solar installation decreases with lower taxes and duties, since its profitability is directly related to the avoided electricity purchase price.

ADAPTING GRID TARIFFS TO CHANGING CONDITIONS

A fixed grid tariff depending only on the maximum load would address the issues raised before regarding the unfair distribution of costs. The resulting significantly lower cost per kilowatt hour (refer to) however decreases the incentive to save energy and to use energy-efficient products. Thus other approaches might be favorable in order to address both, a fairer distribution of costs and maintaining incentives for energy efficiency investments.

Different approaches exist to bypass those shortcomings. EURELECTRIC [22] proposes network tariffs comprising two parts: a part that accounts for the capacity held available and an energy component. Alternatively, EURELECTRIC [22], as well as the German Agora Energiewende [14] propose time-varying grid charges to fairly distribute costs to all stakeholders. At a time of peak load, grid charges should be higher than in times of a low load. This way, incentives for smoothening production and consumption can be set, as well as stimuli for self-consumption at times of peak feed-in. On the other hand, load shifting by large consumers such as industrial plants can be incentivized, since price signals will raise profits of load adapted behavior.

Smart meters and other supportive ICT infrastructure can promote the development of tariffs that set incentives to shift loads to different hours while considering a fair distribution of costs. Changing the way grid costs including supportive infrastructure costs get distributed may have an impact on the grid parity of the different technologies available for self-consumption. Further, expected changes in the reduction of peak loads through self-consumption should be carefully considered when deciding on reforming grid tariffs.

27.5 CONCLUSIONS

Energy policies, regulations, and market conditions for self-consumption in each Member State of the EU are diverse. Introducing specific policies supporting self-consumption should take these different market structures into account and also the state of development of the RES sector. This includes in particular the probability for different technologies to reach grid parity.

To foster self-consumption the national legal framework in each Member State should be revisited. Potential barriers must be analyzed carefully and removed if there is no reasonable justification for not doing so. Apart from the review of current legislation, there are different options to support the market uptake of self-consumption, such as direct support schemes for self-consumption, support to investments in storage, and measures to facilitate demand side management.

Since renewable energies and especially PV are well on track to reach grid parity within the next few years all over Europe, direct support schemes such as a premium on self-consumption might not be necessary in most Member States to foster self-consumption. An additional downside of premiums on self-consumption is the potential interference with energy efficiency efforts: If the mere consumption of energy gets remunerated by a premium, this will rather encourage an increase in consumption.

Supporting the usage of energy storage solutions and demand-side management might be a good measure to promote both the development of related technologies and self-consumption. Furthermore, storage can contribute to balancing services on the grid, if incentives are set right. The implementation of management solutions such as dedicated charging algorithms appears to be crucial for enabling the full grid-related benefits from self-consumption. Similar to the introduction of feed-in tariffs to promote RES, support to technological solutions can lead to market maturity of storage and other demand-side management technologies.

Benefitting from the balancing potentials of self-consumption will require enablers such as smart grid technologies and dynamic electricity tariffs. A delicate topic in this context is the distribution of costs, be it costs of the power grid or additional production costs of RES. Self-consumption tends to reallocate costs from prosumers that can afford the necessary investments to consumers that receive their power only from the common grid. The latter are being charged a higher share of grid costs, levies, and taxes, as those are largely paid in the form of an add-on to grid consumption charges. Alternative tariff structures are thus being discussed, such as time-varying grid charges or charges split by volume and maximum load [14,22].

REFERENCES

[1] R. Luthander, J. Widén, D. Nilsson, J. Palm, Photovoltaic self-consumption in buildings: a review, Appl. Energy 142 (2015) 80−94.

[2] Pöyry, Is the end in sight for renewable subsidies? Available from: <http://www.poyry.com/sites/default/files/imce/files/pov_renewable_subsidies_pn0019_v1_web.pdf>, 2014.

[3] D. Pudjianto, P. Djapic, J. Dragovic, G. Strbac, Grid integration cost of photovoltaic power generation. Available from: <http://www.pvparity.eu/results/cost-and-benefits-of-pv-grid-integration/>, 2013.

[4] B. Schott, J. Binder, M. Felder, B. Matthis, M. Capota, M. Danzer, Optimierung der Systemintegration fluktuierender Stromerzeugung aus erneuerbaren Energien am Beispiel der Photovoltaik auf Niederspannungsebene - Untersuchungen zu Möglichkeiten und Potenzialen zukünftiger Energieversorgungsstrukturen, Zentrum für Sonnenenergie - und Wasserstoff - Forschung Baden - Württemberg (ZSW), 2014.

[5] B. Normark, A. Faure, How can batteries support the EU electricity network? Available from: <http://insightenergy.org/static_pages/publications>, 2014.

[6] G. Mulder, F. De Ridder, D. Six, Electricity storage for grid-connected household dwellings with PV panels, Sol. Energy 84 (2010) 1284−1293.

[7] M. Baumann, B. Zimmermann, H. Dura, A comparative probabilistic economic analysis of selected stationary battery systems for grid applications, 2013.

[8] C. Kost, J. Mayer, J. Thomsen, N. Hartmann, C. Senkpiel, S. Philipps, et al., Stromgestehungskosten erneuerbarer Energien., Fraunhofer Institut für Solare Energiesysteme (ISE), Freiburg, 2013.

[9] M. Baumann, D. Poncette, B. Zimmermann, Evaluation of calculation methods, models and data sources for life cycle costing on the example of stationary battery systems, 2014.

[10] P. Stenzel, M. Baumann, J. Fleer, Database development and evaluation for techno-economic assessments of electrochemical energy storage systems, 2014.

[11] IRENA, Battery Storage for Renewables: Market Status and Technology Outlook, International renewable energy agency, Bonn−Germany, 2015.

[12] C.A.R.M.E.N. (2016) *Marktübersicht Batteriespeicher Informationsangebot* Effective December 2016, Centrales Agrar-Rohstoff Marketing- und Energienetzwerk e.V. Straubing.

[13] G. Fitzgerald, J. Morris, Battery Balance of System Charrette, USA: Rocky Mountain Institute, 2015.

[14] Agora Energiewende, Stromspeicher in der Energiewende - Untersuchung zum Bedarf an neuen Stromspeichern in Deutschland für den Erzeugungsausgleich, Systemdienstleistungen und im Verteilnetz, 2014.

[15] P. Denholm, R. Margolis, Evaluating the limits of solar photovoltaics (PV) in electric power systems utilizing energy storage and other enabling technologies, Energy Policy 35 (2007) 4424–4433.

[16] M. Baumann, B. Simon, H. Dura, M. Weil, The contribution of electric vehicles to the changes of airborne emissions, 2012.

[17] G. Strbac, Demand side management: benefits and challenges, Energy Policy 36 (2008) 4419–4426.

[18] R. Hollinger, B. Wille-Haussmann, T. Erge, J. Sönnichsen, T. Stillahn, N. Kreifels, Speicherstudie. Available from: <http://www.ise.fraunhofer.de/de/veroeffentlichungen/veroeffentlichungen-pdf-dateien/studien-und-konzeptpapiere/speicherstudie-2013.pdf>, 2013.

[19] A. Colthorpe, International firms target UK for 2015 energy storage push, 2014. Available from: <http://www.solarpowerportal.co.uk/editors_blog/international_firms_target_uk_for_2015_energy_storage_push_2694>, 2014.

[20] EURELECTRIC, Analysis of European Power Price Increase Drivers. Available from: <http://www.eurelectric.org/media/131606/prices_study_final-2014-2500-0001-01-e.pdf>, 2014.

[21] Eurostat, Electricity prices by type of user. Available from: <http://ec.europa.eu/eurostat/web/products-datasets/-/ten00117>, 2015.

[22] EURELECTRIC, Network tariff structure for a smart energy system. Available from: <http://www.eurelectric.org/media/80239/20130409_network-tariffs-paper_final_to_publish-2013-030-0409-01-e.pdf>, 2013.

[23] SunEdison, Enabling the European consumer to generate power for self-consumption. Available from: <http://www.sunedison.es/docs/SunEdison_PV_Self-consumption_Study_high_resolution_%2813_Mb%29.pdf>, 2014.

[24] REC Solar Germany GmbH, Study on the profitability of commercial self-consumption solar installations in Germany. Available from: <http://www.recgroup.com/sites/default/files/documents/study_self-consumption_singapore_web_20141027.pdf>, 2014.

DC POWER PRODUCTION AND CONSUMPTION IN HOUSEHOLDS

28

Bo Normark[1], Abhishek Shivakumar[2], and Manuel Welsch[2]

[1]*InnoEnergy Scandinavia, Stockholm, Sweden* [2]*KTH Royal Institute of Technology, Stockholm, Sweden*

28.1 INTRODUCTION

Over a century ago George Westinghouse, with the support of Nikola Tesla, defeated Thomas Edison in the "War of Currents" [1], thereby successfully establishing alternating current (AC) as the primary mode of electricity transmission and distribution. Large power plants such as coal, nuclear, and hydro, are often located far from consumption centers. With transformers, the voltage level of AC power is easily increased to very high voltages, which is preferable for long-distance transmission, before being stepped down again to levels that are safe for consumers to use. Today, however, there is a revival of direct current (DC) for high-voltage transmission, particularly for long distances and for integrating large-scale renewables such as hydro and wind parks.

The past decade has also seen a rapid increase in local electricity generation from renewable sources, such as solar photovoltaics (PV), both globally and in the EU. Solar PV panels generate DC power that is either used to charge batteries or feed into the electricity grid after being converted to AC, with associated losses [2]. Batteries play a crucial role in balancing the variability of solar PV, and are especially well suited to households.

Furthermore, there has also been a shift towards the use of DC power on the demand side. Several household appliances, such as computers, cell phones, and LED (light-emitting diode) lighting use DC power, requiring the electricity from the grid to be converted from AC to DC. One important technical development is that household appliances are increasingly using power converters to convert unregulated AC to constant DC. The DC can then be used to power speed-controlled motors with an increased efficiency. Such modern appliances are, therefore, well suited for direct DC supply.

This chapter investigates the current developments related to DC networks and their feasibility at the household level. By distributing DC rather than AC power, the number of transformations can be reduced, and therefore also the associated losses. Several studies show that cumulative losses of the DC−AC−DC conversion when powering DC appliances through local PV systems are in the range of 5%−7% [3,4]. The losses across the EU from avoiding this conversion could be approximately 120−170 million Euros per year as shown in Table 28.1.

Europe's Energy Transition. DOI: http://dx.doi.org/10.1016/B978-0-12-809806-6.00028-6

Table 28.1 Savings by Avoiding DC−AC−DC Conversion Losses

Solar PV Generation (TJ)	Share of Residential Solar PV Generation (%)	Solar PV Generation, Residential (GWh)	Electricity Price (€/kWh)	Million € (5% Saving)	Million € (7% Saving)
291,120[a]	22%[b]	17,792	0.1376[c]	122	171

[a]Eurostat, Supply, transformation and consumption of renewable energies − annual data: nrg_107a, 2015.
[b]European Photovoltaic Industry Association, Global Market Outlook for Photovoltaics 2014-2018 (2014).
[c]Eurostat, Electricity prices by type of user: ten00117.

28.2 DC NETWORKS
MARKET FOR DC NETWORKS

The first real market where low-voltage DC (LVDC) is expected to be employed is data centers, due to their high DC demand. At present, several pilot installations are testing and demonstrating the value of such LVDC networks [5]. Some of these data center projects have reported that the benefits of DC include a 10%−30% reduction in energy consumption, about 15% lower capital costs, potential increases in reliability, a smaller carbon footprint, simpler design, less physical area requirements, and less cooling demand [6−8]. With the very large and growing energy consumption of these data centers of up to 10% of global electricity consumption in 2013 [9], even relatively minor gains in efficiency can have a significant impact.

In addition to data centers, other potential markets are expected to be nonresidential (tertiary) buildings such as office buildings and supermarkets. These buildings are typically characterized by large electrical DC loads from computers, screens, and possibly lighting (with a shift from fluorescent lamps to LED lighting).

Depending on the success of LVDC networks in these markets, the residential sector may also follow. The main reasons for this potentially delayed market uptake are:

- The benefits of LVDC networks for households have not been clearly evident due to the prevalence of large AC loads and relative lack of appropriate low-cost power converters.
- There is a large stock of households, which are not renovated or refurbished as frequently as data centers and tertiary buildings.

In this respect, the rollout of the latest USB technologies and standards may play a significant role in accelerating the deployment of LVDC in households. With a capacity to deliver up to 100 W of power at a voltage rating of 5−20 V, USB 3.1 may widen the types of household applications that can be powered by LVDC, as discussed in more detail under the subsequent heading "Role of USB."

WHAT DOES A DC NETWORK COMPRISE OF?

The main constituents of a local electricity network can be categorized as:

- Electricity generation and storage (solar PV, wind, fuel cells, batteries);
- Distribution (wiring and electronic control);
- Loads (computers, appliances, lighting).

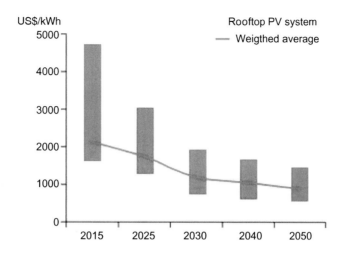

FIGURE 28.1

Cost projection of rooftop solar PV [11].

If two or more of the above constituents of a network are DC-compatible, it is worth exploring the viability, both technical and financial, of a DC network.

On the electricity generation side, the share of solar PV in the electricity generation mix of the EU has increased from 0.3% in 2004 and 0.5% in 2009 to 2.9% in 2013. This has been largely driven by the dramatically falling costs of solar PV technologies [10]. Furthermore, battery costs for residential applications have been steadily reducing. The recently announced Tesla Powerwall comes at a price of 350 $/kWh for a 10 kWh unit, and its Powerblock is priced at 250 $/kWh for a 100 kWh unit.

Figs. 28.1 and 28.2 show cost projections for residential (rooftop) solar PV and Li-ion batteries respectively. With falling solar PV and Li-ion battery costs, they will become more prevalent in households.

On the demand side, several end-uses are likely to be increasingly powered by DC. Fig. 28.3 shows the electricity consumption per household and end-uses across the EU. Within these end-use categories, the following demands could be directly fed by DC:

- Potentially all modern electric appliances using power convertors such as fridges, freezers, dish washers, washing machines;
- All LED lighting;
- Modern air conditioners with power convertors;
- Space and water heating with heat pumps or direct heating.

Today, in 23 of the 28 EU Member States (MS) the share of consumption of electrical appliances represents over 50% of the total electricity consumption (Fig. 28.3). This share of electricity consumption can potentially be met using a DC network, powered by solar PV combined with a Li-ion battery storage and a LVDC network.

According to a study on the energy savings potential when shifting to DC appliances [14], average energy savings of 33% can be achieved with the best DC alternative. However, even with an LVDC network not all DC–DC conversion losses can be avoided. This is due to the several

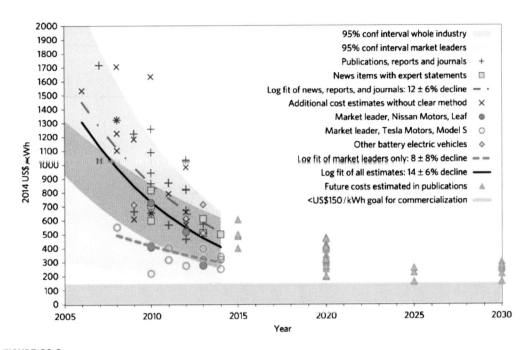

FIGURE 28.2

Cost trends of Li-ion battery technologies [12].

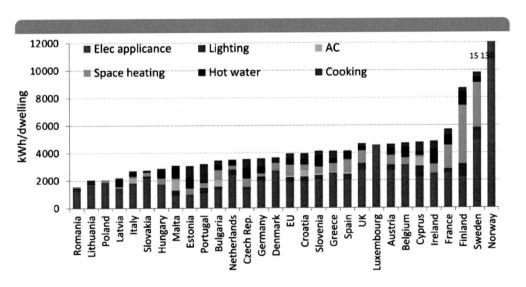

FIGURE 28.3

Electricity consumption per dwelling by end-use (2012) [13].

Table 28.2 Summary of Reasoning to Select a Voltage Level [15]

Voltage Level	Reasoning
Vdc ≥ 220	Adaptability with existing building's grid
Vdc ≤ 238 or 457 (phase-to-phase)	Compatibility with single phase loads
463 < Vdc < 617	Compatibility with three-phase loads
Maximum possible	Efficiency
Vdc ≤ 373	Insulation
Vdc ≤ 350–450	Component and devices matching (rated levels)

different voltage levels required for the operation of the various devices. For instance, a device may run on 1.8 V while its peripherals are powered by 5 V. Therefore some DC conversion losses related to appliances will continue to remain in LVDC networks.

WHAT IS THE RIGHT VOLTAGE LEVEL?

A key issue to consider for DC networks is the optimal voltage level. In recent years, there has been growing consensus on the potential benefits of powering data centers with 400 V DC. Bolstered by the development of associated power products, this has led to new DC electrical standards.

The most important parameter to decide on for an optimal DC voltage standard for households and tertiary buildings is the power to be transferred. Therefore, information on the loads to be connected to the distribution system will first need to be determined and analyzed. Following this, the electricity supply options will need to be studied. The main objectives of the distribution system are to link supply and the consumption in a safe, reliable, and cost-efficient way. A higher voltage will result in less losses and a more efficient distribution. However, it will imply that more safety issues need to be considered and new standards developed.

At present, there is no definitive consensus on an optimal voltage level. Table 28.2 summarizes the main reasons in support of different voltage levels.

In the case of data centers, the Emerge Alliance's standards for 24 and 380 Vdc are becoming the industry standard. To agree on a standard voltage level for households the required power in a room, house, or building will need to be analyzed, taking into consideration the necessary safety features to be defined as part of wiring rules.

ROLE OF USB

Electronic appliances, such as smart phones and laptops, are ubiquitous at the household level and represent a growing share of electricity demand. The simultaneous rollout of the USB 3.1 standard and USB Type-C connector (also called USB-C), starting from 2016, has a direct impact on the use and electricity consumption of these electronic appliances. This development is driven by a large number of companies, securing a very high penetration and fast implementation of the technology. The main features of the USB-C connector are that it is reversible (both ends of the cable are identical), "flippable" (both "up" and "down" orientations are identical), has twice the theoretical throughput of USB 3.0 (increased from 5 to 10 Gbps), and is compatible with the USB 3.1 standard. USB 3.1 will work with three different voltages, 5, 12, and 20 V and the highest current at 20 V will be 5 A, corresponding to a delivered power of 100 W.[a] A standardization of the lower DC voltage levels is thus given by the USB 3.1 specification.

This last feature is particularly relevant to the discussion of LVDC networks. Around 10 billion electronic devices such as mobile phones, tablets, and laptops already use USB cables for charging. For example, both the Apple MacBook[b] and Google Chromebook Pixel[c] are equipped with USB-C ports. In the case of the MacBook, this is combined with USB 3.1. In addition, a host of other small USB-powered devices such as heaters, blenders, and monitors are on the market today.

Following this trend, increasingly aircrafts and hotel rooms have started to provide USB sockets as electrical fittings,[d] which are also being sold at furniture retailers such as IKEA. USB wall-sockets and chargers are easy to install and therefore look set to become the standard in new private houses and office buildings.

At the household level, Table 28.3 lists the electrical appliances present in a typical household and their potential compatibility with USB 3.1 and a DC supply.

POTENTIAL HOUSEHOLD CONFIGURATIONS

There are several possible household configurations that can be considered. One differentiating factor between these alternatives is the varying levels of DC network usage across household electrical appliances. For a transition towards DC households, the most feasible and likely configurations are presented below.

HYBRID AC–DC HOUSEHOLD

A potential solution is that a hybrid system will be installed in some households, where both AC and LVDC networks will operate side-by-side, with high-power appliances (such as washing machines and dishwashers) being supplied by AC (Fig. 28.4). Power from solar PV is converted from DC to AC through an inverter. Medium- and low-power appliances are supplied by LVDC with voltage levels ranging from 12 to 50 Vdc.

DC HOUSEHOLD

Another solution is to power the majority of household appliances through a DC system. 400 Vdc can be used for high-power appliances, 100 Vdc for medium-power appliances, and a few volts (potentially with USB 3.1) for appliances with low-power ratings. This implies that there will be

---

[a]USB 3.0 (also called USB 3.1 gen 1) allows up to 1.5 A at 5 V (max. power of 7.5 W).
[b]https://www.apple.com/macbook/design/.
[c]https://www.google.com/chromebook/pixel/.
[d]The Economist (October 2013).

Table 28.3 Suitability of Typical Household Appliances for Use With a DC Network and USB [16,17]

Appliance	W	DC Suitability	USB Suitability
Lighting	9–72	+	+
Cell phone	3	+	+
Electric razor	5	+	+
Internet router	13	+	+
BlueRay/DVD player	26	+	+
LCD monitor	32	+	+
Laptop	60–90	+	+
Computer	100	+	+
36″ LCD TV	60	+	+
Home theater system	300	+	−
Mixer	220	+	−
Blender	300	+	−
Sandwich maker	750	+	−
Toaster	1050	+	−
Coffee maker	800–1400	+	−
Vacuum cleaner	200–700	+	−
Kettle	2000	+	−
Washing machine[a]	500	+/−	−
Refrigerator[a]	400	+/−	−
Air conditioner[a]	1000	+/−	−
Dishwasher[a]	1200–1500	+/−	−
Electric oven	2150	−	−
Tumble dryer[a]	4000	+/−	−
Microwave oven	600–1500	−	−
Electric stove	1000–3000	−	−

[a]*Modern appliances with a variable-speed drive are better suited for DC supply.*

three LVDC networks to be installed in such a "DC household"—all with the necessary protective measures, switching products, and connections. Fig. 28.5 shows this household configuration.

A key prerequisite for such a household configuration to be feasible is the development of DC power electronic components with high efficiency, reliability, and low costs. This development process has already led to the launch of several DC network-specific products on the market. For instance, Vicor announced the first 400 Vdc to 48 Vdc (nominal) bus converter to use its CHiP (Converter Housed in Package) module technology. The DC input range for the converter is between 262 and 410 Vdc. Its nominal output voltage is 47.5 Vdc, but it can be set for any output voltage from 32.5 to 51.25 Vdc. The converter has a power rating of 1200 W with an efficiency of 98%. It can, however, handle up to a 1500 W peak, with the efficiency remaining over 90% until 10% of its rated power. In OEM (Original Equipment Manufacturer) quantities, it is priced at US

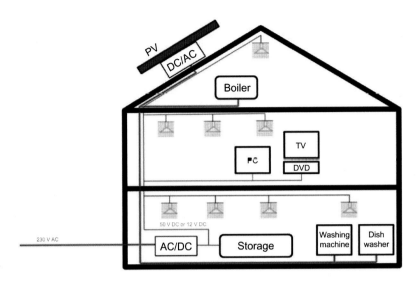

FIGURE 28.4

Hybrid AC−DC solution.

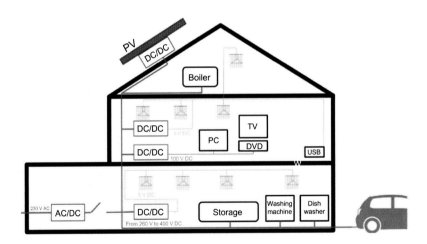

FIGURE 28.5

DC household solution.

$120. Table 28.4 compares the costs of some of the other main components that differentiate the hybrid AC−DC and DC household configurations.

Table 28.4 suggests that, at present, there is no strong justification for a transition to household DC networks. The costs of the required DC converters currently outweigh the cost savings from reduced conversion losses. The savings are compared for the cases of high and low solar irradiation in Table 28.5.

Table 28.4 Cost Comparison of Selected Household Components

	Component	Cost (€)	Hybrid AC−DC	DC
1	USB wall charger	16−20 [19,20]	+	+
2	AC−DC converter (220/230 Vac to 400 Vdc)	243 [21]	−	+
3	AC−DC converter (220/230 Vac to 12/48 Vdc)	45−395 [22]	+	−
4	DC−DC converter (solar PV to 230 Vdc)	33−830 [23]	−	+
5	DC−DC converter (400 Vdc to 48 Vdc)	110−405 [22,24,25]	−	+
6	DC−DC converter (48− >5 V)	32−126 [22]	−	+
7	DC−AC inverter	1420−2750 [26]	+	−
Total cost (€)			1481−3165	434−1624
Total annual savings (€) (high solar irradiation) (compared to hybrid AC−DC−AC configuration, see Table 28.5)			−	46−64
Total annual savings (€) (low solar irradiation) (compared to hybrid AC−DC−AC configuration)			−	24−34

"−" indicates that the component will not be required for that configuration, " + " indicates that it may be required.

Table 28.5 Annual Savings for a Typical Household With DC With (A) High Solar Irradiation and (B) Low Solar Irradiation

	Unit	(A) Spain	(B) Sweden
Solar irradiation[a]	kWh/m^2/year	1700	900
Efficiency	%	0.15	
Solar panel area	m^2	35	
Performance ratio	−	0.75	
Annual solar PV generation	kWh/year	6693.75	3543.75
Electricity savings			
5% loss reductions compared to AC-DC-AC system	kWh	334.68	177.18
7% loss reductions compared to AC-DC-AC system	kWh	468.56	248.06
Electricity price	(€/kWh)	0.1376[a]	
Cost savings			
Savings at 5% loss reductions compared to AC−DC−AC system	€	46.05	24.38
Savings at 7% loss reductions compared to AC−DC−AC system	€	64.47	34.13

[a]*PVGIS © European Communities (2001−2008), Solar energy resource in Europe, JRC. Available from: <http://re.jrc.ec. europa.eu/pvgis/solres/solreseurope.htm#Fig6> [18].*

STANDARDIZATION AND LEGISLATIVE FRAMEWORK

As the use of DC is currently most widespread in data centers, the standardization work in this area has progressed the farthest. The European Telecommunications Standards Institute (ETSI) has developed standard EN 300 132-3-1, which describes the characteristics of a DC bus between 260 and 400 V, and EN 301 605, which describes the earthing and bonding of 400 Vdc data and telecom (ICT) equipment. Further standards have been published by the USA-based Emerge Alliance, the International Telecommunication Union (ITU-T), and the International Electrotechnical Commission (IEC) [19].

For household applications, work has been ongoing for a long time within the Institute of Electrical and Electronics Engineers (IEEE) and the IEC. The activities within the IEC have increased considerably in recent years and a Strategic Group (SG 4) has been set up to recommend technical work to define standards for LVDC networks up to 1500 V. While both the IEC and IEEE are very active in this field, as of now there has been little coordination between these two bodies.

The work within the IEC is currently investigating several options. One solution could be to have 380–400 Vdc for high-power products and 24 Vdc for electronic loads (potentially through USB) for the low-power products.

It is most likely that multiple voltages will be used and it is apparent that on the highest level 380–400 V will be used globally. 400 Vdc facilitates the transition to DC networks as many devices operating on AC today could, without modification, work at that voltage level. That means that the current system with 220 Vac and 50 Hz could be replaced with a common system based on 400 Vdc.

Apart from the 400 Vdc level, the standard for the lower voltage level is set by USB 3.1, and this standard is not expected to be challenged. With a capacity of up to 100 W, it could handle all low- and some medium-power devices. Particularly new electronic devices are likely to come with the USB standard and will thus be directly suited for DC supply via USB 3.1.

28.3 POLICY RECOMMENDATIONS

This leads to the following main policy recommendations to facilitate the transition to DC networks in households:

1. Encourage and support the standardization work driven by the IEC and IEEE. Clear standards are key for the development of DC networks in households.
2. Increase energy efficiency with technologies such as variable-speed drives. DC networks in households have the potential to reduce electricity consumption and can be supported through relevant technologies such as variable-speed drives.
3. Clearer policy direction on self-consumption of renewables (refer to Chapter 27: Self-Consumption of Electricity from Renewable Sources). To foster self-consumption, the legislative framework in each Member State will need to be revisited, since legislation in EU MS varies.

4. Increase support for batteries, other distributed storage technologies, and demand-side management at the household level.
5. Standardization of operating voltage levels and associated components for a household DC network. Mandate USB for power supply to electronics.

The key factors in the choice of a transition to DC networks in households will be the evolution of electricity consumption of different household devices, the penetration of residential solar PV, and the cost of DC power electronics (such as converters). Increased distributed generation from solar PV, distributed storage in batteries, and decreasing costs of DC power electronics are likely to make a compelling case for household DC networks in the medium- to long-term future.

In the case of a long market transition period, DC households may develop in parallel to the current AC system. As pointed out in the previous Section 28.2, a hybrid configuration with installations of parallel networks of AC and LVDC distribution systems is a possible "transition solution," and may turn out to be the best solution if high-voltage DC is found to be infeasible (for technical, economic, or other reasons).

REFERENCES

[1] A. Lantero, The war of the currents: AC vs. DC power. Available from: <http://energy.gov/articles/war-currents-ac-vs-dc-power> (accessed 16.07.15).
[2] K. Zipp, How do solar inverters work? Available from: <http://www.solarpowerworldonline.com/2013/04/how-do-solar-inverters-work/> (accessed 16.07.15).
[3] IEEE Smart Grid, IEEE smart grid experts roundup: AC vs. DC power: a new battle of the currents. Available from: <http://smartgrid.ieee.org/resources/interviews/368-ieee-smart-grid-experts-roundup-ac-vs-dc-power?highlight = WyJhYyIsInZzIiwiZGMiLCJkYydzIiwicG93ZXIiLCJwb3dlcidzIiwiYWMgdnMiLCJhYyB2cyBkYyIsInZzIGRjIiwidnMgZGMgcG93ZXIiLCJkYyBwb3dlciJd> (accessed 16.07.15).
[4] J. Åkerlund, Investigation of a micro DC power grid in Glava Hillringsberg − a smart grid, 2012.
[5] B. Fortenbery, DC power standards. Technical report, March 2011.
[6] R. Adapa, G. Ailee, W. Tschudi, B.T. Patterson, G.F. Reed, B.M. Grainger, Plugging into DC, IEEE Power Energy Mag. 10 (2012) 19−79.
[7] T. Aldridge, Direct 400 Vdc for energy efficient data centers direct 400 Vdc facility vision. Technical report, April 2009.
[8] Electric Power Research Institute, DC power for data centers. Technical report, November 2010.
[9] M. Mills, The cloud begins with coal. Big data, big networks, big infrastructure, and big power. An overview of the electricity used by the global digital ecosystem. Digital Power Group, 2013.
[10] REN21, Renewables 2014 − global status report, 2014.
[11] IEA, Technology roadmap: solar photovoltaic energy (2014 edition), 2014.
[12] B. Nykvist, M. Nilsson, Rapidly falling costs of battery packs for electric vehicles, Nature Climate Change 5 (2015) 329−332.
[13] Enerdata, Energy Efficiency Trends for households in the EU: (as part of the ODYSSEE-MURE project co-funded by the Intelligent Energy Europe Programme of the European Union), 2014.
[14] K. Garbesi, V. Vossos, H. Shen, Catalog of DC appliances and power systems. Technical report, 2011.

[15] H. Pang, B. Pong, E.W.C. Lo, A practical and efficient DC distribution system for commercial and residential applications-240 V or higher? in: The International Conference on Electrical Engineering, 2008, pp. 1−4.

[16] D. Salomonsson, A. Sannino, Load modelling for steady-state and transient analysis of low-voltage DC systems, IET Electr. Power Appl. 1 (2007) 690−696.

[17] M.C. Kinn, Benefits of direct current electricity supply for domestic application, 2011.

[18] PVGIS © European Communities (2001−2008), Solar energy resource in Europe, JRC. Available from: <http://re.jrc.ec.europa.eu/pvgis/solres/solreseurope.htm> (accessed 27.08.15).

[19] <http://www.ebay.com/bhp/usb-wall-outlet-charger> (accessed 20.08.15).

[20] <http://www.amazon.com/RCA-Wall-Plate-Charger-White/dp/B0094E4A86/ref = sr_1_4?s=electronics&ie= UTF8&qid=1439294212&sr=1-4&keywords=usb + wall + outlet > (accessed 20.08.15).

[21] <http://www.vicorpower.com/megapac> (accessed 01.09.15).

[22] <http://www.digikey.com/product-search/en/power-supplies-external-internal-off-board/ac-dc-converters/ 590377> (accessed 20.08.15).

[23] <http://www.altestore.com/store/Voltage-Converters/DC-to-DC-Voltage-Converters/c511/ > (accessed 20.08.15).

[24] <http://www.vicorpower.com/> (accessed 27.08.15).

[25] <http://electronicdesign.com/power/400-v-dc-distribution-data-center-gets-real-0> (accessed 27.08.15).

[26] <http://www.wholesalesolar.com/power-inverters>.

DISTRICT HEATING IN EUROPE: OPPORTUNITIES FOR ENERGY SAVINGS, BUSINESS, AND JOBS

29

Ulrich Fahl and Audrey Dobbins
University of Stuttgart, Stuttgart, Germany

29.1 INTRODUCTION

District heating systems can supply the required heat load for highly efficient combined heat and power (CHP) plants, but also offer the opportunity to employ renewable energy sources. District cooling has also emerged as a promising energy efficient option to provide a cooler indoor ambience in summer time.

Under Article 14 of the 2012 European Energy Efficiency Directive, all Member States of the European Union were required to assess the potential of expanding cogeneration and efficient district heating and cooling (DHC) systems and to investigate adoption strategies to 2020 and 2030. This assessment would entail the development of heating and cooling maps to localize areas of demand as the basis to evaluate cost-effective potentials for heating and cooling technologies [1].

This chapter investigates the state of the art of district heating (and cooling) in Europe (volumes of energy, localization, state of the installation, and level of performance) as well as the technologies, measures, and examples of projects which have the potential to increase the level of performance of district heating. This includes in particular the integration of renewable sources, taking into account regional specificities.

In order to assess the potential contribution of district heating towards the achievement of the EU energy and climate targets for 2020, 2030, and 2050 (GHG emission reduction by 20%, 40%, and 80%−95% compared to 1990, respectively), two key performance indicators are of significance:

1. For the CO_2 emissions per kWh of district heat delivered, the alternative use of natural gas provides a benchmark. Each unit of natural gas used results in 201.6 gCO_2/kWh [2]. With the existing generation mix for district heating in the EU, 297.6 gCO_2 are currently emitted for each kWh of district heat delivered.
2. On the economic side, the district heating prices are comparable to the prices for natural gas. However, natural gas prices are country-specific such that no generalized statement can be made.

The district heating value chain as well as the opportunities for energy savings and CO_2 reductions span across the fuel provision through heat production (supply side) to the distribution (district heating networks) and consumers (demand side).

Europe's Energy Transition. DOI: http://dx.doi.org/10.1016/B978-0-12-809806-6.00029-8

29.2 **CURRENT SITUATION**

Residential and service sector buildings across the EU consumed about 3300 TWh/year in heat in 2010. District heating is estimated to supply about 840 TWh or 25% of this heating demand. Buildings connected to district heating networks account for 430 TWh/year of the total heat demand. The industrial sector's use of district heating for low-temperature applications amounts to about 180 TWh/year. Together, these two main buyers thus consume about 620 TWh annually. Industry further consumers 220 TWh/year of heat that is supplied by its own CHP plants.

It is acknowledged that the precise disaggregation of these figures across district heating systems and industrial CHP plants is difficult, because heat is sometimes used for internal purposes and not reported in statistical sources. The breakdown provided, however, remains a realistic approximation of the use of district heating across the EU [3] as shown in Fig. 29.1.

District heating systems are already well-established across Europe, with a network of distribution pipes of a total trench length of about 200,000 km. Annually, the total revenue for heat sold was about €30 billion [3]. The actual market varies across Member States and is characterized, inter alia, in terms of the type of DHC system, its market share, sales volume and trench length, and the share of the population served [4].

A variety of heating technologies are utilized in the European Union. The most dominant technologies across the majority of Member States include fossil-thermal power plants and CHP

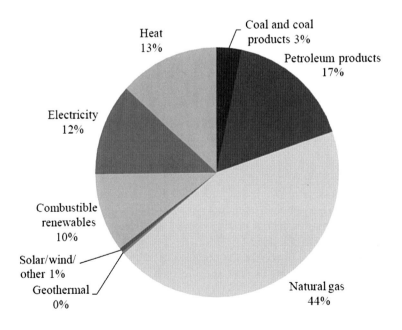

FIGURE 29.1

Composition of heat supply for residential and service sector buildings in the EU in 2010. (The figure does not include indirect heat supply from all indoor electricity use. Labels refer to the standard commodity groups used in the IEA energy balances. Heat denotes mainly heat from district heating systems.)

plants. The share of wood as a fuel source has increased drastically over the past decades. Fourteen percent of German households draw their heat from district heating plants. These are predominantly large CHP plants powered with natural gas or coal, but 10% are fueled by renewable energy sources with a focus on biomass. Half of the Polish heating demand is supplied with district heating generated mostly by coal. District heating enjoys a share of 50%−60% in Denmark produced by a mix of renewables (biomass, solar), fossil fuels (coal, natural gas), and waste. Natural gas (44%) and biomass (38%) supply the heating demand in the residential sector, where district heating comprises 20% of this demand [5].

29.3 DEMAND SIDE

DENSIFICATION AND EXTENSION OF EXISTING NETWORKS

The increased thermal insulation in buildings has led to a reduced need for heating. This decrease in energy demand results in a lower sales potential for district heating. Concurrently, the heat demand during summer is naturally lower. To maintain their business case, district heating networks will therefore need to expand their customer base, e.g., by densifying their networks. Additionally, industrial and commercial customers can benefit from the use of process heat and cooling when the heat demand is controlled over the year through measures such as lower tariffs for heat during the summertime [6].

- In recent years, the German energy supplier MVV Energie AG has densified the existing district heating networks throughout the city of Mannheim. The network was also extended to different areas of the city (red blocks) as shown in Fig. 29.2, with an additional pipeline capacity of about 30 km. This extended network will contribute a 17.6 kt annual reduction of CO_2 emissions and save an additional 115,000 MWh of primary energy per year. About €30 million was invested in this project, where the majority of contractors benefiting were local to the Mannheim region, resulting in an effective employment level of 4000 man-years [7].

CONSTRUCTION OF NEW NETWORKS

The construction of new heating networks offers opportunities for climate protection through local power generation with cogeneration plants and the economic use of biomass in larger units. For this purpose, areas with sufficient energy density for the establishment of district heating networks can be determined with a heat map. With relatively little effort and within a short period, local heat islands can be identified which combine heat loads within close range. These heat islands may serve as profitable locations to develop new networks. The development of larger heating networks in areas with existing buildings is generally associated with technical, social, and economic barriers, and is associated with longer execution times. By upgrading heat islands to an extended network, a gradual build-up can be realized.

- The Olympic Games in 2012 provided a platform for the development of new infrastructure, where district heating was one key option to respond to an array of objectives, such as emissions reductions and harnessing local energy resources. The decision to invest in a district heating system resulted in the installation of two trigeneration plants combined cooling, heat

FIGURE 29.2

Densification of the district heating system in Mannheim, Germany. (This graph shows the existing and future district heating network. Red areas represent the district heating densification areas; dark red (dark gray in print versions) lines represent the district heating transmission network.)

and power (CCHP) in combination with large thermal storage at both Stratford City and Kings Yard on the Olympic Park. The heat provided by these two systems has increased from an existing, small network of 100−200 MW, while cooling has increased from 18 to 64 MW (through a combination of absorption and ammonia chillers), and low-carbon electricity generation has increased from 3.5 to 30 MW. This initiative also included the development of an additional 27.5 MWh of heat storage and 4.7 MWh of cool storage. While these CCHP plants operate exclusively with gas now, they have the potential to run on both gas and biomass, which could lead to savings of 5%−10% for the majority of customers [8].

DISTRICT COOLING

Cooling demand is generally lower than heating demand in buildings. Cooling networks offer lower losses compared to heating networks due to the much lower difference between operating and environmental temperatures. Shopping centers, certain production plants, and laboratories typically have higher cooling demands and offer the opportunity to harness the greatest potential for the use of cooling networks. Yet, very few communal cooling networks have been constructed [6].

Cooling networks can operate either as a closed system or as an ancillary division of a heating network. By linking absorption chillers[a] for the production of heating and cooling energy, high efficiency can be attained for both heating and cooling. Since temporary high thermal loads can arise across the networks, e.g., to power larger events, appropriate planning is required to anticipate the correct sizing of installations. Through the incorporation of storage the necessary size can be reduced, thereby enabling a more efficient use of the chillers [6].

- A district cooling system in France, Paris-Bercy makes use of "free cooling" assistance by taking cold water from the Seine River to provide cooling. This system achieves an increased efficiency of 34% of the average coefficient of performance in the utilized chillers of the 44 MWth cooling facility. The Bercy plant saves an average of 7.4 kt CO_2 annually [1].

29.4 DISTRICT HEATING NETWORKS
EFFICIENCY IMPROVEMENTS

The efficiency and profitability of district heating networks is largely defined by the linear heat density, meaning the ratio of the annual heat demand and pipeline length. Whether a specific area would be suitable to be connected to a district heating network depends on the heating demand, meaning the ratio of the annual heat consumption across the whole customer base and the surface area [5].

Historically, steam networks are referred to as the first generation of heat network. The changeover from steam to hot water networks then led to the second heat network generation, whose net temperature averages up to 130°C. A development of this district heating system is to reduce the supply temperature to around 120°C, while keeping the other conditions of both network operation and heat generation the same. Therefore, these networks are often referred to as 2 + generation.

The term heating networks of third generation is used when the flow temperatures are reduced even further and are in the range of ≤ 100°C. Efficiency in heat distribution can be further improved and distribution losses reduced (to a maximum of 8%) with measures to minimize the cooling of the return flow. This can be achieved, for example, through adaptions to the home equipment and the type of consumer connection (flow line or return flow).

- The corresponding energy saving potential is around 280 PJ in the EU or 11% of the gross district heat production in 2012. This corresponds to a CO_2 reduction of 18.8 Mt.

DISTRICT HEATING SYSTEMS OF THE FOURTH GENERATION

In the long run, the integration of a higher share of renewable energy requires a further reduction in system temperatures. Therefore, the trend is towards district heating systems of the fourth generation, which are operated with a flow temperature of 50−70°C. The benefits of these networks cannot only be seen in an expanded use of existing resources such as waste heat or

---

[a]Absorption chillers use heat to drive the refrigeration cycle, they produce chilled water while consuming just a small amount of electricity to run the pumps on the unit.

renewable energies. By lowering the flow temperature, also the heat losses and the thermal load of the district heating pipes can be decreased. Further, due to the use of smaller but more efficient pumps, operating costs and, potentially, capital costs can be reduced.

29.5 SUPPLY SIDE

There are several possible options to make the supply side of district heating systems more efficient and climate friendly.

ENERGY EFFICIENCY: POWER-TO-HEAT RATIO

One important parameter in cogeneration is the "power-to-heat ratio," which determines the proportion of electric power to heat generated in a single cogeneration system. New technologies with higher power-to-heat ratios include combined cycle (gas and steam) cogeneration plants, block-type thermal power stations, or fuel cells. For those, the power-to-heat ratio is around 1.0 and higher. This compares to ratios for existing plants of between 0.3 and 0.7, e.g., for steam power plants with back-pressure turbines.

- Increasing the power-to-heat ratio of the district heating systems in the EU in general from the current average of 0.45 to 1.0 can lead to an increase in CHP electricity generation of around 310 TWh. This equates to a CO_2 reduction of 106.4 Mt, taking into account the electricity generation mix as given by the European Network of Transmission System Operators for Electricity (ENTSO-E) for 2014. The specific investment cost for the transformation of existing steam power plants with back-pressure turbines into combined cycle cogeneration plants could be around €1000/kW. The potential savings as well as the payback period will vary by Member State due to the prices of electricity and other fuels [9].

RENEWABLE ENERGIES

The DHC networks profit from the incorporation of locally available, carbon-free energy sources. These include solar thermal heat, bioenergy, and waste heat recovered from industrial processes, which can be applied to a district heating network or transformed into cooling capacity through the use of absorption chillers. The network could also integrate the natural environment by incorporating the surrounding bodies of water as cooling sources, such as lakes, rivers, and the sea. Such DHC networks have the potential to attain an energy efficiency that is 5−10 times greater than those of conventional systems [1].

Solar energy systems combined with either short- or long-term storage can also be applied to generate heat. Large residential housing, such as apartment blocks, hotels, homes, hospitals, or residential developments with more than 30 units can benefit from short-term, daily heat storage systems, where the hot water is retained in tanks. Currently, these systems are typically optimized to cover about half of the daily hot water demand. In solar-supported systems with long-term, seasonal storage (from summer to winter), 40%−60% of the energy required for hot water could be

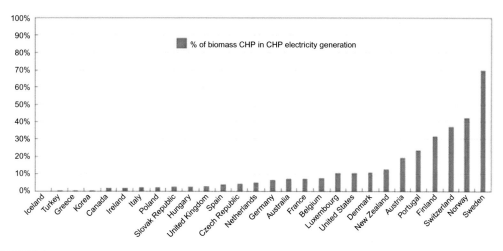

FIGURE 29.3

The importance of biomass cogeneration compared to overall cogenerated electricity production.

covered, but this is usually only economic when connecting 100–250 units due to the high investments in the various technologies [6].

> The Sunstore 4 project is a district heating plant located in Marstal, Denmark. It was developed to demonstrate the production of 100% renewable-based district heating and flexible management of different variable energy sources with the assistance of thermal storage. The plant combines solar thermal, a biomass boiler coupled with an Organic Rankine Cycle, a heat pump, and thermal storage. It is estimated to save 10.5 kt CO_2 annually [10].
> The metropolitan area of Brest, France, is investigating the installation of seawater heat pumps which will use the steady ocean temperatures in winter to deliver 5 MW of heat to its district heating network [8].
> The Markinch biomass project consists of a 60 MWe cogeneration plant at the Tullis Russel paper mill in Fife, Scotland. The CHP unit provides heat and electricity to support the paper production process, and exports excess electricity to the grid. It avoids 250 kt CO_2 per year, provides 40 permanent jobs, and contributes to the national renewable energy target [11].

Fig. 29.3 shows the importance of biomass cogeneration compared to overall cogenerated electricity production [12].

POWER-TO-HEAT

A smart energy system is vital to an electricity system with a high share of variable renewable energy in order to ensure all sectors contribute to balancing supply and demand. District heating systems present an established method to provide this balance. An example of this would be to combine district heating systems with electric boilers and large heat pumps together with thermal storage. This would then allow absorbing surplus electricity (generated in times of high renewable energy generation and low demand) by transforming it into heat and feeding it into the heating network. Therefore, district heating can enable higher penetrations of variable electricity generation in the European electricity grid.

- In January 2013 the Flensburg city utility commissioned a large electro-boiler. This is a relatively primitive technology where six large electric immersion heaters can use surplus power from renewable production to heat up the district heating water to 130°C, which is then fed into an enormous tank containing 29 million liters of water. The hot water can then be used in the district heating grid of the city of Flensburg [13].

29.6 BUSINESS MODELS AND JOBS

Funding remains the major factor in both enabling and hindering a greater implementation of DHC systems across the European Union. Due to the additional equipment required for heat recovery, higher upfront investments are necessary for cogeneration technologies compared to conventional power plant types. Significant investments are also required for the necessary distribution infra-structure from generation to consumers. The development and integration of various energy sources and technologies associated with the DHC network are also cost-intensive. Feasibility studies should monetize environmental and flexibility benefits taking into consideration the local legislative frameworks and market conditions. This holistic method allows for fair comparative assessments of the costs and benefits of these projects compared to conventional technologies.

Currently, business streams aim at satisfying standard supply and demand (from generation to end user) as well as a diverse set of end users, distribution markets, and producers. The business model for a district energy system is specific to each project. However, the design should ensure that all players concerned, from investors, owners, operators, and utilities/suppliers to consumers can benefit from direct profits as well as the greater sustainability gains (economic, environmental, and social).

- Fortum launched the Open DHC business model in Stockholm (Sweden) in 2012 with the objectives of utilizing the most efficient energy sources available and enhancing the profitability of the DHC system by minimizing costs related to heat supply. This is achieved by opening up the network to a wide range of energy sources (Fig. 29.4) [1]. For example, the business model makes use of the large excess heat produced by the city's large data centers, and feeds it into the district heating network. Three types of rates are offered for the surplus heat, depending on the type of line through which heat is being delivered: open spot market price for heating (through feed lines), open returned heating price (through return lines), and open residual heating price (through district cooling return lines during winter). Customers are hereby encouraged to recover their excess heat and become suppliers, which in turn taps into an otherwise unexploited resource through the use of local waste heat. This system does not only offer a market price for surplus heat from consumers, but also ensures sustainability by reducing their heat demand through improved demand-side management or thermal storage. Fortum has also launched several Open DHC pilots in Finland, which have the potential to be reproduced in other networks across the globe [14,15].

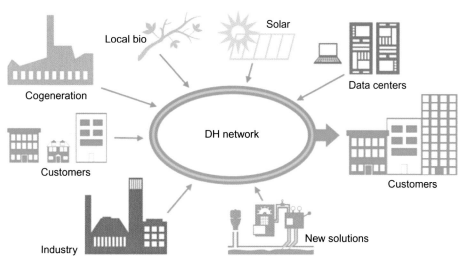

FIGURE 29.4

The Open DHC business model integrates a wide range of energy sources.

In 2012, the district heating sector already employed around 200,000 people across the European Union according to own calculations. This corresponds to 360 employees per TWh of district heat delivered. If the links to upstream and downstream industries are taken into account, an additional indirect and induced employment effect of 500,000 can be associated with district heating. Thus, in total 700,000 employees can be ascribed to the district heating business in 2012. Overall, this corresponds to an employment intensity of 1246 persons per TWh of district heat delivered.

In the "70/70-Strategy" of the German District Heating Association (AGFW), the 70 most populous cities in Germany are considered under the aspect of a consistent development of the district heating infrastructure, fed by cogeneration and renewable energies, with the objective of carbon neutrality by 2050. This could be achieved by a share of district heating in the heat supply of these cities of 70%. The expansion of district heating is primarily an investment in infrastructure, which provides the possibility to react flexibly to any energy policy changes in future. This will create up to 12,000 new jobs by 2030. Another 1250 jobs can be created by the operation and maintenance of the infrastructure. By 2030, through the 70/70-Strategy a municipal value added of €9.6−12.2 billion can be achieved (income tax, net employment, trade tax, and profits). Direct and indirect employment effects ensure a doubling of this value by the year 2050 [16].

29.7 POLICY RECOMMENDATIONS AND OUTLOOK

For the further development and use of district heating in the European Union, taking into account the energy and climate policy objectives, the following three recommendations are of relevance.

1. District heating must become more climate-friendly.

   In all stages of the value chain, efficiency potentials should be harnessed. With regard to the climate change objectives of the EU, the efficiency gains through cogeneration will no longer be enough. Decarbonization in the supply side of district heating must also take place. Comparing a solar-supported gas heating system with a natural gas-fired CHP plant shows an emission factor of 294 gCO_2 per kWh at the break-even point, i.e., the point at which an equal amount of CO_2 emissions is allocated to the heat production of the CHP plant, as the solar-supported gas heating system would entail.

   This is demonstrated in Fig. 29.5. The purple line depicts the emissions for the CHP plant. These vary depending on which of the various existing methods is applied for assigning its total CO_2 emissions to the electricity or the heat production. While not all linear combinations are justified based on currently applied methods, a variety exists, covering the full range from assigning all emissions to the electricity production to assigning all of them to the heat production. The orange (light gray in print versions) line represents a gas condensing boiler combined with solar power supplying 15% of the heat demand. In this case, electricity is assumed to be supplied independently by a grid composed of any possible combinations of supply options, and thus CO_2 emissions. This was done to identify the break-even point with the CHP plant.

   At this break-even point, where the lines cross, the CHP proffers a climate advantage of 13% over the ENTSO-E EU Mix (separated heat and electricity production) of 2014 [17], which stands at 340 gCO_2/kWh_{el}.

   However, this will not be sufficient for a gas-fired CHP to outperform a future low-carbon generation mix that is in line with the EU's climate change mitigation ambitions. With the increasing use of renewable energy for electricity generation there is also an increased need for

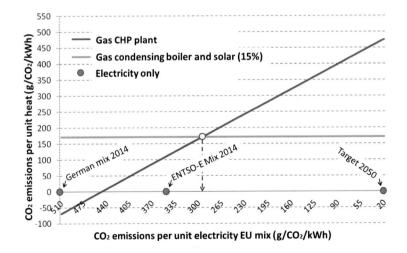

FIGURE 29.5

CO_2 emissions per unit of heat production as a function of the CO_2 emissions per unit of electricity generation.

the use of renewable energies for district heat production as a contribution to the decarbonization of the European energy system.

2. Efficiency gains must be considered holistically, taking into account all stages of the value chain.

   Coupled by the heating network, the production, the transport, and the demand side are mutually dependent on each other in the district heating sector. Accordingly, potential efficiency gains are present and realizable at all stages of the value chain from the demand side to the supply side (power-to-heat ratio and integration of variable renewables by power-to-heat) as well as with district heating systems of the fourth generation. The synergetic effects should be considered when evaluating efficiency measures.

3. The transition to a smart DHC system should be conceptualized, developed, and implemented.

   Information and communications technologies (ICT) offer new opportunities to develop a more effective and complex network for production, distribution, and demand. For all parts of the system, benefits are possible, from production (e.g., through forming virtual power plants), to distribution (e.g., when decoupling and integration different temperature levels), and to the demand side (e.g., when using smart meters to monitor and manage consumption).

REFERENCES

[1] IEA, Linking heat and electricity systems co-generation and district heating and cooling solutions for a clean energy future, 2014.
[2] D.R. Gómez, J.D. Watterson, B.B. Americano, C. Ha, G. Marland, E. Matsika, et al., Stationary combustion, in: 2006 IPCC Guidelines for National Greenhouse Gas Inventories, vol. 2, IPCC, IGES; Hayama, Japan, 2006, page 2.16.
[3] D. Connolly, B.V. Mathiesen, P.A. Østergaard, B. Möller, S. Nielsen, H. Lund, et al., Heat Roadmap Europe 2: Second Pre-Study for the EU27, Department of Development and Planning, Aalborg University, Aalborg, Denmark, 2013.
[4] Euroheat & Power, District heating and cooling barometer, 2014.
[5] T. Nussbaumer, S. Thalmann, Status report on district heating systems in IEA countries, 2014.
[6] M. Fuchs, M. Hegger, T. Stark, M. Zeumer, Energy manual: sustainable architecture, 2008.
[7] MVV Energie AG, THERMA Fernwärme. Available from: <https://www.mvv-energie.de/de/geschaefts-kunden/industrie__handel__gewerbe/fernwaerme/therma_fernwaerme_1/therma_fernwaerme_3.jsp>.
[8] UNEP, District energy in cities: unlocking the potential of energy efficiency and renewable energy. Available from: <http://www.unep.org/energy/portals/50177/DES_District_Energy_Report_full_02_d.pdf>.
[9] IETD, Combined heat and poer in chemical recovery. Available from: <http://ietd.iipnetwork.org/content/combined-heat-and-power-chemical-recovery>.
[10] Sunstore 4, 100% renewable district heating. Available from: <http://sunstore4.eu/>.
[11] Kable, Industry projects. Available from: <http://www.power-technology.com/projects/>.
[12] IEA, Co-generation and renewables—solutions for a low-carbon energy future, 2011.
[13] City of Flensburg, District heating in Flensburg. Available from: <http://www.stadtwerke-flensburg.de/fernwaerme/versorgungsgebiete/flensburg/erzeugungskonzeptflensburg.html>.
[14] R.B. Stockholm, A new generation of energy networks: Nordic Conference Energy Quality Management, 2014.
[15] Fortum, Open district heating. Available from: <http://www.opendistrictheating.com/>.
[16] DBDH, New German 70/70 Strategy. Available from: <http://dbdh.dk/new-german-7070-strategy/>.
[17] ENTSO-E, Statistical factsheet 2014. Available from: <https://www.entsoe.eu/Documents/Publications/Statistics/Factsheet/entsoe_sfs2014_web.pdf>.

ENERGY POVERTY ACROSS THE EU: ANALYSIS OF POLICIES AND MEASURES

30

Steve Pye[1], Audrey Dobbins[2], Claire Baffert[3], Jurica Brajković[4], Paul Deane[5], and Rocco De Miglio[6]

[1]University College London (UCL), London, United Kingdom [2]University of Stuttgart, Stuttgart, Germany [3]InnoEnergy, Brussels, Belgium [4]Energy Institute Hrvoje Požar (EIHP), Zagreb, Croatia [5]University College Cork (UCC), Cork, Ireland [6]E4SMA, Turin, Italy

30.1 INTRODUCTION

Energy poverty, commonly understood to describe a situation where individuals are not able to adequately heat their homes at affordable cost, is an increasingly recognized problem across Member States. Rising energy prices, recessionary impacts on national and regional economies, and energy-inefficient homes are the main circumstances leading to energy poverty. Using data from the EU Survey on Income and Living Conditions (EU SILC), researchers have estimated that 54 million European citizens (10.8% of the EU population) were unable to keep their home adequately warm in 2012, with similar numbers being reported with regard to the late payment of utility bills or presence of poor housing conditions.[a] Such proxy indicators suggest the problem is extensive, and in some regions, such as southern and eastern European states, strongly entrenched [1].

The issue is one that needs to be addressed by European Member States, supported by the European Commission, for three distinctive reasons (articulated in Ref. [2]). Firstly, fuel poverty is thought to be a significant contributor not just to excess winter deaths due to colder homes, but also to wider health concerns, as highlighted by the Marmot Team Review [3]. Healy [4] also linked higher seasonal mortality to energy-inefficient homes and other indicators of a lack of socioeconomic wellbeing. Secondly, households in energy poverty often pay proportionally higher costs for energy, with limited scope for addressing the issue of inadequate heating without additional support. Thirdly, energy poverty can be a barrier to introducing measures to reduce energy use and carbon emissions due to affordability concerns.

The European Commission acknowledges the need for Member States to address energy poverty, with its primary focus on the protection of vulnerable consumers in the energy markets. In its Communication on the Energy Union Package, it states that

> Energy poverty negatively affects living conditions and health. It has many causes, mostly resulting from a combination of low income and general poverty conditions, inefficient homes and a housing tenure system that fails to encourage energy efficiency. Energy poverty can only be

---

[a]Energy Vulnerability Trends and Patterns in Europe: EVALUATE project policy brief no. 1. https://energyvulnerability.files.wordpress.com/2014/06/1brief.pdf

Europe's Energy Transition. DOI: http://dx.doi.org/10.1016/B978-0-12-809806-6.00030-4

> tackled by a combination of measures, mainly in the social field and within the competence of authorities on the national, regional or local levels [5].

However, while the problem of energy poverty is on the agenda, limited coordinated actions at the European level are in place, for three key reasons: (1) the problem is not yet fully understood due to shortcomings in existing indicators; (2) action to date has been guided by the principle of subsidiarity,[b] and (3) the EC competency is focused on vulnerable consumers in regulated markets, not on households in energy poverty across the wider energy system. As a result, its recognition and understanding are limited to a few Member States.

This chapter considers, through assessing the experiences of Member States, how the three problems above can start to be addressed through a more coordinated and comprehensive European response. This is facilitated by establishing indicators that allow for an improved understanding and help target action by strengthening related requirements in European regulation. Further, such indicators will help to broaden the understanding of vulnerability beyond a focus on electricity and gas markets but on the wider system (e.g., including transport). This chapter reviews approaches to defining energy poverty and vulnerable consumers, and the types of actions being undertaken in response across Member States have been reviewed. Based on this review, a set of recommendations are proposed to move the European policy agenda forward.

30.2 ENERGY POVERTY IN EUROPE: UNDERSTANDING OF THE PROBLEM AND POLICY RESPONSE

A EUROPE-WIDE CHALLENGE

Bouzarovski et al. [6] state that outside the UK, limited analysis of energy poverty has been undertaken across Member States to date. Much of what we know of the problem in Europe relates to a specific focus in Member States, notably the UK [2,7,8], Ireland [9], and France [10], and a range of European-funded research initiatives, looking at energy poverty from different perspectives, and across specific Member States [11–13].

The extent of energy poverty in Europe has largely been informed using data from EU-SILC [1,14]. Through the use of these survey-based data regarding living conditions, consensual measures of energy poverty have been developed [14]. A composite index has also been developed by Thomson to better reflect the overall incidence and intensity of energy poverty in each Member State [15].

Particularly when looking specifically at the population *at risk of poverty or social exclusion* (abbreviated AROPE and defined by Eurostat as the population earning <60% of the median income), these indicators suggest that energy poverty is a more significant issue in eastern and southern Europe (e.g., see Fig. 30.1) due to a number of factors. Such regions have been disproportionately impacted by recessionary forces in recent years, increasing problems of energy affordability. They are characterized by higher levels of inefficient housing, coupled with inadequate heating infrastructure to deal with colder periods [1]. This is evident when we look at the statistics on

---

[b]The notion that decisions should be taken as closely as possible to the citizen, with the EU only taking action when this is more effective than at national, regional, or local level.

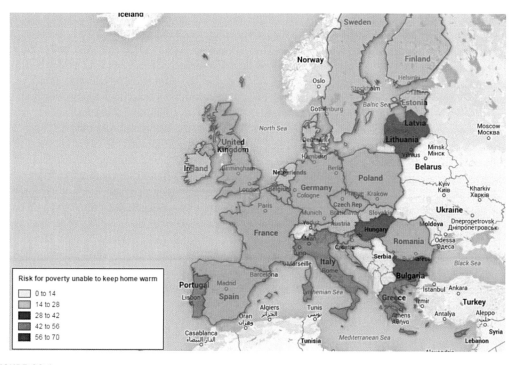

FIGURE 30.1

Share of the "at risk of poverty population" for proxy indicator "unable to keep home warm."

households with central heating systems, and built fabric indicators, such as window U-values indicating the level of insulation [16]. There are also countries in eastern Europe that are moving towards market pricing of energy, through increasing energy sector liberalization. The resulting price increases that households face,[c] coupled with lower energy-efficient homes (underinvested in due to the previously low-cost energy supply) further aggravates the problem.

Several research initiatives[d] across the EU have or are furthering the understanding of energy poverty, quantifying the extent of the problem or addressing the actions required to alleviate the burden experienced by households. The key results and recommendations emanating from the 11 research initiatives reviewed fall broadly into five categories: regulatory and legislation, financing mechanisms, energy efficiency, information, awareness and education, and further research. One of the recommendations is a call for the provision of guidelines by the Commission on how Member States can define energy poverty. Further, there is strong recognition that legislation plays a key role in driving the changes needed to address energy poverty. Regulation could also address the

---

[c]The transition from regulated prices to liberalized markets has seen increases in household prices as a result of: (1) savings from the competitive wholesale market initially not being passed on quickly to households; and/or (2) passive consumers not changing suppliers and thus not encouraging competition; and/or (3) additional taxes and levies.
[d]A summary of the EU-wide research initiatives on energy poverty reviewed is provided in Ref. [17].

infrastructural vulnerability perpetuating energy poverty (such as in southern and eastern Member States) and support the implementation of energy efficiency in housing.

Recommendations also focused on financing investments in energy efficiency and mobilizing the roll-out of energy efficiency refurbishments in housing. Financing schemes were considered in relation to broader structural issues (EU cohesion funds[e]) and in the allocation of national grants or EU Regional Development Funds targeting energy efficiency refurbishments in housing. Furthermore, concrete measures, such as energy audits coupled with the installation of several energy-saving devices, were shown to save monthly energy expenditure in lower-income households.

However, most research and action is ad hoc and not measured against an EU-wide or national benchmark. The issue of the collection of consistent, reliable data is recommended in several of the studies in order to increase information and awareness. Further research is required to assess how the different Member States with their unique circumstances can quantify, address, and monitor the status of energy poverty. Research is needed to inform policy recommendations aimed at improving the energy welfare of households and to ensure other policy objectives do not exacerbate the issue.

It is evident that increased research is being undertaken in this field in recent years. However, a gap in understanding remains, both at the European level, to inform the Commission on how to respond, and at the Member State level, due to issues of limited recognition. There is a clear view from the Commission that the information deficit needs to reduce in order to develop a coherent strategy at the EU level and trigger action across Member States.

THE CURRENT EU POSITION AND APPROACH

The main European legislation in the context of addressing energy poverty is the Third Energy Package (refer to Section 6.1) relating to common rules for the internal electricity and gas markets, under Directives 2009/72/EC [18] and 2009/73/EC [19]. These Directives clearly state that energy poverty is a problem and that Member States should take action. To do this, there is an explicit requirement for Member States to adopt vulnerable consumer definitions and protective measures (Article 3 (8) of 2009/72/EC). Subsidiarity is a key principle in the current approach, where the specific definition of what constitutes a vulnerable consumer and the resulting actions need to be considered in view of a given country context.

A key body for understanding some of the challenges in implementing these provisions is the Vulnerable Consumer Working Group (VCWG). This group was established by the European Commission to help ensure the effective implementation of the Third Energy Package for consumers. Its objectives are to promote an improved understanding of vulnerability in the energy markets, to harmonize its definition and to share good practice in actions to protect vulnerable consumers [20]. Such activities can support the Commission as it shapes its policy position in this area, and Member States as they implement the Directives' provisions.

The European Commission's current perspective on energy poverty is through a focus on vulnerable consumers in regulated markets, reflecting their policy area of competency. Other European bodies have called for a more direct and explicit recognition of energy poverty. In their opinion *For coordinated European measures to prevent and combat energy poverty*, the European Economic and Social Committee [21], a consultative body of the EU, argue for common definitions

---

[e]EU cohesion funds aim at reducing the economic and social inequalities through infrastructure project developments.

and indicators. They suggest that this, coordinated by an observatory, could help develop a European strategy on energy poverty, recommendations echoed by European-focused research studies [11,22].

The development of a broader strategy is gaining some traction at the European Commission. This is reflected in the mainstreaming of the concept of energy poverty in policy documents, such as the Energy Union. Following the publication of research on this issue, including the INSIGHT_E report [17], the Commission is taking forward further research to improve the under-standing of energy poverty at the European level, through development of indicators, and to further assess actions that can be undertaken. This is being done under a project called *Fuel/energy poverty—Assessment of the impact of the crisis and review of existing and possible new measures in the Member States* [21].

It is apparent, based on the research program being formulated and discussion in forums such as the VCWG, that there is a real interest from the Commission in exploring: (1) additional legislative or other types of measures that could be implemented; (2) the extent to which definitions should be consistent to allow for harmonized protection; and (3) how monitoring of the problem can be improved.

30.3 ASSESSING MEMBER STATE RESPONSES: DEFINING THE ISSUES

The purpose of the research described in this chapter section is to establish how Member States are defining the issue of energy poverty, and vulnerable consumers, and the actions being undertaken. Having established the state of play, the objective is to consider the role the European Commission can play, through further research efforts, strengthening legislation, and disseminating awareness of the issues and good practice.

VULNERABLE CONSUMERS AND ENERGY POVERTY: LINKED YET DISTINCT ISSUES

It is important to recognize that the energy poverty challenge and the protection of vulnerable con-sumers are linked yet distinct issues. They are linked in that the extent and/or severity of energy poverty could be exacerbated if vulnerable consumers are not adequately protected. However, they are distinct; in the European context, vulnerable consumers relate to gas and electricity consumers who may not have full access to competitive tariffs or need additional protection and support, for a range of reasons (income, disability, age, being welfare recipients). This focus on regulated markets means that regulators, ombudsmen, and energy utilities are often viewed as the key actors. The types of measures would typically be more short term in nature, and curative, addressing acute access issues, and limited to electricity and gas.

While there are different ways of defining the issue, characteristics of energy poverty typically differ; it goes beyond energy markets to consider affordability issues for energy services, whether they be provided through regulated markets or not. The focus on affordability for energy services means that there is a focus on low-income households and the multiple drivers for energy poverty, relating to energy efficiency, energy costs, and disposable income. This results in measures focused on more structural issues that require longer-term solutions, and require the expertise of multiple stakeholders in the energy industry, but also civic society and government.

This distinction means that different approaches and actions are required—and that an expanded role from the Commission beyond vulnerable consumers is necessary to help address the energy poverty challenge. The linked nature of the two issues however merits that any emerging strategies are synergistic and do not conflict. In the following sections, it is described how these issues are defined by Member States.

DEFINING VULNERABLE CONSUMERS IN ENERGY MARKETS

Provisions under the Third Energy Package require Member States to adopt definitions of vulnerable consumers and to take action to protect such consumers. A Council of European Energy Regulators (CEER) review found that in most member countries vulnerable consumers were protected through a combination of energy-specific protection measures and social security benefits. Furthermore, 17 out of 26 Member States stated that a concept of vulnerable consumers existed in energy law, other law, or a combination of both [23].[f] An Agency for the Cooperation of Energy Regulators (ACER)-led review assessed that 13 out of 26 Member States explicitly define the concept of vulnerable consumers, and in another 12 it is implicitly defined [25].

Vulnerable consumer definitions can be categorized as per Table 30.1. The most common type of definition is based on *receipt of social welfare*, reflecting vulnerability due to social circumstances. Definitions explicitly referencing issues of difficulty with energy cost payments or

Table 30.1 Categorization of Member States' Definitions of Vulnerable Consumers

Definition Type	Member State (MS)	No. of MS by Type
Receipt of social welfare	BG, CY, DE, DK, EE, FI[a], HR, HU, LT, LU, MT[b], PL, PT, SI[c,d]	14
Energy affordability (low income/high expenditure)	FR[e], IT, SE	3
Disability/health	CZ, NL, SK, IE	4
Range of socioeconomic groups	AT, BE, ES, GR, RO, UK[f]	6
Not available/under discussion	LV	1

[a]*Although term not officially recognized.*
[b]*Also has health and income categorizations.*
[c]*Also includes disabled individuals.*
[d]*According to the concept for the protection of consumers fulfilling conditions of energy poverty, new definition and indicators will be based on social (economic) criteria.*
[e]*Under definition of energy poverty.*
[f]*Based on OFGEM definition, not the national fuel poverty definitions.*

---

[f]An earlier review in Ref. [24] suggested that the term vulnerable consumers was not widely used, in fact only in eight Member States, namely Belgium, Bulgaria, Great Britain, Greece, Hungary, Ireland, Italy, and Slovenia.

households incurring high expenditure are categorized under *energy affordability*. Four countries specifically refer to *health and disability* concerns as the main characteristic of vulnerability, although such issues are also often considered under *social welfare* and *socioeconomic group* categories. Finally, some definitions specifically encompass a broader range of *socioeconomic characteristics*, which may include income, age, or health characteristics. At the time of our review, only Latvia was yet to specify a categorization of vulnerable consumers.

The review highlights a divergent understanding of what a vulnerable consumer is. For some Member States, vulnerability is about disability, or due to social circumstances or age, while in other Member States it is about recognizing those that have difficulty in affording energy costs. This matters because actions to protect will be formulated according to the definition. There are two risks; one is that the definition is too broad, capturing too many persons to thus affecting targeted action—or that it is too narrow, missing key groups.

An emerging question is whether there are specific socioeconomic groups in all Member States that should be afforded minimum protection. Such an approach would require additional prescription in the legislation, harmonizing levels of protection across the EU, and ensure Member States had to act. There still needs to be a level of subsidiarity that allows Member States to act according to their policy approach and within the prioritization of their financial budgets.

It is evident from the research that Member States consider issues of consumer vulnerability and energy poverty from different perspectives. They can be categorized according to whether policy and action in this area is "social" or "energy" policy-led. This crude distinction is based on who drives policy, how the problem has been defined, and typically the type of measures undertaken.

For those Member States with a social policy-focus, the issue of vulnerability is often viewed as a function of low income, and therefore poverty (and not as a distinctive issue, e.g., energy poverty). Scandinavian and northern European countries (including the Netherlands, Germany, and Poland) and some selected eastern European countries (Bulgaria, Czech Republic, and Croatia) view the challenge from such a social policy perspective.

Other countries, including those in western and southern Europe, tend to view this as a distinctive energy policy issue, of course recognizing the important underlying social determinants. For some Member States, the approach is mixed, e.g., defined in energy law, but based on socioeconomic criteria, as in Portugal or France. This distinction may be useful in formulating additional policy action in this area, as it highlights the different outlooks on the problem and approaches to addressing the issue.

In summary, it is evident that vulnerable consumer definitions tend to lead to curative, short-term action that affords protection, primarily preventing disconnection, and provide support for welfare recipients in payment of energy costs. As discussed in the beginning of this chapter section, the types of action required for addressing energy poverty are characteristically different.

RECOGNITION OF ENERGY POVERTY ACROSS MEMBER STATES

The recognition of energy poverty, while mentioned under the Third Energy Package, is not prescribed for Member States. Only the UK (in its constituent countries), France, Ireland, and Cyprus have legislation on this issue, and therefore definitions in place, and consider this an issue broader than regulated markets. While only a few Member States have an official definition in place, it is interesting to note the number of other countries[g] where discussion is underway concerning energy poverty, and how it should be measured. It is also worth noting that in many Member States there is a strong civic voice on energy poverty issues, even if not recognized in policies at national or subnational levels. Where the purpose of the definition should be to better identify and target households in need, this also serves to increase recognition of the issue and thereby highlight the need for budgetary allocation.

All the definitions proposed or officially in use by Member States include considerations for income or affordability. About half of them focus specifically on energy for heating, while others take a broader approach to encompass all household energy services. For those Member States with a definition, the UK and Ireland have used expenditure-based metrics, while the French definition sets out to use a mix of expenditure and consensual-based[h] indicators (although such indicators are yet to be operationalized). Of those definitions that are currently under consideration, all are expenditure-based, except for Austria and Malta, which are considering a range of indicators, including consensual-based ones.

Developing energy poverty metrics can be challenging, as shown by the number of considerations (Table 30.2).

At the EU level, there exists no dedicated survey of energy poverty or standardized household data on energy, such as expenditure, consumption, or efficiency. This makes developing a specific energy poverty indicator challenging, and means that most researchers have been using EU-SILC survey-based proxy indicators. In their pilot study, Thomson and Snell [22] explored options for constructing EU indicators of fuel poverty. In their report, useful recommendations on improvements include adapting existing household surveys so that they can be more effectively used for energy poverty analysis in addition to the collection of new datasets.

30.4 ASSESSING MEMBER STATE RESPONSES: POLICIES AND MEASURES

While definitions are critical for orientating action towards the challenges of vulnerable consumers and energy poverty, effective action then needs to be implemented. The focus of the research in this chapter section is to review measures undertaken across different Member States; a full description of measures is provided in the country reports accompanying the report by Pye et al. [17].[i]

In this review, measures constitute those that explicitly provide additional consumer protection to vulnerable groups, and have some targeted aspect to improve the energy welfare of consumers. This includes improvements of the building fabric (thereby reducing energy use), provision of

---

[g]Austria, Italy, Malta, Slovakia.
[h]The consensual method assesses whether a household is in energy poverty via a survey-based approach regarding living conditions, e.g., the ability to keep the home warm, existing problems with building conditions, etc. For the EU, such survey-based proxy indicators are taken from EU-SILC.
[i]Country reports can be accessed when downloading the Policy Report on energy poverty from 2015 on www.insighte-nergy.org

Table 30.2 Issues to Consider in Developing National Energy Poverty Definitions and Metrics

Issue for Consideration	Description
1. Purpose	Does this need to be a high-level indicator measuring the country-scale problem, or local-level indicators that help target households? For example, in Northern Ireland, households spending above 10% of their total expenditure for energy are classified as energy poor, GIS-based algorithms are then used to target specific areas, and finally professionals are then needed to identify specific households, again based on proxies [33] (The following considerations 2–4 focus on high-level national indicators)
2. Broad metric type	What is the type of metric—consensual versus expenditure-based? To a large extent, this will be dependent on data availability, and the requirements of the metric. This is fundamental as it is not useful to develop metrics that cannot be operationalized (The following considerations 3–4 focus on expenditure-based metrics)
3a. Fuel expenditure (FE) thresholds	Nationally appropriate expenditure thresholds need to be considered, with, e.g., 10% as the threshold for household FE specific to the UK situation. The general consensus is that twice the median share of a household's energy expenditure should be used as an upper threshold. For example, the twice median expenditure in Northern Ireland is at 18% [34]. Different thresholds (and metrics) can provide large variation in types of households captured [35]
3b. FE type—relative versus absolute	The original UK 10% metric could be considered absolute, while the new Low Income High Cost (LIHC) metric (relating above average household fuel costs to a minimum residual income) uses a relative expenditure measure. A relative measure makes it difficult to eradicate fuel poverty but can still measure progress in regard to the severity of the problem. Absolute measures can be sensitive to shifts in energy prices
3c. FE type—actual versus required	Best practice suggests that required FE should be used, due to underspending on energy in energy-poor households. However, this has to be balanced against available data; actual expenditure is often available from household budget surveys while required expenditure requires data-intensive modeling
3d. FE coverage	In most metrics, all household energy is included. This is important to reflect total expenditure on energy consumed. This means coverage beyond electricity and gas, and removes the focus from heating only to all energy services, sometimes including transport
4. Household income	There are considerations around whether income should be adjusted across households, and what this should include. Moore [36] notes that subtracting housing costs is self-evident. He states that households cannot spend their housing costs on fuel, any more than they can spend the national and local taxes which are specifically excluded from income

additional information or support, or financial relief in the payment of energy bills. In addition, nontargeted measures include those supporting vulnerable consumers and the energy poor implicitly, by their nature. Examples include measures to reduce energy demand in social housing, to improve access to information on tariffs, and to provide social welfare support and disconnection protection. Without explicitly including this broader set, there is a risk of underplaying the role of nontargeted measures, particularly in those countries which do not explicitly recognize the issue of energy poverty.

Measures are categorized as follows (and detailed in the following):

- *Financial interventions*, introduced to support payment of bills, and primarily focused on short-term relief.
- *Additional consumer protection* for consumers within retail markets.
- *Energy efficiency programs*, targeting improvements to the efficiency of building stock, or energy-using appliances.
- *Information provision and raising awareness*, which improve understanding of consumer rights and information on market tariffs and energy-saving measures.

For each measure, information was gathered, including the type of implementation mechanism, the delivery institution, how targeted they are towards those in need, their effectiveness (where possible to assess), and their time horizon (whether addressing structural or acute problems). Over 280 measures were reviewed; of these, 40% are identified as being specifically targeted on vulnerable consumers or those in or at risk of energy poverty.

FINANCIAL INTERVENTIONS

Over 40% of Member States use financial interventions as the primary basis for support to vulnerable consumers, i.e., this is the stated or implied means (via definitions used or measures proposed) of tackling the issue. Such measures are provided in around 75% of Member States. A large amount of the support is fed through the social welfare system, as a proxy for identifying vulnerability and a mechanism to provide support. Support is either provided via general social welfare payments or through direct payments to help cover the cost of energy (70% of financial measures reviewed, illustrated in Fig. 30.2).

Social tariffs are another measure in this category, in place across a number of Member States including Cyprus, Spain, France, Greece, Portugal, and Belgium. In Belgium, for example, all electricity and gas suppliers are required to offer a social tariff to protected customers (e.g., elderly and disabled persons and those living in particular social dwellings with gas heating) [26]. There is some criticism that such measures should be based on households, not individuals. The French social tariff targets households based on their eligibility for particular medical and health insurances, but large numbers of potential beneficiaries do not take advantage of it as they are not detected in the system [10]. For those consumers that do benefit, its effect is questionable as the average amount of the social tariff support is only 8€/month towards their energy bill [26].

There are a range of different financial interventions, all designed differently based on the national context, and targeted to differing degrees towards those in need. There is a key tension that arises from much of the discussion around such measures, concerning enhanced targeting of vulnerable or energy-poor households versus the administrative complexity that might result. The case of winter fuel payments in the UK, provided to claimants based on age as opposed to other criteria is a case in point [7]. There are also issues around how the measure is implemented, whether the onus is on a household to claim the support, or if it is automatically provided based on given social security criteria.

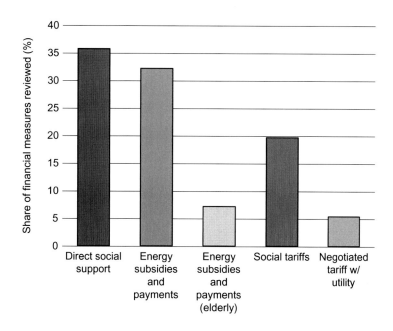

FIGURE 30.2

Share of financial intervention measures reviewed, by category.

What is evident is that financial interventions are crucial for addressing affordability in the short term, and can be used to complement longer-term measures that address the underlying structural issues of energy poverty. For example, in Scandinavian countries and the Netherlands, social support is provided, but also significant effort is being put into improved energy efficiency of social housing stock (as described in the following when discussing energy efficiency interventions). This integrated approach means that financial support does not become the main policy for ensuring affordability, but is rather a transition measure to ensure a safety net.

CONSUMER PROTECTION

Additional consumer protection measures are particularly important for vulnerable consumers in (and with continuing access to) regulated markets. Therefore, National Regulatory Authorities (NRAs) and energy companies play an important role in the implementation of a range of measures. These protections are critical for ensuring that markets operate in a way that does not disadvantage vulnerable consumers.

This category is dominated by the measures to prevent the disconnection of vulnerable consumers (Fig. 30.3), accounting for 40% of measures reviewed in this category. For approximately 20% of Member States, this constitutes the primary basis and often only explicit measure for affording consumer protection. Approximately 80% of Member States have some form of protection from disconnection due to nonpayment, with Bulgaria and Czech Republic as noted exceptions.

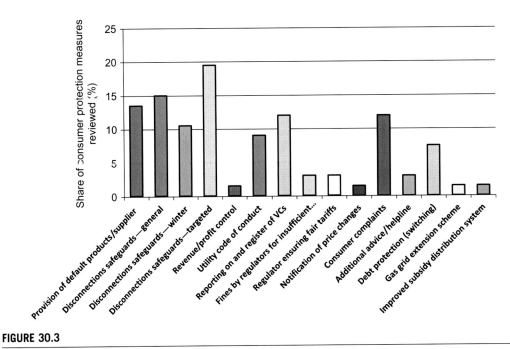

FIGURE 30.3

Share of consumer protection measures reviewed, by category.

In addition to the disconnection safeguards, a number of Member States have specific measures to protect consumers who are in debt, allowing them to switch to other suppliers even if indebted (Denmark, France, Luxembourg, United Kingdom). The measures reviewed also highlight the important role of the energy companies, working alongside the regulator ("NRA controls" and "Information" in Fig. 30.3) in ensuring consumer protection, including the issuing of codes of conduct in dealing with consumers (Belgium, Ireland, Luxembourg, Sweden, United Kingdom), reporting on and registering vulnerable consumers (France, Greece, United Kingdom), and providing additional consumer assistance. In some other Member States, the regulator has the important role of ensuring fair tariffs, monitoring company profits, and fining energy companies for underperforming on specific scheme implementations.

Of all the categories, this is the most heterogeneous (ignoring the role of disconnection protection), with a range of measures specific to given countries. It is also a category of measures most prevalent in open, competitive markets, and will become more important in specific Member States as energy markets become increasingly liberalized.

ENERGY EFFICIENCY INTERVENTIONS

Our review highlights that energy efficiency measures are a key part of a strategy to address energy poverty. Based on the review, 30% of Member States' approaches to tackling vulnerable consumers and/or energy poverty focus on the use of energy efficiency programs. Of the 90 measures reviewed in this category, 65% relate to measures of different types to retrofit buildings (Fig. 30.4), and of these, approximately 30% are specifically targeted on lower-income households.

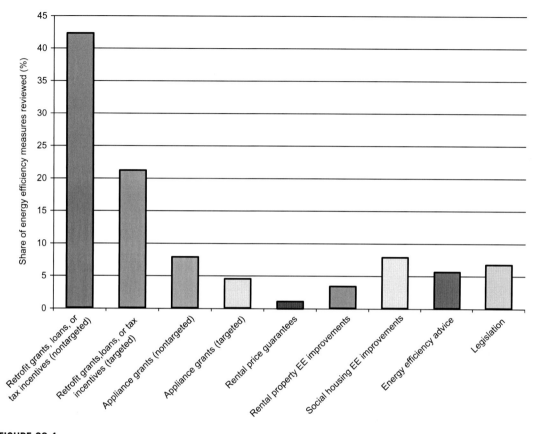

FIGURE 30.4

Share of energy efficiency measures reviewed, by category. "Grants" categories also include loans and tax incentives. "Rental price guarantees" ensure that rental prices will not go up after energy efficiency improvements are invested in by the landlord (see Energy Saving Covenant in Netherlands).

There is therefore considerable scope for improving the degree to which such measures are targeted to those in need, although of course this requires an understanding of which are the energy-poor households. Member State experiences highlight a range of considerations in how such targeted measures should be implemented. These include the Energy savers (*Energiesnoeiers*) project in Belgium [27], the "Living Better" (*Habiter mieux*) program in France [28], the Stromspar-Check (Energy-savings-check for low-income households) in Germany [29], Better Energy: Warmer Homes in Ireland [30], and the Energy Companies Obligation (ECO) in the UK [31]. As described in Table 30.3, there are issues to be considered when developing energy efficiency programs, such as defining the beneficiaries, the approach for delivering and implementing as well as measuring and enforcing the implementation of these measures, and related funding.

The Netherlands and Scandinavian countries have had strong success in targeting measures towards energy efficiency improvements in social housing, where a higher share of lower-income households lives. For example, a covenant on energy savings in the rental sector in the Netherlands

Table 30.3 Issues to Consider in Developing Targeted Energy Efficiency Programs

Issue for Consideration	Description
Targeting approach	Are proxy indicators, e.g., social benefit recipients, good enough to ensure those in energy poverty are reached?
Delivery organization	Delivery by energy companies may mean retrofits are not provided where most needed, but rather "easier" opportunities to fulfill obligations are sought. There may also be an issue of trust, if indeed an energy supplier is also carrying out retrofit measures. Finally, such programs have the potential to offer local employment, which may not be realized if large utilities are monopolizing the market (as under the Stromspar-Check program in Germany)
Implementation approach	Specific studies suggest that area-based (street-by-street) approaches can deliver significant economies of scale, and ensure low-income households are identified and retrofitted (e.g. Refs. [7,31])
Measurement and enforcement	Different proposals in the UK have suggested a minimum efficiency standard for low-income households. If delivered via the market and/or delivered by energy companies, regulators need to effectively enforce targets to ensure progress is made. However, the definition of these targets is critical as well. For example, should a minimum set of measures be offered in order to ensure that renovations result in a significant improvement of energy performance? How should the energy performance be measured?
Funding	If funded through energy bills, this could add to the burden of energy prices on lower-income households, while if funded through general taxation, the funding could be at risk from budget cuts (particularly in times of austerity). If paid for by homeowners/tenants, loan rates need to be attractive and split incentives overcome (between tenants and landlords), while full grants may need to be considered for low-income households. Energiesprong ("Energy Leap") is an innovative scheme in the Netherland focused on social housing that aims to fund the investments in retrofit through bill savings, ensuring no net additional cost to tenants. Another interesting example is Croatia, where the proceeds from the sales of EU ETS permits are ring-fenced under an Environmental and Energy Efficiency Fund to subsidize investments in energy efficiency measures.[a]

[a]*Under the Croatian Air Protection Act (Official Gazette, no. 130/11 and 47/14).*

aims to reduce the energy consumption by 24 PJ by 2020 with measures targeting both the existing and newly built rental housing stock.[j] The transferability of such measures is somewhat contingent on the dwelling stock and nature of tenure. For example, the level of social housing stock in some Member States is much lower, with lower-income households catered for by private rental markets.

There are a wide range of approaches to the implementation of measures in support of energy efficiency improvements. These vary by, e.g., the funding source, the extent of targeting towards those in need, or the implementing body. Such factors need to be considered in view of national circumstances. There are already well-understood barriers to energy efficiency measures. Therefore, strong incentives for low-income households are needed for them to engage in such measures, and measures need to be designed to promote awareness and key benefits.

---

[j]MURE. Available from: http://www.measures-odyssee-mure.eu/public/mure_pdf/household/NLD27.PDF

INFORMATION PROVISION AND AWARENESS CAMPAIGNS

The final category of measures concerns information and awareness, including advice provision and campaigns, and increased information on bills and tariffs through price comparison sites and more transparent billing. Member States with strongly liberalized markets tend to be those that have the most measures relating to price comparison and transparent billing. Where there is a strong civic society movement in relation to energy or fuel poverty, the number of awareness campaigns is higher.

Greater awareness of energy poverty and how to tackle it could come through the roll out of smart meters in various Member States. This offers, subject to data protection, the opportunity for consumers to better manage their consumption, but also for energy companies to identify vulnerable consumers. As smart metering becomes the norm, it will be important to share learning concerning how this technology can help in protecting vulnerable consumers and increasing the affordability of energy use.

To allow for strong participation in energy markets, providing adequate information to vulnerable consumers is critical. Awareness raising of how to increase affordability of energy services is also important. In specific Member States, we see that civic society groups and other nongovernmental organizations play a critical role in both assisting the energy-poor through various measures, but also in pushing the agenda with governments. Such campaigns are important for wider recognition and understanding of energy poverty issues.

30.5 DEVELOPING A COMPREHENSIVE AND COORDINATED EUROPEAN RESPONSE

The review of action to address vulnerable consumers and energy poverty across Member States highlights a number of key features. Firstly, the level of action varies significantly. In most Member States, there are basic protections in place for vulnerable consumers, but few other targeted measures. For example, some 20% of Member States have protection for disconnection but few additional measures in place. In others, there are many more targeted actions, including those focused on issues of energy poverty. This is particularly true for those Member States where the recognition of energy poverty is strongest. Secondly, the types of actions are tailored towards national circumstances, characterized by the policy approach, extent of market liberalization, and physical characteristics of household energy and building stock.

These features make the development of a more coordinated response at the European level challenging. On the one hand, it is critical that all Member States act to address the issues; this could be coordinated by the Commission. On the other, actions need to take account of national circumstances. Being too prescriptive regarding the necessary action may therefore not be effective.

However, it is imperative that a more comprehensive and coordinated response is developed. This can be achieved through better understanding of the problem, by establishing indicators that can help target action, by strengthening requirements in European law, and by applying a broader view of vulnerability, not restricted to energy markets, but encompassing the wider system. To do this, there are a number of recommendations that emerge from this research.

RECOGNIZING THE DISTINCTIVE ISSUES

The issues of vulnerable consumer protection and energy poverty are distinct. Both are important challenges that are linked, but require different solutions. It is important that this distinction is communicated clearly to Member States through legislation, who can then develop effective measures. The European Commission could take the opportunity of the revision of the regulatory framework set-up by the Third Energy Package in 2015—16 (as announced in the Communication on the Energy Union Package [5]) to streamline the dispositions on vulnerable consumers and energy poverty contained in the current Electricity and Gas Directives. In particular, article 3 (paragraphs 7 and 8) and recital 53 of Directive 2009/72/EC could be amended to reflect clearly the specificities of vulnerable consumer protection (along the lines of consumer protection and curative approaches) and energy poverty (requiring a long-term, preventive approach).

Furthermore, the Commission should encourage Member States to develop distinctive yet consistent strategies for both issues. Such documents are important for demonstrating action in these areas, and for ensuring a good understanding across different government departments and agencies, and at different subnational levels.

GUIDANCE ON DEFINING VULNERABLE CONSUMERS

Given the variability in definitions, we propose that the Commission is more prescriptive about who constitutes a vulnerable consumer. For example, in some Member States, the vulnerable are simply those groups at risk of disconnection. Such narrow definitions do not provide broader support to consumers who may have difficulty accessing and participating in the market. Guidance on defining vulnerable consumers needs to be developed, through further research and in consultation with key stakeholder groups such as VCWG, the EU ACER or the CEER. This research suggests that "vulnerability" should reflect concerns of affordability, access, and participation, and acknowledge both socioeconomic circumstances (e.g., being elderly, disabled, or unemployed) and structural circumstances with regards to energy use (e.g., inefficient or expensive heating systems, high tariffs, inefficient building fabric, or off-grid location).

In further prescribing what constitutes vulnerability, it is important to move beyond measures relating solely to ensuring supply, i.e., emergency measures. Rather definitions should ensure improved access to markets for groups in society who need additional support. Guidance should be provided to ensure that vulnerable consumer definitions are more aligned with energy poverty concerns, whilst also covering wider vulnerability issues (not related to affordability). Guidance on definitions could also feature under an implementing act of the revised Gas and Electricity Directives.

The Commission should also state clearly what is required of NRAs in reporting both definitions and measures through a common reporting format. At the occasion of the review of the functioning of ACER and the European Networks of Transmission System Operators for electricity and gas (ENTSO-E and ENTSOG) announced in 2015—16, a stronger mandate could be given to ACER to ask NRAs to report more fully on vulnerable consumer definitions and measures.

DEFINING THE CONCEPT OF ENERGY POVERTY

Given the lack of recognition of energy poverty, the Commission should play a strong role in formulating what energy poverty is and urge Member States to act to alleviate it. This could be done without prescribing the metric to be used by Member States. The Commission should develop a communication document or strategy (as is most appropriate) on their understanding of the energy poverty challenge and what is being done at the Member State level, and urge Member States to develop strategies. Their recognition should provide an overview of the key drivers, the extent of the problem, and the impacts of energy poverty. It should have a scope beyond regulated markets, covering all energy use.

At this stage, the EC should not adopt a specific (consumer or household) expenditure-based metric due to lack of harmonized data, and since it would not necessarily provide any additional insights at this scale [14]. However, they should harness related research using EU-SILC data and take on board recommendations to improve this survey. The Commission should share practices on how different Member States have been developing energy poverty metrics. This would highlight the types of metric and data required to support such a metric. A single metric should not be prescribed; a pragmatic approach would be for Member States to tailor metrics to the best available data, whilst looking to continually improve data in the future.

The process for developing this communication or strategy could be facilitated by a broad group of stakeholders, including the VCWG. It could include NRA representatives, civic society groups, academia, data and indicator providers (including Eurostat), as well as relevant Directorate-Generals (DG) of the European Commission (in particular: DG Health and Safety, DG Energy, and DG Justice and Consumers), and other interested and affected parties. Such a Commission document would provide this issue with the visibility it requires, and the longer-term vision needed to address this challenge. It could also provide the impetus for developing indicators at the EU level that help quantify the problem, and allow for progress to be measured (as described next).

DEVELOP IMPROVED INDICATORS AND DISSEMINATE GOOD PRACTICE

There is an urgent need to develop improved indicators for measuring energy poverty, both at Member State and European levels. In line with the recommendation from other research initiatives, an Energy Poverty Observatory should be established that would help support the development of different indicators, improve current proxy datasets, and hold information on energy poverty research and actions across the EU. This would help to better understand the challenge and assess the effectiveness of strategies to tackle energy poverty. This observatory could also help facilitate exchange of best practices between Member States. It can further play a strong role in information dissemination regarding effective and relevant measures.

The research undertaken here and the associated Member State reports [17], other research initiatives reviewed (see Ref. [17]), and the work of the VCWG provide a useful starting point. Concerning the effectiveness of measures, there could also be an opportunity that the EC impact assessment guidance is further developed to reflect the need for policy appraisal to consider lower-income households and other vulnerable groups.

It will be important to understand appropriate levels of data required for the compilation of different indicators. National experiences will be key, e.g., on the development of indicators in the UK [32] and the development of an observatory in France [10]. Understanding problems with and how to improve existing EU level datasets, such as EU-SILC,[k] will also be critical [14]. Furthermore,

---

[k]Regulation (EC) No 1177/2003 of the European Parliament and of the Council of 16 June 2003 concerning Community statistics on income and living conditions (EU-SILC).

coordination between Eurostat and Member State statistical agencies could help develop a more accurate understanding of what would be required, and how to best harmonize efforts.

PROMOTE THE TARGETING OF ENERGY EFFICIENCY MEASURES TO ADDRESS ENERGY POVERTY

Energy efficiency measures that are more targeted towards low-income households should be encouraged. Mechanisms could include the Energy Efficiency Directive mandating a percentage of funding in this area to tackling energy poverty through energy efficiency refurbishments in low-income households. The Commission could also ensure it allocates a higher share of EU funds to renovation programs focused on fuel poor, low-income, and vulnerable categories of people. These funds should also be targeted towards Member States in central, eastern and southern Europe, where the problem is most entrenched.

30.6 CONCLUSIONS

This chapter provided an overview of how Member States view issues of vulnerability in energy markets and energy poverty, and the actions put in place to address them. It highlighted a quite fragmented European response, both in terms of defining these issues and measures put in place. This is not surprising given the different perspectives on these issues across Member States, the strong position on subsidiarity to date, and the widely differing national circumstances, e.g., regarding the stage of market liberalization, the types of energy systems, or the energy efficiency of buildings.

The fragmented response suggests a stronger role for the Commission, despite the challenges posed by such different national circumstances. We presented a number of ideas that provide a starting point for discussion across the Commission and its stakeholders. Without a more comprehensive program of action through legislative or other routes, there is a risk that lower-income households and other vulnerable groups will be further entrenched in situations of energy poverty, and will not be able to benefit from broader developments in the European energy markets.

There are three key broad areas of action to be facilitated at the EU level: (1) enhancing understanding of the issues through development of improved indicators, and sharing of experiences; (2) greater prescription by the Commission in helping define the issues; and (3) a broader perspective on vulnerability and energy poverty, beyond internal energy markets. Crucially, this review finds there are a range of valuable and effective metrics being used, and measures being undertaken across Member States, supported by a growing body of research in this area. The Commission could play a critical role in bringing these experiences together and formulating a comprehensive strategy that fosters effective policy making across all Member States.

Since this research was published, a number of the recommendations have been incorporated into recent proposals published by the European Commission at the end of 2016 as part of the so-called Winter Package [37]. A key Directive proposed for revision was that on common rules for the internal market in electricity, where a number of changes have been proposed that reflect the above recommendations, namely: (1) differentiating the challenges of protecting vulnerable customers and addressing energy poverty; (2) framing the different causes of vulnerability and energy poverty to help define the issues; and (3) requiring Member States to proactively identify, monitor and support households experiencing energy poverty.

REFERENCES

[1] S. Tirado Herrero, S. Bouzarovski, Energy transitions and regional inequalities in energy poverty trends: exploring the EU energy divide. Available from: <http://papers.ssrn.com/sol3/papers.cfm?abstract_id = 2537067>.

[2] J. Hills, Getting the measure of fuel poverty: final report of the fuel poverty review. CASE report 72, March 2012. Available from: <http://sticerd.lse.ac.uk/dps/case/cr/CASEreport72.pdf>.

[3] Marmot Review Team, Health impacts of fuel poverty and cold housing. Available from: <http://www.instituteofhealthequity.org/projects/the-health-impacts-of-cold-homes-and-fuel-poverty>.

[4] J.D. Healy, Excess winter mortality in Europe: a cross country analysis identifying key risk factors, J. Epidemiol. Community Health 57 (10) (2003) 784−789.

[5] EC, Communication from the Commission to the European Parliament, the Council, the European Economic and Social Committee and the Committee of the Regions—A Framework Strategy for a Resilient Energy Union with a Forward-Looking Climate Change Policy: COM(2015) 80 final, Brussels, 2015.

[6] S. Bouzarovski, S. Petrova, R. Sarlamanov, Energy poverty policies in the EU: a critical perspective, Energy Policy. 49 (2012) 76−82.

[7] I. Preston, V. White, K. Blacklaws, D. Hirsch, Fuel and poverty: a Rapid Evidence Assessment for the Joseph Rowntree Foundation, June 2014. Available from: <http://www.cse.org.uk/downloads/file/Fuel_and_poverty_review_June2014.pdf>.

[8] DECC, Cutting the cost of keeping warm—a fuel poverty strategy for England, 2015. Available from: <https://www.gov.uk/government/uploads/system/uploads/attachment_data/file/408644/cutting_the_cost_of_keeping_warm.pdf>.

[9] DCENR, Warmer Homes: A Strategy for Affordable Energy in Ireland. Available from: <http://www.dcenr.gov.ie/NR/rdonlyres/53F3AC25-22F8-4E94-AB73-352F417971D7/0/AffordableEnergyStrategyFINAL.pdf>.

[10] ONPE, Rapport de synthèse. Définitions, indicateurs, premiers résultats et recommandations, 2014.

[11] EPEE, Tackling fuel poverty in Europe: recommendations guide for policy makers. Available from: <http://www.fuel-poverty.org/files/WP5_D15_EN.pdf>.

[12] FinSH, Financial and Support Instruments for fuel poverty in Social Housing in Europe (FinSH). Project results. Available from: <http://fg-umwelt.de/index.php?id = 88>.

[13] ELIH-MED, Homepage, project description and outputs. Available from: <http://www.elih-med.eu/Layout/elih-med/>.

[14] H. Thomson, C. Snell, Quantifying the prevalence of fuel poverty across the European Union, Energy Policy. 52 (2013) 563−572.

[15] H. Thomson, Exploring the incidence and intensity of fuel poverty in the EU. Available from: <http://urban-energy.org/2015/07/02/workshop-report-fuel-poverty-and-energy-vulnerability-in-europe/>.

[16] ENTRANZE, Project website (cited January 23, 2015). Available from: <http://entranze.eu/>.

[17] S. Pye, A. Dobbins, C. Baffert, J. Brajković, I. Grgurev, R. De Miglio, et al., Energy poverty and vulnerable consumers in the energy sector across the EU: analysis of policies and measures, 2015. Available from: <http://insightenergy.org/static_pages/publications#?publication = 15>.

[18] EC, Directive 2009/72/EC of the European Parliament and of the Council of 13 July 2009 concerning common rules for the internal market in electricity and repealing Directive 2003/54/EC, 2009.

[19] EC, Directive 2009/73/EC of the European Parliament and of the Council of 13 July 2009 concerning common rules for the internal market in natural gas and repealing Directive 2003/55/EC, 2009.

[20] VCWG, Vulnerable Consumer Working Group Guidance Document on Vulnerable Consumers. Available from: <http://ec.europa.eu/energy/sites/ener/files/documents/20140106_vulnerable_consumer_report_0.pdf>.

[21] EC, First Commission interim report on the implementation of Pilot Projects and Preparatory Actions 2015, March 2015. Available from: <http://www.europarl.europa.eu/meetdocs/2014_2019/documents/imco/dv/first_iterim_report_2015_03_04_/first_iterim_report_2015_03_04_en.pdf>.

[22] H. Thomson, C. Snell, Fuel Poverty Measurement in Europe: a Pilot Study. Available from: <http://fuelpoverty.eu/wp-content/uploads/2014/06/Fuel-Poverty-Measurement-in-Europe-Final-report-v2.pdf>.

[23] CEER, CEER status review of customer and retail market provisions from the 3rd package as of 1 January 2012: Ref: C12-CEM-55-04, 2012.

[24] ERGEG, Status review of the definitions of vulnerable customer, default supplier and supplier of last resort: Ref: E09-CEM-26-04. Available from: <http://www.energy-regulators.eu/portal/page/portal/EER_HOME/EER_PUBLICATIONS/CEER_PAPERS/Customers/Tab/E09-CEM-26-04_StatusReview_16-Jul-09.pdf>.

[25] ACER/CEER, Annual report on the results of monitoring the internal electricity and natural gas markets in 2013, 2014.

[26] ADEME, Rapport d'audit sur les tariffs sociaux de l'énergie. Available from: <http://www.ademe.fr/sites/default/files/assets/documents/rapport-audit-sur-tarifs-sociaux-energie-2013.pdf>.

[27] Energiesnoeiers, Energy savers. Available from: <http://www.energiesnoeiers.net/es/english_63.aspx>.

[28] M. Crémieux, Propositions pour renforcer la lutte contre la précarité énergétique. Terra Nova [Internet] 2014, May 2014. Available from: <http://tnova.fr/notes/propositions-pour-renforcer-la-lutte-contre-la-precarite-energetique>.

[29] Stromsparcheck, Energy savings check. Available from: <http://www.stromspar-check.de/>.

[30] SEAI, Better Energy: Warmer Homes in Ireland. Available from: <www.seai.ie/>.

[31] R. Platt, J. Aldridge, D. Price, P. Washan, Help to heat—a solution to the affordability crisis in energy. Available from: <http://www.ippr.org/assets/media/images/media/files/publication/2013/11/Help-to-heat_Nov2013_11562.pdf>.

[32] DECC, The fuel poverty statistics methodology and user manual: URN 14D/148. Available from: <https://www.gov.uk/government/uploads/system/uploads/attachment_data/file/408644/cutting_the_cost_of_keeping_warm.pdf>.

[33] Liddell, C., & Lagdon, S. (2013). Tackling Fuel Poverty in Northern Ireland-An Area-Based Approach to Finding Households Most in Need. http://www.ofmdfmni.gov.uk/de/tackling-fuel-poverty-in-ni-liddell-lagdon.pdf.

[34] C. Liddell, C. Morris, S.J.P. McKenzie, G. Rae, Measuring and monitoring fuel poverty in the UK: National and regional perspectives, Energy Policy 49 (2012) 27−32.

[35] Heindl, P. (2014). Measuring Fuel Poverty: general considerations and application to German Household Data. SOEP Papers 632. 2014.

[36] R. Moore, Definitions of fuel poverty: implications for policy, Energy Policy 49 (2012) 19−26.

[37] EC, Proposal for a Directive of the European Parliament and of the Council on common rules for the internal market in electricity, COM (2016) 864 final, Brussels, 2016.

CONCLUSIONS

Audrey Dobbins

University of Stuttgart, Stuttgart, Germany

Consumers play a central role in the European Energy Transition. This section has highlighted some ways in which consumers can participate in the energy transition in line with options outlined in the Energy Union, and where the Commission can support this process across the European Union. Some of the key outcomes of this section highlighted that consumers have a key role in the energy transition of the European Union towards achieving its overall energy efficiency, climate change, and renewable energy targets.

Consumers can contribute to the energy system by becoming energy producers, reducing their energy consumption, or by using new and innovative methods. For example, DC networks have potential to reduce energy consumption, thereby assisting in achieving energy efficiency targets. Further, self-consumption offers consumers a possibility to contribute actively to the energy transition and has potential to increase renewable energy production in households. Finally, we investigated the role of district heating and cooling networks and their potential to integrate renewable sources, thereby contributing towards the energy transition in one of the largest areas of energy demand.

In terms of energy poverty, related policy responses are largely designed at the national level, and thus vary by country. The Commission could act as the facilitator to bring the various bodies involved together, with the aim to derive more effective and targeted approaches to address energy poverty. This could ensure that vulnerable consumers can participate in the energy markets, and also in the broader energy sector (e.g., transport).

The role for the Commission in all instances is to provide guidance on supportive legislation on the national level and to coordinate an exchange of experiences with formulating and implementing related measures amongst Member States. The Commission can also support further research regarding the potential of enabling technologies within the energy transition (DC networks, self-consumption), including their costs and distribution effects across the entire system, as well as on households unable to afford access to the services these technologies provide.

Particularly in terms of protecting vulnerable consumers, the Commission should take a strong role in broadening the comprehension of the issues of vulnerable consumers and energy poverty, and in assisting Member States to develop related definitions.

The proposals related to vulnerable customer protection and energy poverty in the "Clean Energy for All Europeans" package from end of 2016 have incorporated many of the recommendations arising out of this and other research. This includes particularly the importance of identifying and addressing energy poverty as a specific issue, distinctive from vulnerable customer protection.

Europe's Energy Transition. DOI: http://dx.doi.org/10.1016/B978-0-12-809806-6.00031-6

A stronger role for energy efficiency in buildings to help alleviate energy poverty has also been included. Further, a platform is being created through a newly established Energy Poverty Observatory to help Member States disseminate good practice, develop indicators, and provide better data.

Ultimately, as one of the main objectives of the energy transition, the protection of vulnerable consumers is a pillar on which the success of the transition will need to be measured.

SOCIETY AND CONSUMER DEMANDS—ABBREVIATIONS, ACRONYMS, AND INITIALISMS

AC	Alternating current
AROPE	At risk of poverty or social exclusion
CCHP	Combine cooling, heat and power
CHiP	Converter housed in package
CHP	Combined heat and power
CO$_2$	Carbon dioxide
DC	Direct current
DG	Distributed generation
DH	District heat
DHC	District heating and cooling
DSM	Demand-side management
EE	Energy efficiency
EJ	Exajoule
EU	European Union
EU ETS	European Emissions Trading System
EU SILC	EU Survey on Income and Living Conditions
FiT	Feed-in-tariff
GW	Gigawatt
GWh/d	Gigawatt-hour per day
ICT	Information Communications Technology
IEC	International Electrotechnical Commission
ITU-T	International Telecommunication Union
kt	Kilotonne
kW	Kilowatt
kWp	Kilowatt peak
LCOE	Levelized cost of electricity
LED	Light-emitting diode
LVDC	Low-voltage direct current
Mt	Megatonne
MW	Megawatt
MWh	Megawatt-hour
MW$_{th}$	Megawatt (thermal)
PJ	Petajoule
PV	Photovoltaic
REF	Reference
RES	Renewable energy sources
SC	Self-consumption
SC-CC	Self-consumption with chronological charging
SC-GR	Self-consumption in grid-relief operating mode
SG	Strategic group

Europe's Energy Transition. DOI: http://dx.doi.org/10.1016/B978-0-12-809806-6.00037-7

TWh	Terawatt-hour
V	Volt
Vdc	Volts direct current
c€/kWh	Euro cent per kilowatt-hour
€/kWh	Euro per kilowatt-hour
€/kWh*a	Euro per kilowatt-hour and annum

MS Code	MS Name
AT	Austria
BE	Belgium
BG	Bulgaria
CY	Cyprus
DE	Germany
DK	Denmark
ES	Spain
FI	Finland
FR	France
GR	Greece
HR	Croatia
HU	Hungary
IE	Ireland
IT	Italy
LT	Lithuania
LU	Luxembourg
MT	Malta
NL	Netherlands
PO	Poland
PT	Portugal
RO	Romania
SE	Sweden
SK	Slovakia
SI	Slovenia
UK	United Kingdom

EUROPE'S ENERGY TRANSITION: CHALLENGES AND INSIGHTS FOR POLICY MAKING

INTRODUCTION

32

Steve Pye[1], Manuel Welsch[2], and Aurélie Faure-Schuyer[3]

[1]*University College London (UCL), London, United Kingdom* [2]*KTH Royal Institute of Technology, Stockholm, Sweden* [3]*Institut Français des Relations Internationales (IFRI), Brussels, Belgium*

The Energy Union sets out the key challenges for the European energy sector, namely to deliver to EU consumers (households and businesses) sustainable, secure, competitive, and affordable energy [1]. This will require a fundamental transformation of Europe's energy system. The outcome of COP21, the Paris Agreement which the EU ratified, further underlines the need for such a transition. To deliver on these challenges as set out in the Energy Union, this transition must consider a set of issues: effectively decarbonizing the energy system, ensuring energy security, facilitating integrated and competitive energy markets, and ensuring consumer protection, particularly for vulnerable groups. This will require increased policy cooperation and a governance framework to deliver on the Energy Union's objectives, including consensus around the main elements of the low-carbon transition and supportive instruments. This is no small task, requiring the engagement and action by numerous energy stakeholders in a coherent and cohesive manner over a relatively short period of time.

In Chapter 33, Key Challenges Ahead, we draw on the analyses presented within this book and performed by the think tank INSIGHT_E to shed light on the nature of these challenges. In Chapter 34, Developing the Policy Package, we then turn to the policy needs to meet these challenges. Priorities for future energy research are presented in Chapter 35, Research Priorities, before concluding with reflections on the future role for think tanks.

While INSIGHT_E is independent, its research topics were chosen and work was performed in close dialogue with the European Commission. It thus covered topical areas of direct concern to the European Commission in future years. The concluding thoughts presented in this section therefore prioritize and build on these strategic key areas.

REFERENCE

[1] EC (2015). Energy Union Package. Communication from the Commission to the European Parliament, the Council, the European Economic and Social Committee, the Committee of the Regions and the European Investment Bank. A Framework Strategy for a Resilient Energy Union with a Forward-Looking Climate Change Policy. Brussels, 25.2.2015, COM(2015) 80 final.

Europe's Energy Transition. DOI: http://dx.doi.org/10.1016/B978-0-12-809806-6.00048-1

KEY CHALLENGES AHEAD

Steve Pye[1], Manuel Welsch[2], and Aurélie Faure-Schuyer[3]

[1]University College London (UCL), London, United Kingdom [2]KTH Royal Institute of Technology, Stockholm, Sweden [3]Institut Français des Relations Internationales (IFRI), Brussels, Belgium

33.1 SYSTEM DECARBONIZATION

The Paris Agreement signals a breakthrough in climate negotiations, which had long stalled since the 1990s. This breakthrough was achieved by taking a different approach [1]. Instead of setting commitments centrally, countries were allowed to make their own commitments via nationally determined contributions (NDCs). Together and once further strengthened, these NDCs will aim to deliver the Paris Agreement's overall objective: "to ensure the achievement of the goal of keeping climate change well below 2°C and pursuing efforts towards 1.5°C" [2]. This approach provides the flexibility to set an ambitious global objective while not imposing requirements for individual countries. The eventual success of the agreement will of course be predicated on how parties to the Agreement respond, in terms of ratcheting up ambition in subsequent pledges, and delivering on these pledges. Promisingly, strong leadership is being shown by a range of countries in addition to the EU. This includes the USA and China [3], although the 2016 election makes the future US position increasingly uncertain. Despite this recent political change, the relatively rapid ratification of the Agreement also shows that crucial momentum from COP21 is being maintained.

This context very much frames the action on emission reductions that the Europe Union must implement, and various interpretations exist. The Commission argued that the energy packages in place, including the 40% greenhouse gas emissions reduction target by 2030, are in line with the objectives of the Paris Agreement [4]. However, a number of Member States have suggested that the 2030 climate target needs to be further strengthened [5]. For a 2°C transition, the IEA World Energy Outlook (WEO) [6] puts the required reductions at a significantly higher 54% by 2030, relative to 1990 levels.

This overall level of reduction is critical, as it sets the speed and depth of action to be taken now and in the coming decades. Any climate policy framework which includes longer-term decarbonization goals also needs a set of near- to mid-term policy actions to get on track [7]. These policy actions need to provide the necessary certainty to investors to ensure confidence that the long-term goals are being taken seriously, including those set out in the Paris Agreement and the EU Roadmap for reducing greenhouse gas emissions [8].

A key part of any transition will be a reorientation of Europe's energy supply, with a move away from the traditional fossil-based system to one that is less carbon-intensive. Our research presented in Section III puts this challenge in stark terms, by noting the extent to which fossil fuel reserves would have to "stay in the ground" under a 2°C compliant pathway. For Europe, this translates to 11% of gas, 20% of oil, and as much as 78% of coal reserves remaining unused in 2050.

Europe's Energy Transition. DOI: http://dx.doi.org/10.1016/B978-0-12-809806-6.00032-8

This leads to the key conclusion that national policies orientated towards the maximization of domestic resource extraction are incompatible with a globally economically optimal pathway. Given the long-term commitment of the EU to deep emission reductions of 80%−95% by 2050, prospects for new fossil resource extraction and associated infrastructure will need to be questioned in view of this objective.

33.2 SECURE, RELIABLE, AND COMPETITIVE ENERGY MARKETS

The shift away from fossil fuels to lower-carbon alternatives raises concerns around ensuring security and reliability of supply, and creates the need for Member States to strike an often difficult balance across these two objectives.[a] The current energy security strategy [9] concerns: (1) supply diversification, for both fossil fuel supplies and lower-carbon options; (2) strengthening Europe's position in global markets; (3) developing enhanced cooperation between Member States, including a move towards a fully integrated internal market; and (4) reducing demand through action to improve energy efficiency.

The 2016 energy security package set out a range of new measures aimed at addressing the energy security challenge [10]. A strong emphasis has been put on security of gas supply, as in 2013, 66% of gas used in the EU was imported, with the majority from three countries or regions—Russia (39%), Norway (33%) and North Africa, primarily Algeria, and Libya (22%) [9]. These new measures include proposed regulations on the security of gas supply [11] and a strategy for liquefied natural gas (LNG) and gas storage [12]. Gas supply regulations will target a shift from a national to a regional approach, and a solidarity principle that ensures supply to households and other key services when a country's supply is affected due to a severe crisis.

Chapter 11, Gas Security of Supply in the European Union highlighted a range of issues associated with gas supply security across Europe, which the new regulatory package is trying to deal with. This includes the need to improve interconnector capacity in the south-east Europe region, which is particularly susceptible to supply disruption, increased storage, development of new indigenous resources, and enhanced LNG capacity. There are prospects of expanding indigenous production to address security of supply concerns to some extent through exploiting the potential for shale gas in Europe and new opportunities for gas extraction in the East Mediterranean. From an energy supply perspective, shale gas could contribute towards reducing some of the security of supply risks associated with import dependency. However, in addition to the need for a reduced role of gas in the medium term to meet carbon emission reductions, there are a range of other factors that will require consideration. These include public acceptance and environmental concerns (particularly for shale), the future price of gas, and the wider geo-political situation.

The role of gas in Europe needs to be evaluated considering longer-term energy developments, given the EU's climate commitments and progress on energy efficiency. There are concerns that the current thinking around energy security is too focused on gas supply, and needs to better

---

[a]The integration of variable renewable electricity generation is a central element of the transition to a low-carbon system. This increases the need for system flexibility to maintain reliability, as detailed in Chapter 21, Need for Flexibility and Potential Solutions.

capture the need for a low-carbon transition [13]. A recent report focusing on the role of gas in the UK under climate targets, albeit more ambitious than those currently tabled by the Commission, saw a limited role for gas in the absence of carbon capture and storage (CCS) [14]. Therefore, the role of CCS must be prioritized if indeed long-lived gas infrastructure assets are invested in. However, to date few CCS demonstration plants have been constructed [15],[b] despite the CCS Directive being in place since 2009 and providing a legal framework for such initiatives [16].

Another important dimension is what happens on the demand side, a key element of the Commission's energy security strategy. An analysis by E3G [17] estimates that gas demand in 2014 was 23% below its 2010 peak, due to structural change in the European economy, changing patterns of consumption, and energy efficiency improvements. With historic overestimation of future gas demand, there is a risk of overcapacity in the medium to longer term, and stranding of assets.

Security of supply considerations also extend to the use of more indigenous renewable energy. The EC [9] estimates that some €30 billion on imported fuels are currently saved from the use of renewable resources. However, particularly for power generation, a growing use of renewable energy brings additional challenges to ensuring supply reliability. Generation from wind and solar photovoltaics is characterized by large variability and seasonality. Supplying the residual demand (total load minus variable generation) requires rethinking market and system operations.

For markets, this relates to the need for new market designs and regulatory frameworks to, for example, incentivize flexibility in the system (see Chapter 17, Market Design Options for Promoting Low-Carbon Technologies). Further, the merit order effect resulting in lower wholesale prices requires consideration, as due to their lower operating costs renewable generation pushes some of the fossil fuel-fired generators out of the market. This potentially undermines the ability to ensure fossil-based back-up capacity in the power system, and in turn the conventional generation business model.

For system operation, there is a need to ensure that the relevant systems and infrastructure are in place to manage the grid in a reliable way. Part of the approach to ensuring this is by closer cooperation at the EU level to improve the connectivity of national power systems. Under the framework to deliver the Energy Union [18], the Commission has set out measures to ensure a minimum interconnection target for electricity of 10% of installed electricity production capacity, to be achieved by 2020. The Commission is in the process of considering measures to increase this target to 15%. Increasing connectivity could help secure supply, reduce generation capacity, and manage higher levels of renewables.

The future generation system thus faces the challenge of requiring new market designs that effectively deal with merit order effects, the strong decentralization of generation, and the increasing need for flexibility, including from demand-side options, to ensure a reliable system operation. This is discussed further in Chapter 34, Developing the Policy Package, together with the necessary policy responses.

33.3 AFFORDABILITY FOR CONSUMERS

The costs of supplying energy in a system that is both secure and reliable, and transitioning to a lower-carbon model, will ultimately be paid for by consumers. The challenge is how these objectives can be achieved whilst also ensuring competitive markets that offer consumers fair prices and

---

[b]For further information on current activities, see the European CCS Demonstration Project Network, http://ccsnetwork.eu/

protecting those that are most vulnerable. Building on earlier Commission documents [19], the Energy Union aims at putting "citizens at its core" through their participation in the transition and, as envisioned, by reducing bills through use of new technologies, facilitating full participation in the market, and protecting vulnerable consumers [18]. While stronger efforts are needed, some progress is evident on participation. Consumers are now able to switch more effectively between tariffs in the market, and more are moving to being prosumers, who both produce (e.g., via household solar units) and consume electricity.

However, recent trends in Europe have brought affordability concerns into sharp focus. Firstly, retail prices have seen above inflationary increases since 2008 [20], although having plateaued somewhat in the last 2–3 years [21]. (There is of course large variation between Member States.) Secondly, the European economy has been through a period of economic stagnation, which hit specific regions in southern and eastern Europe particularly hard. Furthermore, ongoing energy market reform has the potential to put additional pressure on retail prices as competitive tariffs are increasingly introduced, replacing regulated prices that provide discounted tariffs to lower-income consumers.

The Energy Union rightly recognizes the need to protect consumers who are vulnerable and, more generally, the problems of energy poverty that are pervasive across specific regions of Europe [22,23]. The current understanding of the problem is at best patchy, but specific indicators suggest a significant proportion of the European population may be experiencing some form of energy poverty [24]. Chapter 30, Energy poverty across the EU: analysis of Policies and measures provided an overview of how different Member States have been seeking to address energy poverty and protect vulnerable consumers, concluding that there was large variation in actions taken. A stronger role for the Commission to intervene or provide guidance might be necessary. At the same time, the data to specifically understand the extent of the problem are lacking [25], and therefore understanding how to take forward the policy agenda is challenging.

REFERENCES

[1] D. Victor, Why Paris worked: a different approach to climate diplomacy, December 2015. <http://e360.yale.edu/feature/why_paris_worked_a_different_approach_to_climate_diplomacy/2940/>.

[2] UNFCCC, Adoption of the Paris agreement, in: Conference of the Parties 21st Session, Paris, November 30 to December 11, 2015. United Nations Framework Convention on Climate Change, December 2015.

[3] White House Press Statement, U.S.–China cooperation on climate change, September 3, 2016. <https://www.whitehouse.gov/the-press-office/2016/09/03/fact-sheet-us-china-cooperation-climate-change-0>.

[4] EC, Communication from the Commission to the European Parliament and the Council. The Road from Paris: assessing the implications of the Paris Agreement and accompanying the proposal for a Council decision on the signing, on behalf of the European Union, of the Paris agreement adopted under the United Nations Framework Convention on Climate Change, Brussels, 2.3.2016 COM(2016) 110 final, 2016.

[5] M. Darby, Germany and Austria call for higher EU 2030 climate ambition, March 2016. <http://www.theguardian.com/environment/2016/mar/04/germany-and-austria-call-for-higher-eu-2030-climate-ambition>.

[6] IEA, World Energy Outlook 2015, International Energy Agency. IEA/OECD, Paris, 2015.

[7] C. Mathieu, R. Hillerbrand, S. Pye, Shaping expectations to foster the low carbon transition: can COP21 be a catalyst for action? INSIGHT_E Hot Energy Topic 11, September 2015.

[8] EC, Communication from the Commission to the European Parliament, the Council, the European Economic and Social Committee, and the Committee of the Regions. A Roadmap for moving to a competitive low carbon economy in 2050, Brussels, 8.3.2011 COM(2011) 112 final, 2011.

[9] EC, Communication from the Commission to the European Parliament and the Council. European Energy Security Strategy, Brussels, 28.5.2014, COM(2014) 330 final, 2014.

[10] European Commission Press Release, Commission presents energy security package, February 2016. <http://europa.eu/rapid/press-release_AGENDA-16-272_en.htm>.

[11] EC, Proposal for a Regulation of the European Parliament and of the Council concerning measures to safeguard the security of gas supply and repealing Regulation (EU) No 994/2010, Brussels, 16.2.2016 COM(2016) 52 final, 2016.

[12] EC, Communication from the Commission to the European Parliament, the Council, the European Economic and Social Committee, and the Committee of the Regions on an EU strategy for liquefied natural gas and gas storage, Brussels, 16.2.2016 COM(2016) 49 final, 2016.

[13] Nature Energy Editorial, Pipe dreams, March 2016. <http://www.nature.com/articles/nenergy201631>.

[14] C. McGlade, S. Pye, J. Watson, M. Bradshaw, P. Ekins, The future role of natural gas in the UK. UK Energy Research Centre, UKERC/RR/RV/2016/01, February 2016.

[15] C. Bauer, K. Volkart, INSIGHT_E Technology Note 1: carbon capture and storage, 2015. <http://insightenergy.org/ckeditor_assets/attachments/44/insight_e_innovation_corner_ccs.pdf>.

[16] EC, Directive 2009/31/EC of the European Commission and of the Council of 23 April 2009 on the geological storage of carbon dioxide and amending Council Directive 85/337/EEC, European Parliament and Council Directives 2000/60/EC, 2001/80/EC, 2004/35/EC, 2006/12/EC, 2008/1/EC and Regulation (EC) No 1013/2006, 2009.

[17] E3G, Europe's declining gas demand—implications for infrastructure investment and energy security, June 2015. <https://www.e3g.org/news/media-room/europes-declining-gas-demand>.

[18] EC, Energy Union Package. Communication from the Commission to the European Parliament, the Council, the European Economic and Social Committee, the Committee of the Regions and the European Investment Bank. A Framework Strategy for a Resilient Energy Union with a Forward-Looking Climate Change Policy, Brussels, 25.2.2015, COM(2015) 80 final, 2015.

[19] EC, Commission staff working paper: an energy policy for consumers, Brussels, 11.11.2010. SEC(2010) 1407 final, 2010.

[20] EC, Communication from the Commission to the European Parliament, the Council, the European Economic and Social Committee, and the Committee of the Regions. Energy prices and costs in Europe, Brussels, 29.1.2014 COM(2014) 21/2, 2014.

[21] European Commission, EU energy in figures: statistical pocketbook 2015, 2015. <https://ec.europa.eu/energy/sites/ener/files/documents/PocketBook_ENERGY_2015%20PDF%20final.pdf>.

[22] H. Thomson, C. Snell, Quantifying the prevalence of fuel poverty across the European Union, Energy Policy 52 (2013) 563−572.

[23] S. Bouzarovski, S. Tirado-Herrero, The energy divide: integrating energy transitions, regional inequalities and poverty trends in the European Union, Eur. Urban Reg. Stud. 24 (2015) 1−18 <http://journals.sagepub.com/doi/abs/10.1177/0969776415596449>.

[24] EC Press Release, Energy poverty may affect nearly 11% of the EU population, June 25, 2015. <https://ec.europa.eu/energy/en/news/energy-poverty-may-affect-nearly-11-eu-population>.

[25] H. Thomson, C. Snell, Fuel poverty measurement in Europe: a pilot study. Eaga Charitable Trust, May 2014. <http://fuelpoverty.eu/wp-content/uploads/2014/06/Fuel-Poverty-Measurement-in-Europe-Final-report-v2.pdf>.

DEVELOPING THE POLICY PACKAGE

34

Steve Pye[1], Manuel Welsch[2], and Aurélie Faure-Schuyer[3]

[1]*University College London (UCL), London, United Kingdom* [2]*KTH Royal Institute of Technology, Stockholm, Sweden* [3]*Institut Français des Relations Internationales (IFRI), Brussels, Belgium*

34.1 EMISSION REDUCTION TARGETS AND THE EU ETS

As was argued earlier, the ambition level of the climate and energy targets in 2030 and beyond are crucial for guiding the type of policy package that is implemented now. This is why it is so critical to adequately reflect the targets set by the Paris Agreement, as ratified by the EU in 2016 [1]. According to the European Environment Agency [2], current progress on greenhouse gas emission reductions in 2014 were estimated at 23% below 1990 levels, up from $\sim 20\%$ in 2013. In part this was due to lower heating demand as a result of warmer temperatures in 2014. This EEA analysis projects that by 2020 emission reductions will stand at 24%, exceeding the target of 20% in that year. These data suggest good progress to date, particularly in relation to the 2020 package. Against the recent trend of declining greenhouse gas emissions since the mid-2000s, a recent estimate by Eurostat however suggests a growth in CO_2 emissions from the energy sector. In 2015, CO_2 emissions from fossil fuel combustion increased by 0.7% compared with the previous year [3].

It is also worth noting that stronger action will be needed to meet the 40% emissions reductions target in 2030, with annual reductions from now increasing to 1.4% per annum from the historic rate of 1% since 1990. After 2030, this will need to further increase by $2-3$ times the pre-2030 mitigation rate [2]. Energy policies will have to be strengthened significantly for these stronger emission reduction rates to materialize. Current estimates by the EEA [2] are that planned policies will deliver a 30% greenhouse gas reduction by 2030, well short of the required 40%.

To date the drivers of emissions reductions have been the decoupling of energy use and economic growth, a reduction in the intensity of the fuel mix through an increasing share of renewables, and a decline in coal consumption [4,5]. From an energy and climate policy perspective, renewables policies proved to be the most effective, although the majority of the reductions observed since 1990 have resulted from a range of factors other than specific climate policies.

THE EU ETS

A central market instrument for delivering future emissions reductions is the EU Emission Trading Scheme (EU ETS, see Chapter 7: A Market-Based European Energy Policy), a cap and trade system whereby emission pollution credits are maintained below an annual EU cap expressed in megatonnes (Mt) of CO_2-equivalent. In operation since 2005 and now in its third phase (2013−20), the EU ETS covers power generation and industrial sources emitting 40%−45% of the EU's

Europe's Energy Transition. DOI: http://dx.doi.org/10.1016/B978-0-12-809806-6.00033-X

295

greenhouse gas emissions. Within those sources covered, the EU ETS targets a 43% reduction of emissions by 2030 (relative to 2005). This compares to much lower reductions of 30% from non-ETS sectors [6]. However, to date, the success of the EU ETS has been limited, a real concern given its centrality in delivering the required reductions. The scheme has performed poorly since its inception largely due to credit oversupplies (also as a consequence of the 2008 financial crisis which slowed down economic growth), and must therefore be strengthened. The current price range of €3−8/tCO$_2$ (between 2013 and 2015) does not provide a meaningful incentive.

The primary structural reform of the scheme is the introduction of the Market Stability Reserve (MSR), as investigated in more detail by INSIGHT_E [7]. Its aim, from 2019 onwards, is to reduce surplus allowances, improve resilience to supply−demand imbalances in the scheme, and enhance synergies with other climate policies. Currently, the cap on emissions imposed by the EU ETS is too high, resulting in a cumulative surplus since 2008 of 2.1 GtCO$_2$ (2014), which is expected to grow to 3 GtCO$_2$ by 2030 in the absence of reform. Modeling the impact of the MSR sees the cumulative surplus level fall to 0.5 GtCO$_2$ in 2030 and a carbon price of €78 per tonne, compared to €62 in the reference case (without the MSR). However, it is worth noting that the MSR is unlikely to impact the 2020 prices due to the timescales of its introduction, and therefore the ability to achieve stronger near-term reductions may be limited. A potential drawback is that the mechanism does not differentiate between surplus arising from abatement efforts and any surplus from exogenous shocks, which may cause some volatility.

In addition to the MSR, the EU brought forward proposals for operational improvements during phase 4 of the EU ETS (2021−30). Under these proposals, allowances will be reduced annually by an increased rate (2.2% vs the current 1.7%). Free allowances will also be better targeted to address carbon leakage issues, to improve alignment with sector production levels, and to support electricity sector modernization in specific Member States [8].

OTHER DECARBONIZATION POLICIES

The EU ETS is at the heart of the EU's efforts to reduce greenhouse gas emissions. However, INSIGHT_E research suggested that it is vital that a range of policy measures are considered, given the limits to what carbon pricing can achieve. Noting the scale of the challenge of decarbonizing the energy system, it has been a range of other policy instruments that have produced most gains (including across EU ETS sectors), compensating some of the current short-falls of the EU ETS (see Chapter 10: Decarbonizing the EU Energy System). Examples include the Renewable Energy Directive, and the Passenger Car CO$_2$ Regulations. The key message here is that carbon pricing has a role to play but due to the size of the challenge, developing an effective policy package that can trigger change on the many different actors will require a broader range of policy instruments.

According to Grubb et al. [9] there are three key policy pillars, all of which are needed to effectively tackle climate change. These include (1) standards and engagement at the level of households and businesses, to influence choices that impact on emissions, (2) markets and pricing at the sector and economy-wide level, and (3) strategic investment to achieve transformative levels of innovation and infrastructure, often driven by governments or large industrial players. The argument here is one of balance; clearly the Commission is developing a mixed policy package (including the Energy Efficiency and Renewable Energy Directives), but there is a risk of overemphasis on delivery of the low-carbon transition through the reformed EU ETS and electricity market reform (through the Third Energy Package).

It is also important to highlight that Member States have distinctive country-specific approaches towards taking forward the decarbonization agenda, as reflected by varying levels of ambition and types of policy mechanisms applied. Therefore, the range of approaches applied at Member State level can provide valuable experience to inform EU energy policy making. For example, Sweden has a road map to achieve net zero emissions by 2050 [10], while the UK has implemented a set of 5-year carbon budgets to realize its long-term greenhouse gas reduction goals, with a strong increase in stringency in the late 2020s and early 2030s.[a] Other approaches range from country-specific carbon prices[b] to measures to enforce phase out of coal in power generation. When assessing the impact of a prospective coal phase out in the UK and Germany [12], it was found that such measures lead to emission reductions at the country level. However, without similar measures in other Member States under an EU wide target, overall emissions could still increase, negating the impact of the specific country-level measures. So in addition to highlighting useful Member State-level policy approaches that are transferable, recognizing the imperative for consistent EU-wide action will also be needed to realize ambition levels to 2030, and in the longer term.

34.2 DELIVERING A HIGHER MARKET SHARE OF RENEWABLE ENERGY

Meeting the EU's decarbonization challenge will require a major shift away from an energy system built on fossil fuels to a low-carbon system by 2050. Fossil fuels will, of course, continue to play a crucial role in the near to mid term for maintaining supply for electricity, heating, and mobility. However, policies related to their import, production, and usage will need to be cognizant of the need for a transition away from these sources of energy. As explained in Section 33.2, gas in particular may be gaining too much attention given the potentially limited future role without carbon capture and storage, the potential overestimation of future gas demand, and environmental concerns beyond climate change, especially for shale gas.

Renewable energy is going to be an important enabler of the shift away from fossil fuels across all sectors. In just 10 years, between 2004 and 2014, the share of electricity from renewables has almost doubled in the EU, from 14% to over 27% (73.4 Mtoe). Of the 13% points of growth, 9% is from solar and wind generation. This success reflects the importance of the EU renewable framework policy, the Renewable Energy Directive [13]. Renewables in transport have also increased over the same period, from 1% to nearly 6% (14.7 Mtoe), while for heating and cooling the increase has been from 10% to almost 17% (87.5 Mtoe).[c] Given the substantial focus of European efforts on promoting renewables and the challenges this brings to the system, a key focus on INSIGHT_E research has been on assessing these challenges.

Whilst recognizing the progress that has been made on renewables, it could be argued that energy policies must provide a stronger focus on the heating and cooling, and transport sectors [14]. The primary reason is that electricity only accounts for about a quarter of total EU energy

---

[a]An overview of the UK carbon budgets can be found at https://www.gov.uk/guidance/carbon-budgets
[b]For example, the carbon price floor for power generation in the UK of £18($\sim$€20)/tCO_2, with France set to follow in 2017 with a €30 price. Other Member States such as Finland and Sweden also have explicit carbon taxes [11].
[c]Latest data taken from the 2014 SHARES tool published by Eurostat, http://ec.europa.eu/eurostat/web/energy/data/shares

consumption, whilst accounting for 42% of total renewable energy. The other 75% of energy consumption is from heating and cooling (50%) and transport (25%), yet these account for only 58% of total renewable energy consumption.[d]

While it is likely that some Member States will exceed their projected shares of renewable electricity (RES-E),[e] it is also evident that RES-E action alone to 2020 and beyond will not be sufficient. This is for a number of reasons; firstly, there may be some technical limits to the level of variable generation that can be integrated into the system. Secondly, a large share of energy demand is not via electricity (as discussed above), and therefore direct deployment of renewable energy for nonelectrified heating and cooling and transport will be needed. To position the EU on a pathway to ambitious emissions reductions for 2030, it is imperative that renewable energy policies target all sectors to increase the contribution of renewable energy. In this context, we considered the types of mechanisms that might be envisaged to strengthen the broader policy framework for renewables [15].

The Renewable Energy Directive target of 20% renewables by 2020 is set to increase to a 27% share by 2030. However, to allow for the most cost-effective strategy, it is questionable whether this will be achieved via specific national or sector-specific renewable targets, such as an explicit biofuel target [6]. Rather, efforts should focus on ensuring Member States develop harmonized policy support packages consistent with the internal market, and on establishing a strengthened EU ETS to also drive investments in renewables. Again, this suggests a strong focus on renewable electricity (in parallel with the reinforced efforts in other sectors), which is projected to rise to 45% by 2030, to help meet the 27% target. This strong push on renewable electricity will result in some key challenges to be overcome for the power system, as detailed in Section IV.

ELECTRICITY MARKETS

One key challenge relates to getting the right market incentives in place to facilitate investments in low-carbon technologies while maintaining the reliability of electricity supply. This is complicated by the merit order effect: prices tend to decrease with increasing shares of electricity generation by variable renewables. These renewables can thus only profit to a limited degree from the higher prices set by conventional generation in times of high demand and low renewable electricity generation. This poses a challenge for investments in additional low-carbon generation in electricity only markets. Chapter 17, Market Design Options for Promoting Low-Carbon Technologies, considered different market designs that might overcome the problems of low wholesale prices due to merit order effects. While many options exist, the required changes and complexity suggest that most Member States will continue with energy-only markets for some time to come, but with specific add-ons to support low-carbon technologies.

A move to smaller-scale investments and a more decentralized system, seen in Germany in particular and emerging in other Member States, could also necessitate changes to policy.

---

[d]This is in terms of Gross Final Energy Consumption (GFEC), as used in the Renewable Energy Directive.
[e]Based on the *National Renewable Energy Action Plans (NREAP), which outline how a Member State will achieve its 2020 renewable energy target.*

Decentralized self-consumption (electricity generated and used on site) may potentially reduce renewable support requirements and allow for strong consumer participation in the markets. However, policies may be needed to help meet the resulting challenges, such as how to ensure a fair distribution of infrastructure costs and maximize the potential through smarter energy solutions (see Chapter 27, Self-consumption of electricity from renewable sources). Effective policy in this area could help alleviate grid balancing issues related to the integration of variable renewables and promote distributed renewable installations on the end-user side.

The European Commission has an important role in ensuring that the internal market for electricity remains competitive and is fit-for-purpose. It needs to cope with higher shares of variable renewables and the challenges it brings for conventional as well as renewable generators and other actors providing system flexibility (via storage, demand side management, etc.) (see Section IV).

HEATING AND COOLING

Moving away from renewable electricity, for heating and cooling the majority of the current share in renewables is delivered by bioenergy, but with growing contributions from district heating and heat pumps. Any post-2020 regime will need to promote these three types of energy sources, in addition to energy efficiency measures that reduce overall consumption. This will be critical given the size of energy demand in this sector, accounting for half of the total system demand. Recent assessments suggest that many Member States have insufficient policies in place to deliver the necessary progress in the heating and cooling sector [16], and therefore the Commission has an important role in sharing best practice and developing ideas in this area. A heating and cooling strategy for Europe would go some way in understanding how best to foster increases in heating and cooling renewable energy.

One important area relates to bioenergy. As the largest renewable source for this sector, and set to grow over the next decade, clear sustainability criteria will be critical to establish. In addition, stronger integration of renewables for heating and cooling into energy networks, such as through solar hot water or advanced heat pumps, will help foster their development. However, this will require a supportive market environment that facilitates such investments, especially by consumers, e.g., through adjusted tariff policies. Further, it would need to address the challenges of an increased electrification of heating and cooling that builds on low-carbon generation, as just discussed under the preceding sub-heading.

TRANSPORT

On transport, the absence of a specific renewable target potentially places uncertainty across the biofuel industry. Possible policy options include a single binding legislative framework while allowing differentiated support mechanisms. For example, a legislative framework on the greenhouse gas intensity of transport fuels could be combined with support for lowest carbon biofuels, green certificates for providing flexibility to meet intensity targets, or policy supporting the uptake of electric and hydrogen mobility [17]. However the policy framework develops, it is critical that it can ensure sustainability of biofuels in particular, which has been a major issue with biofuels to date. It should also ensure that it is aligned with the longer-term framework set out in the EC's Transport White Paper. This sets out the objective to reduce greenhouse gases from transport by at least 60% by 2050 (relative to 1990). In 2030, this means reducing these emissions to around 20% below their 2008 level.

The evolution of policy as it relates to bioenergy will be key to increasing the shares of renewable energy in the heating and transport sectors. For transport, the limited prospect of meeting the renewable target for the sector of 10% by 2020 is related to concerns about the sustainability of first-generation biofuels and resulting political uncertainty, and a lack of commercial availability of alternative, second-generation biofuels [18].

Future reforms of the Renewable Energy Directive, approved by the European Parliament, try to tackle some of the concerns around feedstock sustainability, particularly promoting second-generation advanced biofuels. This includes a 7% cap on food crop-based biofuels for the transport sector and an indicative target of 0.5% for advanced biofuels. Further, to support the following areas, advanced biofuels count double towards meeting the renewable energy target, renewable sources in electric road vehicles count 5 times, and electrified rail transport 2.5 times [19]. If and when adopted, to which extent these reforms will enhance bioenergy use in these sectors to 2020 still needs to be seen. Currently, the Commission is considering the bioenergy support in the post-2020 period.

Specific sectors may also require bespoke policies to incentivize renewables. Unlike surface transport fuels, biojet fuel has not benefited from EU renewable energy policies. Some of INSIGHT_E's research has therefore specifically focused on the issue of biofuels uptake in aviation. The role of biofuels in this sector is well illustrated in Chapter 12, Biofuels for aviation: policy goals and costs, which highlights the potential growth in aviation emissions by 2050 and points to an increase from 151 to 405 $MtCO_2$ from 2005 to 2050. However, the current implementation of the Renewable Energy Directive by Member States, which tends to limit support of biofuels in the aviation sector, and the high costs of new biojet technologies, have resulted in limited progress.

In this context, progress on developing a viable biofuel supply for the aviation sector was analyzed, including both technical and economic challenges [20]. A range of policy mechanisms for incentivizing increased biofuel use were considered, particularly in view of the Commission's goal to realize an uptake of 2 Mt biojet by 2020, equivalent to 17% of total sustainable EU biofuel production today, and 4% of current EU aviation fuel consumption. These include the use of a combined auction-route charging scheme, strengthening of biofuel obligation schemes at the Member State level, or voluntary and/or industry-led approaches.

Whatever approach is taken, it will need to consider the international mechanism that has been proposed by the International Civil Aviation Organisation (ICAO).[f] An ongoing concern for the airline industry is that any EU-based scheme could have distortionary effects due to international competitors not being subject to the same measures, and that it could even be unnecessary given this industry-led global initiative.

---

[f]The recently agreed scheme at the 38th ICAO Assembly is called the Carbon Offsetting and Reduction Scheme for International Aviation (CORSIA), http://www.icao.int/Meetings/a39/Documents/WP/wp_530_en.pdf

34.3 ADDRESSING ENERGY POVERTY AND PROTECTING VULNERABLE CONSUMERS

In view of the continued and rapid change of the European energy system, there is a broad question as to what this means for consumers. In line with the Energy Union's objective to provide affordable energy, there is a need for protection of the more vulnerable consumers in society. There is also the need to ensure consumers can participate fully in the smart systems revolution, both as consumers and prosumers who also generate electricity. This full participation is also required to ensure that all consumers are able to take advantage of technologies that potentially allow for reduced energy bills, such as smart appliances that adjust their consumption based on time of use tariffs. As INSIGHT_E research has highlighted [21], the consumer has the potential to play a leading role in the system transformation, but policy has to facilitate this, particularly in removing some of the key barriers. This includes informational, technical, structural (split incentives between landlords and tenants), economic (lack of incentives), and acceptance-related (aversion to adopt) barriers. In summary, consumer policies must be orientated towards ensuring protection and enhancing participation.

INSIGHT_E research has particularly focused on how the European Commission can address issues of consumer vulnerability and energy poverty. Energy poverty has had a strong policy focus in the UK, Ireland, and France, and increasingly in other Member States such as Slovakia, Belgium and Austria. However, it is only in recent years that it has been increasingly recognized by the Commission as a key challenge requiring policy solutions.

While the issue of energy poverty is now on the agenda of both the Commission and Member States, limited coordinated actions are in place at the European level. This is for three key reasons: (1) the problem is not yet fully understood due to shortcomings in existing indicators; (2) action to date has been guided by the principle of subsidiarity,[g] and (3) the EC competency is focused on vulnerable consumers in regulated markets, not on households in energy poverty across the wider energy system. In Chapter 30, Energy Poverty Across the EU: Analysis of Policies and Measures, a number of policy recommendations were made to strengthen the Commission's impact in this area.

Firstly, to address the problem, the Commission should define the concept of energy poverty, and distinguish it from vulnerable consumers. They are linked in that the extent and/or severity of energy poverty could be exacerbated if vulnerable consumers are not afforded adequate protection. However, they are distinct, as in the European context vulnerable consumers relates to gas and electricity consumers who may not have full access to competitive tariffs or need additional protection and support, for a range of reasons (such as income, disability, age, being welfare recipients). Characteristics of energy poverty typically differ and go beyond energy markets to consider affordability issues for energy services, whether they be provided through regulated markets or not. The focus is often on more structural issues that require longer-term solutions and involve multiple stakeholders in the energy industry but also civic society and government. This is different for action to support vulnerable consumers, which largely just targets regulators and utilities. Explicitly stating what energy poverty is would therefore be a major step forward, without necessarily having to state the metric of measurement which could be best left to Member State decision makers.

---

[g]The notion that decisions should be taken as closely as possible to the citizen, with the EU only taking action when this is more effective than at national, regional or local level.

Similarly, given the observed variability in definitions, the Commission should be more prescriptive about who constitutes a vulnerable consumer. For example, in some Member States, protection for vulnerable households is based on their risk of disconnection. Such narrow definitions do not provide broader support to consumers who may have difficulty accessing and participating in the market.

In the 2016 Clean Energy for All Europeans, which proposed a range of changes to energy sector legislation, the Commission has reflected some of the research recommendations. For example, it has been more explicit about the importance of distinguishing energy poverty from vulnerable consumers, and stating that Member States must measure and monitor this phenomenon (Article 29) [24].

Secondly, improved indicators should be developed and good practice disseminated [22]. There is a recognized deficit in understanding the problem of energy poverty in the EU. Further efforts are needed to develop datasets and metrics that improve this understanding that is required to inform related policy formulation. Alongside improved data, a European energy poverty observatory could provide a platform to collect and disseminate good practice of how energy poverty can be measured and effective actions that can be undertaken. Progress is being made in this context, as a recent report published by the European Commission sets out some proposals for new indicators and different designs for observatories [23]. Following the publication of this report, the Commission have launched a much larger project aimed at establishing an observatory. This observatory will focus on developing energy poverty metrics to help measure and monitor its prevalence across Member States, and facilitating the sharing of best practice, including on policy interventions.

Finally, the EC should promote energy efficiency measures to address energy poverty, particularly targeting low-income households. For example, the Commission could also ensure that it allocates a higher share of EU funds to renovation programs focused on energy poor, low-income, and vulnerable categories of people. These funds should also be targeted towards Member States in central, eastern and southern Europe, where the problem is most entrenched.

Article 7 strengthens the provision for Member States to include targeted social measures for households affected by energy poverty in Member States' energy efficiency obligation schemes. These schemes require energy companies to support final consumers in improving their energy efficiency. Article 7 also requires Member States to take energy poverty into account when designing alternative policy measures for reducing final energy consumption, such as taxes or financial incentives.

As the Commission develops an improved understanding of the challenge of energy poverty, in partnership with Member States, it will be crucial that they continue to assess how countries can be best supported to deliver the necessary measures to support energy customers who are vulnerable or energy poor. While providing leadership and coordination on this issue, action will need to be developed that meets the highly distinctive challenges observed across different Member States.

REFERENCES

[1] EC Press Release, Paris agreement to enter into force as EU agrees ratification, October 2016. <http://europa.eu/rapid/press-release_IP-16-3284_en.htm>.

[2] EEA, Trends and projections in Europe 2015: tracking progress towards Europe's climate and energy targets. European Environment Agency. Report No 4/2015, 2015.

[3] European Commission Press Release, Early estimates of CO_2 emissions from energy use, May 2016. <http://europa.eu/rapid/press-release_STAT-16-1651_en.htm>.

[4] ICF, Decomposition analysis of the changes in GHG emissions in the EU and Member States, April 2016.

[5] Eurostat, Coal consumption statistics. <http://ec.europa.eu/eurostat/statistics-explained/index.php/Coal_consumption_statistics> (accessed 10.05.16).

[6] EC, Communication from the Commission to the European Parliament, the Council, the European Economic and Social Committee, and the Committee of the Regions. A policy framework for climate and energy in the period from 2020 to 2030, Brussels, 22.1.2014 COM(2014) 15 final, 2014.

[7] S. Cail, M. Jalard, E. Alberola, The market stability reserve: assessing reform needs and possible impacts on the EU ETS. INSIGHT_E Hot Energy Topic 12, October 2015.

[8] EC, Report from the Commisssion to the European Parliament and the Council. Climate action progress report, including the report on the functioning of the European carbon market and the report on the review of Directive 2009/31/EC on the geological storage of carbon dioxide, Brussels, 18.11.2015 COM (2015) 576 final, 2015.

[9] M. Grubb, J.C. Hourcade, K. Neuhoff, Planetary Economics, Taylor & Francis/Routledge, London, 2014.

[10] Swedish Environmental Protection Agency, Basis for a roadmap for a Sweden without climate emissions in 2050, Naturvårdsverket, 2012. <http://www.naturvardsverket.se/fardplan2050>.

[11] OECD, Effective carbon rates: pricing CO_2 through taxes and emissions trading systems, September 2016. <http://www.oecd.org/tax/effective-carbon-rates-9789264260115-en.htm>.

[12] H. Yilmaz, Q. Bchini, D. Keles, R. Hartel, W. Fichtner, M. Mikulić, et al., Impacts of a UK and German coal phase-out on the electricity mix and CO_2 emissions in Europe. INSIGHT_E Hot Energy Topic 14, April 2016.

[13] EC, Directive 2009/28/EC of the European Parliament and of the Council of 23 April 2009 on the promotion of the use of energy from renewable sources and amending and subsequently repealing Directives 2001/77/EC and 2003/30/EC, 2009.

[14] S. Pye, B. Ó Gallachóir, P. Deane, Europe's renewable energy policies: too much focus on renewable electricity? INSIGHT_E Hot Energy Topic 4, November 2014.

[15] A. Shivakumar, T. Badouard, D. Moreira de Olivera, J. Dehler, S. Pye, M. Welsch, Analysing RES support mechanisms in the EU post-2020. INSIGHT_E Hot Energy Topic 10, August 2015.

[16] EUFORES, EU Tracking Roadmap 2015. European Forum for Renewable Energy Sources, 2015. <http://www.keepontrack.eu/contents/publicationseutrackingroadmap/eu_roadmap_2015.pdf>.

[17] IEEP, Low carbon transport fuel policy for Europe Post 2020, 2015. <http://www.ieep.eu/assets/1789/IEEP_TEPR_ICCT_2015_Low_Carbon_Transport_Fuel_Policy_for_Europe_Post_2020.pdf>.

[18] EC, Report from the Commission to the European Parliament, the Council, the European Economic and Social Committee, and the Committee of the Regions. Renewable energy progress report, Brussels, 15.6.2015 COM(2015) 293 final, 2015.

[19] EC, Directive (EU) 2015/1513 of the European Parliament and of the Council of 9 September 2015 amending Directive 98/70/EC relating to the quality of petrol and diesel fuels and amending Directive 2009/28/EC on the promotion of the use of energy from renewable sources. L239, 2015.

[20] P. Deane, S. Pye, Biofuels for aviation: review and analysis of options for market development. INSIGHT_E Policy Report 4, February 2016.

[21] C. Jullien, P. Serkine, M. Miller, S. Bubeck, U. Fahl, End-users: the trigger to shape the European Energy System. INSIGHT_E Hot Energy Topic 16, July 2016.

[22] EC, First Commission interim report on the implementation of Pilot Projects and Preparatory Actions 2015, Brussels, 04.03.2015, 2015. <http://www.europarl.europa.eu/meetdocs/2014_2019/documents/imco/dv/first_iterim_report_2015_03_04_/first_iterim_report_2015_03_04_en.pdf>.

[23] K. Rademaekers, · J. Yearwood, A. Ferreira, S. Pye, · I. Hamilton, P. Agnolucci, et al., Selecting indicators to measure energy poverty, Published by the European Commission, May 2016.

[24] EC, Proposal for a Directive of the European Parliament and the Council on common rules for the internal market in electricity. COM (2016) 864 final, Brussels, 2016.

RESEARCH PRIORITIES

35

Steve Pye[1], Manuel Welsch[2], and Aurélie Faure-Schuyer[3]

[1]University College London (UCL), London, United Kingdom [2]KTH Royal Institute of Technology, Stockholm, Sweden [3]Institut Français des Relations Internationales (IFRI), Brussels, Belgium

Emerging from the body of research presented in this book and performed by the think tank INSIGHT_E, and in view of the wider research landscape, there are a number of research areas that could be prioritized by the Commission and other funders of energy research at the European scale. These focus on those challenging areas where an improved understanding is required to inform the policy process. They relate to the following priority areas.

An integrated understanding of the wider low-carbon transition. Analyses that focus on the techno-economic transition of the energy system are crucial. However, a broader understanding is needed, as to what the additional benefits and challenges at the boundary of the energy system and beyond are going to be. This includes benefits in terms of job creation, the associated social cohesion this may bring, and wider environmental benefits, and challenges in terms of vulnerable (emission-intensive) industries, the importance of these industries to society, and public acceptance of the required infrastructure and technology roll out. Identifying these benefits and challenges will be crucial in getting buy-in for the transition by effectively communicating the benefits, and allowing for policy intervention to address the challenges.

Implications of deeper ambition of climate targets to 2030. Following COP21 in Paris, the question emerges whether the proposed 2030 targets are adequate in view of both, the stated EU ambition for 2050 and, beyond this time horizon, the Paris Agreement objectives to achieve net zero emissions in the second half of the 21st century. The implications of stronger action can be profound [1] and need to be recognized in order to reconsider initiatives across a range of policy areas, from energy supply to consumers, from technology support to environmental concerns and market implications. Further, developing new market design options will be crucial to facilitate a transition to a low-carbon electricity system. Future market designs will need to allow for high shares of renewables while ensuring security of supply. They will need to support a radical change towards smarter systems with higher participation by a range of actors, systems that become increasingly interlinked with end-use sectors, such as transport and households.

Reshaping low-carbon policy post-2030. Informed by the preceding research priority, this large area of research is one that is critical in further scaling low-carbon energy supply in the EU. A number of areas of research appear important for supporting EU policy efforts in this area. Firstly, there needs to be an improved understanding of what is good practice in policy making for incentivizing the scale up of renewables in heat and transport. Secondly, in support of this, an improved understanding of how a bioenergy policy framework can best promote low greenhouse gas feedstocks while guaranteeing sustainability is required. It is particularly important that relevant

Europe's Energy Transition. DOI: http://dx.doi.org/10.1016/B978-0-12-809806-6.00034-1

incentives need to be put in place for those sectors where biofuels need to play a role, such as across the heat and transport sectors, and specifically aviation.

Enhanced modeling to explore different strategies for coordinating Member State responses to the different challenges set out in the earlier chapters, including the interconnectedness of electricity systems, cooperation on mitigation activities such as CCS infrastructure investments, social and environmental impacts beyond climate change, etc. Recent enhancement of in-house modeling capacity at the European Commission's Joint Research Centres (JRC) in Petten[a] and Seville[b] are promising developments, as are a range of important modeling projects, such as REEEM to support the SET plan implementation.[c]

Improved assessments of energy poverty issues across Member States to inform policy responses. There is a need for improved understanding of consumer vulnerability and energy poverty across Member States. To date, an understanding is largely informed by EU-SILC survey data[d] on household experiences based on proxy energy poverty indicators. In addition, different projects assessed related issues for specific regions of Europe.[e] However, a more robust and comprehensive understanding requires improved data and metrics. This was enhanced by recent work by Rademaekers et al. [2], and is further supported by a new EC initiative to establish an observatory and concrete metrics that provide a better understanding on the energy poverty challenges in different Member States.

Further work is also needed to build on that undertaken by the think tank INSIGHT_E to identify policy interventions, and determine what has worked in different domestic situations. The build-up of best practice in defining energy poverty and necessary policy interventions would be particularly helpful for the Commission in promoting action on this issue. This also applies to enhancing the understanding of what helps consumers to both participate in the market and be protected if considered vulnerable.

Research on the position of Europe in respect to technology innovation. This will help the Commission and Member States understand where the EU has a competitive advantage, and prospects for developing and strengthening new industries. A useful assessment by INSIGHT_E of the European Union's innovation capacity can be found in Drmač et al. [3]. A focus on how technology innovation can be turned into industrial growth could be a key factor in helping gain further acceptance of the low-carbon transition.

The EU, in support of the low-carbon transition, also needs to focus on critical technologies that will be required in the transition. It has a unique opportunity to facilitate collaboration on such technologies such as CCS, nuclear, hydrogen systems, and electric mobility infrastructure. This

---

[a]The JRC-EU-TIMES model—assessing the long-term role of the SET Plan Energy technologies, http://publications.jrc.ec.europa.eu/repository/handle/JRC85804

[b]POTEnCIA model description, http://publications.jrc.ec.europa.eu/repository/handle/JRC100638

[c]Further information on the REEEM project can be found at www.reeem.org. The SET plan is the European Strategic Energy Technology Plan, which aims to accelerate the development and deployment of low-carbon technologies by improving new technologies and bringing down costs by coordinating research and helping to finance projects.

[d]EU-SILC is the European Union Statistics on Income and Living Conditions, hosted by Eurostat, http://ec.europa.eu/eurostat/web/microdata/european-union-statistics-on-income-and-living-conditions

[e]For example, the EVALUATE project (https://urban-energy.org/evaluate/) focuses on central and eastern Europe, and the REACH project (http://reach-energy.eu/) on south-eastern Europe.

collaboration is needed in terms of innovation, demonstration projects, and developing large-scale systems—and in exploring the policy packages necessary to effect large-scale system change.

Access to policy research that is unbiased, yet responsive. An energy think tank such as INSIGHT_E can play an important role in helping take this research agenda forward. The independence of an academic consortia can bring objective analysis to some of the key energy challenges. This objectivity helps promote credibility with a wide range of stakeholders concerning the research support that is provided to the European Commission. As demonstrated by INSIGHT_E, the reach to stakeholders, both in terms of numbers and diversity, can be significant, and therefore is another key function of such a think tank.

A think tank can also provide an integrated and consistent approach towards informing policy making. Comprising a diverse set of expertise, ideally from various research institutions, a think tank can bring together different research fields that are usually not found within one single research group or institute. It thus allows investigating policy-relevant topics from various angles. This is crucial to ensure that the research informing the emerging policy direction from the Commission is balanced across these research fields and consistently pointing in the same direction across all policy areas. This is not only done through the approach to the research, but also by discussion with and dissemination to the different policy-making bodies and institutions.

Ensuring such an integrated and consistent approach, outward-facing yet responsive research support to energy policy making can be of high value to inform policy making. This research support should be outward-facing by communicating with, and integrating the expertise from, a wide set of external stakeholders. It should further be responsive to the issues of relevance to energy policy and decision makers. Such research support would especially be extremely advantageous in future years as the Commission faces up to the large-scale energy system challenges.

It is our hope that the work performed by INSIGHT_E and this book contribute to providing such support and insights for policy in support of Europe's energy transition to a sustainable and low-carbon energy system.

REFERENCES

[1] J. Rogelj, G. Luderer, R.C. Pietzcker, E. Kriegler, M. Schaeffer, V. Krey, et al., Energy system transformations for limiting end-of-century warming to below 1.5°C, Nat. Clim. Change 5 (6) (2015) 519–527.
[2] K. Rademaekers, · J. Yearwood, A. Ferreira, S. Pye, · I. Hamilton, P. Agnolucci, et al., Selecting indicators to measure energy poverty. Published by the European Commission, May 2016.
[3] I. Drmač, D. Jakšić, N. Karadža, R. Kunze, J. Dehler, R. De Miglio, et al., Exploring the strengths and weaknesses of European innovation capacity within the Strategic Energy Technologies (SET) Plan. INSIGHT_E policy report 3, August 2015.

Index

Printed in the United States
By Bookmasters